THE COMPLETE GUIDE
TO GUNSMITHING

BY CHARLES EDWARD CHAPEL

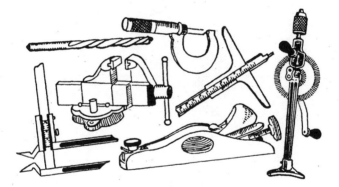

EDITOR'S NOTE

CHARLES EDWARD CHAPEL'S

THE COMPLETE GUIDE
TO GUNSMITHING

by Dr. Jim Casada

Charles Edward Chapel was born in Manchester, Iowa, on May 26, 1904. He attended public schools in Iowa, the University of Iowa, Missouri University (now the University of Missouri), the Polytechnic College of Engineering in Oakland, California, and the U.S. Naval Academy. After leaving Annapolis, he was commissioned as a second lieutenant in the Marine Corps and saw active service in a number of far-flung theaters, including Panama, Cuba, China, the Philippines, and Nicaragua. He was discharged with the rank of first lieutenant in 1937 as a result of wounds received in action.

Chapel began writing while in college and eventually became one of the most prolific firearms authorities of the twentieth century. However, his writings were not limited to that field but also included works on police science (especially fingerprint identification), on aviation, and in other fields. He would ultimately write more than four thousand articles, be the author of twenty-nine books, and contribute multiple entries to the *Encyclopaedia Britannica*. Active to the end, he died on February 20, 1967, having just finished work on a children's book dealing with the life of Henry Deringer of Derringer pistol fame.

As if his literary and other career-related endeavors were not enough, Chapel was also involved in politics. In 1950, running as a Republican for a seat in the California State Assembly, he was elected to that body. He would be elected every two years afterward, nine times in all. He also served as a presidential elector in 1956 and was an alternate delegate to the Republican National Convention in 1964. While serving in the California State Assembly, he was an unsuccessful candidate for speaker.

At one juncture, his penchant for outspokenness and advocacy of Second Amendment rights got Chapel into a patch of legal trouble. In May 1962, while preparing to board an airplane in Sacramento, he jokingly said something to a flight attendant about his briefcase holding a revolver and nitroglycerin. She understandably found no vestige of humor in this and Chapel was convicted of "falsely reporting a bomb on an airliner." The ultimate verdict, a fine of $600 and a two-month suspended sentence, let him off fairly lightly. He could have been convicted of a felony, and had that been the case his political career would have come to a screeching halt.

The written works from Chapel's years as an aeronautical engineer (he was employed at Northrop Aeronautical Institute after he left military service) are mainly concerned with aircraft maintenance and repair. Among those he wrote, edited, or contributed to were *Aircraft Electricity for the Mechanic* (1946; second edition, 1959); *Aircraft Power Plants* (1948; revised edition, 1955); *Aircraft Basic Science* (1948; revised edition, 1953); *Aircraft Weight, Balance & Loading* (1948); *Aircraft Maintenance and Repair* (1949; revised edition, 1955); and *Jet Aircraft Simplified* (1950; new edition, 1954). In connection with this work, he held memberships in the Institute of Aeronautical Sciences and the Aviation Writers Association.

For readers of the present volume, however, it is Chapel's literary endeavors as a gun writer, and perhaps to a lesser degree those as a pioneering forensic scientist, that are of primary interest. In the latter arena he wrote two highly regarded books: *Forensic Ballistics* (1933) and *Fingerprinting: A Manual of Identification* (1941). He was the author of numerous works on various aspects of guns and shooting. These, in chronological order of original publication, included *Gun Collecting* (1939); *The Gun Collector's Handbook of Values* (1940); *Gun Care and Repair: A Manual of Gunsmithing* (1943); *The Boy's Book of Rifles* (1948; revised edition, 1961); *Field, Skeet, and Trap Shooting* (1949); *Simplified Pistol and Revolver Shooting* (1950); *The Art of Shooting* (1960); *Guns of the Old West* (1961); and *U.S.*

Martial and Semi-Martial Single-Shot Pistols (1962). The work presently being reprinted was his final book on firearms.

The nature of guns, and hence that of gunsmithing, has altered appreciably in the more than half a century that has passed since the appearance of *Gun Care and Repair,* as *The Complete Guide to Gunsmithing* was called in its first edition. In truth, even when the second, revised edition (reprinted here) was published in 1962, the word *complete* in the title was misleading. Despite the fact that it runs to almost five hundred pages, the book was designed more as a general primer than a highly detailed, definitive work on gunsmithing. My educated guess is that the publishers (the New York firm of A.S. Barnes and Company along with London- and Toronto-based Thomas Yoseloff Ltd.), not Chapel, chose the title. This would have been done with thoughts on sales potential to the forefront.

The existence of a revised edition attests to this as well as to the changing nature of gunsmithing. The revision itself also went through at least four printings, and I saw listings indicating a sixth printing of the first edition. Two other printers, Gazelle Book Services and Oak Tree Publications, produced modern reprints that, inexplicably, still carry the 1962 date of the second edition.

Whatever the precise nature of the book's history, there can be no doubt it enjoyed what folks in the trade sometimes describe as "a good run." Today it is important for three key reasons: as a milestone in the evolution of gunsmithing literature, as a major work from one of the twentieth century's most prolific and popular gun writers, and as a volume that belongs on the shelves of anyone with a serious interest in books on guns. As such it is a welcome addition to the Firearms Classics Library.

Jim Casada

ROCK HILL, SOUTH CAROLINA

THE COMPLETE GUIDE TO GUNSMITHING

Gun Care and Repair

BY CHARLES EDWARD CHAPEL

Second Revised Edition

Skyhorse Publishing

Dedicated to JULIAN SOMMERVILLE HATCHER,
MAJOR GENERAL, UNITED STATES ARMY, RETIRED

ACKNOWLEDGMENTS

ORIGINAL EDITION

THE original edition of this book was published in 1943 as *Gun Care and Repair: A Manual of Gunsmithing*. Among the many experts who gave the author advice, information, and assistance in the preparation of the text and illustrations were: A. H. Barr, National Rifle Association of America Staff; the author's brother, Robert J. Chapel, Captain, Ordnance Corps, U.S. Army; Walter M. Cline, outstanding authority on the restoration and firing of antique firearms; Frank C. Daniel, now Secretary, National Rifle Association of America; William Fadda, master machinist and gunsmith; Anthony J. Fokker, aeronautical and mechanical engineer; Julian Sommerville Hatcher, Major General, U.S. Army, and Chief of Ordnance Field Service, U.S. Army; Kenneth H. Henson, mechanical engineer; R. J. Kornbrath, master gun engraver; Warren Merboth, then an instructor for the U.S. Army and now an executive of Aerojet General Corporation; F. C. Ness, National Rifle Association of America Staff; Earl Norman Percy, mechanical engineer; Frank Pierce, gunsmith and ordnance engineer; Lindsey Smith, master gunsmith; A. F. Stoeger, Jr., Vice President, Stoeger Arms Corporation; Roy S. Tinney, ordnance engineer; D. B. Wesson, Colonel, Ordnance Corps, U.S. Army, and former Vice-President, Smith & Wesson, Inc.; and Townsend Whelen, Colonel, Ordnance Corps, U.S. Army, Retired.

In addition, the author received advice, information, and help in the preparation of the text and illustrations from many officers and enlisted men of the U.S. Navy, the U.S. Marine Corps, and the U.S. Coast Guard.

PRESENT EDITION

THE author acknowledges with thanks the valuable assistance he has received in preparing the present edition from Alphonzo E. Bell, Jr., Colonel, U.S, Air Force Reserve, and Member of Congress, Beverly Hills, California; Shelley Braverman, Firearms Consultant, Athens, New York; Frank Royce ("Bob") Brownell, Montezuma, Iowa; M. Bigelow Browning, Browning Arms Co., St. Louis, Missouri; William Goldbach, Works Manager, Thompson-Ramo-Woolridge, Inc., Cleveland, Ohio; Julian Sommerfield Hatcher, Major General, U.S. Army, Retired, and Technical Editor, *The American Rifleman,* the official journal of the National Rifle Association of America; Maynard B. Henry, National Secretary, Amateur Trapshooting Association, Los Angeles, California; Alex H. Kerr, President, National Skeet Shooting Association, Beverly Hills, California; R. I. Metcalf, Vice-President, Winchester-Western Division, Olin Mathieson Chemical Corporation, New Haven, Connecticut; O. F. Mossberg, O. F. Mossberg & Sons, Inc., New Haven, Connecticut; Harrie J. Rowe, Jr., Vice-President and General Manager, Harrington & Richardson, Inc., Worcester, Massachusetts; W. R. Weaver, W. R. Weaver Co., El Paso, Texas; and Kenneth R. Johnson, Redondo Beach, California.

The author is exceedingly grateful to H. B. Gibson, Jr., Lieutenant Colonel, Ordnance Corps, U.S. Army, Chief of Armory Operations Division, Springfield Armory, Springfield, Massachusetts; and E. J. Gibson, Brigadier General, U.S. Army, Commanding, U.S. Army Ordnance Weapons Command, Rock Island Arsenal, Rock Island, Illinois, for providing the author with information and illustrations prepared by the Ordnance Corps, U.S. Army, regarding the U.S. Rifle, 7.62-MM, M14, with official permission to use this material in the present edition.

Finally, the author could not have written this book without the patient understanding and intelligent editorial assistance of his wife, Dorothy Jane Chapel.

CONTENTS

ILLUSTRATIONS

PLATE

THE COMPLETE GUIDE TO GUNSMITHING

Gun Care and Repair

I. Shop and Bench

THE important requirements for a gunsmith's workshop are warmth, ventilation, and light. No one can work well if his hands are cold, his brain foggy from foul air, or his eyes tired from too much or too little light. Professional gunsmiths take these facts for granted, but amateurs usually select the first space available for a shop and then wonder why they continue to turn out poor work.

The basement is the worst place for a gunsmith. It is usually poorly heated in the cold months, inadequately ventilated the year round, and devoid of natural light. Dampness causes metal parts to rust. The concrete floor is bad for the feet. If you must use the basement, partition off a section that has a window, obtain one of the modern "daylight" lamps, install a "blower" ventilation system, and lay at least a temporary flooring of planks nailed to two-by-fours.

The attic can be remodeled to eliminate objectionable features. The most serious problem is ventilation, but this can be solved by either a blower system or a fan placed in a hole cut into the roof, with a cover that drops into place to keep out the rain. Be sure to strengthen the flooring where you place the bench and any heavy weights. If there is no flooring, be careful in laying one that you do not break the ceiling plaster of the room below.

The garage is probably the best place of all if it is large enough. There you can pound and saw to your heart's content. A small forge and an anvil can be installed without encountering the opposition that these objects arouse when used in a home. Natural light is already provided or it can be obtained without much trouble and expense. Ventilation is almost too much of a good thing in a garage.

With all these advantages, it is natural to expect some obstacle. Usually it is the absence of a heating system. This can be met with a portable kerosene stove, or an electric heater where the rates are not too high.

Having selected the best location for the shop, its floor plan is the next consideration. Leave 5 or 6 feet of clear space in front of the workbench and the same clear area to the left of the bench if you are right-handed. If you are left-handed, leave the clear space to the right of the bench. When possible, place the power tools, such as the lathe, drill press, etc., well away from the bench.

The bluing equipment should be in another room, or at least as far as possible from the bench, because the fumes, vapors and moisture that accompany many bluing processes are unpleasant to smell and at the same time they promote the rusting of your steel tools and stock.

A surprising amount of wood and metal stock can be stored overhead by providing racks securely fastened to the walls and ceiling, but the material should be arranged so that the vibration from the various gunsmithing processes will not shake it down on your head.

Having laid out the workshop, we turn our attention to the workbench. The one shown in Plate 1 is designed for a man of average size. It is 30 inches wide, 34 inches high, with a top of 1½ x 6-inch pine, and legs 4 x 4 inches. The drawer is square, 18 x 18 inches, and 3 inches deep, all of these being inside measurements. The backboard, placed there to keep tools from falling on the floor, is made of 6 x 1½ inch pine. The bench is assembled with ⅜ inch carriage bolts. At the front, there is a 1 x 8-inch apron board. A 4-inch machinist's vise is mounted at the right and a 6-inch carpenter's vise is at the left.

These dimensions are by no means arbitrary. Design your bench to suit your own requirements. Make the length from 4½ to 6 feet, and the height from 30 to 36 inches, according to your height and whether or not you expect to do most of your work standing or sitting. Work placed in the machinist's vise brings up the operating height a few inches, of course, but you may want a high bench in order to work without straining the back and neck while you are standing. On the other hand, if you expect to make and repair

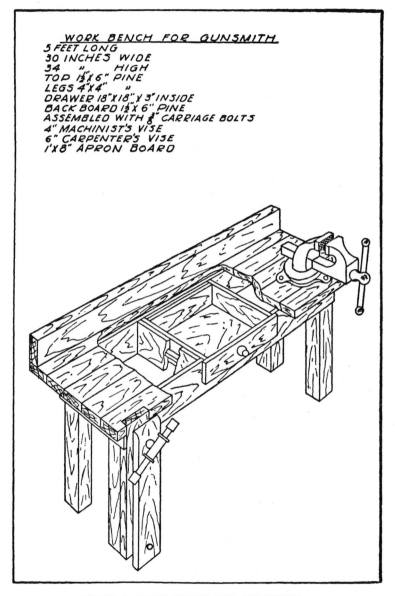

WORK BENCH FOR GUNSMITH
5 FEET LONG
30 INCHES WIDE
34   "   HIGH
TOP 1½"X 6" PINE
LEGS 4"X4"   "
DRAWER 18"X18" X 3" INSIDE
BACK BOARD 1½"X 6" PINE
ASSEMBLED WITH ⅜" CARRIAGE BOLTS
4" MACHINIST'S VISE
6" CARPENTER'S VISE
1"X8" APRON BOARD

PLATE 1. WORK BENCH FOR GUNSMITHS.

small parts while seated, the height of the bench may be as low as 28 inches.

The bench must be substantial. The one illustrated proved satisfactory to the author, but several gunsmiths who copied it added braces across the legs at the ends, and diagonal bracing at the back. Bracing across the front would limit leg action; hence it is not recommended by anyone.

The backboard can be used for the temporary storage of tools by adding cleats and a narrow, thin strip of wood, so that the tools can be placed between the strip and the backboard, and at the same time be separated by the cleats. This idea does not meet the approval of many gunsmiths; instead, they keep their tools in a separate chest or cabinet, or lay them out on a nearby table until the day's work is done.

Length is a desirable characteristic. Some gunsmiths build their benches 8 and even 10 feet long, while others have two benches, one for woodworking and one for metalworking. Obviously, the available space may determine the length more than the nature of the work, but no one has ever complained of having a bench that was too long.

Manual-training benches, such as those used in high schools, can be purchased, but they cost more than twice as much as one made at home and are never as satisfactory, because they are designed for light cabinet-making rather than the heavy loads that a gunsmith may place upon a bench. If you are in a hurry to start gunsmithing, and at the same time want a bench that will fit your needs, you may be able to buy new or secondhand steel bench legs. These are supplied with bolts, screws, etc., ready to join them to a homemade top. Drawers, brackets for attaching a backboard, and similar accessories are seldom sold with the steel legs, and even if they were, you can derive more pleasure from making the apron board, backboard, and drawers according to your own plans.

Most gunsmiths keep valuable small objects, such as screws, bolts, nuts, nails, taps, dies, drift pins, gauges, etc., in cigar boxes, cardboard boxes, drawers, etc., but when they want to find something in a hurry, it is always in the last container. The better course is to keep small objects in screw-top glass jars, where they will be dust-proof and plainly visible. Keep all objects of the same kind in one jar; if there are various sizes, use a separate jar for each size. When your stock accumulates, paste labels on jars for screws, showing the size and thread.

A permissible variation is to keep in one jar objects that are associated with each other. For example, sights, screws, drills and taps may belong together. Likewise, a rifle bolt may be placed in the same jar with extra parts for its repair. It is not so important to select a particular type of arrangement as it is to have some kind of system and follow it faithfully.

Neatness and cleanliness are as important as order. Have a bench brush to clear the bench of sawdust, shavings, metal filings, and broken parts. Keep an old broom handy and sweep the floor around the bench after each job. Throw your trash into a container that is made of metal, for there is a fire hazard in oil-soaked sawdust and shavings, and an added advantage in being able to know where to look for that important missing screw or spring that somehow disappeared.

It is unhandy to keep tools in cabinets or chests while working, but at the end of the project they should be placed under lock and key. Members of the family, or well-meaning neighbors, may borrow your tools while you are gone. Even if you get them back, they probably will have been injured by careless handling. Then, too, children, especially small boys, cannot resist the temptation of gleaming cutlery and whirling wheels. Locking up your tools may bring a few unpleasant comments, but it is one of the first things to be learned by the gunsmith who is serious about his craft.

When the workshop is in a garage or a shed, be sure to place bars or strong wire mesh across the windows and reinforce the door, or someone, sooner or later, will break in to steal tools, guns, or ammunition. Then, if a crime is committed with your guns the law enforcement officials may trace ownership to you and demand an explanation.

In the following chapters, we shall examine the tools and equipment needed for a well-rounded gunsmithing program. At first you will buy only a few tools. As you grow in skill and experience, others can be added.

II. Measuring Tools

THE measuring tools used by the gunsmith include the tools of woodworkers and metalworkers. Some of the tools are common to both trades. We shall first discuss those which are suitable for both metal and wood measuring purposes.

The *Steel Scale or Rule* is absolutely necessary. Obtain one 6-inch and one 12-inch flexible steel rule, graduated in sixty-fourths and hundredths of an inch. You will use these rules for laying out the work preparatory to checkering, inletting, engraving, etching, mounting sights, and for various other measuring tasks. Steel rules can be obtained in lengths from 1 inch to and including 48 inches, with the widths varying from $2\%_4$ inch to and including $1\frac{1}{2}$ inches, but the flexible steel rules are usually made in lengths from 4 inches to and including 24 inches, with widths varying from $\frac{1}{2}$ inch to $\frac{3}{4}$ inch. An ordinary steel rule is shown in Figure 6, Plate 7.

A folding wood or steel rule, at least 3 feet long, is a handy tool for measuring wood and metal stock before it is worked. Obviously, an ordinary yardstick also should be included among our possessions.

Flat material is measured by laying the rule across the top, parallel with the edges if the stock has been squared; otherwise the rule is laid along or parallel to the axis. The No. 1 index mark should be set at the end of the piece, instead of setting the piece to the end of the rule, because this is a more accurate method. Ob-

8

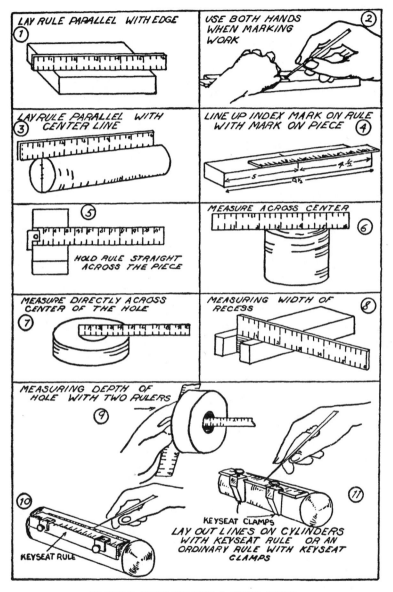

PLATE 2. HOW TO USE A STEEL RULE.

serve the index mark at the opposite end of the piece, subtract 1, and you have the measurement. See Figure 1, Plate 2.

Both hands should be used in measuring or marking the work, as shown in Figure 2, Plate 2. One hand steadies the rule while the other hand holds the pencil or other marking tool.

A round piece, such as a blank for a gun barrel, is measured for diameter by laying the rule on the piece so that the rule is parallel to the center line of the piece and also at right angles to the diameter, as shown in Figure 3, Plate 2. It is better to set the index mark with the 1-inch mark at the end of the work than it is to set the end of the rule at the end of the work, as we have explained in connection with flat work.

Sometimes you may wish to use a 6-inch rule to measure flat stock longer than your rule. Lay the rule on the stock, parallel with the edge, measure 5 inches, with the 1-inch index mark at the end of the work, and then measure again, starting 5 inches from the end of the work. This method was used in Figure 4 of Plate 2.

Figure 5, Plate 2, shows a "Hook Rule," so called because it hooks over the end of the work. When this rule is laid at right angles to the side or end of the work, dimensions are read directly, that is, the end of the rule is set at the end of the work, instead of having the 1-inch index mark at the edge or end.

Figure 6, Plate 2, shows the use of a common rule to measure the diameter of round stock, such as a barrel blank. The rule is placed across the end, directly over the center, with the 1-inch index mark at the edge.

The diameter of a hole can be roughly measured by setting one end of the flexible steel rule against the side of the hole, being sure that the corner of the rule does not go too deep into the hole; instead, the corner should barely catch the side of the hole. Remember that this is only a rough measurement. Elsewhere in this text we shall explain how accurate measurements of holes are obtained. Figure 7, Plate 2, shows the rough method.

The width of a recess is measured according to a similar method shown in Figure 8, Plate 2. Set the end of the rule with the corner barely catching against the side of the recess. Be sure that the rule is at right angles to the material.

The depth of a hole can be roughly measured with two rules.

Hold one across the hole, and set the other rule so that it is not only at right angles to the first rule but also parallel to and inside the channel of the hole. Read the depth on the second rule. This is shown in Figure 9, Plate 2.

Figures 10 and 11, Plate 2, illustrate how to lay off distances and draw lines on curved surfaces, such as gun barrels. The tool used is sometimes called a "Box Rule," but more often it is called a "Keyseat Rule" because it is used principally in laying out keyways on shafts. There are three types: the one-piece, solid keyseat rule; the ordinary rule held in place with two removable clamps; and the type that has two separate rules at right angles, held in place with clamps. Figure 10, Plate 2, is the solid type, while Figure 11, Plate 2, is the ordinary rule with the keyseat clamps.

An *Angle Plate* is an L-shaped piece of cast iron, with each arm about 3 inches long and about 3 inches wide, drilled with horizontal and vertical V-grooves as well as round holes. This tool is used to clamp work in place, to lay out work, and to check measurements. It is by no means essential, but many gunsmiths find it a handy device. It can be purchased from a hardware supply house, but most gunsmiths prefer to make their own according to a design that fits their own, individual needs.

A *Bench Plate,* sometimes called a *Surface Plate,* is simply a large, smooth plate of a close-grained special type of cast iron, reinforced underneath to prevent any tendency to warp. It is used to test and straighten precision tools and instruments, for lay-out work in mounting telescope blocks, for laying out stocks to obtain accurate drop and cast-off, for squaring between machined or filed parts of guns, and for other purposes of a similar nature. One commercial size is $7\frac{7}{8}$ x $11\frac{3}{4}$ inches, while another size is $11\frac{3}{4}$ x $15\frac{3}{4}$ inches; still another size is $19\frac{1}{2}$ inches square. These factory-made precision plates are expensive. The beginner can get along quite well with a large sheet of plate glass laid on a bench free from vibration, with a spirit level used to be sure that the plate is perfectly level at all times. Some gunsmiths think of an iron or steel plate for pounding as a bench plate, but that is a wrong use of the term.

A *Bevel Protractor* consists of a rule with a protractor affixed so that any desired angle may be laid out or read on either wood or metal. It is similar in design and construction to the Combined

Protractor and Depth Gauge; in fact, some gunsmiths use an instrument designed to serve as either a bevel protractor or a depth gauge.

Calipers, both inside and outside types, can be bought in 2-, 3-, 4-, 5-, and 6-inch sizes. We recommend the purchase of a set of both inside and outside calipers in the 2-, 4-, and 6-inch sizes only. Obtain the kind known as "toolmakers' calipers." They are handy for making rough measurements, but when accuracy is essential, micrometer and vernier measuring instruments are used.

Dividers are classed according to their form, as spring, lock joint, and extension, and there is also a special form used for large work, called a trammel, abbreviated to "tram" sometimes, and occasionally referred to as a "beam compass." The gunsmith principally uses spring dividers, sold in a set of three, in 2-, 4-, and 6-inch sizes, usually listed as "toolmakers' roundleg dividers." You can use ordinary dividers when you first start your shop, but the better quality tools are worth the extra cost.

Keep your dividers sharp because if they are not sharp it is impossible to set them for fine work. However, if they have points which are too sharp they become dull easily. It is best to sharpen the points on an oilstone at an angle of about 25 to 30 degrees, being sure that the point is still in line with its leg at the end of the sharpening process. This is done by constantly rotating the point to present new surfaces as it is being ground. This is shown in Figure 1, Plate 3.

Spring dividers are set to a rule by holding the rule firmly on the bench with one hand, while the other hand holds the dividers. One point of the dividers is placed on the index mark of the rule; the thumb and forefinger of the hand holding the dividers are used to adjust the screw. However, if the surface on which the rule is resting is not slippery, one hand may hold the dividers while the other hand adjusts the spring. Do not lean on the dividers; hold them as if you were holding a bird—firmly enough to keep the bird from escaping, yet lightly enough to avoid choking it to death. Finally, when setting dividers, place the points so that an imaginary line between them lies parallel to the edge of the rule. Figures 2 and 3, Plate 3, show how to set and adjust dividers.

It is advisable to set the dividers to parallel lines in an orderly

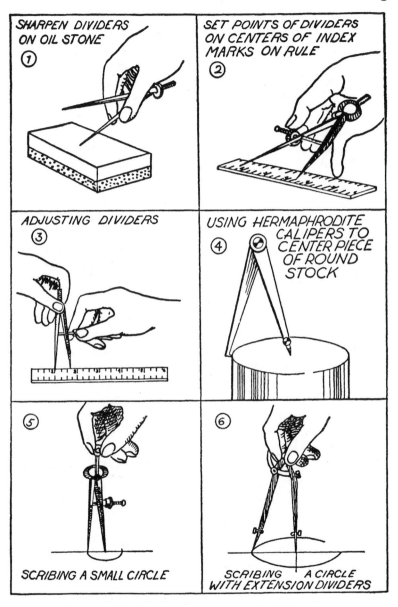

PLATE 3. HOW TO USE DIVIDERS.

manner. First, hold the dividers at right angles to the surface of the work and at right angles to the parallel lines. Second, set one point of the dividers on one of the two parallel lines. Third, lower the other point and turn the adjusting screw slowly until the point being lowered comes to rest on the other line. An imaginary line through the points of the dividers should be at right angles to each of the two parallel lines.

Figure 4, Plate 3, shows the use of hermaphrodite calipers in roughly centering a piece of round stock. First, the legs are adjusted so that the distance between their ends is a little greater than the radius of the circle. Second, the bent leg is hooked over the edge. Third, the scriber (marking leg) is adjusted so that it is not quite as long as the bent leg. Fourth, the scriber is swung in a short arc near the center of the circle from its present position, and the process of swinging the arc is repeated from three more positions, each about 90 degrees from the former. The center of the circle is in the center of the enclosure formed by the four arcs.

Hermaphrodite calipers, it must be explained, are also called "phrodites" and "morphodites." They are not used for accurate work, but are very useful for laying out work and transferring dimensions from one surface to another where rough measurements are sufficient. The scriber should be kept sharp; in use it should be held as nearly perpendicular to the surface being marked as possible. The use of hermaphrodite calipers is not restricted to centering the end of round stock, but the one illustration is sufficient to emphasize the rough character of measurements taken with this tool.

Figure 5, Plate 3, shows a small circle is drawn with the dividers. The dividers are first set to the radius of the circle on a rule. One leg of the dividers is then set in the center of the circle (marked with a center punch in most cases), and a short arc is swung on both sides of the center. A line is drawn through the center of the circle and through these two arcs, and a rule is used to measure the distance between the points where the arcs cross the center line. If the distance between the two points is the desired diameter, the complete circle is drawn. When the distance between the two points is greater or less than the diameter, the dividers are adjusted to correct the error and the trial process is repeated until the desired diameter is obtained.

Figure 6, Plate 3, shows a circle being drawn with extension dividers. The legs are first adjusted so that they are equal in length and then they are tightly clamped in place. The half-moon-shaped object near the top of the dividers is the quadrant, which has its own clamp that can be adjusted for roughly setting the points of the dividers to the desired radius. The final and accurate adjustment is accomplished with the adjusting screw on the other leg. Trial arcs are swung across a center line, and the diameter checked, as explained before.

When measurements are marked on a finished surface, some protective covering is desirable. Copper sulphate, whiting (a powdered chalk mixture), and other substances are commonly made into solutions which are painted on the surface with a brush and allowed to dry before being marked. Obviously, the substance used must be one which does not itself harm the surface. Adhesive tape, either surgeon's adhesive tape or the Scotch cellulose tape, can be used to protect the surface while measurements are being marked.

A *Center Punch* is shown in Figure 5, Plate 4. The ordinary machinist's center punch is about 4 inches long, tempered at both ends, with a point carefully ground to an angle. A set of five of these punches, in a case, costs very little. The diameter at the top of the tapered point, in inches, varies from $\frac{1}{16}$ to $\frac{7}{32}$ in the usual set of five.

An automatic center punch looks like an ordinary machinist's center punch except that the handle is larger because it is really a sliding sleeve containing a spring and a trip. A downward pressure releases the trip and makes the impression. The depth of the impression is uniform, the punch seldom slips off the mark while the blow is being struck, and a clean, sharp mark is left. Automatic center punches are made in different styles, lengths, and diameters; some have removable points which can be replaced if broken or taken out for grinding. A hammer should never be used with an automatic center punch.

Prick punches resemble center punches so much that the two types are usually mentioned as belonging to one class. Small ones, about 3 or 4 inches long, can be cut from worn-out Swiss needle files, hardened, and kept ground sharp, although you will not want all of them to be equally sharp, since some types of work require comparatively dull punches. Still smaller prick punches can be made from discarded dental burrs. Even the punches turned out by the famous manufacturers may prove too soft for your purpose, so you will learn to temper your tools according to methods explained in a later chapter.

Drift pin punches, with ends having diameters ranging from $\frac{1}{16}$ inch up to $\frac{3}{16}$ inch, can be bought, or they can be made from drill rod. Small ones can be made from old dental burrs. These punches should be annealed first and then hardened again, but they must not be as hard as center or prick punches or they will break in use. The reason is that drift pin punches, as the name indicates, are used to push pins in or out; they have to "give" while they are being eased along their route. In tempering, oil is used, and the temper is drawn at a blue color, between 600 and 700 degrees Fahrenheit, as explained later in the text.

Nail punches are bought, ready-made, in various sizes to fit the ends of drift pins which have ends showing on a gun, such as the round-headed pins in some shotguns. These punches have cupped ends so that they will not mar a finished pin. Anneal them, reharden, and draw the temper as you did the drift pin punches. Before rehardening, it is advisable to turn down the ends, so that the point extends straight back for about 1 inch. Finally, polish the cupped end carefully with crocus cloth.

Wood punches are not mentioned often. They are simply punches with cupped ends which are used for giving a beaded effect to a stock. They can be made from drill rods, in any diameter desired for stock-checkering operations.

Strictly speaking, the drift, nail, and wood punches do not belong in a classification with measuring tools, but we have described them along with the center and prick punches because all punches are customarily grouped together in a manufacturer's catalog.

A *Center Gauge* is shown in Figure 6, Plate 4. It is used for setting thread tools in the lathe when screw threads are to be cut, and for checking lathe centers when they are being reground. Tables on the center gauge indicate the size of tap drills for American, National, or United States Standard threads, showing in thousandths of an inch the double depth of thread of tap and screw of the pitches commonly used. The angles used on these gauges are 60 degrees for the American, National, or United States Standard and 55 degrees for the Whitworth or English Standard. For this reason separate gauges are made for the 55-degree and the 60-degree angle requirements.

A *Combination Square* is shown in Figure 7, Plate 4. It can be used to lay off a slot in flat stock, to lay off a dovetail slot, to check the length of a number of pieces, as a depth gauge, to determine if adjacent sides of a piece are at right angles to each other, and for many other measurements. This tool can be obtained with removable, interchangeable heads. One type has one head for measuring right angles and 45-degree angles, and another head for centering, with a spirit level built in so that a barrel, for instance, can be placed absolutely vertical in a vise. It is also possible to obtain a head with a bevel protractor that can be used to lay out any angle.

Other squares needed by the gunsmith are (1) a try square, such as the one illustrated in Figure 3, Plate 7; (2) a die-maker's square (this has three or four blades, each 2½ inches long: a standard blade, a narrow blade, a bevel blade with 30-degree and 45-degree angles at the ends, and an offset blade); (3) a solid, thin steel square, for metalwork (obtain two, one with 3 x 2-inch blades, and one with 6 x 4-inch blades); and finally, (4) an ordinary carpenter's square, with arms of 1 foot and 2 feet, respectively; this last square is especially useful in making stocks.

It should be understood that a careful gunsmith should have a small "standard" square for testing purposes only; that is, this square is reserved for testing the accuracy of other squares and is never used on the work. Squares of this type, hardened, ground to absolute 90-degree angles, are usually listed as "toolmakers' squares," and are more expensive than less accurate squares.

A *Depth Gauge* (or *Gage*) is shown in Figure 1, Plate 5. It is used to measure the depth of holes, projections, etc. There are several types of depth gauges, but all of them are basically alike in having two parts, a rod or blade, and a head. The accuracy of the construction and the delicacy of the measurement indicator are factors in determining the cost of a depth gauge, for prices range from three or four dollars to fifty or sixty dollars.

A *Drop Measurer* is shown in Figure 5, Plate 5. The long tube is laid flush upon the barrel and the drop may be read off the scale, both at the comb and at the heel. You can copy this design and make one yourself from wood, brass, or steel.

A *Toolmaker's Steel Clamp* is shown in Figure 4, Plate 7. This is used to hold work square and parallel for laying out surface plates, fitting or drilling. A piece of round stock may be held rigidly in two of these clamps and drilled on an upright, central, or parallel, as desired. These clamps are made from drop forgings, casehardened, with take-up blocks to slip on or off the end of the screw. Supply houses customarily sell these clamps only in pairs.

Steel Parallels, Adjustable Type, are illustrated in Figure 5, Plate 7. They are used with milling, planer, and shaper vises, taking the place of the large number of tool steel parallels usually required. They are also used for leveling up work on a planer, drill press, etc., and for a support for grinding or milling of square or hexagonal stock on centers, since they may be adjusted and locked to micrometer measurements from ⅜ inch to 2¼ inches.

Tool Steel Parallels of the usual type are made from a special grade of tool steel, hardened and ground on four sides. They are sold in pairs according to thickness and width, but all of them are customarily 6 inches long. A complete set of eight pairs permits many possible combinations.

A *Trigger Pull Tester* is shown in Figure 4, Plate 8. This is patterned after the British Army model, and is marked to read by ¼ inch up to 16 pounds. Its principle of operation is simply that of pulling against a spring. Some gunsmiths like this type of instrument, but we prefer the use of weights, as explained later in the text in connection with trigger adjustments.

V (or *Vee*) *Blocks and Clamps,* illustrated in Figure 3, Plate 5, are used for accurately laying out work in connection with an angle iron, a knee, or a surface plate. They are very handy for holding barrels, fitting scope blocks, etc. They are made of hardened tool steel, accurately ground with parallel sides and V-grooves ground central and parallel to the bottom and sides. They are made and numbered in pairs so that the V-grooves in the blocks having the same numbers are always aligned.

A *Screw Pitch Gauge* is shown in Figure 8, Plate 6. The type illustrated has 51 blades, and covers all pitches of V-threads, including pipe threads, threads per inch, and American, National, and United States Threads.

Other Gauges needed by the gunsmith are: (1) the Surface Gauge, for laying out work with the surface plate; (2) the Auger-bit Gauge, which is clamped on a wood auger bit to determine the depth of the hole; (3) the Marking Gauge, which is the ordinary device for marking a straight line parallel to a side (especially by carpenters and gunstock makers); and (4) the Thickness or Feeler Gauge, which has leaves of various thicknesses, and is used by toolmakers, machinists, automotive mechanics, and gunsmiths, the latter using it to measure clearances between parts.

A *Vernier Caliper* is shown in Figure 4, Plate 4. The Vernier feature was named for its inventor, Pierre Vernier. It is applied to calipers, depth gauges, height gauges, micrometers, and protractors. In principle, the vernier scale has a line of known length divided into a certain number of parts; the length of these parts or divisions is then compared with divisions made on a line of equal length but with one less division than the number on the first line.

A *Micrometer Caliper* is illustrated in Figure 8, Plate 5. Micrometers are made in various sizes and shapes. They may be classified as inside, outside, and depth micrometers. The construction principle is that the advance of a screw is recorded for any part of its turn or for any number of turns. It should be noted that both the vernier and micrometer principles may be applied in the same instrument to give extremely accurate readings.

Since gun measurements require accuracy to one-ten-thousandths of an inch, it is advisable to buy a micrometer with a measuring range from 0 to 1 inch by thousandths of an inch on its sleeve and thimble scales, and readings in one-ten-thousandths of an inch with the vernier scale on the sleeve.

Rough measurements can be made with various gunsmith tools, but for accurate readings, vernier and micrometer instruments are required. A small thumbpiece is part of the typical precision measuring instrument, made with a click, so that the instrument can be accurately set with uniform tension. Skilled gunsmiths are sometimes able to set their instruments accurately and uniformly without the click device, but the beginner does well to advance a step at a time and not attempt to take any short cuts.

III. General Tools and Equipment

THE tools, instruments, and equipment, other than measuring tools and power tools, will be described in this chapter. They are presented in alphabetical order to give the reader a broad view of the mechanical means at his disposal. The use of the various tools and instruments will be explained in separate chapters, in connection with the various gunsmithing processes. For instance, the use of checkering tools is explained in the chapter on checkering the stock. Once more, we wish to remind the reader that it is not necessary to acquire all of these tools before he can start work as a gunsmith. Furthermore, many gunsmiths work for forty or fifty years without using more than one-half of the tools mentioned in this book. They could do more work, and do it faster and better, if they had more tools, but for one reason or another they manage to earn a living with a set of tools that could be carried in a suitcase.

Alcohol Lamp.—This is handy for the heat treatment of small tools, and to melt small quantities of substances when other sources of heat are not available or desirable. You can improvise your own from odds and ends. A common method is to cut part of the spout off an oilcan and insert a wick.

Anvil.—The usual blacksmith's anvil is illustrated on Plate 25, and described in the chapter on blacksmithing. One weighing between 40 and 70 pounds is heavy enough for any of the gunsmith's processes: forging springs, making special hammers, and assembling auxiliary equipment, such as target carriers. An excellent substitute for an anvil is a short piece of railway rail or a piece of shafting, but whatever you use as an anvil should have at least one flat, level surface, and it should be both hard and heavy. Many gunsmiths have a 10- or 15-pound anvil for handling small work.

Bench Brace.—Two types of bench braces are illustrated in Figure 1, Plate 15. Make these yourself. Their use is explained in the chapters on making and checkering stocks.

Bending Apparatus is used on gunstocks to increase the drop, lessen the drop, put cast-off into the stock, or put cast-in onto the stock. (These terms are explained fully in later chapters.) The stock-bending apparatus shown in Figure 1, Plate 8, is made of aluminum with steel screws and three wooden blocks. Remember that it is better to properly design and make a stock in the first place than it is to attempt to bend it into a new shape after it has been finished.

Bits.—These are needed for boring into wood. Do not economize on bits, because the wood used in gunstocks is hard and it will dull cheap bits quickly. You can get along with only auger bits, but eventually you will also want Forstner bits, which do not have a spur in the center and hence make a smooth, flat-bottomed hole, suitable for cutting out wood for magazines, locks and trap-butt plates. To start a hole for the accurate location of the Forstner bit, a center bit is required. Eventually, you will acquire one or two center bits, five or six Forstner bits, and a set of auger bits. The usual set of auger bits consists of thirteen bits, one each, $\frac{4}{16}$, $\frac{5}{16}$, $\frac{6}{16}$, $\frac{7}{16}$, $\frac{8}{16}$, $\frac{9}{16}$, $\frac{10}{16}$, $\frac{11}{16}$, $\frac{12}{16}$, $\frac{13}{16}$, $\frac{14}{16}$, $\frac{15}{16}$, and $\frac{16}{16}$ of an inch in diameter, but a cheaper and less complete set that will be satisfactory consists of one each, $\frac{4}{16}$, $\frac{6}{16}$, $\frac{8}{16}$, $\frac{10}{16}$, $\frac{12}{16}$, and $\frac{16}{16}$ inch.

Blacksmith Tools are shown on Plate 25, and described in the chapter on blacksmithing.

Bluing and Browning Tools and Equipment are shown on Plate 23, and described in the chapter on that subject.

Braces are used with auger bits. The ratchet brace, shown in Figure 4, Plate 6, is the type preferred by gunsmiths. A breast drill, such as the one shown in Figure 2, Plate 4, is also needed. One of the principal uses of the brace, particularly a plain brace without a ratchet, is with a screwdriver bit; this is necessary in loosening connecting screws in rifles and in assembling shotguns.

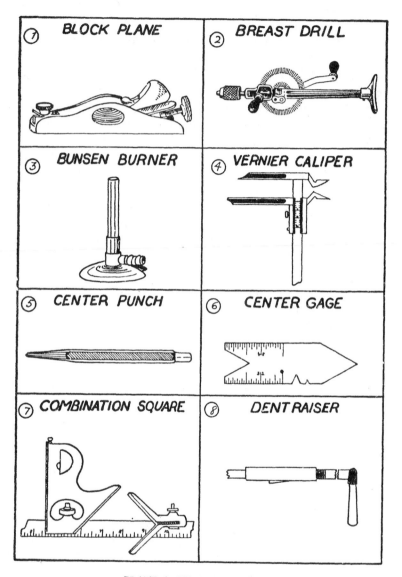

① BLOCK PLANE	② BREAST DRILL
③ BUNSEN BURNER	④ VERNIER CALIPER
⑤ CENTER PUNCH	⑥ CENTER GAGE
⑦ COMBINATION SQUARE	⑧ DENT RAISER

PLATE 4. GUNSMITH TOOLS.

Brazing Tools are illustrated on Plate 24, and described in the chapter on soldering and brazing.

Bunsen Burner.—The usual type of bunsen burner is illustrated in Figure 3, Plate 4. The typical one for bench use has a cast-iron base, is about 6 inches high, has a base diameter of about 3 inches, and uses 6 cubic feet of gas per hour. The same burner, bent to a 45-degree angle, is also available. Both of these improved burners have a simple adjustment whereby the length and temperature of the flame can be controlled by simply turning the burner tube. A cheaper type of burner has a fixed orifice and is controlled by adjusting the air shutter. In appearance, it closely resembles the more elaborate type.

Catalogs are not tools in the mechanical sense, but they certainly form a valuable part of the equipment of a gunsmith's shop. Obtain them from retail dealers, jobbers, wholesalers, and manufacturers of hardware, firearms, ammunition, tools, lumber, optical instruments, and other materials and instruments. Frequently an illustration of some special tool, such as a stock-straightening apparatus, for example, will give you an idea for solving a perplexing problem. You may need a replacement part; consult the catalog. If you cannot afford to buy the part, you may be able to design and make your own from the illustration and description in the catalog. Aside from their information, old catalogs, particularly old catalogs of firearms and ammunition, are often sold at a premium. Gun collectors, gunsmiths, museums, antique dealers, and others have frequent occasion to refer to the old catalogs.

Checkering Tools are illustrated on Plate 20, and explained later in the text in connection with checkering processes. A typical set of checkering tools consists of one tool for laying out lines, one for making the border, and two sizes for the actual checkering. But you can get along with one tool or build up a vast collection, just as you wish.

Chisels.—Wood chisel blades are illustrated on Plate 17; Die Sinkers' Chisels are shown on Plate 20; and the use of the Cold Chisel for cutting steel is shown in Figure 2, Plate 9.

Chisels are sometimes divided into classes, such as bottoming tools, carving tools, cold chisels, firmer chisels, gouges, and socket chisels.

Bottoming tools are chisels designed to reach into deep recesses, such as the holes cut for shotgun actions, where ordinary tools will not reach. Wait until you have attempted to make one or two gunstocks before you buy or make your bottoming tools. To make your own, forge and file ¼ inch drill rods to the length and shape you find desirable for making your deep cuts, harden and temper, sharpen on an oilstone, and then fit into wooden handles. Keep the heat at a cherry red while you are working it and draw the temper to a purple. These colors used in heat treatment are explained fully in a later chapter.

Carving tools, in the trade sense, are special tools, usually done up in sets. A typical set consists of nine tools, two sharpening slips and a small oilstone. The tools include firmers, corner firmers, V-gouge, scroll, hollow and extra flat gouges. The most famous maker of such carving tools has been F. V. Addis & Sons, London, England, but tool makers in the United States have gradually captured this trade. The reason for the supremacy of the Addis Co. in the past is that there was a limited demand for wood carving in America.

Cold chisels are necessary if you do much metalwork. There are four general types of cold chisels generally used. These are: (a) the ordinary flat chisel, usually called a "chisel," for chipping flat surfaces; (b) the cape chisel, used for cutting keyways and grooves and for chipping flat surfaces in narrow places; (c) the diamond-point chisel, used for cutting holes in solid metal and similar purposes; and (d) the round-nose chisel, sometimes called a "gouge," used where a sharp corner is not wanted, and for other special purposes.

Cold chisels are classed as to size according to the width of the cutting point. The length of chisels varies greatly and depends upon the purpose for which they will be used. When you start your tool collection, obtain a ¼ inch chisel; follow this with a ½ inch chisel. Add various sizes and types as you find the need for them. It is difficult to advise a beginner about the selection of cold chisels because no one knows the kind of work he will attempt. Chisels can be made from old files or from pieces of hexagonal tool steel.

Firmer chisels are ground on both sides so that cuts can be taken in any direction without changing the grip on the tool. Firmers come in various widths and lengths, some being 1 inch wide while others are as narrow as the hyphen (-). When wood carvers speak of "firmers," they do so to distinguish their own chisels, which are sharpened on both sides, from the carpenter's chisels, which are sharpened on one side only, and cannot be used easily for many wood-carving cuts because they must be turned constantly to avoid spoiling the work. "Skew chisels," "skews," or "corner firmers" are ground off diagonally with an edge that has a sharp point on one side.

Gouges are chisels but all chisels are not gouges. The difference lies in the shape of the blade; the gouge has a concave-convex cross section, which may also be described as "scoop-like." Gouges are made in all widths and in varying degrees of curvature, starting with the extra flat, which has very little curvature, through the scroll gouge, which has more curvature, to the hollow gouge, which has a semicircular cutting edge or one which follows the curvature of a circle. Small hollow gouges are called veiners. Still smaller hollow gouges are called eye tools.

Gouges can be made from drill rods having diameters from ⅛ inch to ½ inch, progressing by 16ths, that is, after the ⅛ inch rod comes the ³⁄₁₆ inch rod, etc. Using a file, work the drill rod down to a taper so that the shape at the cutting end will be that of a semicircle, and then file out the inside, harden and temper. Turn down the opposite end enough to fit it into a wooden handle. When finished, the gouge should project about 4 or 4½ inches from the handle, which means that about 6 or 6½ inches of drill rod is needed for each gouge.

Socket chisels are short carpenters' chisels for rough work. They are subclassified as Socket Butt, Socket Firmer, Socket Framing, Socket Pocket, etc. Socket Butt chisels run from ¼ inch to 2 inches wide; Socket Firmer chisels run from ⅛ inch to 2 inches wide; Socket Framing chisels run from 1 inch to 2 inches wide; Socket Pocket or Cabinet chisels run from ¼ inch to 2 inches wide. The blade is usually from 2 to 5½ inches long, with an average of about 3½ or 4 inches. These figures are, of course, general; the actual dimensions vary among the manufacturers.

Special Wood Carving Knives, Wood Chisel Blades, and Inletting Chisels are shown on Plate 17. The Special Wood Carving Knives illustrated on that plate are designed from patterns which originated in Sweden. Only a few of the many shapes are shown. The blades vary in length from 2½ to about 5 inches, with an average length of about 3 inches for the majority of patterns. They are made with a tang that extends through the handle and is riveted.

The Wood Chisel Blades on Plate 17 illustrate the principles of chisel design already discussed. The Inletting Chisels are for stock-makers. A set of eleven, similar to those shown on Plate 17, is considered necessary for all-around work.

Having explained the better known types of chisels, we can now consider briefly the engraving tools shown on Plate 20. The Die Sinkers' Chisels are so called because they are the type of tool used by die sinkers, who are engravers of dies, for stamping coins, medals, etc. These chisels are made from the finest tool steel, according to old, established patterns. A set of twelve shapes provides enough variety for most difficult cutting or engraving. The Flat Engraving Tools shown on Plate 20 are likewise professional tools. Explanations of the use of such professional engraving tools are given in the chapter on etching and engraving, together with suggestions for making your own tools.

Clamps.—These tools are used wherever parts must be brought together, as by a screw or screws, for holding temporarily or for compressing. See Figure 3, Plate 26. "C" Clamps can be bought for a few cents in any "dime store"; they are useful for various temporary holding purposes, such as the welding operation on Plate 26, for gluing horn, wooden insets, ebony, plastic material, or ivory to forearm tips or pistol grips; for holding down work on a power tool, such as a drill press, and for many other operations.

In addition to the C clamps, there are carpenters' and machinists' clamps, the better grade of the latter being called toolmakers' clamps; all of these have two parallel jaws and two clamping screws. Each of the clamping screws works inward. Carpenters' clamps are available in both wood and steel, but machinists' and toolmakers' clamps are carefully made of casehardened steel.

Toolmakers' Steel Clamps for holding work square are different from the parallel type described above; they are discussed in another chapter, as are V (or Vee) blocks, drill blocks, and clamps, and similar tools which can be classified for some purposes as measuring tools.

A *Dent Raiser, or Dent Remover,* is shown in Figure 8, Plate 4. This is used in shotgun barrels and it is made for 12-, 16-, and 20-gauge shotguns, respectively. We have shown the tool sectionalized to save space. The principle of operation is simply exerting leverage against the dent.

Shotgun Rectifying Cylinders are made in sets of five for each shotgun gauge. The diameter of one cylinder is .006 inch less than the true barrel size; the second is .004 inch less; the third is .002 inch less; the fourth is true caliber size; the fifth is .002 inch over-size. Many gunsmiths prefer these to the Dent Raiser because they are less likely to injure the barrel when properly used and they cost about one-half as much.

Dies.—The beginner will not use thread dies and even the professional gunsmith will not have many occasions when he will need dies unless he is attempting to do a great deal of advanced work. Screws can be cut better in a lathe than in a thread die. On the other hand, numerical and alphabetical dies are almost a necessity for the professional gunsmith. These are merely sets of punches bearing numerals or letters of the alphabet; when pounded against metal they leave the desired mark.

A *Draw Knife* is shown as "f" in Figure 1, Plate 9. This is useful in the rough-shaping of a gunstock in the early stages of its manufacture.

A *Drill* is shown in Figure 2, Plate 5. This happens to be a type known as the Straight Shank Wire Drill, made of carbon steel, or high speed steel, in wire gauge sizes. A drill for drilling in solid metal has two grooves or flutes; one for enlarging a hole has three or four grooves; oil-hole drills have internal holes or ducts for carrying oil, or some other cutting compound, to the drill point; these last drills are used for deep holes where it is difficult to supply the point of the drill with enough oil or cutting compound, due to the tendency of the chips to carry the fluid back with them before it reaches the bottom of the hole.

Drill sizes are classified as numbered (for a certain range of small sizes); lettered (for a range of somewhat larger diameters); and fractional (for a large range of sizes). In the letter class, A is smallest and Z is largest. In the numbered class, No. 1 is the largest and No. 80 is the smallest. The fractional class lists drills according to their actual diameters in fractional readings, such as, for example, from ⅛ inch to 1¾ inches, advancing by 64ths.

A Breast Drill is shown in Figure 2, Plate 4.

A *Drill and Wire Gauge* could be classed with the measuring tools, but we mention it here because it is so intimately connected with drills. A gauge of this type is simply a polished steel plate about ¹⁄₁₆ inch thick, 2½ inches wide and about 6 inches long, with holes punched in it and tables embossed to give the correct drill for any common size machine screw tap, the size of tap, pitch of thread, and size of hole required and size of drill for making a hole through which the outside diameter of a tap will pass. There are variations of this gauge. Some are made on the circumference of a circle and some are made to resemble dividers. Some give decimal and fractional equivalents and other handy tables.

Files.—Plate 9 shows several illustrations of files. Figure 3 shows the correct way to file round surfaces. The file is held with the handle up at the start of the stroke. As the stroke advances, the hand is lowered so that the hand is in the lowest position at the end of the stroke. On the return stroke, the file is raised. At the beginning of each stroke it is laid on very easily, so that the file glides over the surface instead of striking it at an angle. This produces a fairly smooth, round surface, if done properly.

Figure 4 of Plate 9 shows *draw filing*. Select a perfectly straight and true file; be sure that it has not been bent by laying it on a perfectly flat surface and looking for the light underneath. Hold the file in both hands and push it straight across the work, bearing down just hard enough to make the teeth cut. Rub the file back and forth, keeping it at right angles to the work at all times. This should give a flat surface.

Figure 5, Plate 9, shows cross sections of files. The thin rectangular shape is a warding file. The thick rectangular shape is the hand file, and the medium thick shape is the common flat file. The other shapes have obvious names, such as square, triangular (also called 3-square), half-round, and round.

Files for adjusting triggers and actions, etc., are shown in Plate 31; they have such names as crossing, knife, sear notch, square, round, etc. The various uses of these special files are explained briefly in the captions under the pictures on the plate, and also in the chapter on adjusting trigger pulls, etc.

A *File Card,* also called a file cleaner, or a file brush, is an inexpensive but important piece of equpiment. Lay the file flat on the bench and work the brush back and forth across it in a direction parallel to the cuts on the file. This will preserve the life of the file and also enable you to do better work.

File Handles should be used on the files. There is nothing "sissy" about refusing to use a file without a handle. The tang of an unprotected file may slide into your hand or wrist and carry with it a serious infection. Furthermore, you can exert more pressure when there is a handle.

General Discussion of Files.—The file is the most important of all the gunsmith's tools. It can be used to make other tools and it can serve as a substitute for many of them. It is a metal-cutting tool with many cutting points and it is driven directly by the hand. Progress with the file seems slow to the beginner, but the experienced gunsmith knows that accuracy and speed seldom go together in hand work.

Files may be described according to their cut, name, or kind, and length. They may also be named for their shape. A round or rat-tail file may also be called a mouse-tail file if it is small. A diamond-shaped file may be termed a slitting file because of its use, which is remembered better than its shape. There is no system to the nomenclature of files. A lozenge file is actually more diamond-shaped than lozenge-shaped. To avoid errors, in ordering a file, give as much descriptive information as you possess and then draw the outline of its cross-sectional shape.

The file cut may be single or double. A single-cut file has single, unbroken, straight teeth or chisel cuts running at an angle across its surface. A double-cut file has another set of straight teeth cut diagonally across the first set.

Each style and cut has several degrees of coarseness, such as coarse, bastard, second-cut, smooth and dead smooth. The smooth is sometimes called fine, and the dead smooth may be called superfine. Double-cut files are often called bastard files, but the term "bastard" should refer only to the size of the teeth, disregarding whether the cut is single or double. Finally, coarseness varies with the length; the longer the file, the coarser the cut. Coarseness is designated by numbers starting with No. 00, the coarsest, and running to No. 6, the finest.

A rasp is a coarse file with raised points instead of lines. The teeth on a rasp are not connected to each other in any way; each tooth is made by a separate operation where the old system is followed. Rasps, like files, have different degrees of coarseness. The rasp cut used most by gunsmiths is the smooth cut, also known as the cabinetmaker's rasp, which is used to rough-cut wood where no other tool will work. See Plate 6, Figure 3.

The beginner can start his collection of files with the following: one flat bastard file, 12-inch; one half-round bastard file, 12-inch; one round bastard file, 10-inch; one mill file, 10-inch; one set of 5½ inch needle files; and one half-round wood rasp, 12-inch. Gradually, as finances permit and the need arises, others can be added.

A *Gasoline Torch* is a handy source of heat, along with the alcohol lamp and the bunsen burner. A blacksmith's forge is another source of heat. When the shop expands, an electric or gas furnace may become necessary eventually.

A *Hacksaw* is illustrated in Figure 4, Plate 5. There are two types of hacksaw frames, adjustable and solid. With the adjustable type, the blade can be held in any one of four positions; with the solid frame type, the frame is not adjustable for length and therefore it is necessary to use a blade of the correct length. Hacksaws come in different sizes and shapes. The size is determined by the largest blade the frame will take; it may be anywhere from 8 inches to 16 inches, in even lengths. Care must be taken with the blades, for if they are allowed to bend they may break. The hacksaw, like the file, cuts only on the forward stroke; lift it clear when it is returned to the starting position, but do this without too much loss of energy by lifting it just clear of the work.

A *Hammer* is shown in Figure 6, Plate 5. This is a special gunsmith hammer, of the correct shape and proportions for our work. It can be obtained in various weights from 3½ ounces up to 18 ounces. Several weights are desirable for the professional gunsmith, but a beginner can get along with a 7-ounce or 9-ounce hammer.

A *Lead Hammer* for straightening barrels is shown in Figure "F",

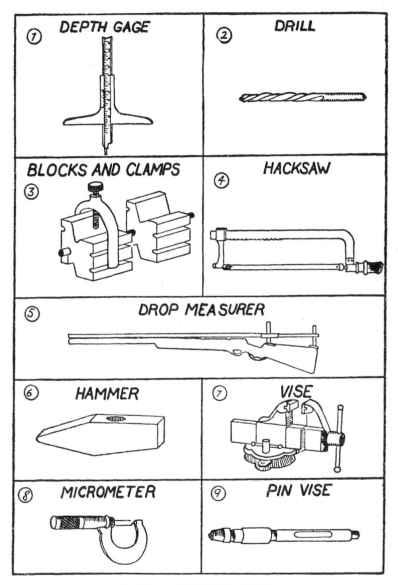

PLATE 5. GUNSMITH TOOLS.

Plate 27. This can be made in your own shop by pouring lead in a mould around a steel handle. Other soft hammers are made of metals such as babbitt, copper, soft brass, and even rawhide. The lead and babbitt hammers can be made solid or they can be made of some hard material with a core to receive the soft metal poured into the end. Copper and brass hammers can be made in the same manner. Still another soft hammer can be made by inserting a piece of round fiber in a brass tube of a suitable diameter and length, with some of the fiber projecting from each end of the tube.

Machinists' Hammers include not only the soft hammers already mentioned, but also sledge hammers, riveting hammers, and the common machinist hammer. The latter is further divided into round peen, straight peen, and cross peen classes. Figure 2, Plate 9, shows the use of a hammer and a cold chisel for cutting steel. The face of the hammer is parallel with the chisel butt, not at an angle to it; the handle is grasped firmly, the arm is raised straight away from the chisel, and then brought down with a sharp, quick blow, striking fair and true, not at an angle.

Magnifying Glass.—This is needed for trigger, action, hammer and other adjustments where you are working with small objects. By rigging a holder for the magnifying glass, you can examine your work and still have both arms free. A magnifying glass is shown on Plate 31.

Mallet.—A wooden mallet, or one of the soft hammers previously described, is necessary for both metal and wood work.

Matting Tools.—These tools are used to give a rather rough, interwoven, basket-like decoration to wood or metal. They are usually purchased from a jeweler's supply house, but if you are handy with tools you can make a matting tool out of a ¼ inch square drill rod. Use a fine slitting file to cut sharp rows of teeth at right angles to each other, and evenly spaced. Harden this tool after the teeth are cut and draw the temper when the steel has a very deep straw color, as explained in the chapter on heat treatment.

A *Miter Box* is an apparatus for guiding a saw at the proper angle. Many carpenters and cabinetmakers construct their own, but highly accurate ones, suitable for cutting angles carefully, can be purchased.

Oilstones for trigger, hammer, and other small-part adjustments **are** shown on Plate 31. They are obtainable in a vast variety of shapes so that the proper shape can be selected to fit the part being worked. A large, ordinary oilstone, suitable for sharpening chisels, knives, etc., is shown in Figure 1, Plate 3, where it is being used for sharpening the points of dividers.

The Truth About Surface-Coated Abrasives.—An abrasive is a substance used for wearing away by friction. Emery is an excellent example of an abrasive. There are only five abrasives in general use; these are Aluminum Oxide, Flint, Garnet, Silicon Carbide, and Turkish Emery, but these five abrasives are commonly marketed in the United States of America under more than forty-five different private trade names or "brands." About one-fourth of the commercial abrasives are really Silicon Carbide, and nearly one-half are actually Aluminum Oxide, leaving about one-fourth of the commercial brands for the other three abrasives.

Natural Stones.—The Arkansas stone is a natural stone composed of pure silica. It is probably the best sharpening tool available for engravers, watchmakers, dentists, surgeons, and others who use very fine-edged tools and instruments. The gunsmith uses the Arkansas hard stones (there are two grits, hard and soft) for giving the final finish to hardened surfaces, such as cutting tools, sears, triggers, reamers, etc. Either oil or water can be used with this stone.

The Washita is a medium-priced natural oilstone used by carpenters and other woodworkers for giving a keen, lasting edge to their tools. The Lily White Washita is a better grade of the same natural stone; it cuts faster and gives a better edge but costs more. Either oil or water can be used with either of the Washita stones.

The India, or Hindustan, is another coarser stone, but it should be used only with water, not with oil. The medium grade is used for the initial smoothing and cleaning, before using another stone for the final finish, on rifle sears, ejectors and sears on shotguns, small round stocker's chisels, the inside of rifle bolts, the inside of bushings, barrel bands, and in other preliminary work.

Planes.—The best plane for the gunsmith is a Block Plane, such as the one illustrated in Figure 1, Plate 4. It is 7 inches long, with a 1⅜ inch cutter, and a weight of about 1½ pounds. In addition, you will need a jack plane and a smooth plane. If you buy a plane that is not made by a well-known manufacturer, be sure that the parts are interchangeable with those of other manufacturers or you

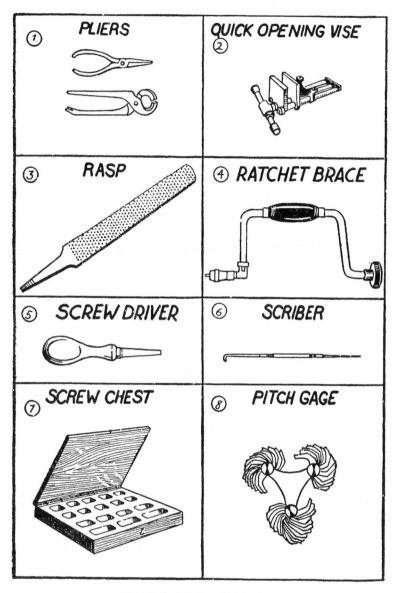

PLATE 6. GUNSMITH TOOLS.

may have an "orphan" on your hand some day. This advice applies with equal force to the selection of many other tools.

Pliers are necessary for gunsmithing. Buy these tools as you need them, one or two at a time. Some of the types to be considered are: standard side cutting plier, long chain needle nose plier, end cutting nipper, woodworker's pincer, short chain nose mechanic's plier, curved needle nose plier, barrel and tube plier, diagonal cutting plier, etc. See Plate 6, Figure 1.

Saws.—Plate 9, Figure 1, shows the gunstocker's saw, the dovetail saw, the stockmaker's saw, the stockshaper saw, and the inletting saw. In addition to these special saws, you will need an ordinary rip saw and an ordinary cross-cut saw.

A *Gunsmith's Screw Chest* is divided into milled compartments for the most popular screws, sights, small springs, firing pins, and other small parts. See Figure 7, Plate 6.

Screwdrivers for gunsmiths are sold in sets of twelve different sizes and shapes, but be sure to buy the best quality because the cheap ones will break and spoil your work. You can well make a set of gunsmith's screwdrivers yourself from octagon chisel steel. File the end to fit a screw, but without any taper to the end because a taper allows it to spring when under tension. Make a set with a different screwdriver for each size and shape of gunscrew you expect to encounter. See Plate 6.

Scriber.—Plate 6, Figure 6. This is for measuring and marking.

Soldering Tools are illustrated on Plate 24, and described in the chapter on soldering and brazing.

The *Sight Spanner* is shown in Figure 1, Plate 7. It is fastened into a vise and used to hold very small parts, such as tiny pins, the front sight, etc.

A *Spray Gun* for applying lacquer to a gunstock is shown on Plate 19, but it is important to remember two things about this illustration: First, we do not recommend the use of lacquer for a finish on a gunstock; second, the spray gun is used for applying lacquer but not for applying the oil finish that is described in connection with Plate 19.

The *Spring Spanner* is illustrated in Figure 2, Plate 7. This is the adjustable type which costs about four times as much as the non-adjustable kind. Spanners serve as clamps in handling springs. The

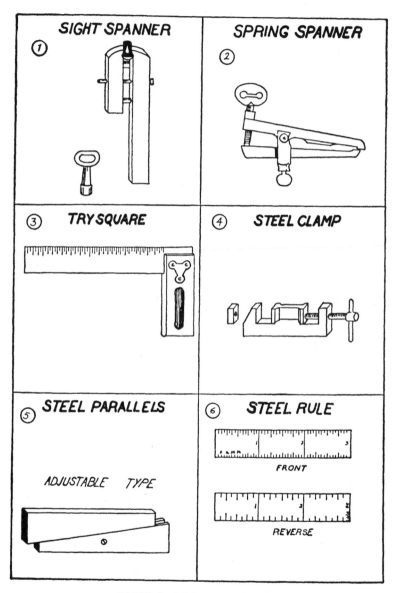

PLATE 7. GUNSMITH TOOLS.

adjustable type can be used for the smallest pistol springs or the largest rifle or shotgun springs.

Taps and a Tap Wrench.—A tap is a tool for forming an internal screw. In Figure 2, Plate 8, are shown a machine tap and hand taps, while Figure 3 of the same plate shows a tap wrench.

Templates or Templets are patterns, made when the same size and shape of work is to be repeated. Templets may also be gauges, such as depth gauges, radius gauges, etc., where the proper size and shape must be verified quickly and accurately. A third meaning is that of moulds, but this use of the term is not found in gunsmithing.

Tongs are shown on Plate 25, for blacksmithing.

Tweezers of various sizes and shapes are needed for picking up and handling small screws, springs, and other parts that are difficult to hold between the fingers.

A *Vise* is indispensable. Plate 1; Plate 5, Figure 7; and Plate 31 show vises of the usual types. A Pin Vise is shown in Figure 9, Plate 5. A Barrel Vise or clamp block is shown in Figure 6, Plate 29. A Gunsmith's Hand Vise is a little tool for working on small parts, springs, etc.

A typical bench vise for the gunsmith should have the following among its characteristics: jaws made of tool steel, accurately machined and heat-treated; gripping surfaces machine-knurled; handles with ball ends made of one piece from cold rolled steel; a hardened steel washer under the screw head to prevent wear and end play; a base of the swivel type, but made to lock positively in any position; a forged steel lock bolt equipped with teeth which mash into the gear-like corrugations in the bench plate. The base should be flat and require no cutting into the bench top for fastening. The weight may vary from 12 to 30 pounds for the beginner, but the professional will want one weighing as much as 45 pounds.

A Gunstocker's Vise is a woodworking vise. It should be constructed along simple lines, simple, durable and reliable, with the fewest possible parts. There should be a heavy steel screw with a double fast round thread to provide positive action. The handle should be of hardwood; the jaws should be drilled for wood facings; the jaw size should be either 4 x 7 inches, or 4 x 10 inches, and the

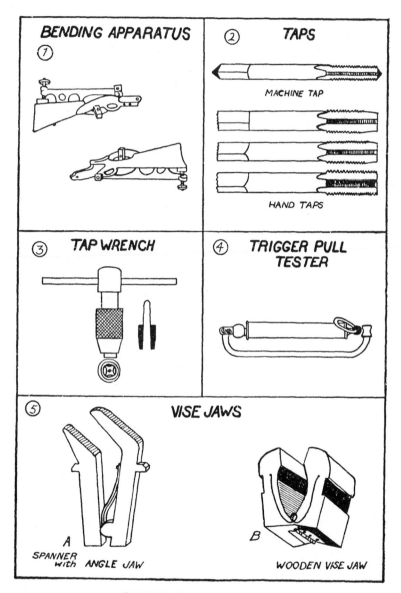

BENDING APPARATUS
①

TAPS
②
MACHINE TAP

HAND TAPS

TAP WRENCH
③

TRIGGER PULL TESTER
④

VISE JAWS
⑤
A
SPANNER with ANGLE JAW

B
WOODEN VISE JAW

PLATE 8. GUNSMITH TOOLS.

weight should be from 22 to 30 pounds. A quick-opening wood-working vise is shown in Figure 2, Plate 6.

Vise Jaws.—No matter how smooth they are, the jaws of a vise disfigure the work. To prevent this, it is usual to use false jaws such as vice blocks, lead jaws, brass jaws, copper jaws, babbitt metal jaws, and leather or paper-faced jaws. These can be purchased or you can make your own. Plate 8, Figure 5, shows a spanner with an angle jaw, and a wooden vise jaw. False jaws or jaw caps can be made of wood first, the wooden jaws can serve as patterns, and then molten metal can be poured into a mould. The faces of these metal jaws are filed smooth and flat.

Still another method is to bend sheets of brass, lead, copper or some other soft metal around the jaws of the vise in shapes adapted to each job. See Plate 29.

Vise blocks are usually made of wood and covered with some material softer than the work. For example, if a wooden stock is to be held, the blocks should be covered with felt, leather or paper, but if metal is to be held, then the blocks may be of soft metal. It is well to design a vise block with a U-shaped cut-out, the top of the cut-out made so that it will ride the slide for the movable jaw of the vise; the top edge of the vise block should be flush with or slightly above the jaws of the vise. In other words, make the vise block to fit the vise and handle the work. See Plate 29.

Welding Tools are illustrated on Plate 26, and discussed in the chapter dealing with welding.

Wrenches of various types are illustrated on Plate 29, such as the Monkey Wrench, the Billings Pipe Wrench, the Soft Jaw Wrench, and the V-Jaw Wrench. The same common-sense precaution followed in the use of a vise must be observed here. Be sure that the jaws of the wrench are covered with some substance softer than the material being worked, if you wish to avoid marring the work.

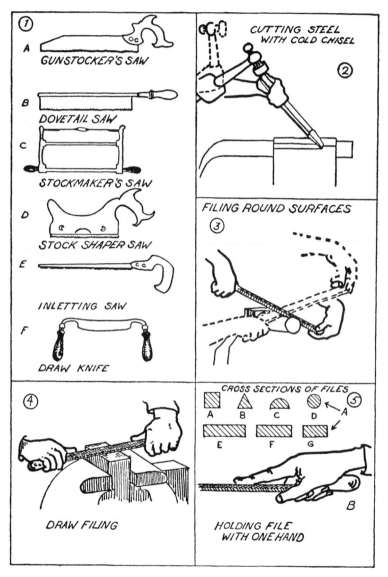

PLATE 9. TOOLS IN USE.

IV. Power Tools

POWER tools are not necessities for the amateur gunsmith, but they enable him to turn out accurate work faster and more economically than he can do with hand tools. The professional gunsmith, and even the semiprofessional gunsmith, needs every help that he can obtain to lighten the burden of performing the monotonous tasks that unavoidably accompany the more pleasurable phases of his work.

The drill press is probably the most valuable of all power tools owned by a gunsmith. It is used for drilling or sanding wood, bone, metal, plastics, or hard rubber. It is used for boring horn, mounting telescopic sights, doweling buffalo fore-end tips, drilling receivers for micrometer sights, routing and mortising wood, and for inletting rifle and shotgun stocks.

A bench drill press is made to rest on a bench, while a floor drill press is mounted on a column which rests on the floor. The parts are the base; the vertical support called the column; the movable head, which carries the movable steel quill; the vertical steel spindle running on bearings in the quill; the chuck which is at the lower end of the spindle; an adjustable table for holding the work, with a lock lever to control it; the stepped pulley; a bracket fastened to the head; and a motor secured to the bracket. The motor recommended is one of ¼ or ⅓ horsepower, 1,740 revolutions per minute.

Drill presses are customarily sold without a motor, although a motor can be acquired at the same time. We mention this because beginners sometimes fail to understand that the motor price is quoted separately. Bench drill presses for the amateur and semi-professional are ordinarily found in three grades. The lowest priced one is strong and stable; it is as accurate as the more expensive models, and although it is not intended for routing or shaping on a commercial basis, it is satisfactory for the occasional piece of work. Mortising cannot be performed on the typical low-priced drill press.

The drill press in the intermediate price range should cost about 50 per cent more than the one in the bottom group. It will handle mortising, and can be used for routing or shaping on an industrial basis. It is somewhat lighter in weight and has less capacity than the machine in the higher priced group, but on the whole it will be quite satisfactory.

The best of the three grades should cost about twice as much as the lowest grade. It is heavier and has more capacity than the intermediate type, but both the intermediate and the top quality machines should have a 6-spline spindle, which reduces vibration; and four ball bearings, two of which are in the quill, one above the pulley and one below the pulley.

The usual attachments for the drill press are a mortising attachment, a collet chuck for holding bits, a hold-down and guide, a threaded adapter for shaping cutters, a ¼ inch bit, a ½ inch bit, a ¼ inch hollow chisel, a ⅜ inch hollow chisel, and a ½ inch hollow chisel.

The *bench grinder,* run by a motor of from ¼ to ⅓ H.P., is needed for sharpening tools, working down rough metal, fitting recoil pads, buffing, polishing, cleaning, grinding and many other important operations of the gunsmith's shop. A typical grinder within the reach of the amateur has a ⅓ H.P. motor, 3,450 R.P.M., 110 volts, A.C., 60 cycles; with two grinding wheels, 6 inches in diameter, ¾ inch wide. Guards mounted over the grinding wheels permit the operator to handle his work easily, watch it through windows in the guards, and at the same time avoid personal injury. The bearings are the grease-sealed type. Both the motor and the bearings are almost entirely protected from dirt and dust.

The grinder wheels can be removed and hardwood discs substituted. These discs may be covered with sandpaper, felt, muslin, canton flannel, chamois, buckskin, leather, sheepskin, emery paper, or any other cleaning, surfacing, polishing or grinding material.

Likewise, wire wheels can be substituted for either or both of the grinding wheels.

The *belt and disc surfacer,* also called a sander, performs many of the jobs that are ordinarily done on the bench grinder, but it also permits the sanding and polishing of flat surfaces. It is especially useful in fitting recoil pads. It is true that the lathe, shaper, drill press, or almost any other power tool having a rotating spindle or a shaft can be used for sanding and polishing, but the belt and disc surfacer does the job better and easier, since it is designed and constructed especially for sanding and polishing. The stationary belt sander has a sanding belt running over rubber-covered wheels which are held in line by steel rods fastened to a cast-iron base. On the other hand, there is another type, called a portable belt sander, that is pushed over the work instead of bringing the work to the machine, as is done with the stationary sander.

The *jig saw,* operated by a ¼ H.P. or a ½ H.P. motor, is used for cutting out silhouette designs of all kinds, butt plates, targets, shotgun fore-ends, pistol grips, and other nonmetallic objects. It should be able to cut wood nearly 3 inches thick and metal up to ¼ inch thick. Special blades are provided for cutting solid wood, veneers, plywood, moulded plastics, celluloid, fiber, bone, hard rubber, and various metals. The power should come from a direct-drive motor, mounted as part of the unit. Where two or more speeds are possible, finger-tip control of speed, together with an adjustable blade tensioner and other control features, enable the gunsmith to perform with more safety and efficiency.

The *band saw,* operated by a ⅓ H.P., 1,740 R.P.M., motor, is used for cutting gunstocks roughly to shape from either planks or rough blanks, for shortening gunstocks, and for all similar operations where curves and contours must be cut on a larger and heavier scale than is possible with a jig saw. In addition to the woodworking type, which is the one usually seen in a gunsmith's shop, there is a metalworking band saw. The latter is belted to a countershaft driven by a motor in order to reduce the speed. It can be used to cut aluminum, bronze, iron, soft steel, and various other materials.

The *circular saw* is used to rip lumber, that is, to saw it lengthwise, with the grain; to cross-cut lumber, that is, to saw it across the grain; to saw metals; and to groove, rabbet, and tenon lumber. It is by no means an essential power tool for the amateur or intermediate gunsmith, but like other tools for general wood and metal working, it has its place in the professional shop. The saw may be of the 7-, 8-, or 10-inch size, and the motor may be either ¼ or ⅓ H.P., depending upon the amount of heavy work that is being turned out.

The *jointer* or *planer* is another power tool that you can get along without in the beginning, but it is needed where gunsmithing is on a production basis as distinguished from incidental repair work. The planer, as most men remember, is a power tool for smoothing the surfaces of boards; when it is small and intended principally for smoothing the edges of stock so that the edges will fit together neatly, and for smoothing narrow boards, it is called a jointer. In use, the board is fed along so that it comes in contact with the rapidly rotating cutter head of the tool; blades in the cutter head plane the board smooth, as a hand plane would do, but more accurately, swiftly, and easily. Like other power tools, it is operated by either a ¼ or a ½ H.P. motor. If it planes stock up to 4 inches wide and ¼ inch deep with one cut, or if it planes 6 inches in width and ½ inch deep, it is satisfactory for the usual gunsmith's shop. Besides planing, the jointer can be used for making mouldings, beveling, rabbeting, taper cutting, and chamfering.

The *power spindle shaper* is a third power tool that you will not absolutely need until you become a busy professional, but it is better to know about such tools early in your gunsmithing career, for you may find an opportunity to take one in trade for work or buy it at a bargain price. The power spindle shaper has several names; it is variously referred to as a vertical spindle shaper, spindle shaper, or shaper. It is a woodworking tool with a cutter head mounted at the upper end of an upright rotating spindle; it is used principally for shaping, which is divided into two kinds. These are straight shaping, which is the cutting of straight shapes; and curved shaping which is the cutting of curved surfaces. Other uses include the cutting of tongues and grooves, cutting reeds and flutes, cutting panels, and sanding, the latter being possible when sanding spindles and sanding drums are fitted to the tool. The motor should be either ⅓ H.P., running at a speed of 3,450 R.P.M., or ½ H.P., running at the same speed. Reversing switches are used.

Portable electric drills are used for both metal and wood working. Like other power tools, they are used when the amount of work to be done is great enough to justify the expense, but they require more care and skill than hand tools and are more likely to injure the operator. They should be lubricated only in accordance with the manufacturer's instructions. Too much lubrication ruins electric motors.

A portable electric drill is illustrated in Plate 10. It has a small, high-speed electric motor geared to the chuck through reduction gears. It can be obtained in various sizes. The size indication of an electric drill refers to the largest size hole it will drill in mild steel. Common sizes are ¼, ⅜, and ½ inch. The speed at which an electric drill runs depends upon its size. Large twist drills must rotate slower than small ones, to prevent overheating.

The chuck of an electric drill is made so that it will not accommodate a twist drill larger than the motor can drive. This is done to prevent overloading the motor and stalling the drill. Drills smaller than the maximum capacity of the electric drill can be held by the chuck, but it is not a good practice to use a very small twist drill in a large electric drill. It is best to use the smallest electric drill that will hold the particular size twist drill being used. A large electric drill is heavier and harder to hold; it runs slower; and it does not cut as fast as a small drill.

A heavier portable electric drill is called the *breast drill*, and gets its name from a breast plate that rests against the operator's chest. It has a pistol grip and also a side handle so that the operator can use both hands to guide and steady the drill. The side handle is removable for close work. Common sizes are ½, ⅝, and ¾ inch. The large model, with the proper twist drill in the chuck, will go right through the toughest and hardest wood and most metals. It can be used on many jobs where it would be impossible to use a drill press.

In addition to drilling holes in metal and wood, all portable electric drills can accommodate accessories such as brushes, mandrels, files, rasps, polishing wheels, and sanding discs for many purposes, such as carving, routing, sanding, grinding, inletting, and inlaying.

A *flexible shaft* attached to either a line shaft or a motor transmits mechanical power to a rotating tool and can be used for similar work.

The *milling machine* is a power-operated, stationary, revolving cutter with which metal is brought into contact by a traversing table. When equipped with attachments such as the rotary table, vertical head, dividing head, slotting device, etc., it can be used to cut grooves, slots, reamers, spiral flutes in twist drills, and otherwise turn out work of any shape, regular or irregular. If you own a milling machine and all the other tools mentioned in this book you can manufacture all types of firearms. You may not be able to compete successfully with the large companies for a few years, but most of them started originally with much less equipment.

A *lathe* is useful but not essential for the beginner. Intermediate and professional gunsmiths are unable to succeed financially without a lathe. A metal-turning lathe is used for turning down or polishing barrels (inside and out), making firing pins, removing choke from shotgun barrels, turning bushings and threading nuts and rods with tap and die, rifling barrels, and other tasks too numerous to mention. A wood-turning lathe is used for rounding up a piece of wood into a symmetrical shape; stocks, pistol grips, side plates, butt plates, and other nonmetallic objects may be made in part or entirely on the wood-turning lathe.

A wood-turning lathe which is built heavy enough and accurate enough can be used as a metalworking lathe when it is equipped with a compound slide rest. This object combines two simple motions to produce a compound motion, hence its name. It comprises a compound rest feed screw and a cross feed screw in the saddle. In order that these terms may be clearly understood, we shall examine the parts of a typical wood-turning lathe.

The four principal parts are the bed, the headstock, the tailstock, and the tool rest. The bed is the base which holds the other parts. The headstock is fixed rigidly at one end of the bed; or it may be made as one piece with the bed. The headstock may be considered as a frame that supports the spindle which runs in bearings. The spindle has a cone pulley at the outside end, and a face plate or spur center screwed on the inside end; this holds one end of the material to be turned.

The tailstock holds the other end of the material to be worked. It can be moved along the bed and clamped tight at any desired point. It has two adjustments, rough and fine. The rough adjustment permits the tailstock to be moved along the bed until it is located at a point where the distance between the headstock and the tailstock is just a little greater than the length of the material to be worked. Then, the fine adjustment is used. This is a spindle which is threaded at one end and has a sharp point at the inside end to hold one end of the material to be turned.

A typical, low-priced lathe which is within the financial reach of the average amateur gunsmith, and is still good enough to be used for both wood and metal turning, can be described as follows:

10-inch Medium Duty Lathe.—It has a swing of 10 inches. It is 37 inches between centers, which means that you can turn material having a length of 37 inches or less, and you can turn longer pieces by adding a bed extension. Instead of having two flat ways, such as are found on light duty lathes, there is one V-shaped way and one flat way. These are carefully machined so that a compound slide rest can be used when the wood-turning lathe operates as a metal-turning lathe. The headstock has a ¾ inch spindle that runs on self-lubricating sleeve bearings. There is a thrust ball bearing at the end to cut down friction, thus reducing power consumption and increasing smoothness of operation. The spindle projects at its outer end so that turning can be done from the outside end of the lathe, as distinguished from the work normally done between the centers. The height of this lathe is 10½ inches, its over-all length is 47 inches, it weighs 42 pounds, and it is driven by a ⅓ H.P. motor.

There is a great variation in prices for lathes, depending upon the accuracy of construction and design, the weight, the number and quality of the accessories and attachments, the reputation of the manufacturer, and the profit added by the retail dealer. Before buying a lathe, the reader is cautioned to obtain the catalogs of all manufacturers of lathes, prices from retail dealers, and also catalogs from the outstanding mail-order houses. Investigate the reputation of the firm from which you buy your lathe. If they are unknown to machinists, woodworkers, and gunsmiths, pass up the opportunity to buy what may be a piece of junk.

Motors for Power Tools.—Electric motors may be classed as direct-current motors; alternating-current motors; and universal motors, which run on either direct or alternating current. Alternating-current motors are in turn divided into two groups: single-phase motors and three-phase motors. Single-phase motors are further divided into two kinds: synchronous motors and induction motors. The latter are the ones usually used to drive amateur power tools, and they are commonly made to deliver ¼ or ⅓ H.P. For heavy duty work, a three-phase motor is needed; the smallest of this type is the ¾ H.P. motor. Small motors ordinarily operate on 110 volts, alternating current, but the heavier ones are built for 220 volts, alternating current.

Starting and Reversing Switches.—A starting switch is a rheostat; it is a device for cutting resistance coils in and out of the circuit to increase or decrease the strength of the current. In simpler terms, the strength of the current is increased gradually to prevent the current from burning up the coils in the motor when it is started.

A reversing switch is a double-pole, double-throw switch, used to reverse the direction of the current flow into the motor and thus change the direction of its rotation. It is especially needed when metal is being turned on the lathe.

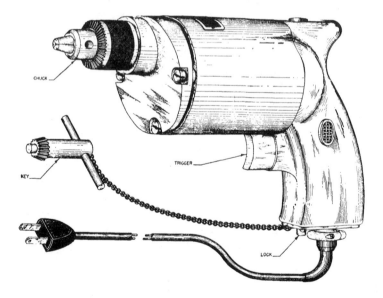

PLATE 9A. PORTABLE ELECTRIC DRILL.

V. Drawings and Blueprints

ALL gunsmiths should know how to read drawings and blueprints. An independent gunsmith, whether he is an amateur or a professional, frequently finds it necessary to make a new part for a gun. An old part may be missing or unserviceable, and a replacement may not be obtainable from the factory. Where the old part is at hand, the gunsmith can work directly from the part, but he will save time and effort by making a drawing and working from that. If no part is available for copying, he must either obtain a drawing or blueprint from some source, or make one himself.

A gunsmith employed in a factory or an armory cannot advance far unless he can work from drawings and blueprints, which are nothing more than instructions presented in the form of lines, figures, and symbols which he must be able to interpret. Since they are recorded on the flat surface of the paper, he must use his imagination to form a mental picture of the object represented, note the dimensions given, understand the meaning of the various initials, abbreviations, and symbols, and then construct the required part without any further instructions, oral or written. The information supplied by the drawing or blueprint includes not only the shape and size of the part to be made but also the material to be used, the finish of each of the surfaces, and the number of pieces to be produced.

In an armory or a factory, the original drawings are not sent to the shop for the gunsmiths to use, since the drawings would soon become soiled, torn, and lost; hence it is necessary to have some cheap and rapid means of reproduction. Blueprints are made by laying the inked drawing (called a tracing) in a frame or blueprinting machine with the inked side next to the glass and the sensitized blueprint paper on the other side. When the hand frame is used the paper is exposed to strong sunlight; when the blueprint machine is used the paper is exposed to an electric light. The length of the exposure depends principally on the type of paper used and the intensity of the light. The original black lines of the tracing appear as white lines on a blue background on the blueprint, hence the name.

Blueprints are rarely used today because there are many methods of reproducing drawings which are easier, faster, less expensive, and more legible. Even during World War II, most aircraft and ordnance factories did not require their draftsmen to ink their drawings because they used reproduction methods that gave the pencilled lines the same effect as inked lines. Regardless of whether you work from blueprints or drawings reproduced by modern methods, the fundamental principles are the same.

THE EXPLODED DRAWING

An *"exploded" drawing* is frequently used today to show the relationship between the various assemblies, sub-assemblies, and parts. A good example of this type of drawing is Plate 9B, which represents the Colt Official Police Revolver, made in caliber .38 Special for service; and also manufactured in caliber .22 Long Rifle for target practice. In addition to the "exploded" drawing, which occupies most of Plate 9B, there is a *side-view drawing,* showing the left side of the revolver, in the upper right-hand corner of the Plate. Incidentally, the barrel is marked on the left in two lines: "OFFICIAL POLICE" over ".38 SPECIAL CTG." The numbers beside each sub-assembly or part are used to follow instructions for assembly and dis-assembly, and also in ordering replacements from the factory or a dealer.

PERSPECTIVE, OBLIQUE, ISOMETRIC, AND ORTHOGRAPHIC DRAWINGS

Plate 9C consists of several illustrations which represent different methods of drawing the same object. Figure 1 is a *perspective* draw-

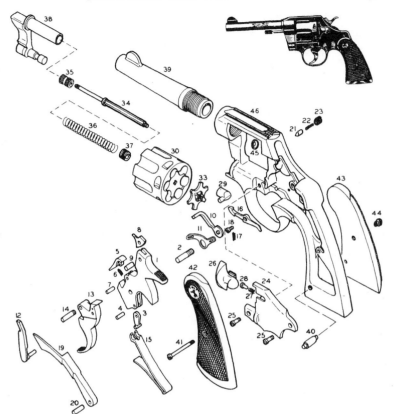

PLATE 9B. COLT OFFICIAL REVOLVER, AN "EXPLODED DRAWING."

ing or view. It represents the object as it appears to the eye, but it does not provide the information needed by a gunsmith. Lines which in reality are parallel, if extended far enough, eventually come together just as railway tracks seem to be closer together at a distance. Lines farthest from the observer are shorter than those near the observer in a perspective view.

Figure 2 is an *oblique view* of the same object shown in perspective in Figure 1, but in this oblique view the line representing the edge farthest from the observer is drawn exactly the same length as the line nearest the observer. Parallel lines are actually parallel and do not come together even when extended. Furthermore, parallel lines in an oblique view are of the same length in the drawing (if they are of the same length on the object), yet the farthest from the observer seems to be no longer because of an optical illusion. Therefore, it can be said that an oblique view is a perspective view with equal distances on the drawing representing equal distances on the object.

Figure 3 is an *isometric* drawing, also called an isometric *projection*. It is fundamentally an oblique view presented without the optical illusion. The object appears distorted, but it shows equal distances on the drawing representing equal distances on the object, thus making the dimensions clear to the reader.

The "exploded" drawing, the side-view drawing, the perspective view, the oblique view, and the isometric projection, are all helpful but the gunsmith who wants to make or repair a gun part needs more than one view, and each view should be drawn without distortion. This can be accomplished by means of an *orthographic* projection, such as the one in Figure 4 of Plate 9C.

Figure 4 is not a gun part, but it is a bracket that could be used for holding one end of a shoulder arm. A pair of brackets, if suitably designed and mounted, can be used for holding a shoulder arm on display in a cabinet or on a wall. There is a front view, a top view, and a right side view in this orthographic projection of a bracket. The *front view* is what you see if you stand directly in front of the bracket. If your eyes are on a level with the front view, you cannot see the top, bottom, or sides.

The *top view* is what you see if you look directly down on the bracket in such a manner that you cannot see the front, the back, the bottom, or any surface except the top.

The *right-side view* is what you see if you look directly at the right side in such a manner that you cannot see the top, the bottom, or any surface except the right side of the bracket.

In Figure 4, solid heavy lines show the outside edges. All edges and sharp corners are projected from one view to another as outlines or visible edges if they can be seen in the particular view under examination. A line or an edge which is not visible in any particular view is called an *invisible edge* or a *hidden line,* and it is represented by a series of short dashes. In the front view, there are no invisible edges or hidden lines. The top view has two series of short dashes which represent edges not visible from the top. The right-side view has one series of dashes which represent a hidden line—that is, a line not visible from the right side.

THE MEANING OF LINES IN ORDNANCE DRAWINGS

Figure 5, Plate 9C, shows several of the types and forms of lines used in preparing mechanical drawings for ordnance, aircraft, and other technical inspection, maintenance, repair, and construction. Most drawings use three intensities or weights of lines: heavy, medium, and light. There always is a pronounced difference between a heavy line and a light line. When a medium weight line is used, its intensity is somewhere between the heavy and the light line.

The *visible outline* is a heavy line which represents edges and surfaces seen when directly viewing an object. The *invisible outline,* sometimes called a *hidden line,* is a medium-weight line of short dashes, sometimes called a *dotted line.* It represents edges and surfaces behind the surface viewed and hence not visible to the observer.

The *center line* is of light intensity and consists of short and long dashes spaced alternately and used to divide a drawing into equal or symmetrical portions. Also, it establishes the centers of arcs and circles. The *dimension line* is of light intensity and is not broken except where necessary to indicate a dimension. This is done by placing a number or a fraction in a break in the dimension line to indicate length, width, or height. The *phantom line* is of medium intensity; it consists of a series of long dashes with two short dashes between the long dashes, and indicates an adjacent part for a location reference.

The *broken material line,* also called a *broken line,* is used to save space in a drawing. The draftsman draws a line of medium intensity with freehand zig-zags for long breaks. If he did not have this symbol, the drawings would run off the end of his paper. When there are short breaks, he uses a heavier, freehand wavy line, especially where he has removed an outer surface to show what lies underneath. Another use for the broken material line is to avoid drawing the second half of a symmetrical part, even though there is sufficient room on the paper.

The *alternate position line* is of medium intensity and consists of a series of long dashes. It is used to indicate the alternate positions of a moving part. When the same type of line is used to indicate the relationship between a part and a sub-assembly, or the relationship between a sub-assembly and the whole gun (or other object), it may be called an *adjacent line,* but the two terms refer to the same series of long dashes.

The *cutting plane line* is a heavy, broken line consisting of one long dash followed by two short dashes, repeated. It is used to refer to another view and direct the reader's attention to a *section* ("slice") of the interior, behind the surface, but this must not be confused with the *broken material line,* which is drawn differently and for a distinctly different purpose.

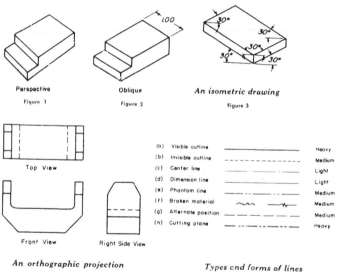

Perspective
Figure 1

Oblique
Figure 2

An isometric drawing
Figure 3

Top View

Front View

Right Side View

An orthographic projection
Figure 4

(a)	Visible outline		Heavy
(b)	Invisible outline		Medium
(c)	Center line		Light
(d)	Dimension line		Light
(e)	Phantom line		Medium
(f)	Broken material		Medium
(g)	Alternate position		Medium
(h)	Cutting plane		Heavy

Types and forms of lines
Figure 5

PLATE 9C. PERSPECTIVE, OBLIQUE, ISOMETRIC, AND ORTHOGRAPHIC DRAWINGS.

SECTIONAL DRAWING OF HARRINGTON & RICHARDSON "SPORTSMAN" REVOLVER

Plate 9D is a *sectional drawing;* that is, it shows how the Harrington & Richardson "Sportsman," Model 999 (Tip-Up Model) Caliber

.22 Revolver would look if portions were cut away, or sliced. Also, it is a left-side view. The various straight, diagonal, curved, solid, and broken lines all have significance because they were drawn to help everyone understand the design, construction, inspection, maintenance, and a repair of this revolver. Of course, there are other drawings of the same revolver. We have selected this particular drawing because it illustrates several features found in many gun drawings.

Almost all drawings made for technical work have legends or title blocks. They may state are scale of the drawing, part number, name of part, assembly number, material, stock, quantity required, unit weight, finish, heat treatment, whether it is a left- or right-hand view (when this is not obvious), and the names or initials of the draftsmen, engineers, etc. However, all these details do not necessarily appear on each view.

The revolver illustrated in Plate 9D is equipped with checkered American walnut side grips, a semi-thumb rest, wide hammer-cocking spur and adjustable sights. The front sight has elevation adjustments. The rear sight has positive windage adjustments. The revolver has a top-breaking action, hence the term "tip-up model." There is an automatic ejector. It weighs 30 ounces. It is chambered for all caliber .22 ammunition, has a 6-inch barrel, and can fire nine shots without reloading. Only a few of these features are readily recognized in Plate 9D unless the reader understands something about mechanical drawing or already knows the revolver and what to look for.

In Plate 9D, at the left appear in three lines the following: "6 INCH BARREL," "9 SHOT CAPACITY," and "DOUBLE ACTION." The lower portion of the drawing consists of the legend, also called the title block. Starting at the left, it shows that the drawing was made by "M. C. RAY," but the blanks for scale, date, and "check" (place for draftsman's superior to sign his name or initials) are not filled. Moving to the right, after "NAME" appears "HARRINGTON & RICHARDSON." Underneath, after "MODEL" appears "SPORTSMAN." Next comes a rectangle with the symbol of Brownell Industries, owned by F. R. ("Bob") Brownell, Montezuma, Iowa, whose staff actually prepared this drawing in the form illustrated. To the right of the Brownell symbol there are two rectangles, one over the other. The upper reads "DRAWING NO. 25," and the lower reads "CALIBER .22."

HATCHING

Hatching consists of lines which represent the material used. Originally, a series of evenly spaced fine lines drawn diagonally at an angle of about 45 degrees from the horizontal, extending from the lower left to the upper right—that is, slanting upward to the reader's right—meant that the material was cast iron, but this no longer holds true. Such hatching is now widely used in detail drawings to show sections (slices) regardless of the material used, and the diagonal lines may slant upward to the reader's left. This type of hatching is used in Plate 9D, with the diagonal lines slanting upward to the reader's right for some parts and upward to the reader's left for other parts or sub-assemblies. In addition, anyone familiar with revolvers will recognize the symbols for springs, screws, bolts, pins, and other parts.

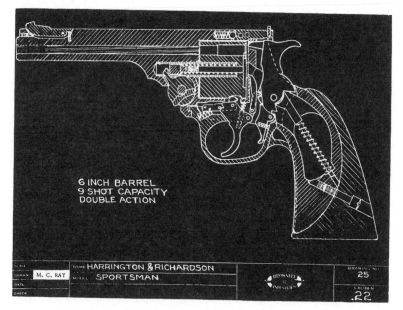

PLATE 9D. SECTIONAL DRAWING OF HARRINGTON & RICHARDSON "SPORTSMAN" REVOLVER.

VI. Woods for Gunstocks

Introduction.—The gunsmith always has been a worker in wood and probably always will be, unless our forests become depleted and we use plastics in place of wood. At one time the gunsmith was called upon to prepare the rough lumber from the logs he had felled. He dried the boards in his attic or shed, cut out the stock, and followed through all the interesting but laborious tasks of inletting, fitting the action, fitting the butt plate, checkering, etc. In these days, however, factories are doing a great deal of this work, such as the cutting of rough blanks, the production of stocks roughly inletted, the manufacture of finished stocks, and even the complete job of fitting the customer's gun to any stock he orders.

The old-time, all-around gunsmith is giving way to the modern specialists whose electrically driven machinery has largely replaced the plane, saw, chisel, file, and hacksaw of the past. Nevertheless, the principles upon which the art and science of gunsmithing are based have not changed. Amateur and semiprofessional gunsmiths will certainly continue to use hand tools to a considerable extent for reasons of economy. Professional gunsmiths will employ hand tools wherever quality and not speed or price is the criterion, for many operations cannot be performed as well by machinery as by hand.

The gunstock maker has always found it to his advantage to understand the physical characteristics of wood and its action after it has been put in place. In order, therefore, to use wood intelligently, it is necessary to know how it grows, the way it acts after the tree has been felled, its seasoning or drying, and how it is prepared for use. No two woods are exactly the same in structure, they do not behave the same under the same circumstances, and they must be selected carefully for the purpose and place where they are employed.

No two woods are identical in structure, but they have some common characteristics. They are composed of a vast number of small pockets filled with a fluid. These little pockets are called cells or fibers. The size, shape, and organization of these tiny pockets vary in the different woods; this variation accounts for the differences in appearance, texture, durability, hardness, weight, etc. When dry, all woods have approximately the same composition; by weight, this consists of the following elements: carbon 49 per cent, hydrogen 6 per cent, oxygen 44 per cent, and ash 1 per cent. The large amount of carbon explains the readiness with which it takes fire and the heat which it gives off when burned. There is also a considerable quantity of water. Green wood contains from 30 to 35 per cent of water. Air seasoning reduces this to 12 to 15 per cent. Artificial seasoning or kiln-drying reduces the water content to less than 10 per cent. However, even seasoned wood, if left in a damp place, will absorb some moisture from the atmosphere.

In the building trades, a distinction is often made between lumber and timber. Timber is the name given to wood in its natural state, before the trees are cut down, while lumber is the word used to describe the wood after the trees have been cut down and sawed up into pieces. Timber, however, may be applied to large beams, though those beams are ready for use, or even if they are already incorporated into a structure. In shipbuilding, for instance, the word is applied to a rib branching outward from the keel, usually composed of several united pieces. In gunsmithing, we do not use the word timber much, but we are interested in timber to the extent of observing the various classes of trees, the manner of their growth, the details of wood structure, and the conversion of timber into lumber.

Classes of Trees.—Trees may be divided into four kinds or classes for structural purposes. Two of these, the palms and the bamboos, may be disregarded by the gunsmith, although it is interesting to remember that the Filipinos made not only gunstocks but also gun barrels from bamboos before, during and after the Spanish-American War and the subsequent Filipino Insurrection. The two kinds suitable for gunsmiths are the so-called broad-leaved trees and the leaved trees; the latter are called conifers. The broad-leaved trees are usually referred to as hardwoods while the conifers are often called softwoods, but these terms have no reference to the actual softness or hardness of the wood. Many hardwoods are softer than the usual softwood.

Growth of Trees.—Taken together, the conifers and broad-leaved trees are described as exogenous, which means that they grow by addition to the exterior. There are two kinds of growth. First, the tree increases in height and its branches become longer by process of shooting forth a bud which becomes a twig and then a little branch that itself sends forth a bud to continue the extension process. Second, the sap passes up and down between the leaves and the roots, and new layers of wood are formed under the bark, increasing the diameter of the tree.

Structurally, there are three main parts to a tree. First, there is the bark, which may be from ½ to 2 inches or more in thickness. It has no value to the craftsman except for fuel and is removed when the tree is felled to avoid decay. Second, inside the bark is the sapwood which is the growing part of the tree. Third, inside the sapwood is the heartwood which gives the tree rigidity and strength. This heartwood is harder and denser than sapwood because it is older and has been squeezed so much while the tree has grown that its pocket-like pores have become filled. Sapwood is lighter in color and softer because it is newer and has not been subjected to much compression. Sapwood eventually becomes hardwood. Finally, we note that at the very center of a tree there is a small, whitish, loose, spongy tissue called pith.

When a tree is felled, a cross section of the trunk reveals a series of rings, one inside the other. These rings are called annual rings, sometimes called annular rings, because the wood was formed in concentric rings through the gradual growth of the trunk, one layer of wood being formed each year. A rapid growth in the spring, followed by a slow growth in the summer and an almost complete stoppage of growth during the winter months causes the rings to appear.

These annual rings are crossed at right angles by other lines which start at the pith and almost reach the bark, alternating with still other lines which start at the bark and almost reach the pith. All these lines are called medullary rays; sometimes they are called pith rays. In quarter-sawed lumber they appear as shiny, smooth spots. They are more common in the broad-leaved trees such as the oaks and chestnuts than in the pines and other conifers.

Grain.—The arrangement, appearance, and direction of the fibers in wood is called the "grain." This word is also used as a substitute for the word "fiber." When the fibers are not parallel to the main axis of the piece, it is cross-grained. When the fibers are curly, the wood is called curly-grained. When the fibers follow a winding course, the wood is termed spiral-grained. Wavy-grained wood has fibers arranged to resemble waves. Along the grain is the same as in the direction of the fibers. Fine-grained wood has small fibers; this wood may also be called close-grained. Hardwoods are usually fine-grained. Actually, this means that the annual rings are narrow and close together.

Defects and Blemishes.—A defect is an imperfection that may reduce the strength of the wood. A blemish is an imperfection that mars the appearance of the wood. Pieces cut from the same tree, or even the same log, may vary greatly in appearance, hardness, and strength. Likewise, they may have different defects and blemishes. Only a careful inspection of each piece of lumber purchased will enable the gunsmith to avoid serious losses of time and money.

Defects may be due to wind and weather or irregularities occurring during the growth of the tree. Defects of this type include knots, starshakes, heartshakes, and windshakes. These defects are permanent, that is, they will not spread. They exist within sharply defined areas. The areas containing such defects can be removed, leaving the remainder suitable for some use or other.

Another class of defects includes diseased conditions such as dry rot and wet rot. These defects will spread. Their areas of infection may become larger. The disease spreads from one part to another within the same piece of lumber or timber and it may spread from one piece of timber or lumber to another piece by even a slight contact.

We shall first consider in detail the first-mentioned type of defects, those not due to disease, and with these defects we shall also discuss a few characteristics of woods which are not necessarily defects.

Bark pockets are patches of bark partially or entirely enclosed in the wood.

Bird's-eye figures are those marked with spots suggesting birds' eyes, such as bird's-eye maple, and sometimes French and Italian walnut.

Burls are wart-like growths containing fibers running in every direction. When the presence of burls does not weaken a board structurally the resulting figure may increase the attractiveness of the board to the gunsmith.

Butt-wood is cut from the upper roots or the lower part of the trunk.

Checks are cracks along the grain of wood, the greater part of which takes place across the annual rings. An end check is one at the end of a piece of lumber. A heart check starts near the pith and reaches toward the surface without actually touching it. When several heart checks come in the same area they may form what is called a star check. A surface check is one on the surface of the lumber. There are several other terms for checks, all of which are more or less self-explanatory.

Collapse is a breaking down at the surface. It may be in streaks caused by the too rapid drying of wet wood. Other breakdowns may occur. A cross break, for instance, may come from some external force or it may result from uneven shrinkage. Cracks occurring inside a piece of wood, called honeycombing, may not be visible on the surface and yet they may render a piece of lumber utterly useless except for fuel.

Figure is the form, shape, outline, appearance, pattern, design, or whatever you choose to call the arrangement of the grain, together with the various lights and shadows of the colors and shades of the wood.

Gum Spots are streaks and patches of gum-like material in the wood.

A *Knot* is a small piece of dead wood found in a log with sound wood surrounding it. It was formed during the growth of the tree where a branch left the trunk or another branch. The branch may break away, leaving the stub to be surrounded by new growth. If a knot is tight and small, it may add to the appearance of a gunstock, but large, loose knots are obviously undesirable. There are several trade classifications for knots but they are of slight interest to the gunsmith.

A *Mottled Figure* is a pattern of wavy, irregular, cloud-like arrangements of the fibers of the wood, regarded as attractive for gunstocks.

A *Pitch Pocket* is a crack containing pitch. Pitch pockets are classified in the lumber trade according to length and width, but all pitch pockets are ruinous for gunstocks.

Shakes are cracks or separations along the grain of the wood, the greater part of which occurs between the annual rings. They are classified as fine, slight, medium, open, and through. A heartshake is found at the center of the trunk, at the heart, usually in an old tree. There is a small cavity at the center, with cracks reaching toward the bark.

A *Windshake* has moon-shaped separations, hence it is sometimes called a cupshake from the resemblance of the cracks to cups or bowls. The term windshake came from the belief of the people that high winds produced the cracks, but there are authorities who believe that the windshake may be caused by the expansion of sapwood and a resultant separation of the annual rings from each other.

A *Starshake* resembles a heartshake, but with this difference: a heartshake shows decay in the center, indicated by a large round hole, while a starshake appears to be entirely sound.

A *Raindrop Figure* is a pattern sometimes found in walnut, so called because it has the appearance of a surface streaked by falling drops of water. Like other rare patterns, it increases the value of a gunstock.

A *Ribbon Figure* consists of stripes, of various widths and lengths, rarely found in board-sawed lumber but sometimes found in quarter-sawed boards. It rivals the raindrop figure in popularity.

A *Wane* is a defect found on a corner or an edge of a piece of wood; it may be the absence of bark where bark ought to be, or more often it may be the presence of bark where none is desired.

Warping is a turning or twisting from a true surface, resulting from the evaporation of water from the wood cells and the subsequent shrinkage. Warping can be prevented by drying the lumber properly and then storing it where it will not gain or lose more moisture.

Molds and Stains Caused by Fungi affect mostly sapwood which is not selected for gunstocks. The discoloration of the wood from this source may appear in specks, spots, streaks or patches, but it has little effect on the strength of the sapwood, hence such wood can be used for ordinary building purposes and need not be wasted.

Decay, Dry Rot, and Wet Rot.—We have so far considered a number of favorable, attractive characteristics of woods, and also several defects due to structural weaknesses of wood. We are now ready to observe the defects due to the deterioration of the wood brought on by fungi.

Decay, also called "dote" and "rot," is caused by fungi which destroy wood. When "advanced, typical decay" is present, the wood is punky, stringy, spongy, crumbly, pitted, and ring-shaked, with streaks of discolorations and bleaching. When the next lower stage of decay is present it is called "incipient decay"; here it has not gone far enough for the wood to soften noticeably, but there may be some discoloration or bleaching. Also, there may be conditions described as "firm red heart" and "water-soaked." When the term "firm red heart" appears, it means that there is a peculiar reddish color in the heartwood, especially in the pines, which are not suitable for gunstocking, whether they are sound or not. The "water-soaked" condition, sometimes called "water-stained," is an incipient state of decay in hemlock and a few other woods, where there is a water-soaked area in the heartwood.

Dry Rot is dangerous because it is a disease which spreads from one part of the wood to another, causing it to lose strength long before the defect is observed. It can be avoided to a considerable extent by keeping the wood either entirely submerged in water or entirely dry. The name is misleading because no wood rots while it is dry. While the wood is in the form of timber, dry rot attacks the heartwood more readily than the sapwood, but after the timber has been cut, the dry rot attacks the sapwood part of logs or boards easier than the heartwood.

Wet Rot is another form of decay, but it is apparently confined to growing trees which have absorbed great quantities of water from a stream, swamp, bog, or other water supply. It spreads rapidly on contact between pieces of wood and in many respects resembles dry rot.

Cutting Timber into Lumber.—The central figure (No. 5) of Plate 10 shows several methods of cutting planks from a log. First it is cut into quarters; this gives what is called quarter-sawed lumber. Then the planks can be cut out in any one of the four methods shown, and each of the resulting planks or boards will be quarter-sawed.

The method shown in quarter "A", the upper left-hand quarter, is fairly good. The planks are cut more or less along radial lines; the cost of such cutting is cheaper than the method shown at C and more boards can be obtained.

The method shown in quarter "B", the upper right-hand quarter, is a common one. Only the board nearest the center is on a radial line, but it is almost as good a method as that used in "A", and has the advantage of being simpler.

The method shown in quarter "C" the lower left-hand quarter, is the best because all of the boards are cut so that they radiate from the center of the log. There is no warping or splitting. This method is expensive because each board must be squared up after being cut. It is obvious that considerable waste results, but the lack of splitting and warping tendencies makes this method desirable in spite of the cost and waste.

The method shown in quarter "D", the lower right-hand quarter, is the worst of the four because the boards have a strong tendency to twist and warp.

Figure 1, in the upper left-hand corner of Plate 10, has its two upper quarters quarter-sawed while the lower half is "board-sawed" or "plain-sawed," that is, it is simply sliced. Plain- or board-sawing gives the boards a tendency to curl. After a board has curled it is almost impossible to flatten it out, and it is then useless for gunstocking.

Figure 2, of the same plate, shows a variation on plain-sawing. Figure 3 shows a wasteful method of quarter-sawing which is ex-

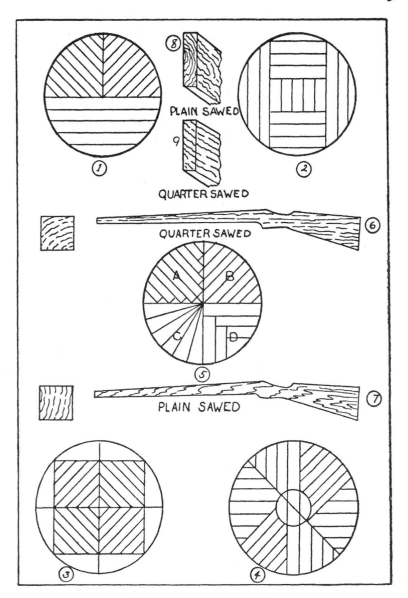

PLATE 10. SAWING WOOD.

pensive but productive of beautiful boards. Figure 4 shows a variation of quarter-sawing called the "6-point method."

Other terms applied to sawing are "flat-sawing," which means the same as board- or plain-sawing; and "rift-sawing," which means the same as quarter-sawing. The product of quarter-sawing is sometimes called "edge grain," while the product of plain-board-sawing is sometimes called "flat grain." Figures 6 and 7, Plate 10, show quarter-sawed and plain-sawed stocks.

Another way to explain quarter-sawing is to say that the annual rings are cut in a radial direction as much as possible, as contrasted with board-sawing, where the timber is cut at right angles to the annual rings as much as possible. Quarter-sawed boards shrink and crack less, wear more evenly and smoothly, and produce less slivers; furthermore, they have a prettier appearance.

Most gunstocks break at the small of the stock, that is, where the right-handed man grasps the stock with his right hand in shooting. Board- or plain-sawed stocks resist the breaking strain at this point better than the average quarter-sawed board which has been made into a stock, but if the stock is laid out so that the grain runs parallel to the grip and the bottom edge of the stock, rather than the top edge, the stock will be almost as strong as though it were made from a quarter-sawed plank. Acting on the same principle, a curly-grained board should be laid out so that the extremely curly patterns are in the butt with other lines following the curve of the pistol grip at its lower edge and then following the straight, lower edge of the forearm.

Rotary Cut Boards.—A newer method of cutting a log is to place it on a movable carriage which causes the log to whirl around rapidly against a long fixed blade which slices off strips around the circumference. We have not seen any boards for gunstocks cut by this method, but it prepares beautifully figured wood for veneers which can be used for ornamental inlays in gunstocking.

CHARACTERISTICS OF WOODS

General Characteristics.—The wood selected for gunstocking must be hard, tough, flexible; able to resist cleavage; able to resist shrinking, twisting, and warping after having been seasoned; able to withstand the deteriorating effect of oil and grease; of moderate weight; and possessing beautiful grain. We use these words and phrases to express our ideas of the mechanical and esthetic properties of the ideal gunstock wood, or of its probable behavior under conditions of stress and strain. In order that we may all agree as to the precise meaning of these terms we shall now examine them individually.

Hardness.—This is the ability to resist indentations. A wood is very hard when it requires 3,000 pounds pressure per square inch to make an indentation $\frac{1}{20}$ inch deep; examples are maple, elm, hickory, and oak. A wood is hard when it requires 2,500 pounds per square inch to do the same thing; examples are ash, birch, cherry, and walnut. A fairly hard wood is indented by a pressure of 1,500 pounds per square inch; examples are pine and spruce. Softwoods, such as butternut, hemlock, redwood, and poplar, require much less pressure and are not important to the gunsmith.

Toughness.—This is a quality of withstanding shocks and jars without shattering; it includes both strength and pliability. It is also defined as the ability to withstand high unit stress together with great unit deformation without complete fracture. In plain words, it is flexible without being brittle.

Flexibility.—Timber that adapts itself readily to change of shape, (opposed to being brittle or rigid) bends before it breaks. Hickory is probably the most flexible of all woods. In general, broad-leaved trees are more flexible than the conifers.

Cleavage.—This is the tendency to split. Conifers split more easily than the broad-leaved trees. Seasoned wood does not split so easily as green wood. Gunstock makers should remember that all lumber splits more easily along radial lines. By observing the direction of the grain and laying out the stock carefully, splitting can be avoided.

Air or Natural Seasoning.—Natural seasoning is the exposure of boards to a free circulation of air so that they may be dried to prevent shrinking and decay. The boards are placed under cover in a dry place, with the bottom layer at least 2 or 3 feet from the ground. Pieces of scantling 1 inch or more thick are laid at intervals between layers of lumber, and there should be open air spaces all through the pile to permit the free circulation of air around each piece of lumber. Air seasoning sometimes takes as long as three years, depending upon the character of the lumber, its dimensions, the structural quality to be expected from the wood after seasoning, the size of the pile, and other factors. Green wood may contain 30 per cent water before air seasoning and 15 per cent at the end of the seasoning process, but it is difficult to give any rules that will always work.

Kiln-drying or Artificial Seasoning.—Timber is stacked in a drying kiln and subjected to currents of hot air, sometimes accelerated by vacuum pumps. The time required and the temperature to be used depend upon various factors, such as the kind of lumber, dimensions of the boards, etc. Hardwoods cannot be kiln-dried immediately after cutting because then the outside would dry too fast while the inside would remain damp. This would result in the formation of checks and a condition known as "casehardening." For this reason, hardwood is dried in the open air for 3 to 6 months and then artificially dried in a kiln from 6 to 10 days, depending upon various factors. The preliminary natural drying can be avoided by using steam in the kiln, but this method is expensive and authorities do not agree that it equals the usual process. Softwoods can be placed in the kiln without being given a preliminary natural seasoning. The temperature ranges from 100 degrees F. for oak to as high as 200 degrees F. for pine. Kiln-drying can reduce the moisture content of wood to less than 10 per cent, which is obviously lower than the natural drying percentage figure of 12 to 15 per cent, but the advantages of kiln-drying are somewhat offset by the increased cost and the danger of casehardening which reduces both the elasticity and the strength of the lumber.

Shrinkage of Lumber.—The greatest shrinkage takes place in the cross section of the fibers running at right angles to the annual rings; this is known as circumferential shrinkage. Quarter-sawing cuts the medullary rays across the length, in which the shrinkage is least. Plain- or board-sawing produces lumber which cracks and checks when it shrinks. Shrinkage in the length of a board, called longitudinal shrinkage, is usually less than .1 per cent. Shrinkage in width varies in hardwoods on radial lines from 2 to 5 per cent, and on tangential lines from 4 to 7 per cent; in softwoods, it varies from 1 to 4 per cent on radial lines, and from 2 to 6 per cent on tangential lines. Since the longitudinal shrinkage is slight, the change in volume is due almost entirely to radial and tangential shrinkage, and it must be remembered that shrinkage takes place in two directions by approximately equal amounts. Opposite to shrinkage in effect is the swelling of lumber from the absorption of moisture, from the air or from contact with the ground or some direct source of water, such as a stream.

Plywood for Gunstocks.—Plywood is made by fastening together an odd number of thin layers of wood with glue, with each layer having its grain at right angles to the grain in the next layer. To prevent warping, the layers must all be sawed the same way from the timber and the moisture content should be approximately the same for all layers. Many German stocks are made of plywood.

The strength of plywood is easily explained. The tensile strength of wood parallel to the grain is greater than the strength perpendicular to the grain; sometimes the ratio is as great as 20 to 1. Next, the shearing strength parallel to the grain is far lower than the shearing strength at right angles to the grain. In plywood the layers are placed with the grain at right angles; this makes the strength about equal in all directions and is approximately equal to the average of the strength with the grain and the strength across the grain. The increased labor cost is justified by the increase in strength and beauty, for combinations of colors and figures can be easily arranged. Thin sheets of the best quality of basswood, redwood, poplar, maple, birch, and red gum have been used successfully in the manufacture of airplanes, automobiles, boats, and railway cars. The use of plywood is sound from the engineering viewpoint. It is a logical field for research and development by gunsmiths.

WOODS FROM BROAD-LEAVED TREES

Apple.—This wood is durable, strong, close-grained, and homogeneous but lacking in ornamental figure or grain. It was used occasionally by pioneer gunstockers, but it is not commercially available today and hence its use is rare. It should be seasoned for several years. When sharp tools are used, it inlets and checkers beautifully.

Beech.—This wood is heavy, hard, strong, and serviceable. It was a usual substitute for walnut in pioneer days because many of its characteristics are similar to those of walnut. Military, muzzle-loading musket stocks were made of this wood. Its interlaced fine grain works slowly, but it checkers and inlets beautifully with little danger of splitting, and it takes a high polish. In color, it is light brown and sometimes almost white. During the seasoning process it tends to shrink and check, but once it is dried out it offers little trouble. Industrially, beech wood is used for making tool handles, shoe lasts and some furniture, but it is such a homely, utilitarian wood that it has never been popular as a gunstock material.

Birch.—This is a hard, heavy, strong, firm wood of uniform texture, which takes a finish resembling that of mahogany or walnut, depending upon the method followed. There are two kinds, the red birch and the white birch, both taken from the same tree, but the red birch consists of more and older heartwood, which can be used for gunstocks, while the white birch is the sapwood or young heartwood, which cannot be used for gunstocks. Birch has not been used much for making gunstocks in the past, and we mention it here only as a possible substitute for the better woods.

Cherry.—This wood was used in the early days, especially during the percussion (cap-and-ball) period, by amateur gunsmiths, but the professional gunsmiths usually preferred other woods. When first cut it is pink or light red in color, with a close, firm grain, capable of receiving a very high polish. A few modern gunsmiths consider that if the heartwood is selected and carefully seasoned it is to be preferred to mahogany for stocks. They recommend that a little filler be used before the oil finish is applied. Incidentally, the wild cherry is not considered as strong as the cultured variety.

Gumwood.—This is a heavy, hard, tough, close-grained, compact wood, used mostly in the manufacture of furniture, wagon hubs, and hat blocks. It has a tendency to shrink and warp badly while being dried. It is light brown in color, tinged with red, and takes a high polish. The variety commonly called "Red Gum" has been used occasionally by stock makers, but it is not popular, probably because it is hard to work, is not durable when exposed, and warps and checks badly. Since the grain is very close, some pieces are so regular in figure that they can be stained to imitate black walnut and used for gunstocks, furniture, and cabinetwork.

Mahogany.—The true mahogany comes from Cuba, Mexico, the West Indies, and Central America. Formerly it was obtained in great quantities from Santo Domingo and Honduras, but these two countries no longer export so much mahogany. Other kinds of mahogany are obtained from Africa and India, especially from Africa. Mahogany is strong, durable, and flexible when green but brittle when dry. If the seasoning takes place too rapidly, deep shakes result, but in general it is free from shakes and it is less liable than most woods to attacks by worms or fungi. It comes in a great range of color, from light cherry to reddish brown, and it becomes darker and richer in tone with advancing age. As a cabinet wood, its beautiful figure and grain make it very desirable for veneers and fine furniture, but its light weight (comparatively speaking), and its brittleness make it undesirable for a gunstock that may be exposed to the elements and to stress and strain. Instead, it belongs on presentation pieces, in inlays, and any place where beauty is more important than utility.

Maple.—This wood is sometimes divided into two classes—Hard Maple and White Maple. Hard maple is hard, heavy, strong, tough, and close-grained, with small but distinct medullary rays, and a color ranging from yellow to very light brown. White maple has much the same characteristics except that they are usually more pronounced and the wood is much lighter in color than hard maple. When there is a fine, wavy grain, the wood is called "curly maple." It may have other features, such as the "bird's-eye" effect, or a so-called defect called a "blister." These variations from the normal are hard to describe but they may be explained as the result of twisting the fibers which compose the woody structure of the timber. Our ancestors favored the maple for gunstocks during the flintlock period and far into the cap-and-ball period.

Myrtle.—Strictly speaking, this is a genus of *shrubs,* but the term has also been applied in the United States to various plants. Wood described as "myrtle" and sold for gunstocks may be anything, but sometimes it is a species of wood imported from Australia, having a close grain, fine texture, and capacity for taking checkering and polishing well. When buying "myrtle," first ask the seller where he obtained it and what its true name may be. Some of the lumber sold as myrtle is well suited to stock making while other pieces marketed under this name are junk.

Osage Orange.—This wood gets its name from its color, which ranges from bright yellow or orange to brown. It is hard, strong, flexible, lustrous, pliable, elastic and durable. It checks and shrinks to a certain extent, but it takes a beautiful polish. The timber grows principally in the Gulf States and is seldom found north of the Mason and Dixon Line. It is principally used for making poles and posts, but originally it was called "bois d'arc" (bow wood), since it was a substitute for yew wood in making bows. It has been used in the past for making ramrods for muzzle-loaders, but it could be used for gunstocks.

Rosewood.—This wood is much too heavy for gunstocks, but it is ideal for inlay work and for making furniture. Most of it is imported from British India, hence it is also called East Indian, Bombay, and Malabar Rosewood, and sometimes it is termed Bombay blackwood. The color ranges from a light red to a deep purple, but no matter what color or shade may predominate there are streaks passing through the wood of every imaginable color, shade and combination —golden yellow, purplish black, pink, lavender, etc. This wood is dense and hard, close-grained, brittle, and not easy to work unless one's tools are very sharp.

Walnut.—The most popular of all woods for gunstock making is walnut. It is tough, relatively strong, and elastic. Its weight is such that it absorbs much of the recoil without being so heavy as to be a burden to the shooter; furthermore, it balances nicely. It is comparatively free from shrinkage, splitting, checking or swelling after it has been properly seasoned. It is hard enough to resist denting. The texture and hardness are uniform throughout; this permits working the walnut into the desired shapes, checkering it, and giving it a fine polish.

Black Walnut, the North American kind, is usually a rich dark brown, but it can also be described as a rich purplish brown, depending upon your idea of colors. Some experts believe that the best of the black walnut is grown in California, Texas, and other states having a warm, fairly dry climate, especially if it is grown on high, rocky ground, since this gives a harder, finer-grained, lighter-figured wood. These men claim that walnut grown in Iowa, New York,

Pennsylvania, and other northern states, where it is cold in the winter, is too porous, but still another group of experts prefer black walnut from Missouri, Kansas, and Indiana. *The truth is that each piece of lumber must be selected on its own merits; the place of its origin does not guarantee its quality.*

Circassian walnut originally came from Circassia, the region in the West Caucasus, between the Black Sea and Mt. Elbruz, formerly occupied by the Cherkesses or Circassians, but now included in the Russian province of Kuban. It is beautifully figured in the better grades, but it is characterized principally by sweeping dark lines that deepen into black when polished. These lines often assume fantastic shapes. Curly Circassian walnut usually comes from the butt or crotches of the tree, like any other curly wood, but the wood from the main trunk may be straight grained.

Most of the so-called Circassian walnut sold today is not Circassian. Furthermore, there are poor grades of genuine Circassian walnut just as there are poor grades of domestic walnut. The name "Circassian" sounds good to people who buy by the label.

English Walnut is mostly grown in California and Oregon. Spanish, Italian, Turkish, French and other foreign varieties may, or may not, come from the country whose name is on the tag. Most so-called "Circassian" and "English" walnut sold today is actually French walnut. Circassian walnut has not been imported for many years and English walnut is practically non-existent, and little more than a London gunmaker's term for fine walnut. Actually, the French walnut from the south of France is probably equal to the best Circassian.

Those desiring more information about wood should buy the bulletins issued by the U.S. Department of Agriculture, and sold by the Superintendent of Public Documents, Washington, D.C. In addition to the U.S. Department of Agriculture, and the departments of agriculture of the several states, the other outstanding source of information is the Forest Products Laboratory, Madison, Wisconsin, a nonprofit institution whose reports are constantly cited by other scientific bodies.

VII. Stock Design

THE stocks on rifles and shotguns as they arrive from the factory are made to fit everyone fairly well. If they fit the buyer accurately it is an accident. That is why there is a big demand for tailor-made stocks. Discriminating shooters want stocks that conform to their bodies, just as horsemen are particular about their saddles.

The easiest way to design a stock is merely to copy one that the shooter likes, but it is not always possible to find a suitable model. The first step is to cut a "blank" from a plank. Ready-cut blanks are obtainable from several dealers in gun supplies, but here again the shooter may wish to select the plank from which the stock is cut and follow through the various steps in the manufacture of the stock.

Figures 1, 2, 3, and 4 of Plate 11 show rough blanks. Figure 5 shows a finished stock for a Springfield, checkered, presented here to give you an idea of what can be accomplished. Figure 6 gives the principal dimensions for cutting a blank for a Springfield with a pistol grip. Figure 7 shows the method of laying out a rifle blank on a plank before the first cut is made. The dimensions given in Figure 7 need not be followed exactly, for they are there merely to show that distances are laid out along the top edge to various points; from these points perpendiculars are dropped and distances from the horizontal line are laid out on these perpendiculars. To give a really fine lay-out, more perpendiculars would be dropped than the number we have shown, because the more there are, the more accurate will be the curved lines forming the bottom of the blank. A good rule to follow for this purpose is to have few perpendiculars where

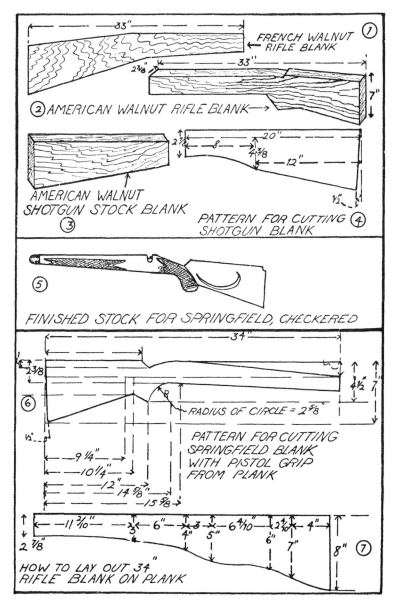

PLATE 11. HOW TO CUT STOCK BLANKS.

the slope is gentle, and many perpendiculars where the curve changes direction sharply.

A knowledge of nomenclature is necessary before we proceed further. Plate 12 not only shows how to design stocks, but it also illustrates nomenclature. The more important parts of a rifle that are closely associated with the stock design are shown on Plate 33, a Springfield Rifle, and Plates 40 and 41, a Garand Rifle, but it is not imperative to refer to them at this point.

Refer to Plate 12, Figure 1. Using the conventional nomenclature and abbreviations, "FT" is the forearm tip. "A," the part just behind the forearm tip, is the forearm, forestock or fore-end, whichever term you prefer. "G" is the grip, sometimes called a "hand" or a "hand grip," as you please. "PG" stands for "pistol grip," which is the lower part of the grip. Just behind the upper part of the grip is the "Comb," abbreviated "CO," as we have shown. The part of the stock to the rear of the grip is the "butt," marked thus on the drawing, and also labeled "B" to follow the gunstocker's custom. The heel of the butt is marked "H" and the toe of the butt is marked "T." The Cheek Piece is so marked, and also labeled "C." The center of the trigger is also marked "C" but this should not cause any difficulty. The Sight Line, marked "S" at each end, runs from the top of the front sight, at the muzzle, through the center of the rear sight, to the point where a perpendicular line drawn downward would hit the end of the butt. This sight line is drawn with the sights set as they would be for the usual range at which the rifle would be fired. This range is usually 100 yards because most game shot with a .30 caliber rifle is killed at that distance.

Notice the line drawn at right angles to the line of sight and just touching the heel of the butt. Next, notice that the toe of the butt is at a little distance from this perpendicular line. This distance is called the "Pitch." When the rifle is rested with the butt on the ground, the pitch will be the distance from the front sight to a line drawn perpendicular to the ground.

Refer to Plate 5, Figure 5, where a Drop Measurer is shown. The drop is the distance measured from the line of sight to the top edge of the heel of the butt; likewise, it may be the distance from the line of sight to the comb of the stock. A Pitch Measurer can be made by fastening a wooden or metal extension to a steel square, as shown

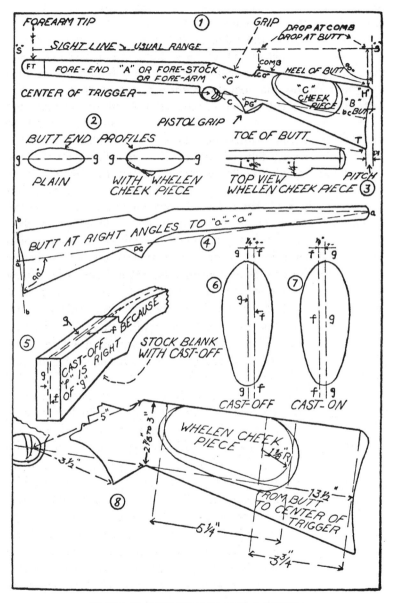

PLATE 12. HOW TO LAY OUT A STOCK.

in Figure 2, Plate 15. These devices are handy if you intend to make many stocks, but they are not essential.

Refer to Plate 12 again, where there is a line drawn from the center of the trigger to the forward edge of the cap on the pistol grip, in Figure 1. This is one of the important dimensions in stock design. When there are two triggers, the center of the forward trigger is used as a starting point. Notice that in Figure 1 there is also a line drawn from the center of the trigger to the center of the butt, marked "bc." This is another important dimension. Measurements also may be taken from the center of the trigger to the toe of the butt, and from the center of the trigger to the point of the comb.

Figure 2, Plate 12, shows butt end profiles. The one on the left is a plain butt end profile, while the one to the right is the profile of a butt having a Whelen Cheek Piece on its left side. This cheek piece was named for Colonel Townsend Whelen, U.S. Army, Retired, who is one of the greatest authorities on military and sporting rifles. A top view of the Whelen Cheek Piece is shown in Figure 3. From the heel of the butt (before the butt plate is added), measure forward about 3¾ inches on the average butt, along the top edge. Drop a perpendicular from this point, and measure downward 1⁵⁄₃₂ inches. This will be the center of an arc that will give the curvature for the rear part of the raised surface of the cheek piece. Draw the curve. At the rearmost part of the curve, draw a perpendicular up to the original. From the point where this perpendicular cuts the horizontal, measure forward 5¼ inches, and drop a perpendicular. This will cut the forward part of the curve marking the front part of the raised surface of the cheek piece. Smooth out the curves and you will have the outline of the raised part of the cheek piece as seen from the side. Looking at it from the top, as shown in Figure 3, the raised surface extends out from the center line of the butt about 1¼ inches, at a point 3¾ inches from the heel of the butt. At a point about 7 inches from the heel of the butt, the raised surface projects out to the left about ⅞ inch. Obviously, the raised surface gradually falls away until it merges with the butt proper. The actual distances vary. The ones given here are for a butt measuring from 5 to 5¼ inches from heel to toe; which is also from 13½ to 13¾ inches from the center of the trigger, on a line drawn from the center of the trigger to the center of the butt plate. The cheek piece on Figure 1 gives a good idea of the side view of the Whelen-type design. Figure 8, Plate 12, gives the details of the same thing. Remember that you should vary the dimensions to fit the needs of the shooter. The ones given here are for an average man.

Figure 4, Plate 12, is the method for laying out a stock recommended by Clyde Baker, one of America's foremost gunsmiths. He usually makes the butt at right angles to the center line of the whole stock. The center line is shown as "a-a" and the butt line is shown as "b-b" in Figure 4. This gives a stock designed for offhand shooting when hunting, and it permits the stock designer to disregard the question of pitch, since this method takes care of the pitch without further trouble.

Figures 5, 6, and 7 of Plate 12 illustrate Cast-Off and Cast-On. The line "g-g" in Figures 5, 6, and 7 is the center line of the stock; it is in a plane which passes through the center of the bore. In Figure 5 the center line of the butt (marked "f") is to the right of the center line of the stock (marked "g"), and hence the stock is said to be "cast-off." In Figure 6 the center line of the butt ("f") is ¼ inch to the right of the center line of the stock ("g"), hence it is also cast-off. To the contrary, the center line of the butt in Figure 7 ("f") is to the left of the center line of the stock ("g"); hence, it is described as "cast-on." In both Figures 6 and 7, the distance between the center line of the stock and the center line of the butt is ¼ inch. There is no definite rule. The minimum amount is usually ⅛ inch and the maximum is usually ½ inch, depending upon the physical characteristics of the shooter and his method of aim. Furthermore, some stock makers make the amount of cast-off or cast-on from ³⁄₁₆ inch to ¼ inch at the heel of the butt, and from ⁵⁄₁₆ inch to ⅜ inch at the toe of the butt.

A right-handed person naturally shoots from the right shoulder; he requires a butt with "cast-off." If it did not have cast-off, when he brought his rifle to his shoulder the front sight would be too far to the left for correct aiming. Of course, he could swing the rifle to bring the front sight in line with the rear sight, but valuable time would be lost in firing; instead of doing this, he has his butt made with cast-off. For a similar reason, a left-handed person, who shoots from the left shoulder, will require cast-on.

Having mastered a few of the more important terms, we can

turn to details of design. One of the troublesome questions is that of pitch. You will remember that when the butt is on the floor, the pitch is the distance the front sight is off from the perpendicular line to the floor. The exact amount of pitch depends upon the habits of a shooter and his build. A person who uses a rifle a great deal for target shooting usually prefers about a 3-inch pitch for both target shooting and hunting, while for one who does not do much target shooting but spends most of his ammunition in offhand firing in the field, it may be well to provide from 3 to 4 inches of pitch. The average person will usually compromise between the two extremes and choose a pitch somewhere between 3 inches and 3½ inches. A big, barrel-chested man (or a normal woman) who stands very straight when he fires may want as much as 5 inches, while a small woman who leans over when she fires from the standing position might need as little as 2½ inches of pitch. These dimensions refer to rifles. The pitch of the shotgun for the average man is from zero to 2½ or 3 inches.

We return now to the subject of cheek pieces. A shooter who does not have a cheek piece on his rifle or shotgun invariably cocks his head over to the right while lining up the sights (assuming that he is a right-handed person). The amount that he cants his head to the right does not seem to vary with the thickness of the comb (the upper edge of the butt, just back of the small of the stock). When a cheek piece is added, he naturally cants his head the same amount every time he aims, and if it is properly designed, he is able to hold his firearm more firmly and hence he receives less shock from the recoil.

Refer to Figure 3, Plate 12, where you will observe that the cheek piece is made so that it gradually grows thinner toward its forward end. This causes the recoil to exert less force on the face, whereas a cheek piece that is not designed in this manner may bring severe punishment. Also, refer to the right part of Figure 2, Plate 12, where it is shown that the cheek piece is built in a straight line from the top to the bottom edge; it does not bulge inward or outward. The line from the rear edge to the front edge is also straight, but some gunsmiths have given this line a slightly concave effect without experiencing any discomfort from recoil.

Figures 1 and 8, Plate 12, show that the front end of a cheek piece is a little distance back from the comb. This distance depends upon how far forward the comb is from the heel of the butt, but normally the front end of the cheek piece is from 1 to 2 inches behind the comb. However, if the shooter is in the habit of holding his head well forward when he aims, a different type of piece may be desirable. Figure 2, Plate 16, happens to be a cheek piece that is applied to the stock after the stock has been finished, but it illustrates a good form of cheek piece for the person who gets his nose close to the cocking piece of his rifle. The relationship between this type of cheek piece and the comb is well illustrated in the corner drawings on Plate 16, although that plate is intended to illustrate the checkering and carving of stocks. There it is shown that a cheek piece can be made so that its forward edge reaches the comb, instead of stopping short an inch or two behind it, as is the case with the Whelen type.

Figure 3, Plate 15, shows how a cheek piece can be inlaid in a butt, but the technique of this operation belongs in a later chapter.

Our next problem is the design of the comb. This part of the stock is immediately behind the small of the stock; it is the forward top portion of the stock against which the face is rested in firing. Figure 1, Plate 12, shows the comb clearly. Figure 8, Plate 12, shows that the distance from the center of the trigger to the point of the comb may be 5 inches for a military-type rifle, although it may be as short as 4¾ inches. For a shotgun the distance from the center of the trigger to the point of the comb may be from 5 to 5½ inches, measuring from the forward trigger.

A rule-of-thumb advocated by some gunsmiths is to measure with a ruler from the tip of the index finger of the shooter's hand to the crotch of his thumb. That is, grasp the ruler so that it is all the way back between the thumb and index finger, resting against the flesh separating the two digits. Where the tip of the index finger is found on the ruler, the distance from the center of the trigger to the point of the comb is determined. This may be from 4½ to 5 inches, more or less.

The origin of this rule is that when the shooter grips the small of the stock his thumb is supported at its base by the comb, and the index finger is in position on the trigger, preferably with the second joint of the index finger pressing against the trigger, although some shooters get into the habit of using the first joint. This may result in placing the point of the comb over the rear part of the pistol grip, or over the middle of the pistol grip.

A shooter who keeps the thumb on the right side while firing may prefer a comb from ⅜ to ½ inch forward of the location of the comb for a shooter who wraps his thumb around the small of the stock, just behind the cocking-piece of the bolt-action type rifle. The latter shooter ought to learn not to place his thumb in such a position, but it is the job of the gunsmith to cater to the whims of the shooter, not to teach him marksmanship.

The thickness of the comb depends upon the shape of the face of the shooter. A thin-faced man needs a thick comb, while a full-faced person needs a thin comb. The thinnest comb is usually about ⅜ inch while the thickest is about ⅝ inch, giving an average thickness of about ½ inch.

The drop of the comb is its distance below the line of sight, as shown in Figure 1, Plate 12. On a bolt-action rifle this is determined by making the drop to the point of the comb just enough so that the under surface of the bolt will clear the comb as it is withdrawn. This distance may be from 1⅝ inches to 1⅞ inches, usually the latter, but it obviously depends upon the type of sights mounted on the firearm.

The pistol grip is our next problem. The top and side views of a typical pistol grip cap are shown in Figure 3, Plate 13. The stock in Figure 6, Plate 11, has a pistol grip, and there is one on the stock in Figure 5 of the same plate. Likewise, Figures 1, 4, and 8 of Plate 12 show pistol grips. All of the stocks shown in Plate 16 have pistol grips, and Figures 4, 5, and 6 of Plate 15 show pistol grips.

Figure 6, Plate 11, shows how a pattern is laid out for cutting a Springfield blank stock from a plank. On that figure, it is 10¼ inches from the left to the rear edge of the cap of the pistol grip, and 12 inches to the forward edge. The radius of the circle for the under side of the small of the stock is 2⅝ inches. These dimensions would have little meaning unless the stock was cut out according to the plan shown in that figure.

We have already mentioned that in Figure 1, Plate 12, a line is drawn from the center of the trigger to the nearest edge of the

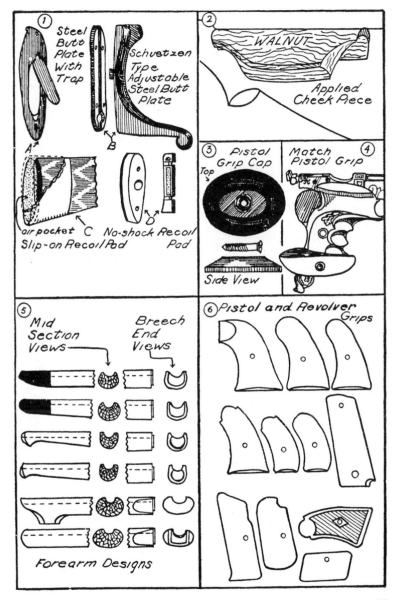

PLATE 13. BUTT PLATES, FOREARM DESIGNS, GRIPS AND CHEEK PIECE.

pistol grip cap, and that this is one of the important stock dimensions. In Figure 8, Plate 12, the distance is given as 3½ inches. Sometimes this distance is cut to 3⅛ inches or 3¼ inches, but 3½ inches is the generally accepted distance. The greatest distance of which we have ever heard was 4 inches, which was for a very big man.

The shape of the point of the butt of the pistol grip, that is, the point from which the distance to the center of the trigger is measured, should be approximately a right angle. This is clearly shown in Figure 1, Plate 12, and also in Figure 4. The point in Figure 6, Plate 11, seems a little too sharp; it would be better if it, too, were a 90-degree angle. Notice also that the angle formed between the lower edge of the butt of the stock and the butt of the pistol grip is an obtuse angle, in fact it is an angle of about 135 degrees. In cross-sectional shape, the pistol grip should be an oval, not a circle. Its size depends upon the size of the shooter's hand. Make it a little larger than you think necessary and then trim it down to fit. A safe rule is to make the oval 2 inches high and 1⅜ inches wide. If that is too big, as it often is, you can still reduce the dimensions from 1⁄16 inch to ⅛ inch in each direction, depending upon the way it fits into the shooter's hand.

The forearm, forestock, or fore-end, whichever name you prefer, comes next. This part of the stock is plainly marked in Figure 1, Plate 12. Side and cross-sectional views of several styles of forearms are shown in Figure 5, Plate 13, where six designs are illustrated. They are not numbered in the illustration, but by calling the top one No. 1, and numbering down, we can refer to them without difficulty.

No. 1 is found on almost all of the finest rifles. No. 2 is favored by those who have a tendency to cant their rifles when firing, but it is a little more difficult to make along graceful lines. No. 3 is cylindrical in cross section. No. 4 is similar to No. 3. No. 5 is oval-shaped with the long dimension horizontal. No. 6 is commonly described as a "full beaver-tail" type.

The length of the forearm on the average rifle may be one-half the length of the barrel, provided the barrel is not more than 25 inches long. Another way to figure forearm length is to make it about one-half the distance from the receiver to the end of the barrel, but never more than 12½ inches. In general, the forearm is usually between 9½ and 11 inches long. However, consider the location of the forward sling swivel. If the swivel base is to be mounted on the barrel there is no problem, but if the swivel is to be placed on the forearm it must be carefully located. This may make it necessary to lengthen the forearm, but no definite rules can be given for choosing the correct forearm length in this situation.

The forearm tips take various forms, as shown by the column of six tips to the left in Figure 5, Plate 13. They may be flat, blunt, sharp, or shaped like a bird's beak. The tip may be part of the forearm, or it may be a separate part, made of bakelite, ebony, horn, ivory or plastic. It may be plain or ornamented. Practically, the shape and material are not as important as most gun lovers like to pretend.

The butt stock is our next problem in stock design. Plates 11 and 12 show the shapes and the general lay-out methods. The stock back of the grip should have the same thickness as the grip. The bottom edge behind the grip should be full, rounded out, and narrowed toward the toe of the butt in a straight taper that conforms to the shape of the butt plate. On the contrary, the upper edge of the stock is narrow toward the comb and thickens in a straight taper to a fully rounded shape at the butt. The shape and thickness of the butt are determined by the butt plate, which is oval, about 5¼ inches long, and about 1⅜ inches wide. A conventional steel butt plate with a trap door is shown in the upper left-hand corner of Figure 1, Plate 13, marked "A." The Schuetzen-type adjustable steel butt plate is marked "B." In the same figure, "C" is a slip-on recoil pad with an air pocket, laced over the butt; and "D" is a "no-shock" recoil pad made of rubber with an inner cushion of a jelly-like substance.

A recoil pad is very desirable for women, children, and frail men; also, anyone who is firing for a long period of time needs one. There are many men with narrow shoulders who find a pad necessary; otherwise, they hold the butt against the outside edge of the shoulder and bruise the arm. However, military rifles are issued with steel butt plates, corrugated to prevent slipping. In firing on the range, soldiers habitually pin a towel under the shirt or wear a padded shooting jacket.

A steel butt plate with a trap door is mounted on the butt after a recess is cut into the butt stock. This hole is a handy container for a little oilcan, a cleaning brush, and a piece of line for cleaning in the field. Sometimes the hole is made big enough to hold matches, extra cartridges, a firing pin, springs, etc. Even when the hole is not needed for storage purposes, it may be drilled to lighten the stock and hence throw part of the weight forward to obtain proper balance. When this is done, the hole may be closed by inserting a wooden plug, tightly sealed to keep out moisture.

When the butt plate is mounted, it must fit the stock smoothly at all points. If the wood has been cut to an exact fit, this is no trouble, but where the parts of the butt plate project from the smooth lines of the butt, they can be ground down, although the best course is to make sure that the plate will fit before the butt is finished. Figures 4 and 6, Plate 13, are self-explanatory.

We have chosen the bolt-action rifle stock for our discussion because it embodies most of the features of stocks for other shoulder weapons, as well as some points that are ordinarily considered peculiar to the Springfield type but which are really adaptable to other weapons. The bolt-action stock, as we have shown, is a one-piece stock. Two-piece stocks are found on many single-shot rifles, but their design and construction follow the principles already explained.

Single-shot rifles are usually found in two classes: first, .22 caliber rifles, both in the cheap grade for children and beginners and in the target grade; second, target rifles of various calibers designed for expert marksmen. There is a strong tendency on the part of manufacturers to assume that .22 caliber rifles are bought more for children than adults; they therefore make the stock too small to fit the average man. If the rifle barrel and action are inferior or mediocre, there is no point in mounting them in a carefully made stock, but when they are superior in quality, the owner may find it necessary to acquire a stock made according to his personal needs. It seems obvious that an experienced target marksman will prescribe the specifications for the stock when he orders a match rifle, hence a different stock will not be needed until the possession of the rifle passes to another person.

General rules for making stocks for single-shot rifles are few. One is that the comb must be cut farther back when there is a long upper tang. When the lower tang is straight, it may be bent to form a grip unless action parts extend to the rear into the stock. (The tang is the finger-like projection at the rear of the receiver.) Common faults of single-shot stocks that are brought to the gunsmith are: stock too short; butt plate too small; too much drop at the heel; comb too low and too thin; fore-end too short, too thin, and poorly shaped. The fore-end may have no taper, it may taper from front to rear or from rear to front, but the majority of gunsmiths agree that it should taper from front to rear to give the shooter a better grasp when he instinctively pulls backward with the left arm while it is grasping the forearm (assuming that he is a right-handed shooter).

A shotgun stock is different from a rifle stock, but the differences are matters of degree rather than kind. Ordinarily, the shotgun stock should be straighter and longer. The comb is usually set farther back on a shotgun stock, but mere custom should not dictate its location; the stockmaker should locate it according to the same methods that he would use for a rifle stock. The pistol grip on a factory-made shotgun stock is often too small to have any value. Since most shotguns have two triggers and the pistol grip is located with reference to one of the triggers, the pistol grip is in the way when the other trigger is squeezed; therefore it seems advisable not to have a pistol grip on a shotgun, but if the owner insists on having one, it is better to locate it according to the position of the rear trigger and be sure to make it a full pistol grip and not merely a wart.

The shotgun is usually fired without taking deliberate aim. This indicates a need for a little more cast-off than one would have on a rifle; about ⅛ inch more is about right in most cases. Another result of quick, instinctive aiming is a need for about the same drop at the heel of the butt and the comb, but if the shooter finds that this brings the butt too high on his shoulder, the butt stock should be given a "Monte Carlo" effect. This is done by bringing the comb back horizontally and then dropping the comb to the heel abruptly.

It gives the butt the appearance of having had a curved "bite" taken out of the butt at the heel. It is thus possible to have a high, horizontal comb and at the same time have enough heel drop for the butt to fit into the hollow of the shoulder. The Monte Carlo stock is advisable for people with long necks and for those who wear glasses.

Having explained the design of the parts of a stock, we can refer once more to Plate 11, and discuss the dimensions for stocks. Figures, 1, 2, 4, 6, and 7 give the impression that blank cut from planks should be 33 inches long or 34 inches long for rifles, and 20 inches long for shotguns. These are typical, average dimensions, but the stock should have a length that fits the shooter. A good way to determine the proper lay-out is to visit a gun shop and examine various arms.

A test for stock dimensions and design is to place a target on a wall, with the center of the bull's-eye in the line of normal aim. Assume a correct, standing, firing position. Bring the rifle to the shoulder and aim at the bull's-eye. Then, lower the rifle, close the eyes, and bring the rifle to what you believe is the correct aiming position. Open your eyes and see where you would hit if you had fired a shot. Repeat this several times until your results are fairly uniform. If you are aiming low, there may be too much drop. If you are aiming high, the comb may be too high or the stock too straight. If you are aiming right or left of the bull's-eye, cast-off may be needed. If the trigger must be squeezed with the first joint of the trigger finger, the distance from the center of the trigger to the butt is too great; you should be able to use the middle joint.

Remember that the size and shape of the shooter are the first considerations in stock design. If he has been properly trained according to the standard military methods, he should assume correct firing attitudes when shooting from the standing, sitting, kneeling, and prone positions, but if he is self-taught, or "bull-headed," his individual peculiarities must be taken into account. Mechanical details, such as the length of the barrel, are of less importance than the shooter's size, shape, and aiming habits. Finally, accuracy, comfort and speed are the three objectives of stock design.

VIII. Checkering and Carving Stocks

CHECKERING, also called "checking," is the cutting of squares and diamonds for decoration and to prevent slipping. Examples of checkering are shown in Plate 16. The equipment needed consists of a checkering table and stand, shown in Plate 14, checkering tools, and a three-square file, more correctly described as an American-Swiss, three-square escapement file, with its point bent slightly.

We shall first discuss the checkering table, cradle, and stand, shown in Plate 14, which can be made in the home workshop at small expense. The purpose of the cradle is to hold a gunstock between its centers. The stand holds the cradle, although some gunsmiths prefer to hold the cradle in their lap, and others choose to hold it in either a quick-opening carpenter's vise, such as the one shown in Figure 2, Plate 6 (a similar one is at the left of the workbench shown in Plate 1) or in the machinist's vise, shown in Figure 7, Plate 5 (also shown at the right of the bench in Plate 1).

The best material for the cradle and stand is some hardwood, such as oak. The parts are 3 x 3 inches, except the horizontal board in the stand, which is made wide enough to hold the kingbolt; it, too, should be 3 inches thick. Enclosing boards, shown in section at the bottom of Plate 14, should be 1 x 3 inches. The stand itself is square. The cradle is made long enough to accommodate the stocks being checkered, which means that it should be at least 10 inches longer than the stock. Thus, a stock 34 inches long requires a cradle frame 44 inches long, while a full-stock intended for some types of rifles may be 42 inches long and require a frame that is 52

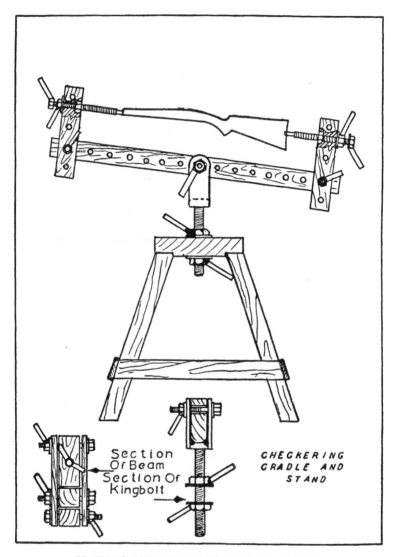

PLATE 14. CHECKERING CRADLE AND STAND.

inches long. To play safe, make your cradle frame long enough to hold any stock of reasonable length.

The kingbolt is a standard 1¼ inches black bolt, 18 inches long, with ear-plates ⅛ inch thick, welded on each side of the bolthead. All clamp-bolts are standard ½ inch black bolts. Clamp-nuts are shown with handles welded, but a wrench may be used instead. The centering-bolts are ¾ inch by any desired length. They run in nuts imbedded in the uprights and are steadied with jamb-nuts. The boltheads and jamb-nuts are shown provided with handles, but wrenches may be used if preferred. The centering-bolts should have cupped ends instead of pointed ends, like the usual wood-lathe centers. Washers must be placed under all nuts.

The cradle is universal in motion, that is, it will swing in any dimension and may be adjusted vertically for height. The maker can design the stand according to his own build and preference. Some work sitting down, but the best work is done standing. Study Plate 14 carefully and you should have no difficulty in building your own appliance. Remember, you can start checkering stocks without a checkering cradle, but if you are going to checker a stock there should be no halfway measures. Nothing looks worse than a poorly checkered stock. The beginner needs every possible means for improving the character of his work.

If you insist upon checkering without a cradle, something must be used to protect the wood if it is held in an ordinary machinist's vise. Sheets of lead, bent to fit, shown in Figure 1, Plate 29, are satisfactory. Wooden blocks, faced with felt or leather, shown in Figures 1 and 2, Plate 29, are still better because they can be used in either a machinist's vise or in a carpenter's quick-opening vise. Lacking these, wrap rags around the stock where it fits into the vise.

A professional-grade set of checkering tools is shown in Figure 2, Plate 20, together with a barrel-inletting rasp, which does not actually belong in a checkering set but falls into the general class of woodworking tools. The cutting-out tool is for English style flat checking; there are two lines of teeth and there are 16, 18, or 20 lines to the inch, depending upon whether fine or coarse checkering is desired. The mullering tool is for cutting a border and general embellishing. The scoring tool is for cutting checkering on the butt plate and similar surfaces. The scoring file is for deepening and cleaning the scoring. The checker smooth (sometimes spelled "chequer") is for deepening, smoothing, and cleaning after the use of cutting-out tools. The steel checker file is for filing checkering on metal. Usually, we think of checkering as being done on wood only, but it is also used on metal to improve the appearance and prevent slipping.

The diamond checker at the bottom of Figure 2, Plate 20 is used, as its name indicates, for cutting diamond patterns. While your attention is directed to this part of the plate, we may mention that the barrel-inletting rasp is used to open the barrel groove or channel in the forepiece of a rifle stock, and for inletting the forepiece of a shotgun stock.

The beginner can do simple checkering with three homemade checkering tools plus the American-Swiss, three-square, escapement file. The common names for these tools are "line-spacer," "V-tool" or "deepening tool," and "border-cutter." All three can be made from $5/32$ inch drill rod, or drill rod that is $1/8$ x $1/4$ inch, whichever is available, the rod being cut into lengths of 6 or 8 inches, heated at the end to a cherry red, forged flat, and then bent about 1 inch from the working end to whatever angle is desired. The question of the correct angle will be discussed further. The rear end is sharpened and forced into a wooden file handle. When drill rod is not obtainable, cut up old umbrella ribs, file them to shape and use them to cut the checkering lines. The results obtained will not be as good as though professional tools, or those carefully made from drill rod, were used, but at least you can get a start.

The line-spacer is bent so that if you laid the main arm of the tool flat the working end would rise from the horizontal at an angle of from 20 to 30 degrees. Another way to express this is to say that if the cutting surface is flat on the material, the rest of the tool rises from the horizontal at an angle of 20 to 30 degrees. After it is bent, cut a groove along the working surface about .04 inch wide, with the three-square file that you will later use for checkering, or, better, use a die sinker's knife-edge needle file, if one is available. Having cut the groove, cut teeth along the sides of the tool but not across the bottom. Some gunsmiths cut the teeth so that they lean forward, while others make them straight, and still others make them lean backward. The angle to which the teeth are cut depends largely upon the nature of the wood to be worked; those which slope back-ward slightly do not catch in the wood easily. Having cut the teeth on both sides of the groove, heat the working end cherry red again, dip it in water and then in linseed oil, and draw the temper by "flashing off the oil" once. (Heat treatment is explained more fully in a later chapter.)

A well-equipped shop has milling cutters for making checkering tools, and for other purposes. These resemble circular saws and are used to mill out the cutting teeth, after which they are filed to their final shape, but the beginner can learn more by confining himself to simple methods and equipment. Softwoods are cut with teeth which number 16 to the inch, while very hard woods are cut with teeth numbering 24 to the inch. The number of teeth is expressed as "lines" to the inch, rather than teeth. The best way to cut the teeth evenly is to first cut a few with a file on soft metal and then place the resulting pattern on the line-spacer.

The "V-tool," or "deepening tool," is made next. It is forged to a shape so that the working end curves down about 1 inch from the end, its under surface forming an angle of about 110 or 120 degrees with the main arm of the tool. With a file, make it about ⅛ inch thick at the end, and then bevel back the edge until it is about ¼ inch thick, thus giving it a V shape, with an angle of about 27 degrees between the sides of the V. Do not cut a groove in the working end, but cut teeth on the side in the same manner as you did on the line-spacer. These teeth should be very fine; 24 teeth to the inch is by no means too fine. Arrange the teeth so that they will be exactly opposite each other on both sides of the tool. Follow-ing the usual methods of heat treatment, harden and temper the working end of the tool, and then smooth the teeth with an Ar-kansas stone.

The border cutter is similar to the line-spacer in construction except that it has two grooves rather than one. These grooves are on both sides of the center line of the tool, giving a sharp, V-shaped cutting edge on each of the outside edges and a rounded cutting edge in the center. Teeth are cut across the bottom so that there will be teeth on the middle cutting section. These mid-section teeth resemble those of a cross-cut saw. Teeth are also cut on the side sections, just as though you were cutting teeth on a line-spacer.

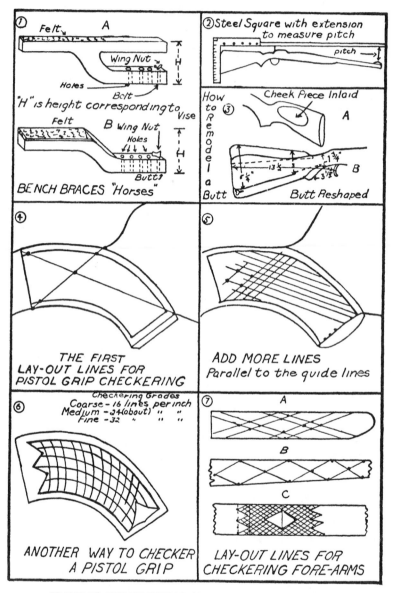

PLATE 15. STOCKMAKING AND CHECKERING DETAILS.

In addition to the three checkering tools, you should have a bent file, preferably of the American-Swiss, three-square escapement type. The easiest way to bend the file is to use boneblack, so called because it is a black substance made by calcining bones in close vessels. Coat the file with a mixture of boneblack and oil, heat to a cherry red, and bend on a block of hardwood with a steadily increasing pressure. Having bent it, coat it with boneblack and oil again, heat it once more to a cherry red, and dip it into a solution of salt and water. Next, brush out the boneblack with a file card. The boneblack and oil mixture must be placed over the teeth of the file for protection. If salt water is not handy for the quenching after the second heating, cold water will do. Only about ¾ to 1 inch of the working end of the file need be bent.

When the checkering cradle and stand, the checkering tools, and the bent file are at hand, we can actually start to checker a gunstock. Figure 5, Plate II, shows that the pistol grip and the forearm are the parts to be checkered. Plate 16 shows four ways to checker the pistol grip and one example of checkering on forearm, pistol grip, and butt stock. Figures 4, 5, 6, and 7, Plate 15, show the lay-out lines for getting started.

Refer to Figure 4, Plate 15. First draw the diagonal line that runs from a point just behind the trigger guard to the point where the upper surface of the butt begins to curve away from the upper surface of the grip. This line runs from the lower left to the upper right. Second, draw the diagonal line that runs from the upper left to the lower right; another way of describing this line is to say that it runs from the point above the rear of the trigger guard to the rear point of the grip cap. Third, draw your border lines which follow the curves of the pistol grip about ¹⁄₁₆ inch or ⅛ inch inside the curved lines. Fourth, refer to Figure 5, Plate 15, and add more lines parellel to the guide lines. Fine checkering may be 32 lines to the inch; medium checkering may be 24 lines to the inch; and coarse checkering may be 16 lines to the inch, as indicated in the caption in the upper part of Figure 6, Plate 15. The number of lines to the inch is not arbitrary. These figures are only approximate, but they are followed more or less by all checkering experts. Notice that in Figure 6, Plate 15, the lay-out lines were first laid out as curves which followed the curves of the pistol grip, and then the other lines were drawn parallel to these guide lines, with two V-shaped indentations at the front of the checkering and one large V-shaped indentation at the rear of the pattern.

It is well to draw the design on paper or cardboard before drawing lines on the grip or forearm, keeping in mind that the checkering will follow a curved surface. Make two patterns for the grip, one for each side, and one pattern for the forearm. The butt is usually not checkered, but if it is there should be a pattern for each side. Lay the patterns against the wood and cut light lines with the bent file. Ordinarily, it is necessary to cut only the guide lines with the help of the pattern, but a beginner may find it necessary to use the patterns until not only the guide lines but also several of the other lines are established. After that, lines can be drawn with the aid of a flexible steel or celluloid ruler. Another means of laying out the pattern is to drive pins into the wood at the points and connect them with wire or string (piano wire is best, but any wire is satisfactory).

Lay-out lines for forearms are shown in Figure 7, Plate 15. A pattern should be used by the beginner, but the expert can work directly on the wood. In Figure 7, "A" shows a side view of a forearm laid out for checkering, "B" shows the first lay-out lines for the under surface, and "C" shows how the lay-out lines are followed by numerous lines parallel to the original guide lines. Remember that there are as many designs as the imagination of the gunsmith can suggest, but all designs are based upon either squares or diamonds, or both. Plate 16 shows how beautiful checkering can be, but it should be kept in mind that the basic reason for checkering is to give the shooter surfaces that will not slip while he is firing.

Having laid out the designs, actual checkering can be started, but the beginner ought to practice on either an old stock or some inexpensive wood that has no other use. If an old stock is handy, practice with the V-tool (deepening tool) on the forearm. Start at the rear of the checkering and push the tool forward in one of the checkering lines, working back and forth as if you were filing, but advancing a fraction of an inch with each stroke, being careful not to deepen the groove but merely clean it out the first time it is gone

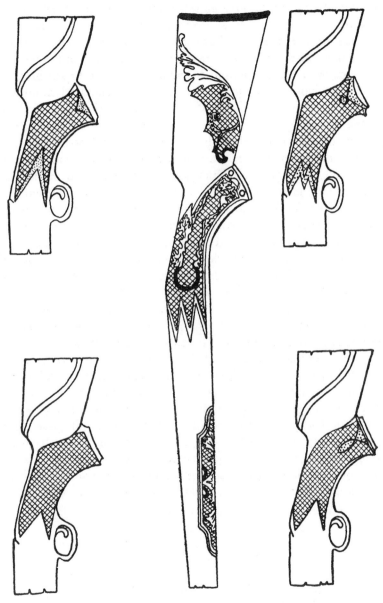

PLATE 16. CHECKERED AND CARVED STOCKS.

over, and stop at the end of the line so that the border is not damaged.

Hold the V-tool in the right hand, the thumb wrapped around the handle, the forefinger extended along the side of the shank. The shank of the tool is thus held in prolongation of the forearm and wrist. Do not exert pressure with the right hand. Place the left hand with the fingers under the part being checkered and the thumb over the tool, at the point where the working end is bent, so that the thumb can act as a guide and at the same time exert a slight pressure on the tool. Do not let the tool slide out of the main axis of the groove or jump into another groove. Keep the tool in front of the center of your body. Stand erect with the elbows braced against the sides of your body to steady your arms. From time to time, bend over and look along the groove being cleaned out to be sure that the line is kept straight. Brush out each groove after it has been worked. Repeat the process with all lines running in the same direction, turn the checkering cradle around and clean out the lines running cross-wise to the first ones cleaned. Clean each groove for its entire length at one operation; do not stop part way and then come back from the other end, because this may result in a groove that has a dip in the center.

If the wood is very dry, place a few drops of linseed oil or some other light oil on your bench brush. Get the habit of brushing out the grooves. When the groove is free of dust you can be sure that you are not overrunning the lines. The oil on the brush will give the wood a shine that reflects the light and it also absorbs the very fine dust that would not be picked up by a dry brush. If too much oil is on the brush, the excess should be removed with a rag. Better, have two bench brushes, one for oil and one that is kept free of oil.

The most difficult checkering to clean out is that on the pistol grip because of the contours that are constantly changing. Just as you would do with a forearm, go over the lines running in one direction and then work on those going the other direction. Turn the stock in the cradle as you progress in each groove, to permit holding the tool in the same position at all times. Be sure that you do not depart from the lines or the appearance of the checkering will be spoiled.

Having cleaned out the checkering with the V-tool, repeat the process with the bent file which we described earlier in this chapter. Hold it in the same manner as you did the V-tool, and follow the same methods throughout, but this time you will sharpen the lines, especially where they cross each other to form squares or diamonds. Constantly brush out the lines. We repeat this instruction because failure to keep the grooves free of dust is the most common cause of failure in checkering.

You have now acquired practice with the V-tool and the bent file, leaving only the line-spacer tool and the border-cutting tool to be mastered. There is no advantage in going over an old stock with these tools, unless you select a surface that has not been checkered already, but it is advisable for the beginner to practice with the line-spacer and the border-cutter on a piece of scrap lumber before using them on a good stock.

Actually, the V-tool is not the first tool used in checkering, but we recommend practicing with it first because it is the most difficult one to use. If you have mastered the technique of the V-tool, the others are easy to handle, whereas bad habits acquired with the line-spacer, the border-cutter, or the bent file show up immediately when the V-tool is mishandled.

The first checkering with the line-spacer should be with one that cuts 16 lines to the inch, which is the coarse cut. Later, as you become more experienced, you can safely use the medium (24-line), or the fine (32-line) tool. Of course, the choice of a line-spacer does not depend entirely upon the skill of the gunstocker. We have already mentioned that a coarse tool should be used on softwoods, while a fine tool can be used on hardwoods.

To use the line-spacer, sit or stand erect in front of the cradle, with the stock held firmly in place. Hold the tool in the right hand, thumb under the shank, forefinger over the shank and exerting a light pressure; the right hand, wrist, and forearm are used to guide the tool. Place the left hand in front of the tool, with the first and second fingers of the left hand exerting a slight pressure on the end of the tool, but not guiding it the least bit. Keep the left thumb out of the way. With a filing motion, such as used with the V-tool, advance along a line with strokes about 1 inch long, being sure to keep the cut straight. Do not try to cut deep with this tool, because, as its name indicates, it is intended simply for spacing the lines of checkering and not for cutting out the grooves.

When one cut has been made along its entire distance, move the cradle and cut another. Continue to cut parallel lines running in the same direction until all of them have been completed; then, cut the lines running in the other direction. Since both edges of the line-spacer are alike, you can work from right to left across the wood, or from left to right, as you please. Do not let the lines either fan out or converge; they must be kept straight. This is difficult, because the stock has rounded surfaces at nearly all points where checkering is applied, but by using a constant filing stroke that steadily advances, inch by inch, and by repeatedly brushing the work and sighting along the lines, even a beginner can keep the lines straight if he is patient.

When the lines have been spaced, go over them very lightly with the V-tool, using no more pressure than you would apply in cleaning out the checkering on an old stock. If you cut the lines to their full depth the first time the V-tool is used, the lines running in one direction may be well cut, but the points where they cross the lines running in the other direction will be dulled and it may be impossible to complete a satisfactory job of checkering. Having gone over all the lines once, go back and go over them again with the object of finishing them to their full depth. Next, sharpen the corners of the squares or diamonds with the bent file.

The bent file is also used for cutting short curves and angles where the line-spacer and the V-tool cannot enter successfully. By tipping the line-spacer or the V-tool upward, it is possible to get into the curves and angles that cannot be cut in the normal manner, but the safest course is to save such places for the bent file.

Finally, we can finish the checkering job by going around the checkered area with the border-cutter previously described, or if you do not have this tool, cut a single-line border around the edge of the checkered area with the V-tool, and finish with the bent file for the sharp corners and small curves. Clean out the lines with an oiled brush, wipe out any excess oil, sweep out the lines with a clean, un-oiled brush, polish the edges, and you are done.

There are many little details that could be discussed, but we have presented the essential steps. One of the things that is left to the taste of the gunstocker is the depth of the checkering. If the checkering is too shallow, it will wear away early in the life of the gun; if it is too deep, the sharp corners of the squares and diamonds will break off. Somewhere between $\frac{1}{32}$ inch and $\frac{1}{8}$ inch deep is correct, with $\frac{1}{16}$ inch being a good general average for the depth at the completion of the job.

Another debatable topic is that of laying out the design. The measuring tools shown in Plates 2 and 3 will prove handy. Although we discussed the lay-out of the checkering design earlier in this chapter without direct reference to a center line, there are many gunstockers who believe that it is imperative always to draw a center line, whether the checkering is being placed on a forearm or on a pistol grip. Having drawn a center line, they measure on each side of that line with dividers.

Still another topic that should be explained is the best way to hold the stock in the cradle. Blocks of hardwood, carved to fit between the bearing surfaces of the metal and the ends of the stock, will prevent any damage done to the stock if the bearing surfaces exert a little too much pressure. However, it seems obvious that the stock is held in the cradle with just enough pressure to keep it in place and not enough to bend or break it.

CARVING

Simplicity is a prime requisite for beautiful wood carving. The simplest and easiest design to carve is the so-called "chip pattern," which consists of triangles formed by diagonal and straight lines crossing each other; the diamond-shaped carving similar to checkering is merely a variation of the chip pattern. A little more difficult is the beaded design, which is formed by placing circles inside the diamonds or triangles. The "fish-scale pattern" consists of ogival-shaped figures placed, row upon row, like bricks. Still more difficult to execute are oak leaves, elaborate scrolls, and flowers. Unless they are held in restraint, elaborate carvings tend to give a gaudy appearance and detract from whatever beauty a gun might otherwise have by reason of excellent checkering and metal engraving. In the opinion of the author, the stock in the middle of Plate 16 has about as much work on it as good taste will permit. Even the simple "C" monogram detracts from the beauty of the checkering because it interrupts the smooth flow of the lines. Actually, we do not have this monogram on any of our stocks; it was placed in the drawing to illustrate our contention that too much decoration kills beauty. On the other hand, the simple, floral-like lines at the rear of the stock harmonize with the rest of the ornamentation because they streamline into the checkering on the butt.

Special wood-carving knives are shown in Figure 2, Plate 17. These are only a few of the shapes adapted to master carving. In addition to knives, wood carvers use chisels which they call "firmers," in order to distinguish them from carpenters' chisels, since a carpenter's chisel is sharpened from one side only (as shown in Figure 1, Plate 17), while the wood-carver's chisel is sharpened from both sides. Firmers are ground on both sides to permit taking a cut in any direction without changing the grip on the tool. Carpenters' chisels cannot be used well in carving because they must be turned constantly to avoid overrunning the lines of the design. In size, firmers come in a variety of widths and lengths, some being as narrow as $\frac{1}{64}$ inch while others have a 1 inch blade. Corner firmers are also called skew chisels or "skews." They are ground diagonally to give the edge a sharp point on one side.

Gouges are distinguished from chisels principally by the shape of the blade. Gouges are chisels in the broad sense of the term, but gouges are more or less rounded. They are made in various widths and lengths, and in different degrees of curvature, starting with the "extra flat" which has almost no curve, and ranging through the "scroll gouge" with a little more curvature, to the "hollow gouge" which has a cutting edge shaped like a semicircle. Small hollow gouges are called "veiners"; when the veiners are very small they are called "eye tools."

A professional wood-carving kit, which can be used for practically any job of wood carving and not merely for carving stocks, consists of nine tools, two sharpening slips, and a small oilstone. The tools are: $\frac{1}{2}$ inch firmer, $\frac{1}{2}$ inch corner firmer, veiner (also called a parting tool, or V-gouge), bent-shank $\frac{1}{2}$ inch scroll gouge, $\frac{1}{4}$ inch hollow gouge, $\frac{3}{8}$ inch hollow gouge, $\frac{3}{4}$ inch extra flat gouge, $\frac{1}{2}$ inch scroll gouge, and $\frac{1}{2}$ inch hollow gouge. The sharp-

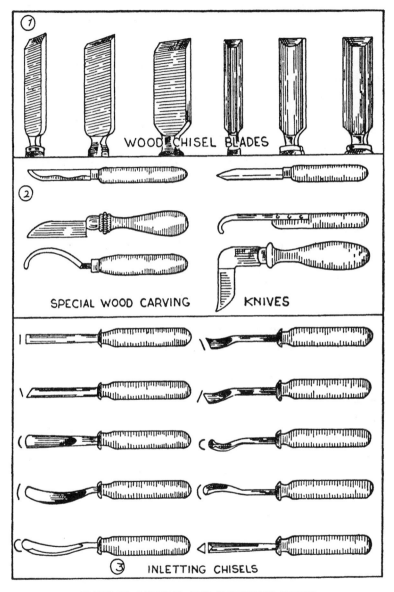

PLATE 17. CARVING AND INLETTING TOOLS.

ening slips are the V-slip and the U-slip. There is also a flat oil-stone.

Gouges are used for rough-cutting. A gouge is held with the handle grasped securely in the right hand, with the forefinger extended along the handle to guide the tool. Notice that the forefinger is not placed along the blade. The left hand is used to guide the tool, also, with two or three fingers on the shank of the gouge, the thumb and remaining fingers being placed underneath.

A firmer is held in a different manner. In cutting an edge, the left thumb is curled behind the shank to steady it against the first two fingers which are bent over the shank. Still a different method is followed in using the spoon gouge made with a bent shank. The whole left hand grips the shank, with all of the fingers above and only the thumb below. There is no fixed rule about holding wood-carving tools. Some carvers hold all of their tools with the four fingers on top, as we have explained for the spoon gouge.

In carving, the work must be held still. The use of the checkering cradle solves this problem, but when one is not available, a "C clamp," such as the one shown in Figure 3, Plate 26, can be used to hold the stock on the bench, being sure to place some soft material between the bearing surface of the clamp and the wood.

Wood carvers also use tools called the scratch, the router, macaroni tools, knuckle bends, tracers, and stamps. The scratch is usually a broken piece of a saw ground squarely across the edges and finished with an oilstone; it is used to scratch long straight lines and grooves.

The router is a kind of plane, like a carpenter's router, but in miniature. It is used to follow up and flatten wood previously roughed out with chisels. Macaroni tools are small tools with cutting edges shaped like three sides of a square, or, in some cases, like three sides of a square that have had the sides spread outward. They are used to remove wood on the sides of a cut when leaves or veins are being carved. Knuckle bends are gouges with curved ends, so called because they are bent like a knuckle. Tracers are tools with a spadelike blade at one end and a sharp point at the other; they are used to outline a background, or to cut little dots and holes in the wood. Stamps are merely dies with cutting edges shaped like hearts, crosses, stars, etc.; they are pounded into the wood with a mallet.

Chip carving was mentioned before. This is accomplished in various patterns formed by squares, triangles, and diamonds. A skew chisel or a firmer can be used to make three cuts, diagonally toward a common point, thus cutting out a little pyramid, and giving a triangle-shaped recess on the surface. Two more cuts from the other side of the base of the triangle will form a diamond-shaped cut. One of the special carving knives shown on Plate 17 can also be used for chip carving, or you can make your own. Circular cuts can be made with a hollow gouge, or with a knife with a semicircular cutting edge. Since wood carving is an art and not a science, it must be learned by experimentation rather than precise instruction.

IX. Stock Finishing

A NEW stock is prepared for its final finish by sanding it with No. 1 sandpaper until all file and rasp marks are removed, being careful to sand in the direction of the grain. This sanding process leaves its own marks, and it also drives into the pores of the wood tiny slivers of wood which are variously described by gunstockers as "fur," "fuzz," or "whiskers." These whiskers must be removed and at the same time the stock must be made still smoother.

One way to do this is to wipe the stock thoroughly with a rag or a sponge full of water, soak up most of the water with a dry rag, and then hold the stock near a source of intense heat to convert the water remaining in the stock into steam that will raise the whiskers. Another method is to soak an old piece of canvas in water, place it on the stock, and go over it very quickly with a hot iron. Whichever method you use, give the entire stock the same amount of heat and work quickly to avoid scorching the wood, especially where it is thin, such as along the edges of the barrel channel and the action mortises.

Examine the stock as soon as it is dry. There may be coarse marks left by the No. 1 sandpaper, as well as whiskers raised by the steam. Now use No. 0 sandpaper to remove any scratches, and to make the surface even smoother than it was before. Do not wrap the sandpaper around a block, but fold a small piece of it in the hand and lightly run it over the wood in the direction of the grain. When the sandpaper becomes worn, throw it away or it will drive the whiskers back into the pores instead of cutting them off. Wet the stock again, wipe it lightly, steam the stock, and sandpaper with

No. o again. Repeat this process over and over again until no more whiskers can be raised. Then wet and steam the stock for a final time, but do not use the sandpaper again, since the final steam treatment is to open the pores.

Before an old stock can be given a new finish, the old coating must be removed. The original finish, on cheaper weapons, is often varnish. This can be removed with ordinary commercial varnish remover applied with a swab, as shown in Figure 1, Plate 18, or you can make your own by adding two heaping tablespoonsful of lye to a gallon of boiling water, as illustrated in Figure 2, Plate 18. This hot lye solution is rubbed briskly over the stock with a scrubbing brush, and then the stock is rinsed several times with clean, warm water.

When commercial varnish remover is used, wipe it over the whole surface of the stock with a rag, lay the stock to one side for an hour, and then give it a second treatment with the remover. The first application softens the varnish, and the second loosens most of it. Wipe off the old varnish with a rag (No. 3 steel wool is even better), as shown in Figure 3, Plate 18, and scrape off any stubborn patches of the old coating with a putty knife, as shown in Figure 4, being careful not to gouge the wood with the corners of the knife. Give the stock another application of the remover, wash it off with warm water, and you are then ready to treat the old stock in the same manner as a new one. Figures 5 and 6 of Plate 18 show the steaming and sanding steps already described.

Varnish should not be used on a gunstock, especially on one made of walnut. Shellac is almost as bad. These finishes crack, chip, and peel; they are neither useful nor ornamental after the stock has been exposed to hard service. A good finish for the gunstocker who is in a hurry is lacquer, but it must be sprayed on the stock; brushed lacquer will not smooth out, and it is torn away by the bristles. Use either a painter's airbrush, or a hand sprayer that can be bought for a few dollars. See Figure 1, Plate 19. Lacquer will dry in an hour or less; it is waterproof; it withstands hard knocks; and it has all the advantages of varnish without any of the disadvantages. It works best on clean, dry wood that has not been stained, but it can be used fairly well on stained wood. It is not successfully applied to a stock that has been given an oil finish.

PLATE 18. STOCK REFINISHING—FIRST STEPS.

Staining must be done, if at all, before the stock is lacquered or given an oil finish. Staining results cannot be prophesied unless trials are made upon pieces of the plank from which the stock was made. These samples should be exposed to varying degrees of temperature and humidity for several days, and even then the tests may not clearly indicate how the stock will look after an oil finish has been applied and the stock exposed to the weather on hunting trips or at the target range.

Tannic acid diluted with water and brushed on a stock produces a brown stain. Nitric acid, full strength, produces a reddish-brown stain; diluted with water, it produces colors ranging from reddish yellow to lemon yellow, depending upon the amount of water. Potassium permanganate crystals, when dissolved in water, give varying degrees of brown. Potassium chlorate, dissolved in water, produces a stain ranging from light gray to black; it has been used sometimes by gunstockers who wanted to give wood an aged, weathered effect. Copper sulphate has an effect similar to that of potassium chlorate. Gunstockers, as a class, shun any artificial aging processes, since such methods smack too much of the "faking" associated with the less ethical members of the antique trade.

One of the most practical stains that can be made in the home workshop is obtained by hanging the stock in a closed box over bowls of ammonia. The fumes from the ammonia turn a walnut stock, no matter how light it is at first, into a dark brown that is permanent. Unlike many other staining processes, this method will not raise the grain of the wood. The time for exposure varies from 8 hours to 24 hours, depending upon the strength of the ammonia, the density of the wood, and other factors.

Maple and other light-colored woods can be darkened with ordinary commercial stains of the "acid" type, as distinguished from stains of coal-tar derivation. Commercial names for the usual colors are Walnut, Mahogany, Mission Oak, Weathered Mission Oak, etc. A mixture of one part of one of these stains to one or two parts of another color may give the exact shade desired; experimentation on sample blocks cut from the same plank as the stock is necessary to guide the gunstocker in his work. The stain is applied with a brush, allowed to dry for an hour or less, rubbed with a clean, dry rag, and examined. If it does not seem dark enough, a second and even a third coat may be necessary.

Stains are not popular with experienced gunsmiths because they tend to hide the grain, and hence the figure of the wood. This is especially true in the case of walnut. The oil finish which we shall next describe is the best possible finish. In itself, it darkens the wood but does not hide the grain; on the contrary, it seems to bring out the grain and point up the beauty of the figure in the wood. We have discussed stains only because there are always a few people who know something about finishing furniture and think that the same methods ought to be applied to finishing gunstocks, forgetting that furniture is protected from the elements while gunstocks are subjected to sudden changes of temperature, humidity, stress, and strain.

The oil finish is obtained by mixing 1 pint of turpentine with 2 pints of raw linseed oil and heating them together until the boiling point is almost reached (212 degrees F. or 100 degrees C.). Then the solution is swabbed over the stock. If the stock itself has been slowly warmed near some source of heat before the oil is applied, penetration is hastened. Swab the hot oil and turpentine solution liberally with a rag swab on the end of a stick over every part of the stock. Rub the swab vigorously over the wood while applying the oil and keep the stock warm if possible. Stand the stock in a pan, first on one end and then on the other end and let it drain. Continue to swab it with hot oil for about an hour, applying fresh oil every few minutes, with repeated draining periods between applications. At the end of the hour, let the stock dry for one or two hours, remove excess oil with a dry rag at the end of that period, and let the stock stand overnight. See Plate 19.

On the second day, repeat the hot oil and turpentine treatment as on the first day, but this time rub the wood with the palm of the hand after each application of the solution, working the solution well into the wood. It is possible to use the checkering cradle during most of the treatment, except that the ends of the stock do not receive their share of the solution unless the stock is removed from the cradle for each application. This is why many gunstockers prefer to pivot the stock in a pan while the stock is slowly turned, first

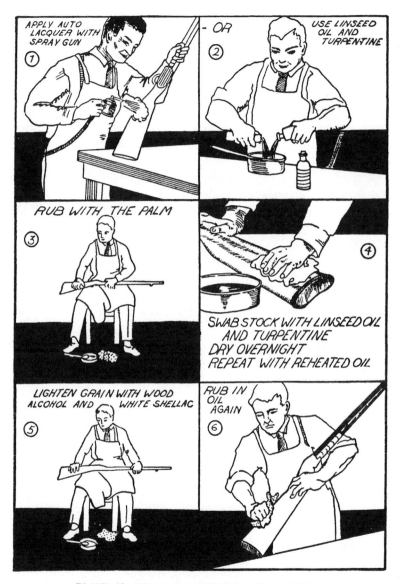

PLATE 19. STOCK REFINISHING—FINAL STEPS.

one way and then the other, now resting on the butt and later on the forward end of the stock.

The constant reheating of the oil and turpentine makes the solution thicker and darker, with the result that the stock becomes darker. The first applications are generous, but as the solution continues to soak into the wood, it is absorbed more slowly, leaving the later coats to form the surface finish. If the solution is too thick for fast absorption, or if it is darkening the wood too much, close the pores of the wood by brushing the stock with thin white shellac cut in alcohol.

When the wood has apparently absorbed all of the oil solution that it will take, probably on the second or third day of the treatment, let the stock stand for two or three days before giving it the final coat. At the end of this waiting period, rub the stock lightly, with the grain, using very fine sandpaper, and then repeat the hot oil applications at 15 minute intervals, rubbing the solution into the wood with the hand until you are sure that the wood will never take another drop of oil. Now put the stock away for a week.

At the end of the week, swab the stock with hard automobile cup grease. Next, remove the oil coating which has been built up on the surface of the wood. This can be done by rubbing with No. 3/0 steel wool; it can also be accomplished by sprinkling powdered pumice over the surface and rubbing away the pumice and the surface coat of oil with a coarse rag, such as part of a gunny sack. Grind the surface coat down the wood; you may fear that you are ruining all your hard work, but you are not hurting the stock a bit, for the surface coat is merely the excess oil that the wood could not absorb. Having removed the surface coat, rub the stock with your bare hands, using a little oil or grease on them to avoid friction, if you desire, but be sure to rub the stock perfectly dry. You now have an oil-finished stock that is as nearly perfect from the standpoints of beauty and utility as it is possible to obtain anywhere. You have spent only a total of three or four hours of labor, but the work has been spread out over two, three, or possibly four weeks, depending upon your anxiety to finish the task.

Some gunstockers follow the rubbing with steel wool or pumice with a rottenstone treatment. Rottenstone is a decomposed siliceous limestone used for polishing. It is placed in a box, and applied to the stock with rubbing pads made by gluing or tacking felt to pieces of wood, being sure that the tacks, if used, do not come into contact with the surface of the stock. Dip the felt pad into water and then into the rottenstone, and rub it over the stock in long, straight strokes with the grain of the wood. Wash the pad in clean water when it becomes caked and change pads frequently. When the surface coat of oil has been removed, give the stock the hand-rubbed treatment previously described.

If you contemplate finishing many stocks, construct a shallow tank large enough to hold the longest stock that you can reasonably expect to finish. Make it of sheet iron, about 6 or 8 inches deep, and weld the seams; do not solder them. One gallon of the linseed oil and turpentine mixture is enough to cover the average stock. Set the tank over a gas burner or on a stove, but keep the temperature of the oil bath just under boiling, as we explained before. It is a good idea to keep a thermometer in the tank so that you can turn off the heat or remove the tank from the stove when the solution has reached a temperature of 180 or 190 degrees F. Of course, you could let it reach a temperature of 200 degrees, but that would be only 12 degrees under boiling, and hence too hot for safety and economy.

When the oil in the tank has reached the required temperature and the heat has been turned off, place the stock in the tank. If the stock has been previously warmed it will absorb the oil faster. Leave the stock in the tank until the liquid has reached room temperature, then remove the stock and drain off the excess oil. Otherwise the use of a tank does not deviate from the oil treatment already explained.

Linseed oil is obtained from the seed of flax. It should not be adulterated with cottonseed oil, fish oil, or any other oil. It may be "raw" linseed oil or "boiled" linseed oil. Furthermore, the so-called "boiled" oil may be merely raw linseed oil combined with some dryer, such as litharge, a substance found in silver-bearing lead ore. In any case, whether the linseed oil is raw or boiled, it should be clear and free from sediment. By "boiled" oil, we mean oil that has been boiled by the manufacturer before being placed on the market. Actually, genuine boiled linseed oil is seldom available; the gunstocker usually works with raw linseed oil whether he realizes it or not.

Time and labor in the oil finish process can be saved by the use of muslin wheels on a motor grinder. The safety glass shields and the grinding wheels are removed; in place of the wheels are mounted cloth buffing wheels, sometimes called muslin wheels because they are covered with muslin. The hot oil and turpentine solution does not seem to work well on such wheels, but the rottenstone paste can be applied by this method. Also, the cloth wheels can be used instead of rag or hand rubbing at various stages of the finishing process.

When the wheels are used, hold the stock against them at an angle of about 45 degrees with the stock held on the underside of the wheels and passed so that the stock is rubbed lengthwise with the grain. Keep the pressure even and be careful that the wood does not become hot, because the friction between the high-speed wheels and the wood can easily scorch the wood and may even set it afire if continued too long.

One of the serious problems of finishing is that of stopping the penetration of the oil. Wood that is porous may continue to soak up oil indefinitely; it may never take a high finish and if the gun is mounted in such a stock the oil will continue to ooze out on hot days to the danger and discomfort of the shooter.

Soft, porous wood, swabbed with the following mixture, will cease absorbing oil in great quantities and will fill up in the outer pores so that it can be polished.

Linseed oil	½ pint
White shellac cut in alcohol	⅓ pint
Spar varnish	⅛ pint
Venice turpentine	20 drops

(Venice turpentine is a thick, gummy substance which is added to varnish where cracking must be prevented. In this formula, it aids in sealing the pores.)

Hard, close-grained wood may be swabbed with the following:

Linseed oil	½ pint
Spar varnish	¼ pint

Turpentine   1 fluid ounce
Venice turpentine   15 drops

If the stock continues to absorb oil too fast after this solution is applied, wait an hour and then apply the solution prescribed for soft, porous wood. Gunstockers frequently insist that the linseed oil used in these formulas should be "boiled," but they, themselves, use raw linseed oil which someone has labeled "boiled." Apparently it makes little perceptible difference whether the linseed oil is raw or not. To speed up the oil finish process, use either of these solutions between applications of oil and go ahead with the usual hot turpentine and linseed oil treatment in the manner described, except that the waiting periods between applications will be cut down.

Each gunstocker has his pet formula for making this solution. Obviously, since it slows up the penetrating powers of the oil process, it can be used as a final oil finish in itself. Variations of the above two formulas are found as follows:

    16 fluid ounces boiled (?) linseed oil
    2 fluid ounces spirits of turpentine
    200 to 400 grains carnauba wax
    2 to 4 teaspoonsful Venice turpentine
    ½ to 3 ounces Japan dryer
    100 to 300 grains burnt umber

If desired, the Japan dryer and the burnt umber may be omitted. Heat all the substances together until the mixture begins to bubble; turn down the heat slightly and let it simmer for about 15 minutes; set it aside to cool; then bottle it for future use. It can be applied hot, between regular oil applications, or it can be rubbed into the wood cold, using the palms of the hands, as a final finish after the last of the hot oil applications has been made. Notice that the quantities of carnauba wax, Venice turpentine, Japan dryer, and burnt umber vary considerably. A gunstocker who intends to do much finishing should experiment with different combinations of these substances brushed on samples cut from planks used for stocks. Exposure of the samples to various conditions of temperature, humidity, and rough handling will indicate the best formula for his work.

The stock should not be finished until all of the checkering has been accomplished. When an old stock, already checkered, is given a new finish, any solution, no matter what it is, applied to the stock, should be brushed out of the recessed portions of the checkered parts as fast as it is put on. If this is not done, the cut-out places in the checkering or carving will be filled with materials that may become gummy and hence destroy both the beauty and the usefulness of the checkering.

Some kind of a wood filler is useful when the wood is very porous. When it is not used, the pores absorb so much oil in the finishing process that the stock becomes very dark, with the result that the grain of the wood is obscured. This is not a detriment to a poor stock, but it is foolish to pay a high price for a stock and then spoil its appearance with a dark finish.

A white, or nearly white, wood filler is used when the stock is to be oiled, but a dark filler is used when varnish or some other nondarkening finish is applied. The correct formula for the filler depends upon the chemical structure of the wood and it can be determined accurately only by experimentation. The simplest step is to buy ready-prepared, commercial wood filler. It should be worked into the wood with a rag swab and the excess removed with a clean, dry rag. Generally, the filler should be applied before the hot oil treatment is started, since it shortens the process of finishing and keeps the wood fairly light.

One formula for a wood-filler paste is as follows: equal parts by weight of whiting, plaster of Paris, pumice stone, litharge, and silica; these solids are mixed with 1 part Japan dryer, 2 parts boiled linseed oil, 3 parts turpentine. This makes a light-colored filler. The addition of Vandyke brown or sienna will give it a brownish color, the depth of the color depending upon the amount of such material used.

A simpler formula is to finely grind rye flour, wheat flour, cornstarch, or Paris white, depending upon what is available. Mix the resulting powder with boiled or raw linseed oil (preferably boiled linseed oil if you can get it); if it is too thick, thin it with turpentine. The correct thickness is that of ordinary starch paste.

Throughout this chapter we have suggested that tests be made with the various substances, solutions, and mixtures before they are used. It takes a little more time to stop for an experiment before each operation, but good gunsmithing is always a comparatively slow, cautious process. Much of the income of professional gunsmiths comes from those who could do their own work if they only possessed that most important trait—patience.

FINAL CAUTION ON FINISHING

Pure linseed oil is difficult to obtain. Some drug stores and supply houses for artists stock it. The linseed oil generally obtained from paint and hardware stores is usually not pure linseed oil unless you insist on no substitute and know the integrity of the store. It is recommended that you be cautious in the selection and use of all materials. Linseed oil is only one example.

X. Stock Repairs and Alterations

THE beginner may want to make a new stock but feels that he must first gain more familiarity with tools and materials. The repairing and altering of old stocks offers him an opportunity to become skillful in woodworking and at the same time improve his weapons.

Lengthening the Stock.—One method of lengthening the stock is to cut out pieces of leather, fiber, ebony, hard rubber, or some plastic material, coat them on both sides with the appropriate glue or cement, clamp them in place, let them dry, and then buff the added material on a sandpaper wheel until the new surface is a continuation of the butt. Each of the pieces is cut to the same shape as the end of the butt, and although it is possible to cut them to the required size, the beginner is less liable to make mistakes if he cuts them too large and then works them down.

A variation of this method is to glue a number of plies of thin wood to the end of the butt, each sheet being a "veneer" less than $\frac{1}{10}$ inch thick. The adjacent layers of wood are laid with the grain at right angles to each other, thus producing a plywood equally strong in two directions. Where the thin sheets are not obtainable, plywood boards can be cut to shape and glued to each other.

Another method is to cut a block of the same kind of wood as the stock, saw off the butt square, glue the block to the butt, clamp it in place, and buff it down when the glue has dried. An effort may be made to cut the block so that the grain will run in the same direction as the stock, but it is almost impossible to match the grain of the stock and block well enough to justify the additional labor.

Instead of cutting off the butt square, it is well to cut it square for part of the distance and then cut out a "step" at either the heel or the toe of the butt. The block is then cut to fit with a projection that fills the step. By cutting two or more projections in the block and recesses in the butt, drilling holes for dowels, and inserting seasoned dowels swabbed with glue before the block is glued and clamped in place, a good union can be effected.

When the recesses are sawed out of the butt there is danger of accidentally sawing into holes, such as screw holes or the large hole in the butt of the Springfield used as a storage space. Such holes should be plugged with wooden blocks of the correct size and shape that are swabbed with glue and hammered into a tight fit with a mallet.

Patching.—A pistol grip is sometimes added to an old stock by an amateur who hollows out a block of wood to fit the original grip. Glue alone will not hold, especially if the stock has had an oil finish. A dowel may be used, or a long screw, but either of these fastening devices will eventually work loose. A pistol grip added after the stock has been completed is better held by dovetailing, but no method of joining is mechanically sound.

Instead of adding a pistol grip, it may be decided that an original pistol grip should be removed. Place the stock in a vise, saw off the pistol grip, and use a rasp to bring the exposed surface down to the desired shape and smoothness, being especially careful not to destroy any checkering on the adjacent surface. Sandpaper the bare area, remove and straighten the trigger guard, carry the old checkering design (if there is any) through the new surface, and then finish it.

The trigger guard is made of soft steel or iron that can be reshaped cold, but if it is casehardened, anneal the trigger guard before you straighten it, or it may break. To straighten the guard, lay it on a piece of wood or a lead block, and pound with a mallet made of rawhide, lead, or some other soft substance. If the tang is not the right shape, it should be bent, but in any event the tang is screwed to the guard and then inletted into the stock.

Checkering the bare wood to make it fit the design of the rest of the stock is extremely difficult. Sometimes it is necessary to remove all of the old checkering and apply a new design that will cover the place where the pistol grip was removed without making that area look botched. For much the same reason, it may even be advisable to refinish the whole stock rather than attempt to give the newly revealed surface a finish that will not blend into the old.

A more difficult problem arises when a piece of wood has broken off from either the toe or the heel of the butt. A wooden patch will not afford a solution, since these parts of the butt are subject to rough handling. The remedy is to cut out a clean recess where the wood has broken away, drill and countersink for two screws, insert a metal patch, screw it in place, and file down any rough edges or any part of the patch that does not conform to the shape of the butt. A wooden patch would be temporarily satisfactory, but it is far inferior to a metal insertion, preferably one made of casehardened steel held in place with casehardened screws.

On a very fine stock, the owner may object to ordinary plugs for filling screw holes. To improve the appearance, plugs can be cut from the same kind of wood as the stock and inserted with the grain showing on the exposed surface, or they may be cut from ivory, horn, or some other attractive substance. The old holes are drilled and counterbored deep enough to avoid the risk of the plugs working loose. This danger is further avoided by cutting the patches in rectangular, oval, diamond, or octagonal shapes, since they will not turn in their holes as easily as round plugs. The plugs must fit tight, but not so tight as to split the stock.

Where the plug is to be the exact shape of the recess, as for an inlay, cover the stock around the recess with lampblack and press against it a piece of white paper. Lay the paper on the wood from which the plug is to be cut and trace the required shape on the wood. Then, in making the plug, if both the recess and the plug taper inward slightly it will give a better fit. After coating the recess and the plug with glue, ordinary clamps may be used, or the plug can be held tight in the recess while it dries in the bench vise, which should have a jaw swiveled to turn at an angle, but if it lacks this feature place a wedge between the vise and the stock.

Broken Stocks.—Bolt-action rifle stocks usually either break across the grip on a line starting at a point near the trigger and extending upward and to the rear of the upper surface of the grip, or they split vertically at the rear of the tang screw. The first break may be due to the grip (small of the stock) being too small, it may be caused by building the stock so that the grain of the wood slopes downward toward the trigger guard in the grip, it may be brought about by striking the butt too hard against the ground in falling to the prone position, or it may be a result of two or more of these causes. The vertical split to the rear of the tang is caused by not inletting the action properly, not fitting the recoil shoulder tightly enough to give support against the shock received from the recoil; and not relieving the radius enough at the end of the tang, the latter being another way of saying that the action is too tight against the wood on the sides of the receiver in the area where the tang tapers to the rear.

The first type of broken grip can be repaired to keep it in service, but eventually the recoil will rupture it again. Coat the broken surfaces with hot glue and clamp them together very tightly. When the glue is dry, sometime between 36 and 48 hours later, you are ready to reinforce the grip with wood screws, dowels, brass plates, closely wrapped wire, or a combination of several of these methods.

Drill holes to receive brass wood screws at each end of the break, or drill holes and insert ¼ inch hickory dowels. If brass plates are to be the reinforcing medium, recess the wood to receive the plates on each side, drill holes for machine screws, and hold the plates tightly on the sides with screws extending through the grip. If wire is the reinforcing medium, use uncoated copper wire, from No. 22 to No. 26 in B. & S. gauge size, lay the end under for several turns at the beginning, wrap tightly for more than the length of the break, and force the free end under the last few turns. Coat the winding with solder so that the wires are all joined to one another, smooth the surface with emery cloth or an emery wheel, and polish.

The second type of break, a vertical one behind the tang, requires two important steps: first, the break must be repaired; second, the cause of the break must be found and cured as much as possible to prevent an early repetition.

The repair of the break follows the basic principles of joining together the adjacent parts of any broken piece of wood, that is, the broken ends are covered with hot glue, fitted together, held in a clamp or vise, and then reinforced. However, since this second type of break is at right angles to the longitudinal axis of the stock, it is subject to great stresses and about the only method for reinforcing securely is to run a long screw at right angles to the break.

The cure of the cause of the break takes place at the recoil shoulder of the stock. Remove enough of its surface with a chisel to eliminate oil-impregnated wood, since the latter cannot be successfully glued to another surface. When dry wood is exposed, score it with a rough rasp to let the glue have a more porous surface of attachment. Next, build up the recoil surface so that the recoil shoulder will fit tightly against the tang by gluing in place one or more thicknesses of wood or fiber of the required shape and thickness. The stock, action, and trigger guard are now assembled and it will be found that they mutually hold one another in place.

A little thought about the cause and cure of both of the above types of grip breaks will lead to the conclusion that a new stock is the only reliable, permanent solution to the problem. A well-made repair may last a lifetime, or it may give way at the precise moment when the rifle or shotgun is needed the most. We mention both weapons because splitting or breakage at the small of the stock is by no means the exclusive characteristic of rifles.

Reshaping the Forearm.—Reshaping the forearm (also called the fore-end) is a comparatively simple and easy operation, especially on military stocks, because there is usually enough wood so that part of it can be removed without weakening the rest. Various shapes for forearms have been discussed previously; additional shapes may be observed on weapons in shops or illustrated in catalogs.

If wood is removed, take out enough to give a new surface that is free from oil and make the recess of such shape that the added wood is held securely, not only by glue but also by the interlocking effect of dovetailing, tongue-and-groove, or similar wood-joining device. When hand or finger grooves along the sides of a military stock are removed, cut them out either square or in a wide V-shape at least ¼ inch deep, plane wood to match, attach the inserts with hot glue, clamp tightly in place, and do not remove the clamps for at least

24 to 36 hours. Do not depend upon glue to fill gaps where the wood does not fit closely. This form of careless workmanship can be avoided by cutting the inserts a little too large at first, coating with chalk or lampblack, fitting them temporarily, and then working them down where the coloring substance shows high spots.

Channels cut in the forearm, under the barrel, of military stocks for lightening the weight, are exposed when the length is reduced to form a sporting-type forearm. A piece of the wood removed at the forward end, where there is no channel, is cut to fit the exposed channel and glued in place. Where wood from the forearm is not long enough, or otherwise unavailable, a piece from matching material is prepared. Some gunsmiths hold such a piece in place with both glue and nails from a cigar box, while others are stoutly opposed to using nails or screws in any stock joint where glue will apparently hold strongly enough to withstand the usual stresses.

Cheek Pieces.—Figure 3, Plate 15, shows how to inlay a cheek piece in a butt, and Figure 2, Plate 13, shows how to apply a ready-made cheek piece obtained from one of the many dealers specializing in stock work. These have been very briefly discussed already. We shall now offer further suggestions for doing this work.

First, cut out the cheek piece to the desired size and shape from a piece of wood that matches the stock, having the grain in the cheek piece run in the same direction as that in the stock, or with a grain that contrasts artistically and hence adds to the beauty of the weapon. It should be at least ⅛ inch thick along the lower left side, about ¼ inch thick at the upper edge, and overlap at least ½ inch on the right side.

Second, lay the cheek piece on the butt and mark lightly around it with the point of a penknife or a sharp scriber.

Third, cut out the recess in the butt, removing slightly more wood at the upper edge than at the lower edge. Do not cut too deep at first, but work slowly with shallow cuts. After each cutting, place the cheek piece on the stock and find the high spots yet to be removed by coating the under surface of the cheek piece with chalk or lampblack. Fourth, when the cheek piece and the recess fit perfectly, glue together, clamp, and let the clamps remain for at least 24 hours. Remove the clamps, and shape the cheek piece so that it streamlines with the shape of the stock and at the same time fits your face. Whether you hollow it out to fit your cheek or leave it straight is a matter of personal choice. In case of doubt, leave it straight until you have tried the weapon in the field or on the range.

Monte Carlo Comb.—A Monte Carlo comb can be added to shotguns such as the Winchester Models 12 and 97, Browning automatic, and Remington Model 10, but it should not be attempted where there is a recoil spring in the butt, an attachment screw extending through the grip from the butt, or any other important part in the butt. Under such conditions, an entire new stock is required, designed and made with the Monte Carlo comb as part of the stock.

Where the comb can be added in accordance with the above restrictions, it is cut from a block of matching wood and fitted into the stock by a wedged dovetail, or by any of the other approved wood-joining methods, including glue, of course. Where the tang extends well to the rear, the comb is carried farther forward than it would be otherwise.

Inserting a wooden block may weaken the stock somewhat. This can be avoided if the Monte Carlo comb is part of a large L-shaped block joined to the butt with the long arm of the L along the upper surface and the short arm of the L overhanging and joining the butt at the rear, where the butt has been previously shortened and cut square. By this means, holding the butt to the shoulder in firing reinforces the joint between the added piece and the stock when the stresses come during firing. When this is not done, there is a tendency for the Monte Carlo comb to shear off during recoil and at the same time come loose from shock and vibration.

Reshaping the Butt.—The lower part of Figure 3, Plate 15, is clear enough to illustrate the principles of designing a new butt, bearing in mind that the reshaped butt must fit the butt plate you already have or else you must either make or buy a new butt plate.

In the illustration, wood is removed from the original butt from the heel well forward into the grip, preparatory to adding a new piece to the upper surface. Also, wood may be removed from the lower surface near the trigger guard, but this is not always necessary. The newly exposed wood and the surface of the wood where nothing has been removed are both gone over with a rasp to make them rough enough to receive the glue, and to remove any oil-soaked wood. Usually, wood is removed from the lower surface of the butt only to conform to the new stock lines, or to prepare for adding a pistol grip, since the main purpose of reshaping the butt is generally the raising of its upper edge and not the lowering of the under edge.

The addition to the upper edge is cut from a block of matching wood to the desired size and shape and held in place with glue and at least two dowels, one near the heel of the butt and the other near the forward end of the addition. These dowels need not be very long and they should never extend upward high enough to enter the thin upper edge of the addition, hence they are both strong and invisible.

Where there is no cast-off, a center line is drawn on the addition to conform to the center line of the stock; where cast-off is desired, it is drawn on both the addition and the stock according to the principles of cast-off previously explained in this text and illustrated on Plate 12.

Removing Dents.—Figure 5, Plate 17, shows how dents, nicks, and gouges are removed from a stock by running a hot iron over a wet cloth placed over the injured surface of the wood. This has already been discussed, but we shall now offer further suggestions for meeting this problem.

Deep gouges cannot be remedied by the steam method. The beginner will immediately think of using wood filler, or perhaps plastic wood, but neither of these materials work well where they come into contact with the metal parts of the weapon, and they do not present such a good appearance as gunmaker's shellac.

To make gunmaker's shellac, place 6 ounces of shellac (technically known as "seed lac") in a wide-mouthed, clean bottle; add 4 ounces of pure grain alcohol, and let the alcohol dissolve the shellac. In a separate bottle, place ½ ounce of turpentine and 2 ounces of resin, and let the turpentine dissolve the resin. When the shellac and resin have been dissolved in their respective bottles, mix the contents of the two bottles and slowly bring the mixture to the boiling temperature over a controlled heat, such as a bunsen burner or an alcohol lamp. (The mixture can be boiled on an ordinary cook stove, but there is the danger that it may get too hot and burst into flames.) Boil until the mixture becomes a thick paste and then pour into moulds to form cakes, bars, or sticks when cooled.

Deep gouges are prepared for the gunmaker's shellac by first warming them near a slow, controlled source of heat. The cake of shellac is held over a gouge, a warm iron is held against the cake, and the melted shellac is allowed to run into and fill the gouge. Let the wooden part having the gouged surface stand for 10 or 20 minutes until the shellac has cooled, after which it can be used as freely as though the defect never existed, provided, of course, that the gouge is not one that weakens the structure.

Another method of filling deep gouges is to use powdered wood. Place a block of wood like that used in the gouged part in a vise and work a fairly fine bastard file against the grain to produce the powder. (The beginner is tempted to use shavings, sawdust, or coarse filings, but none of these pack together tightly enough to properly fill a gouge.) Swab the gouge out with cold glue (or some strong, cold cement) and fill the gouge with a mixture of glue and powdered wood. Tamp the mixture into the gouge with a soft wood stick, level the surface with a putty knife, tamp in more of the mixture and let a little mound accumulate at the surface. Press against the mound with the flat of the putty knife as hard as you can and then let the filling and the mound dry. When it is thoroughly dry, file the mound down to the original surface, sandpaper, and refinish.

Plastic wood, or wood filler, is successfully used to vary the shape of a pistol grip, a stock, or some other surface that touches the body, but it is a very inferior substance for filling gouges where appearance counts. When dry, it does not take the same finish as wood, and although it is possible to add coloring matter near the surface of a gouge filled with this material, the presence of any appreciable amount of coloring matter inside the gouge will weaken the filling substance. These statements are made with a reservation that it is possible that a plastic wood, or a wood filler, adaptable to gouge-filling purposes, may eventually be produced commercially, but nothing of this description is known to the author.

GLUES

Glues have been developed by the aircraft industry for the joining of wooden parts far beyond the stage reached in the gunsmithing profession. Aircraft glue must keep its strength when wet, hot, or attacked by fungus, and it must not deteriorate materially with age. The rate at which it sets, the temperature requirements, the dulling effect on tools, and the tendency to stain woods are all important characteristics. Since these features are also ones of primary value to gunsmiths, we shall present here the latest and most reliable findings of the aeronautical engineers.

Animal Glues.—Animal glues are made from the bones, hide, or sinews of animals, by boiling in water, concentrating the extract and jellying by cooling. When needed, the dry glue is soaked in cold water for several hours, heated in a closed vessel at a temperature between 140 and 150 degrees F., and kept at the same temperature while in use, but if it is heated for more than 4 hours it should be regarded as unfit for first-class work.

The proportion of glue to cold water during preparation is variable; it is at least 1¼ pounds of water to 1 pound of glue, but normal consistency is usually obtained with a ratio of 2¼ to 1. The strength when dry is very high; the strength when wet is very low; the rate of setting is rapid; the effect of the temperature of the glue, the wood, and the workshop is important; the dulling effect on tools is from slight to moderate; and the tendency to stain wood is extremely slight. Taking everything into consideration, animal glue is inferior to either urea formaldehyde resin glue, or casein glue.

Urea Formaldehyde Resin Glue.—This is an excellent all-purpose glue, available commercially as a dried powder marketed under several trade names principally by aircraft-supply houses. It is dissolved in cold water in accordance with the manufacturer's recommendations, which are simple to understand. The strength when dry is very high; the strength when wet is at least 75 per cent of its dry strength, which is a remarkable feature of this glue; it sets rapidly; its working life in the shop is about 4 hours, like animal glue; it must be heated to at least 70 degrees F. in preparation, should be brought to a temperature of 140 degrees F., and does not work well if heated beyond the latter temperature; it has practically no dulling effect on tools; and it has no tendency to stain wood.

Casein Glue—Casein glue is obtained from curdled milk and other materials in combination; it is sold as a powder, and must be prepared exactly as prescribed by the manufacturer. Its dry strength runs from high to very high; its wet strength is from 25 to 50 per cent of its dry strength; it sets rapidly; its working life in the shop should be only a few hours, but it may extend to several days; the temperature requirements are not important; it has a dulling effect on tools varying from moderate to extreme; and it has a very pronounced tendency to stain some woods.

Casein glue is prepared as follows: The powder is either sifted or sprinkled into a vat or vessel while a paddle is turned at the rate of about 100 revolutions per minute, either by hand or mechanically. As soon as all of the glue has been added to the water, the speed of the paddle is reduced to 50 revolutions per minute, and paddling is continued long enough for the mixture to become smooth and even, gradually reducing the speed of paddling toward the end to discourage the formation of air bubbles.

A gunsmith using this glue should prepare only enough to fill a paper cup, throw the cup away when its contents are more than 4 or 5 hours old, and then prepare a fresh cupful. Wooden parts joined with this glue must stand for at least 5 hours; a drying period of 12 hours is a safe practice.

Blood Albumin Glues.—Blood albumin glues are made from the albuminous base of the blood from slaughter houses, mixed with lime, caustic soda, sodium silicate, or similar chemicals, and marketed as powder, to which water is added in the shop until the desired consistency is reached.

These glues have a dry strength ranging from low to high; they have a wet strength ranging from 50 per cent to almost 100 per cent of the dry strength; they dry very fast in the presence of heat; the working life in the shop may be only a few hours or it may be several days; it is better to use them while warm; the dulling effect on tools is almost nil; and the darker forms of these glues may deepen the color of certain woods, especially veneers.

Blood albumin glues give better unions if the two wooden parts being joined are kept under pressure and at a temperature as high as 160 degrees F., for a period ranging between 15 and 30 minutes, depending upon the temperature of the room, the temperature of the glue, the temperature of the wooden parts, the consistency of the glue, the structure of the wood, etc. Steam-heated plates are used to keep up the temperature of the joint in a factory, but the gunsmith can approximate this method with well-wrung-out steaming towels, or with a steam pot.

Bending Wood.—Wood can be bent mechanically or by steam. Figure 1, Plate 8, shows a mechanical bending apparatus for changing the shape of a stock. Steam bending in a gunsmith shop is sometimes accomplished by supporting the part to be bent over the steam outlet of some vessel in which water is being boiled, the length of time being approximated by the rule of allowing one hour of steaming for each inch of thickness of the wood.

A note of caution is needed here: It is correct to bend a board by steaming, but bending a gunstock is extremely perilous. The recesses cut out for the action and other parts will warp unevenly in every direction, and any knots or burls may become separated from the surrounding wood.

Far safer than the steam pot is the use of rags wrapped around the place to be bent; hot linseed oil is poured over these rags and the stock can then be bent enough for ordinary purposes.

Bending by lamination is a mechanical process developed in the aircraft industry that will eventually be adopted for certain purposes by the gunsmiths. A number of layers of wood, cut fairly thin along the desired radius of curvature, are glued together, clamped to a form, and left there until the glue is set and wood dries in the required shape. When hardwoods are used, they may be first bent by steam to the approximate shape while they are still thick in the cross section, after which they are bent by lamination.

XI. Inletting the Action and Bedding the Barrel

INLETTING is the process of fitting the principal metal parts of a rifle or shotgun to the stock. Since the Springfield rifle is the weapon most frequently restocked, we shall start with a description of those wooden and metal parts directly connected with inletting. The reader is asked to refer to Plates 32 to 39, inclusive, and to read the chapter on the Springfield if he is not already familiar with that firearm. Illustrations for the Springfield Rifle are grouped together, although they are referred to in various parts of this text.

The stock is shown on Plate 38 as it appears before the rifle is assembled. Figure 84 is the top view and Figure 85 is the right-side view. The parts are the butt "A"; small of the stock (called simply "small") "B"; magazine well "C"; barrel bed "D"; air chamber "E," which reduces the charring effect of a heated barrel on the stock; hole for butt plate screw, small, and seat for the butt plate tang "F"; butt swivel plate seat "G"; mortise for receiver tang lug and hole for rear guard screw "H"; mortise for sear and slot for trigger "I"; cut-off thumbpiece recess "J"; mortise for recoil lug on receiver "K"; bed for fixed base "L"; grasping grooves "N"; shoulder for lower band "O"; bed for lower band spring "P"; shoulder for upper band "Q"; channels for decreasing weight "R"; upper band screw hole "S"; and the stock screw hole "T." The large hole in the butt is for decreasing weight, and the smaller one is a pocket for the combination oiler and thong case or spare part container. The initials of the inspector and the year of fabrication are stamped on the left side in the rear of the cut-off thumbpiece recess.

The Hand Guard, Figure 86, Plate 38, right-side view, and Figure 87, bottom view of inner surface, has the swell "A" for the protection of the rear sight; the shoulder "B" for the lower band; the shoulder "C" for the upper band; the rear tenon "D" which enters the undercut in the fixed base; the front tenon "E" which enters the undercut in the upper band; the clearance "F" for the windage screw knob; air chamber "H"; and recess "I" for the Hand Guard Clips, one of which is shown in Figure 88. The hole shown in the cut near the rear end of the inner surface is made for convenience of manufacture. At the swell "A," a groove is cut for sight clearance.

The Butt Plate is represented in Figures 89 and 90. The parts are the toe "A"; tang "B"; cap hole "C"; cap ears "D"; through which are the pin holes; spring lug "E"; hole for butt plate screw, large, "F"; and hole for butt plate screw, small, "G." A notch is cut into the edge of the cap hole to facilitate the opening of the cap. For this purpose the flange of the head of a cartridge case can be used. The butt plate is checked for the purpose of insuring a firm seat at the shoulder in firing.

Figures 91 to 103, both numbers inclusive, are shown on Plate 39. The Butt Plate Cap, Figure 91, Figure 92, and Figure 93, has the pin hole "A," and the thumb notch "B." The cap is hinged between the ears of the butt plate on the butt plate pin and is retained either closed or open by the free end of the Butt Plate Spring, Figure 96, which bears on the heel "C." The cap is checked to match with the butt plate. The Butt Plate Pin, Figure 95, after being driven into the holes in the ears of the butt plate and cap, has its ends slightly upset. The Butt Plate Spring Screw, Figure 94, secures the spring to the lug on the butt plate and is firmly screwed against the spring.

The Stock Screw and Nut, Figure 97, are assembled transversely through the stock between the magazine well and slot for trigger. The thread end of stock screw is upset when in place. The large and small Butt Plate Screws, Figures 98 and 99, secure the butt plate to the stock. The Butt Swivel includes the plate, swivel, and pin assembled. The Butt Swivel Plate, Figure 100, has the holes "A" for the swivel screws; "B" for the swivel; and "C" for the swivel pin. The Butt Swivel, Figure 101, is retained in the plate by the Butt Swivel Pin, Figure 102. The Butt Swivel Screws are the same as the butt plate screw, small (Figure 98).

The Upper Band, Figure 103, has the bayonet lug "A"; the ears "B" in which are the holes for the stacking swivel screw; the upper-band screw hole "C"; and the undercut "D" for the front tenon on the hand guard.

The Upper Band Screw, Figure 104, Plate 38, secures the band to the stock, the thread under the head engaging the hole in the right side of the band. The Stacking Swivel, Figure 105, Plate 38, is hinged by the lug "A," between the ears "B," of the upper band, on the Stacking Swivel Screw, which is like the screw shown in Figure 106, but slightly longer. The threaded end of the screw is upset, after assembling, to prevent its being lost.

The Lower Band Swivel, Figure 107, is hinged by its lug "A" between the ears of the lower band, on the Lower Band Screw, Figure 106. The threaded end of the screw is upset when in place. The Lower Band, Figure 108, has the ears "A" and the screw holes "B"; the front or upper end is designated by the letter U. The lower band and swivel are split between the ears in order to give better adjustment to the stock and hand guard and permit removal of the band without marring the stock. The Lower Band Spring, Figure 109, has the notch "A" which holds the band in place, and the spindle "B" which retains the spring in the stock.

Machine-Inletted vs. Hand-Inletted Stocks.—An inletted stock has its wood cut away to receive metal parts. Where the shape of the metal is convex, the stock should have a concave shape at that bearing point; likewise, where the metal is concave, the stock should be convex at that spot. However, a stock cut by a machine may have more wood cut away than is absolutely necessary, due to the mechanical limitations of the machine, whereas a stock cut by hand has wood removed only where wood is to be displaced by some metal part. A handmade stock is stronger, resists recoil better, and withstands vibrations more effectively than one cut on a machine.

In order that any action may fit into any stock, the wood is cut by the machine with tolerances which provide for slight variations in the size or shape of metal parts. Such tolerances are not needed when the stock is inletted to receive only the action which will be mounted in that particular stock. To overcome the weakness resulting from cutting away an excessive amount of wood, machine-made stocks need stock screws which can be eliminated on a home-made stock in most instances.

INLETTING

The magazine and trigger guard are fitted into the solid stock blank as a unit on the Springfield and Mauser rifles. Where the magazines are separate from the trigger guard on bolt-action rifles such as the U.S. Model 1898 Krag-Jorgensen; the U.S. Rifle, Model 1917 (Enfield); the Model 54, Winchester; and the Model 30, Remington, the action or receiver must be fitted first and the trigger guard last.

Plate 19 shows the wood chisel blades, special wood-carving knives, and inletting chisels used by professional stockmakers. Plate 9 shows the gunstocker's saw, the dovetail saw, the stock shaper saw, the inletting saw, and the draw knife used by stockmakers. The depth gauge, shown in Figure 1, Plate 5, and other tools illustrated in this text are also used. The bunsen burner, shown in Figure 3, Plate 4, or an alcohol lamp, can be used in coating the surface of metal parts with a smudge of lampblack, although many gunsmiths prefer to blacken metal parts by holding them over a burning piece of camphor.

Refer back to Plates 11 and 12. Assuming that your stock has been laid out and cut to a profile similar to that of Figure 6, Plate 11, clamp the stock upside down in the bench vise and mark a center line the entire length of the bottom side of the stock. Continue this center line around both ends, turn the stock over and run the center line down the top surface of the stock. The stock, of course, should previously have been planed square on the sides and smooth along the top and bottom surfaces before the center line is laid out, leaving ample wood on the sides for the final finish. Check the accuracy of the center line with a marking gauge (which can be used to draw the line, if you wish), a die-maker's square, a combination square, or any other tool adaptable for this purpose.

The measurements for drop are usually taken from one side of the center line only; it makes no difference whether you take them from the right or left side as long as you always measure from the same side. Since you determined the position of the center of the trigger in designing the stock, place the magazine and receiver, together with the trigger assembly, beside the stock and locate the positions of the front and rear guard screws. Refer to Figure 30, Plate 36, where the letters H and I indicate the holes for these screws. Carry lines from these screw positions around the stock to the under side, hold the trigger guard (of which the body of the magazine forms a part) over the bottom of the stock and check the location of the guard screws.

Mark the location of the tang of the receiver and the end of the trigger guard on the under side of the stock. Using the try square (Figure 3, Plate 7), carry lines to the sides and top of the stock blank for reference points. Also take the dimensions of the magazine, both horizontally and vertically. Run lines along the bottom of the stock blank, up the sides, and on the top surface to determine where you will cut away wood for the magazine. Figure 30, top and right views, Plate 36, and Figure 84, Plate 38, will give you a good idea of the relationship between the trigger guard, the magazine, and the stock.

Most gunsmiths start the inletting process by making a "templet," which is merely a pattern of brass or iron, shaped like Figure 30, Plate 36. This can be copied from an old Springfield trigger guard. The principal over-all longitudinal dimension is 8.386 inches; the distance between the centers of the trigger guard screws, front and rear, is 7.7254 inches. The trigger guard you use as a model might not measure exactly the same, but you will find that there is very little variation. Lay the templet on the bottom of the blank, being sure that the center line of the templet corresponds with the center line of the stock and that the centers of the holes for the trigger-guard screws are correctly located. Mark around the templet, first with a scriber (Figure 6, Plate 6), and then with a pencil. If you do not have a scriber, a nail is a good substitute.

You should now know where the wood must be cut away to admit the magazine. With the blank in the vise, remove the center part of the wood by boring a series of holes with a ½ inch bit, if you are a novice at woodworking, but if you are an expert a ⅞ inch bit will take away more wood, thus leaving less to be removed with chisels. Do not bore all the way through the wood, but just enough for the point of the bit to appear on the top part of the blank; then turn the blank over and bore from the top down. This will avoid splitting the wood. Also, do not get closer than ⅛ inch to your guide lines. Notice especially that the magazine tapers from top to bottom.

Using chisels of different sizes, remove wood slowly and carefully. Use broad flat chisels for the sides, narrow ones for the ends, and round gouges for the corners. Keep the chisels very sharp so that they cut and not merely tear or dig the wood.

Mix lampblack with light oil and apply it to the magazine with a brush or a swab. Another way to accomplish the same purpose is to hold the magazine in the smoke from burning camphor, just as you would blacken sights before firing on the rifle range, but most gunsmiths prefer the mixture of lampblack and oil. Having blackened the magazine, lower it into the mortise you have cut with the chisels. Do not use force. As soon as the magazine has entered as far as it will go, take it out and notice where smudges of lampblack were left on the wood. These are the "high" places that must be removed with the chisels. Reblacken the magazine after you have cut away more wood, insert it in the mortise again, and once more remove it and chisel away any high places on the wood. Keep this up until you can seat the magazine deep enough so that the magazine enters evenly without force. Use a try square to be sure that the magazine does not enter the blank at an angle. If the guard falls below the surface of the wood, as it will if you have left a little extra outside dimension all around for finishing, the surplus wood is trimmed away on the outside.

Always cut the wood across the grain. Unless especially directed to do so in these instructions, do not use a hammer or mallet to drive the chisels. Instead, hold the chisel firmly in the hand and push it steadily in the desired direction, taking short, shallow cuts. Guide the point of the chisel with the index and middle fingers of the left hand, the left forearm resting against the stock to steady the left hand.

There is a projection on the forward tang of the trigger guard that will not go all the way into the stock. Blacken this projection and tap it with a mallet to leave an impression on the wood. Locate the center of a hole for this projection and bore a hole ½ inch deep and ½ inch in diameter, which will take care of the tang projection, but do not bore the hole too deep or only the sides of the hole will support any load thrown on the metal at this point.

Before inletting the guard, provide the cut-out near the magazine that enables the floor-plate catch to operate freely. Place the guard and then bore through the front guard-screw hole with a ¼ inch bit, using the guard-screw hole as a guide. Remove the guard, enlarge the hole to $\frac{9}{32}$ inch, and replace the guard. Connect the long screw, lay out the lines for the receiver, and then fasten the screw through the front guard-screw hole.

Check the center of the rear end of the trigger guard to see if it is on the center line of the stock. If it is not, draw a new center line and place on it the center line of the receiver tang.

The guard and magazine should be inletted by now. The next step is to inlet the barrel and receiver. Professionals usually do this by separating the barrel and receiver and fitting the receiver by itself before the barrel is fitted. Beginners seem to prefer to fit the barrel and receiver together, as a unit, probably because novices lack confidence in their ability to remove a barrel. The removal of barrels is explained clearly in another chapter of this text, but we shall explain the unit method, knowing that it will meet the needs of more people.

The stock is in the vise, top surface uppermost, the guard and magazine are in place, and the front guard screw is lined up with the forward guard-screw hole of the receiver. Guard, magazine, and receiver are now properly related to each other. The top surface of the stock touches the receiver only at the recoil lug and the under, rear projections of the receiver. Run a sharp pencil around the parts of the receiver that rest on the wood and cut away the inside areas of the outlines thus drawn, thus permitting the barrel and receiver to rest on wood at all points of their lower surfaces. Be sure that the barrel tang and the receiver tang are located with their center lines on the center line of the stock. Hollow out some of the wood to permit the barrel and receiver to sink part way into the stock.

Remove the barrel and receiver. Coat the lower half of each of these parts with lampblack and light oil, just as you coated the action. Replace the barrel and receiver, being sure that they are lined up just as they were before. Hold them firmly down against the wood, remove again, and observe the smudges left by the lampblack. Cut away the wood wherever it is blackened to make a channel for both the barrel and the receiver, being sure to take shallow cuts for the whole length. Remove the barrel and receiver, blacken, replace, observe the smudges, cut away wood, and keep repeating this process until the channel is semicircular in shape, with a radius equal to the radius of the barrel for the barrel groove, and equal to the radius of the receiver for the receiver channel.

There are several ways to check the accuracy of the size and shape of the channel. One of the best is to make a semicircle of brass or scrap iron with the same radius as the channel and slide this pattern (templet is the technical name) back and forth while the channel is being cut. The only objection to this is that some gunsmiths believe it best not to cut the channels to their full depth and width until toward the last. When this policy is followed, the templet will not fit until the channels are finished. The solution is to make a number of semicircular templets, each one used having a slightly greater radius than the one used before, so that the semicircular shape will be kept true from the first to the last cut. Each cut is made with a chisel having a razor edge. Take shallow, even cuts, using a 1 inch No. 3 Addis chisel, or even a common 1 inch socket-firmer chisel. Finish with fine sandpaper wrapped around a round stick.

Some gunsmiths screw an iron or steel rod, threaded at one end, into the receiver, and then lower this rod from the top through the forward guard-screw hole in the guard to line up the guard, magazine, and receiver properly until the barrel is seated about one-half of its final depth in its channel. At that point, the rod is removed and in its place the forward guard screw is inserted. This screw is then tightened whenever it is desired to bring the magazine and receiver together while the barrel is being fitted to its channel. Finally, when the barrel channel is about completed, the rear guard-screw hole is bored in the appropriate spot. If you have a lathe, it can be used to drill the guard-screw hole accurately, but if you use a hand or breast drill, make the hole a little smaller than required and finish it with a small file. The reason for this is that the hand or breast drill has a tendency to deviate from a line perpendicular to the wood.

The magazine, barrel, receiver, and trigger guard are now assumed to be fully seated. The rear guard-screw bushing must be inserted very tightly in its hole in the wood, and so exactly aligned that the receiver and barrel are not leaning either to right or left. Both the rear guard-screw bushing and the rear guard screw must be tight in the wood. It is important that the wood around the rear tang of the guard and the rear tang of the receiver fit snugly, except that the wood back of the rear radius of the receiver tang need not be so tight that it will permit the stock to split lengthwise at the small of the stock or the pistol grip. The rear guard screw must be tight to bind the guard and receiver, for if it comes loose the rifle will not shoot accurately.

The back surface of the recoil shoulder on the under front part of the receiver must bear evenly and tightly against its own back vertical contact with the wood. The flat lower surface of the receiver back of the recoil shoulder must bear level on its seat on the wood. If the seat is not perfectly level it will not hold the barrel and receiver evenly, and there may be a tendency for them to lean one way or the other when the front guard screw is tightened. Thus, the seat on the stock assists the rear guard screw and bushing in the performance of their functions.

Before the guard screws are tightened, when the barrel and receiver are being fitted to the stock, there should be a gap of about $\frac{1}{32}$ inch between the flat lower surface of the receiver in the back of the recoil shoulder and its flat seat on the wood. If this condition exists, the front guard screw pulls up the stock to meet the receiver when the guard screws are tightened, and at the same time the tip of the fore-end is squeezed against the lower surface of the barrel.

The forearm touches the barrel only at its tip on most military rifles that have a full-stocked forearm, and at the upper band the forearm presses upward against the bottom of the barrel. In assembling the rifle, there is a gap of about $\frac{1}{32}$ inch between the top half of the barrel and the upper band.

On the other hand, when the Springfield stock has a pistol grip of the type described officially as Model 1923, and there is a short forearm, the tip of the forearm does press upward against the bottom of the barrel. For this reason the lower band should hold the barrel and forearm snugly, but if the barrel band goes all the way around the barrel it must not have such a tight fit that it interferes with the lengthwise expansion of the barrel that takes place when firing heats the barrel.

METAL PARTS MUST HAVE CORRECT
RELATIONSHIP WITH STOCK

Having inletted the action and bedded the barrel, refer to other chapters in this text in order that you may be sure that the metal parts bear their correct relationship to the stock. If you have any doubt about the correct procedure in any phase of gun care and repair up to this point, read the entire text to the end and then come back and reread any instructions which were not perfectly clear at the first reading. This is the logical approach to learning any new subject or advancing in any profession or trade. Very few people, regardless of their intelligence or formal education, obtain a perfect understanding of any non-fiction publication with only one reading.

XII. Etching and Engraving

ETCHING is the production of designs on metals, glass, etc., by lines eaten in by a corrosive, such as nitric acid. Engraving is the production of cut or raised figures on hard material, especially on metal or wood. However, in the usual sense of the term, we think of engraving as the cutting of designs on metal with chisels. Wood engraving is commonly referred to as carving. Etching is comparatively simple, easy, and inexpensive. Engraving is relatively complicated, difficult, and expensive. We shall first explain how to etch designs on firearms and then describe elementary gun engraving.

Gun etching, like other gunsmithing tasks, should be done first on sample material. Find an old firearm that has little value; even part of an old, broken gun will do, especially if it has a surface large enough for ornamentation. Remove the rust with steel wool and some weak acid solution, such as vinegar or a very dilute solution of sulphuric acid. Rinse the acid solution off with water, and dry with a clean rag. Grease and oil should also be removed before etching is started.

Next, choose a simple design. A plain monogram, without shading, such as the "MK" on Plate 21, is a good choice for the first experiment. Having chosen the design, decide whether you want to etch in relief or in intaglio. In relief etching, the design is drawn or painted upon the surface with a liquid etching ground that covers the metal which will not be exposed to the etching fluid, so that after etching and the removal of the etching ground, the design appears raised. In intaglio etching, the whole surface of the metal is covered with the etching ground, and the design is cut through the etching ground with a needle; the ground being thus removed along the lines forming the design, the latter, after etching and the removal of the etching ground, is sunken.

Referring to the "MK" monogram on Plate 21, if you want it to appear in relief, draw a rectangle that encloses the monogram. Cover the monogram with the etching ground and also protect the metal outside of the rectangular border with the ground. Leave the area between the monogram and the border entirely unprotected. When the etching fluid is applied, it will eat away the metal between the monogram and the border, causing the monogram to appear in relief, that is, the design stands out from its background.

Again, if you want the monogram to appear in intaglio, protect everything except the monogram with the etching ground. (It is not necessary to enclose the monogram with a border in this case.) Be sure that the area within the monogram is entirely clean. Expose the metal to the etching fluid; the monogram will be eaten away by the acid and thus appear depressed below the surface of the surrounding metal.

Copy the design you desire on tissue paper and paste it on the metal to guide your hand in the removal of the etching ground. Thin paper is used because it will lay flat and it can be easily removed. Remember, the tissue paper pasted on the metal is used only as a pattern; it will not protect the metal from the etching fluid.

A simple etching ground, sometimes called a "stopping-out varnish," is made as follows:

2 ounces white shellac
5 ounces pure grain alcohol
25 grains methyl-violet dye

Dissolve the shellac in the alcohol and then add the dye. This formula will work fairly well if the etching fluid is weak, but it is frowned upon by the professional etchers.

Another simple formula is:

1 part asphalt
6 parts benzol

Still another formula, much preferred by gun engravers, is:

> 1 part mastic
> 1 part white beeswax
> 2 parts pulverized Syrian asphalt

The latter is prepared as follows: Melt the beeswax and mix it with the mastic by stirring in a pan over a constant heat. When the beeswax and the mastic are thoroughly mixed, add the pulverized Syrian asphalt and keep stirring until the three materials are entirely dissolved. Pour the mixture into water and mould it into little cakes with the fingers before it cools. These cakes are kept in a glass jar until needed. To use them, shave off slivers and dissolve these slivers in pure spirits of turpentine.

The first two etching grounds can be painted on the metal with a brush, preferably a fine, camel's-hair brush, but the third formula works better when applied with a coarser brush. Unlike the first two etching grounds, it cannot be used to protect fine lines in relief etching; instead, it is coated over the metal and then removed where the etching fluid is to act.

A fourth formula, which produces a very hard etching ground, is made as follows:

> Burgundy pitch, 5 parts
> Rosin,   5 parts

Melt the pitch and rosin together; add 4 parts walnut oil; boil the mixture until it can be drawn out in long threads.

A fifth formula, which produces a soft etching ground, is made as follows:

> Mastic,   4 parts
> Burgundy pitch, 12 parts
> Melted beeswax, 30 parts
> Melted asphalt, 50 parts

Add these materials in the order named, and then, after cooling, add 125 parts turpentine oil. If it is desirable to make the etching ground deep black, add lampblack as needed. A smaller or larger quantity can be made by varying the number of parts but keeping them in the proportion given.

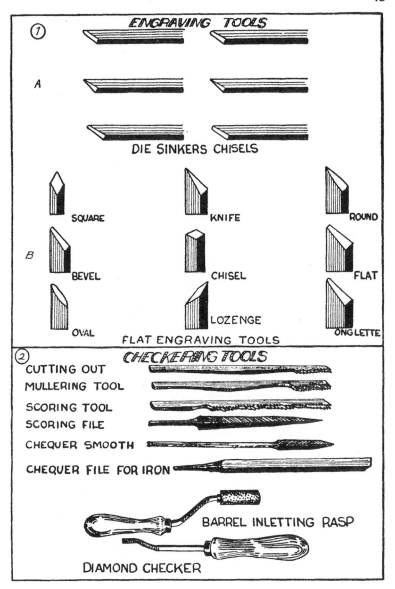

PLATE 20. CHECKERING AND ENGRAVING TOOLS.

The etching fluid is the next consideration. It may be poured over the whole object, or the object may be put into the fluid; in either event, all of the object must be covered with the etching ground. After etching, the object is rinsed in pure, running water, dried with clean rags, and finally washed off with turpentine oil or a light volatile camphor oil, to destroy the last vestige of the etching fluid.

Another method is to treat only the part to be etched with the etching fluid. This is done by applying the etching fluid to the exposed metal with a glass rod. This method is slower but it is less likely to result in a ruined gun.

Etching on steel is usually done with nitric acid. Start with 1 part nitric acid to 6 parts water, as an experiment to see what can be done; this weak mixture is also used where part of the design has not been removed enough. Decrease the amount of water until you are able to etch with equal parts of nitric acid and water. By parts, we mean parts by volume, and not by weight. Etchers use varying ratios of acid and water, such as 1 part acid to 4 parts water, 1 part acid to 3 parts water, etc. There is no fixed rule.

Measure the water and pour it into a clean bottle; then add the acid. Never pour the water into the acid or it will generate heat and crack the bottle. This is a fixed rule, the violation of which may produce acid burns on your clothing and body.

After adding the acid to the bottle, wait a few minutes for the mixture to cool before inserting the cork or stopper in the bottle. If the action is too strong, pour from the first bottle into a second bottle containing the necessary quantity of water for diluting the acid. Notice that again we caution against adding water to the acid, even though the acid is already diluted with water. Another way to reduce the force of the acid is to drop a small ball of steel wool into the bottle, but it is better to dilute by the former method.

Hardened steel, such as hardened steel receivers on rifles, can be etched with a mixture of 2 parts nitric acid to 1 part acetic acid. High speed steel may require 3 parts nitric acid to 1 part acetic acid. When acetic acid is not obtainable, vinegar will prove a fairly good substitute.

Brass is etched with the following: Add 1 part nitric acid to 10 parts distilled water. Next, dissolve ½ part potassium chlorate

PLATE 21. MONOGRAMS FOR ETCHING AND ENGRAVING.

in 10 parts distilled water. Pour the first mixture slowly into the second and use on brass in the same manner as the nitric acid is used on steel.

Bronze, which is an alloy of copper and tin, may be etched with a solution of 20 parts nitric acid mixed with 1 part hydrochloric acid.

Copper may be etched with a saturated solution of bromine in dilute hydrochloric acid; or with a mixture of potassium bichromate, ½ part; water, 1 part; and crude nitric acid, 3 parts. Another fluid for etching copper is made thus: A boiling solution of potassium chlorate, 1 part, in water, 10 parts, is poured into a mixture of pure hydrochloric acid, 1 part, with water, 25 parts.

Electro-etching is done with a bath which is too weak in itself to affect the metal seriously, but is made capable of eating the metal by an electric current. The work done by this method is finer, sharper, and more accurately controlled by the operator. The surface to be protected is covered with the stopping-out varnish or etching ground in the same manner as in ordinary etching. A conducting wire is fastened at an uncovered place by soft soldering, or with a metal clamp, and the connection is covered with varnish. The metal object is then suspended in the acid bath and acts as an anode, while another similar metal object acts as the cathode. Gradations in etching are accomplished by removing the metal objects, rinsing, and covering parts already etched enough with etching ground; after that, they are returned to the acid bath.

In electro-etching, steel can be etched with a green vitriol solution, or with an ammonium chloride solution. Copper is etched with a solution of 1 part sulphuric acid to 20 parts water.

Etching tools can be made in the home shop. Sewing needles, set in ordinary penholders with sealing wax, are used to cut fine lines through the etching ground. Phonograph needles, similarly mounted, are used to cut lines that are a little coarser. Heavier lines can be cut with dental burrs that have been ground down, their flutes removed, and their ends stoned to a high polish. Dental burrs are too big to be mounted in penholders, hence special handles should be cut from softwood for these tools. Another tool that can be used is the scriber, shown in Figure 6, Plate 6.

Most of your etching tools should be blunt and round on the end so that they will not catch in the metal, but a few of them, such as the sewing needles, should be sharp for cutting fine lines. Sharp points can be removed by working them over an Arkansas stone at right angles to the stone. When it is necessary to use sharp-pointed tools, be careful not to damage hardened steel surfaces; the tools are to cut away the etching ground; they are not intended for the actual cutting of the metal in the etching process.

Scrapers are handy for removing etching ground in places where it has been accidentally applied to the metal. An old, flat needle file can be converted into a flat scraper by grinding it down to a sharp cutting edge on the end, setting it in a handle and then stoning it. Since grinding affects the temper, heat and draw to a dark straw color before mounting it in the handle, according to the method described in the chapter on heat treatment. Of course, if you do not object to continually sharpening your tools, tempering is not essential. Some etchers merely use a miniature putty knife as a scraper.

Engravers tools such as burnishers and gravers, described later, can be used to improve the appearance of the etching. The burnisher removes scratches and rough places, while the graver (burin) is used to cut lines which were not brought out in the etching process.

The acids and acid solutions are kept in white glass bottles, so that the strength of the acid may be judged by the color. Glass stoppers are preferred. The bottles should be labeled "Poison," with a skull and crossbones, and directions for making and taking an antidote. They should be kept on a high shelf, away from children.

When an entire object is to be etched, an acid bath is used. For this purpose a receptacle that is not affected by acid is needed. The dish, tray, trough or tub should be large enough to hold the part to be etched. It should be made of some smooth, nonporous material, such as porcelain, glass or rubber. When these materials are not available, a liquid-tight wooden box, with melted wax in all of the joints and several coats of varnish all over its interior, will be satisfactory. It is not advisable to use a kitchen sink or a washbowl for this purpose; they are too large, they are the wrong shape, and they have metal fittings that will be affected by the acid.

Rubber gloves should be worn while working with acids, as well as a heavy oilcloth apron. There should be ventilation to remove the acid fumes, and an ample supply of water for stopping the action of the acid on the parts being etched, or on the body if any acid is spilled. Still better than water for neutralizing the acid is liquid ammonia. This can be applied to places on the metal with a glass rod or an eye-dropper if the etching fluid is working too strongly on certain spots; it is also used to counteract acid spilled on the clothing or body.

Finally, when you have experimented on an old firearm, or on a piece of scrap steel, you can proceed to etch more complicated designs on a good gun. Etching is another of the gunsmith's arts. Each man must find his own way and follow his own methods. A handbook can never be more than a guide.

ENGRAVING

Figure 1, Plate 20, shows two groups of engraving tools: Die Sinkers' Chisels and Flat Engraving Tools. Die Sinkers' Chisels are made from the finest tool steel; they usually come in a set of twelve different sizes and shapes, with cutting edges that are generally wedge-shaped, rectangular, elliptical, or combinations of these three shapes.

Engraving tools have various forms. Flat engraving tools, like those illustrated in Figure 1, Plate 20, are usually numbered from 0 to 14. Pointed onglette tools are numbered from 0 to 6. Knife-edge and half-point tools are available only in one size for each, but there are half-point tools for both the right hand and the left hand. Flat chisel tools are in three sizes, numbered from 1 to 3; and there are also flat tools numbered from 36 to 49. Square and lozenge-shaped tools are numbered from 1 to 8. Bevel tools are numbered from 1 to 6. Lining tools are made in thirteen sizes, ranging from No. 8, which is the coarsest, to No. 32, which is the finest; usually there are two lines to the No. 8 and twelve lines to the No. 32. Most of these tools are made in Europe and therefore are fairly expensive, but the beginner can make his own if he exercises patience and a reasonable amount of skill. The finest quality of tool steel is used, and a keen edge is given with a fine Arkansas or Washita stone.

Each tool is mounted in an ordinary file handle, but a metal plug should be inserted in the base of the handle, preferably made of cold-drawn steel. This plug receives the blows of a special hammer that has a head the size of a half-dollar and about twice as thick; the head is at the end of a short shaft with the end of the hammer handle joined to the shaft at right angles. The end of the handle is the shape of a small egg where it fits in the hand. You can use any ordinary small hammer and turn out excellent work, but eventually you may wish to acquire the professional engraver's hammer.

Engravers use a special swivel vise designed for their work, but any machinist's vise that swivels is better than one that is fixed. This is true because there are usually many curved lines to be chiseled; you can chisel as far as you can go in the same direction, swing the vise, and continue to chisel in the same direction from another part of the curve.

You can work either standing up or sitting down, but it is better to work standing, for then your body can more naturally follow the line that is being cut. The wrist of the left hand, which holds the engraving tool, guides the work while you strike the butt of the tool handle with the hammer held in the right hand.

To avoid cutting too deep, do not hold the tool high; let it slant against the work while you cut shallow grooves. Although the wrist and body bend to follow the direction of a curved line, no wrist or body movement is required in chiseling a straight line. Shading is done with a lining tool that cuts a single line; by tipping it slightly to one side or the other, varying depths can be given to the shading. Of course, there are also lining tools that cut several lines at once, but they are not well adapted to the finest quality of shading.

Like etching, engraving can be done in relief or in intaglio, but the cut-away portions of the metal should be shallow or they will collect grease and dirt, with the result that the gun looks worse than one lacking in ornamentation. For this reason, some engravers hammer 24-karat gold wire into the recess produced by engraving, using a flat punch. This must be done carefully or the vibration of firing will loosen the gold, which will then protrude from the gun and eventually drop out.

Many rifles have receivers that must be annealed before they can be engraved. After engraving, the receiver must be properly hardened again. When a barrel is fitted to an action, the receiver is annealed, engraved, and rehardened before being fitted; after that, the barrel can be engraved.

Another problem is that of the government markings on fire-arms originally owned by the United States government and then sold to civilians. Some gunsmiths make quite a point of removing such markings, probably because it creates more employment, but the removal of any government markings, particularly the serial numbers, raises a suspicion on the part of subsequent owners and others that the weapon was illegally acquired.

This is true to a lesser degree in the case of firearms that have never been government owned. Furthermore, weapons that have the same serial number on several parts are recognized as genuine, whereas the presence of different serial numbers creates an impression that the firearm may have been assembled from junked parts, although this is not necessarily always true.

Removing the serial numbers and markings from a government weapon takes away from $\frac{1}{32}$ to $\frac{1}{16}$ inch thickness at a place where strength is seriously needed. Those who suddenly find themselves with bulged or burst rifles should not complain about the results of their own folly.

Screw heads should be decorated with a double knife-edge needle file. Hold a screw between lead sheets in a vise (see Figure 1, Plate 29) to protect the threads of the screw and file straight lines across its head. You can also place the file in the vise, hold the screw in a pin vise (Figure 9, Plate 5), and work the screw head against the file. If you find difficulty in holding a screw in the machinist's vise (Figure 7, Plate 5), place the screw in a sight spanner (Figure 1, Plate 7), and clamp the sight spanner in the machinist's vise.

If you have a lathe, you can cut fine circles on the screw heads, either by themselves or in combination with straight lines cut with the file. Do not cut either the circles or the straight lines very deep or they will collect dust and dirt. Notice how the slots of the screws of a high-quality gun are all lined up in the same direction. Remember this when you place the decorations on the screw heads and arrange your ornamentation to harmonize with the rest of the gun. When you replace the screws, put them back so that the slots are set as they were in the beginning.

Damascening, when applied to firearm ornamentation, usually means the decoration of metal parts with overlapping circles having centers on the same straight line, although it is also used to describe steel having wavy lines, and further employed as a term for the inlay of various metals to give the appearance of colors woven together.

The overlapping rings are made with a hard rubber (or hard fiber) tool with a circular working end, placed in a drill press. Optical emery mixed with olive oil is spread over the surface to be decorated. The handle of the drill press is brought down with just enough pressure for the hard rubber tool to produce a circle, then the handle of the drill press is lifted, the work is moved, the handle of the drill press is brought down again, and a second ring, overlapping the first, is made. The size of the circle and the amount of overlapping are matters of personal taste; usually they are determined by the size of the object being decorated.

The Matting Tool, so named because it leaves an interwoven, mat-like design, is used to ornament both metal and wood, as well as to give a surface that will not slip. Jewelers' supply houses sell them, or you can make your own by tapering one end of a $\frac{1}{4}$ inch square drill rod, filing out the end with a slitting file to make rows of sharp teeth, hardening it, and then drawing the temper to a dark straw color. The exact design made by the teeth is left to your own taste.

This tool is used in place of checkering or engraving. Around the matting there should be a border, which can be put on with a center punch (Figure 5, Plate 4), a fine prick punch, or a ground-down dental burr. These three tools can also be used to produce matting, since that is nothing more than a series of tiny points, but it is done easier, faster, and better with a matting tool.

Returning to the subject of engraving, the beginner is cautioned again to experiment on old guns or scrap metal before he attempts work on good guns. Furthermore, he should start with something easy, such as the "MK" monogram on Plate 21, which was recommended for the first practice in etching. Then, when he can do the simple designs well, he can progress to more difficult ones, such as the other monograms on Plate 21.

CAUTION ON ETCHING AND ENGRAVING

Etching and engraving anything, including firearms, is an art, trade, or profession. Anyone who has read this chapter and has good common sense can execute average work if he takes his time, practices on metal of little value, and then etches or engraves firearms or other metal objects. However, no one can become a great etcher or a great engraver unless he was born with aptitude for this work.

If money is important and if you develop into an engraver of the first magnitude, you can make more money working for the U.S. Bureau of Printing and Engraving, U.S. Treasury Department, than you can ever make engraving firearms.

XIII. Cleaning Guns and Removing Obstructions

A CLEAN tooth may decay, but a clean, well-lubricated firearm never rusts. Manufacturers of ammunition sometimes advertise that it is not necessary to clean and oil weapons in which their cartridges, made with noncorrosive primers, are fired, but manufacturers of firearms, controlled by the very same holding companies that own the cartridge factories, give away pamphlets which include detailed instructions for cleaning weapons in which noncorrosive primer cartridges have been shot.

Like cleaning your teeth, taking care of your firearms is largely a matter of habit. To make it easy, we shall present the subject in easy steps that should be taken at the end of each day's firing.

First, soak a flannel patch in powder solvent and place it on the end of a cleaning rod. Insert the rod and patch in the barrel, from the breech, run the rod forward until the patch comes out of the muzzle, and then pull the rod backward until the patch comes out at the breech. Repeat this bore swabbing several times, ten or fifteen times is not too often. Throw the patch away when you are through. The barrel should be held in a cleaning rack or in a vise, but the muzzle may be rested on a clean piece of paper placed on the floor.

Gun instructors always say that the barrel must be cleaned from the breech, and never from the muzzle. The author experimented with rifles cleaned repeatedly from the muzzle and discovered that cleaning from the muzzle will change the location of the shot-group on the target, but it will not change the size of the shot-group. Cleaning from the muzzle, if not carefully done, will cause inaccuracies. Therefore, always clean from the breech.

Powder solvent can be made at home by mixing equal parts of the best grade of turpentine, pure sperm oil, and acetone, illustrated in the upper left-hand corner of Plate 22. Let your neighborhood druggist mix these together for you and place the solvent in a bottle with a glass stopper, this being necessary because acetone evaporates rapidly. Commercial powder solvents contain a little alkanet root which has been soaked in turpentine; this gives a red color to the mixture, but it does not materially add to the cleaning properties of the solvent.

The second step in cleaning is to run a brush through the bore, working from the breech to the muzzle, and back again, three or four times for a rifle or revolver, more often for a shotgun, especially if the shotgun is badly leaded. There are three types of rifle-cleaning brushes: the steel brush, the bronze-bristle brush, and the bristle brush. The best one for general purposes is the bronze-bristle brush, (not made in U. S. A.) sometimes called a brass-wire bristle brush. It is made in sizes for rifles, revolvers, and shotguns. Also, for shotguns there are patented cleaners, such as the "Tomlinson Shotgun Cleaner," that are excellent.

The third step is to put a fresh flannel cleaning patch on the ramrod and swab the bore again with powder solvent, for the purpose of removing any powder fouling and lead loosened by the brass-wire bristle brush in the second step.

The fourth step is to wipe the cleaning rod dry and use it to run several clean, dry flannel patches through the bore until it is bright and shiny when the barrel is held to the light. (If you clean a barrel without removing it, hold a small piece of white paper in the breech to reflect the light while you inspect the bore.) Five or six cleaning patches should be enough for this operation.

The fifth and last step in the normal cleaning process is to swab the bore with one flannel patch soaked in gun oil. Generally, you can safely set the firearm away for several days, depending upon the humidity, but the safe rule is to run a clean dry patch through the bore, followed by an oiled patch, each day for ten days after the last

PLATE 22. HOMEMADE CLEANING MATERIAL.

day of firing, and then apply gun grease if you intend to set the weapon away for a long period.

Gun oil can be bought in any hardware or sporting goods store, but it is cheaper and more fun to make your own. Mix 1 ounce of pure cocoanut oil with 16 ounces of pure sperm oil. Usually it is necessary to heat the mixture of the two oils slowly and let it simmer for 5 to 10 minutes over a low flame. The ingredients are represented in the upper right-hand figure of Plate 22. If impurities are present in the oils, scrape or file a block of pure lead and place the particles of lead in the bottle of gun oil, which is then set in the sun until the impurities in the oil collect on the lead shavings, after which the oil is poured into a clean bottle through filter paper.

Gun oil protects the bore for short periods. It can also be used on the action. Simply wipe any dirt and moisture off the action, and apply a light coat of gun oil. Too much oil will interfere with the proper ignition of the cartridge or shotgun shell; it will spatter back in your eyes when the gun gets hot from firing, and it may become gummy and interfere with the moving parts. In addition to the bore and the action, use the gun oil on all exposed metal parts.

Before firing again, run several clean, dry patches through the bore and remove any excess oil from the action. Oil in the bore tends to make the first few shots strike wild of the mark, and it also increases breech pressure. A great excess of oil or grease may even cause a burst barrel, with danger to the life of the shooter.

When the gun is put away for storage, take it apart and put a heavy coat of gun grease on all parts, especially the bore. One way to make gun grease is to melt together, over slow heat, equal parts by weight of pure white vaseline and anhydrous lanolin, the latter being refined grease from sheep wool, but be sure that you actually obtain anhydrous lanolin or moisture will collect and rust the gun. The making of this gun grease is illustrated in the two center figures of Plate 22. If at any time this grease seems too heavy, it may be lightened by the addition of sperm oil. Leave no sweat, fingerprints, or other moist marks on the gun before it is stored.

Careless cleaning methods, or the use of bullets with cupro-nickel jackets, may leave metal fouling in the bore, indicated by spots and streaks of gray in contrast to the shiny background when the bore is examined against the light. Rust may develop under the metal fouling, and in any event the accuracy of your marksmanship will be reduced.

Metal fouling is removed by means of a metal-fouling solution, illustrated in the lower left-hand figure of Plate 22:

Ammonium Persulfate,	220 grains
Ammonium Carbonate,	100 grains
Distilled Water,	60 c.c.
Stronger Ammonia (28%),	90 c.c.

The first two ingredients are powders which should be mixed together and then dissolved in the water; the ammonia is added last. Pour the solution into a large, strong bottle with a rubber cork. Be sure that the bottle is large enough so that the solution occupies only about one-half of its volume, for a gas is generated which might break the bottle. Keep the bottle tightly corked except when you pour out the solution. The strength of the solution decreases steadily, hence it is not advisable to mix more than you need to last for a month at the most.

To use the metal-fouling solution, clean the bore of oil and grease, cork the breech with a rubber stopper, and fill the bore with the solution. Stand the gun upright to one side, let it stand for 15 minutes at least; one-half hour is long enough. Pour out the solution; it will probably be dark blue in color; this shows that it has dissolved the metal fouling.

Knock out the rubber cork with a ramrod; pour boiling water through the barrel; wipe dry with several patches; and follow immediately with a light coat of gun oil. However, if an inspection of the bore shows that any metal fouling remains, run a bronze-bristle brush through the bore, repeat the metal-fouling treatment, clean, dry, and oil before putting the gun away. The slightest amount of metal fouling may ruin the bore.

Military-type rifles, in which ammunition loaded with potassium chlorate primers are fired, may rust from salt deposited in the bore from the primer. Like table salt, this primer salt absorbs moisture from the air. Neither oil nor powder solvent removes it. Simply pour boiling water through the bore several times, run dry patches through until the bore is clean, and finish with a light coat of oil. Actually, the important thing is not whether the rifles are of the military type but whether they use potassium chlorate primers or "noncorrosive" primers. If the former primers are used, boiling water is needed; if the latter primers are used, follow the five-step method given before.

When bolt-action rifles are cleaned with hot water, the bolt is removed and a funnel inserted at the breech. This funnel should have a bent nozzle that can be made by any tinsmith for a few cents. Lever-action rifles should have the breech block lowered to facilitate cleaning by this method. The rifle is held, muzzle down, over a wash-tub or bucket; several dippersful of boiling water are poured into the funnel and allowed to run back into the container. In this way the same hot water can be used several times.

A cleaning rack is a handy accessory for cleaning by the five-step method, or for keeping weapons out of the way while waiting to clean them by the hot-water method. The one illustrated in the lower right-hand figure of Plate 22 is one of the simplest and best racks that can be made. Its dimensions depend on the size of rifles used. The height should be such that a cleaning rod can be used comfortably. The end elevation, or side view, shows how the rifle is held in the rack, barrel sloping downward. The rear elevation shows the slots of proper size to hold the rifle stocks snugly. The top plan shows that there are slots for the stocks opposite holes through which the muzzles are placed.

When a rack is not available, the barrel can be held between the jaws of a vise, but it should be protected by either the lead sheets or the felt-faced blocks shown in Figures 1 and 2, Plate 29. The grooved wooden block placed in a vise, illustrated in Figure 3, Plate 29, can also be used. Still another way to hold a barrel for cleaning is to make a barrel vise or clamp block of two pieces of steel, as shown in Figure 6, Plate 29. This barrel vise may be bolted to the bench top, fastened to the frame of a lathe, or mounted in a machinist's vise. In any case, the bolts that hold the upper part in place are loosened, the barrel is inserted, and the adjusting bolts are then tightened.

Cleaning rods should be made of steel. Brass rods are soft, bend easily, and scrape against the bore when sprung out of shape. A piece of metal fouling or hard grit embedded in a brass rod has the same effect as emery powder in scraping away the steel.

Jointed rods may break just when you need them, or the threads at the joints may strip. The only excuse for owning a jointed rod is that it can be carried easily, but this defense is countered by the fact that "pull-throughs" are just as convenient to carry and much more reliable. These are pieces of cord with steel slots at their ends. The slot is dropped through the bore and pulled back with a patch inside. It takes more time to use a pull-through than a jointed rod, but it is practically indestructible. However, there is no substitute for a straight, solid steel rod, preferably one with a handle that permits the rod to revolve as the patch follows the twist of the rifling. Obviously, this revolving feature is not needed for a shotgun cleaning rod, since there is no rifling.

Three types of ramrod tips are shown in the lower right-hand figure of Plate 22. These are the slot, button, and jagged types. The single slotted tip is best because it always holds the patch, but it sometimes jams when the direction of movement is reversed in the bore, and it occasionally rubs the bore when the patch gets twisted over to the other side. The button type, sometimes called a plain-jag tip, reverses without trouble and always presents a uniform cleaning surface, but it comes loose if carried beyond the muzzle or the chamber. The jagged tip, sometimes called a roll-jag tip, can be used with a patch wrapped or rolled around its surface, but if the patch comes off the jagged tip will scratch the bore. There are other types of tips, but they are merely variations of the three basic types described here.

Cleaning patches should be made of medium weight canton flannel, previously moistened thoroughly with water and wrung out several times to make it more absorbent. The flannel is cut into squares of a size depending upon the caliber or gauge of the gun, and the size of the cleaning-rod tip. It should give a snug fit in the barrel, but not require more than 4 or 5 pounds pressure to drive it through the bore.

A badly neglected, partly rusted barrel presents a serious problem. Sometimes scrubbing it out with hot water and soap, using a brass-bristle brush, will help. A stronger treatment is to lap it out with a mixture of Vienna lime and paraffin oil, using a brass-bristle brush wrapped with a canton flannel patch that has been soaked in the mixture. An even stronger treatment is to lap it out with finely ground emery powder and olive oil. If this fails, desperate measures are required; swab the bore with equal parts sulphuric and nitric acids, rinse in clear water, dry, rinse with ammonia, rinse with clear water, and dry again; follow this with a light coat of oil.

Lead fouling can be removed with mercury. Clean the bore of all oil and grease, place a cork or wooden plug in the chamber, rest the butt of the gun on the floor, fill the bore with mercury, and let the weapon stand for about an hour. Pour the mercury from the bore into a bottle for future use. Remove the plug, clean the bore, and inspect it against the light. If there is any lead fouling left, run a brass-bristle brush through the bore and repeat the mercury treatment.

Most appliances and devices sold by reputable manufacturers and dealers are useful, but the so-called "anti-rust ropes" designed for shotguns, rifles, and revolvers are a source of trouble. When saturated with the correct kind of oil, they tend to exclude air and moisture and make it difficult for the barrels to rust or become pitted. However, the oil with which such ropes are saturated dries out, the owner feels secure for life, and he fails to inspect his guns, with the result that he finds a collection of junk in the gun cabinet when the next shooting season opens.

Canvas, leather, sheepskin, and wooden gun cases are all good for storing or transporting firearms, provided the owner inspects his arms frequently, making sure that no rust has begun to form in the bore. Wool-lined cases are particularly susceptible to moisture. An airtight wooden wall cabinet is probably the best storage medium for the average gun-owner; a steel cabinet has the advantage of being fireproof but it is usually far from airtight. Probably the only safe storage method is that used by the armed services. Weapons are disassembled, cleaned, dried, and greased liberally with cosmoline, after which they are reassembled and given another coat of cosmoline. This grease is unpleasant and difficult to remove, as all veterans know, but at least it is thoroughly dependable.

The removal of obstructions from the bore requires considerable ingenuity, for shooters have quaint ideas about cleaning materials and are inclined to use rags that are too big for the bore; then, when the rags get stuck, they resort to frantic measures that only increase the difficulty. There is an old military adage to the effect that it is bad enough for a soldier to use the sleeve of his overcoat for a cleaning rag, but it is unforgivable if he forgets to remove the buttons.

Homemade bullets are often too big for the bore. Their removal can be accomplished with a drill (see Figure 2, Plate 5) about .01 inch smaller in diameter than the diameter of the bore, measured between the lands. The drill is then sweated on a piece of drill rod of the appropriate length and diameter; and the rod is used in a ratchet brace (Figure 4, Plate 6), or a breast drill (Figure 2, Plate 4). On rare occasions, it may be necessary to rig a device like the barrel rifling setup shown on Plate 28, using a drill instead of a rifling head.

The drill should be ground to a sharp, cone-shaped point, and kept in the center line of the bore or it may slip to one side and spoil the rifling. Although the drill, itself, should be smaller than the bore diameter between the lands, the drill rod behind the drill should closely approach the bore diameter; this tends to keep the drill on the center line of the bore, where it belongs, whereas a drill rod that is too small permits the drill to wobble.

Do not use a drill to remove a cloth obstruction. First, plug one end of the barrel, pour light paraffin oil in the other end, and plug it when it is full; then reverse the barrel, remove the other plug, fill that end with paraffin oil, and replug. Let the barrel stand overnight, full of paraffin oil. On the following day, try to poke out the cloth with a drill rod nearly as large as the bore. If the cloth does not come out easily, use a "wormer." This tool is simply an ordinary wood screw, of an appropriate size, soldered to the end of a steel rod, with a wooden handle at the other end, mounted at right angles to the rod. Another way to make this tool is to file threads in the end of a piece of drill rod and mount a handle at the other end. Screw the wormer into the cloth, little by little, just as you would work a corkscrew into a cork; if the whole obstruction will not come out at one swoop, remove it piece by piece. As a matter of fact, some gunsmiths weld a corkscrew to the end of a steel rod and use that as their wormer.

Amateurs often try to pound an obstruction out of a barrel with a rod and hammer, but they only succeed in expanding the obstruction and making it stick tighter to the walls of the barrel. Some gunsmiths use a large, flat-headed rod, and pound it through the bore with a heavy hammer, but we do not recommend this procedure for several reasons. One is that it is especially bad in the case of shotguns, which have thin walls that will bulge or break under such treatment. Another reason is that the presence of any harsh material in the obstruction damages the rifling if it is pounded through the bore. For some reason or other, even professional gunsmiths seem to forget that they have a vise when they try to pound out an obstruction and hold the gun in one hand while they pound a rod into the bore with the other. If you insist upon rough-house methods, at least clamp the barrel in a vise while you are pounding the rod.

The removal of obstructions from shotgun bores follows the same procedure as that for rifles and revolvers, except that it is better to use a special shotgun wormer, sold by all gun-supply houses, and made with two "worms" that run in opposite directions, sometimes described as a "reversed" worm. Since shotgun walls are thin, it is safer to mount the worm on the end of a hardwood rod that is almost as large in diameter as the shotgun bore.

When the base of a cartridge is removed by the extractor of a rifle, leaving the body of the case in the chamber, load a "ruptured cartridge extractor" into the rifle, just as though it were a cartridge, close the bolt, open the bolt and work the bolt to the rear, just as though you were extracting a fired cartridge case. If the ruptured case does not come out, repeat the process, but this time, just before you open the bolt, insert a rod in the bore through the muzzle and tap downward. This pushes the ruptured cartridge case up against the ruptured cartridge extractor and at the same time it may loosen the broken case from the walls of the chamber. Open the bolt and you should now have your broken case free from the chamber.

When a ruptured cartridge extractor is not available, or when it fails to function, resort to the "worm" idea described for removing cloth obstructions, but this time cut a sharp point with a file on the end of a steel rod, put notches on the sides of the point, and screw the point into the neck of the broken cartridge case, using a tap wrench (Plate 8, Figure 3). The rod should be slightly larger in diameter than the neck of the cartridge, but also smaller than the chamber. Hardening and tempering the working end of the rod will improve its performance. Obviously, this treatment must be given from the rear of the chamber.

If in spite of trying everything already recommended the broken cartridge case remains in the chamber, disassemble the rifle and remove the barrel. Place the barrel in a vise or clamp, try to pry the rear edges of the broken case loose from the chamber with small screwdrivers or chisels, and then try to poke the broken case backward with a rod inserted from the muzzle. If the rear edges of the case have been loosened, the broken case should now come out without any more trouble; if not, repeat the process, but be careful not to damage the walls of the chamber with either the rod or the tools used to pry loose the edges of the case.

SPECIAL PROBLEMS

In cleaning and removing obstructions from any firearm, it is important to first understand the fundamentals of design and construction of that particular weapon. This chapter is correct and as complete as any instructions of this length can be, but if you want highly specialized information you can purchase at comparatively small cost paper-bound pamphlets and manuals from both the National Rifle Association of America, 1600 Rhode Island Avenue, N.W., Washington 6, D.C., and the Superintendent of Documents, U.S. Government Printing Office, Washington 25, D.C. It is recommended that in writing to either of these two great national organizations you specify the weapon or weapons for which you want pamphlets or manuals, and ask for the price list.

XIV. Temperatures

TEMPERATURE is the degree of heat or cold. It may be measured with a thermometer. Ordinarily this instrument consists of a glass tube, closed at both ends with a bulb at the lower end. The lower end of the tube and the bulb contain mercury which, when exposed to cold or heat, contracts or expands in proportion to the temperature change. The top of the mercury column rises or falls with the expansion and contraction of the mercury. Since the rise and fall is directly proportional to the temperature change, the marks on the thermometer scale are the same distance apart from top to bottom. A thermometer for accurate work should have its scale engraved on the tube itself, and not on a metal plate to which it may be attached, because the metal plate itself will expand and contract with heat and cold.

Each thermometer has two fixed points. These are the freezing point and the boiling point, sometimes called the ice point and the steam point. The freezing point is found by putting the instrument in finely chopped ice which is melting. The boiling point is found by placing the thermometer in steam from boiling water at normal atmospheric pressure. Having determined these two fixed points, the distance between them is divided into equal parts, the number depending upon the type of scale to be used, that is, whether it is to show Fahrenheit or Centigrade degrees.

The Fahrenheit thermometer has a scale with the distance between the freezing and boiling points divided into 180 divisions, called degrees. Thirty-two more divisions are laid off below the freezing point, and the lowest point is marked zero. This makes a total of 212 degrees between the zero point and the boiling point. Note that the freezing point is 32 degrees. The scale may be extended above the boiling point and below the zero point, if desired. A point below zero, such as 30 degrees below zero, is read —30 deg. F., while a point above zero, such as 40 degrees Fahrenheit, is read 40 deg. F.; it is not necessary to say "plus 40 deg. F."

The Centigrade scale has the freezing point marked 0 and the boiling point marked 100; the distance between them is divided into 100 equal divisions or degrees. As in the Fahrenheit scale, the Centigrade scale may be extended above the boiling point and below the freezing point. A point above zero, such as 30 degrees, is read 30 deg. C.; a point below zero, such as 10 degrees, is read —10 deg. C.

Changing from one scale to the other is easy if we remember a few simple facts. Remember that the number of degrees between the freezing point and the boiling point on the Centigrade scale is 100, and on the Fahrenheit 180, hence 1 deg. F. equals $^{100}/_{180}$ deg. C. or $\frac{5}{9}$ deg. C. In a like manner, 1 deg. C. will equal $^{180}/_{100}$ deg. F. or $\frac{9}{5}$ deg. F.

Note:—The following rules do not involve algebraic addition or subtraction.

When the given Centigrade temperature is above zero, to obtain the Fahrenheit temperature, multiply the Centigrade temperature by $\frac{9}{5}$ and add 32. We add 32 because the freezing point on the Fahrenheit thermometer is 32 degrees. For example, let us find the Fahrenheit temperature which corresponds to 100 deg. C. Multiply 100 by $\frac{9}{5}$, which gives 180; to this add 32 and we have 212 deg. F., which we already know to be the boiling point on the Fahrenheit scale, corresponding to 100 deg. C., the boiling point on the Centigrade scale.

When the given Centigrade temperature is below zero, to obtain the Fahrenheit temperature, first multiply by $\frac{9}{5}$. If the product is 32 or less, subtract that product from 32. If the product is greater than 32, subtract 32 from the product. The former will give a Fahrenheit reading above zero while the latter will give a Fahrenheit reading below zero, which, of course, is a negative reading. Examples of these last two situations will now be given.

Given a reading of —10 deg. C., to find the corresponding Fahrenheit temperature, we multiply 10 by 9/5, which gives a product of 18. Since this is less than 32, we subtract it from 32 and this gives 14, or 14 deg. F.

Given a reading of —45 deg. C., to find the corresponding Fahrenheit temperature, we multiply 45 by 9/5. This gives 81. Since this is greater than 32, we subtract 32 from 81, which leaves 49, hence the reading is —49 deg. F.

To change from Fahrenheit to Centigrade, when the Fahrenheit temperature is 32 deg. or more, we subtract 32 from the Fahrenheit reading and multiply the remainder by 5/9. For example, given a Fahrenheit reading of 212 deg., we subtract 32, which gives 180; this is multiplied by 5/9 and the product is 100. Therefore, the Centigrade reading corresponding to 212 deg. F. is found to be 100 deg. C.

When the Fahrenheit temperature is between zero and 32 deg., to change to Centigrade subtract it from 32 and multiply the remainder by 5/9. For example, given a Fahrenheit reading of 5 deg. F., subtract 5 from 32; the remainder is 27; multiply 27 by 5/9; the product is 15; therefore the corresponding Centigrade reading is 15, but it must be preceded by a negative sign because we know that the Fahrenheit reading of 5 deg. was below the Fahrenheit freezing point; hence, the Centigrade reading must be below the Centigrade freezing point. The answer is —15 deg. C.

When the Fahrenheit reading is below zero, to find the Centigrade temperature, add 32 and multiply the sum by 5/9. For example, given a Fahrenheit reading of —22 deg. F., we add 32, which gives 54. Multiply this by 5/9; the product is 30, and it must be negative because the original Fahrenheit reading was below the freezing point, hence the answer is —30 deg. C.

Absolute Temperature.—We can easily understand the wisdom of giving the freezing point on the Centigrade scale a reading of 0 deg., but the corresponding reading of 32 deg. on the Fahrenheit scale puzzles many people. The reason for the selection of 32 deg. F. was that when the Fahrenheit scale was devised the lowest possible temperature so far obtained was 32 deg. F. below the freezing point. Since that time, however, experiments and calculations have led to the belief that the point where there is absolutely no heat is 459.69 degrees (practically 460 degrees) below the zero on the Fahrenheit scale and 273.16 (practically 273 degrees) below the zero on the Centigrade scale. The point where there is no heat is called the absolute zero. Temperature measured from that point is called Absolute Temperature.

Letting T represent the absolute temperature and t represent the ordinary thermometer reading, we find:

On the Centigrade scale, T equals t plus 273.

On the Fahrenheit scale, T equals t plus 460.

Obviously, we can rewrite the above equations, thus:

On the Centigrade scale, t equals T minus 273.

On the Fahrenheit scale, t equals T minus 460.

A few examples will show the working of these formulas. First, given a temperature of 32 deg. F., find the absolute temperature. Solution: Add 460 to 32 and the sum is 492 deg. F. absolute, usually written 492 deg. F. abs. Second, given a temperature of 0 deg. C., find the absolute temperature. Solution: Add 273 to 0; the sum is 273; hence the reading is 273 deg. C. abs.

When the temperature is below 0 on the Centigrade scale, subtract it from 273 to find the absolute temperature. Likewise, when the temperature is below 0 on the Fahrenheit scale, subtract it from 460 to find the absolute temperature. In showing absolute readings, be sure to indicate the scale used, whether it is C. or F.

Precautions for using a thermometer.—Before using a thermometer, examine it to see that the column of mercury is not broken apart. If it is, hold the thermometer in the hand with the arm fully extended, bulb downward, and swing it up and down several times. Always carry the instrument with the stem right side up, to keep the column of mercury from parting. When not in use, the thermometer should be kept in its case. Be sure that it is clean and dry before taking readings. Avoid exposing it to any source of cold or heat other than that of the body being measured. The sun's rays, the proximity of a hot stove, a cold draft through an open window—these are only a few of the many things that detract from accuracy if overlooked.

For many years the manufacturers of mercury thermometers removed as much air as possible from the space in the tube above the mercury, leaving an almost perfect vacuum. This lowered the boiling point of the mercury in the instrument far below its ordinary temperature of 356.9 deg. C., and made it impossible to use the mercury thermometer for measuring temperatures much in excess of 260 deg. C.

This difficulty has been overcome by filling the space above the mercury in the thermometer tube with a gas under high pressure, since the increase in pressure raises the boiling point of the mercury. However, it is necessary to use some gas which will not combine with mercury; one of the best for this purpose is nitrogen. By this method it has been possible to take accurate readings with a mercury thermometer up to a temperature of about 482 deg. C.

Pyrometers.—Since mercury thermometers cannot be used to measure very high temperatures, other instruments, called pyrometers, have been developed. There are various types of pyrometers, such as electrical resistance, mechanical, optical, and thermoelectric pyrometers. The action of these instruments is based on various heat effects, such as the variation of the electrical resistance of metals with the temperature, the generation of voltage by the thermocouple, the expansion of gases, the contraction of clay blocks, the expansion of metal, and the change of color of the heated object as compared with a standard.

The electrical resistance pyrometer consists of a coil of pure, fine, annealed, platinum wire placed in an electric circuit through which a small current from one or more electric cells flows while the circuit is exposed to the temperature being measured. Increasing the temperature of the platinum increases its resistance to the flow of the current. A sensitive instrument, based on the Wheatstone bridge, measures the change in resistance, and it is so arranged that it gives direct readings of temperature.

The thermoelectric pyrometer operates on the principle that an electromotive force is set upon heating the junction of two dissimilar metals. For moderate temperatures, copper-nickel and iron are used to make the joint; for extremely high temperatures, rhodium and platinum are used. Thermojunctions of wires of platinum with alloys of platinum-rhodium or platinum-iridium are variations of the same idea. This pyrometer consists of the thermocouple, which is arranged so that it can be placed in the heat, and an indicating device connected to the thermocouple by long, insulated wires that enable the operator to take the readings in comfort and safety. The thermocouple may be built in the form of a long, slender tube, while the indicator resembles an ordinary voltmeter. Many variations and improvements are possible, such as an attached apparatus for ringing bells at certain selected temperatures, recording devices, etc.

A mechanical pyrometer acts on the principle that different substances expand at different rates, even when subjected to the same temperature. Cast iron, for instance, has a coefficient of linear expansion of .00000617, and brass has a coefficient of linear expansion of .00001037. (The coefficient of linear expansion is the ratio of the increase of length to original length for an increase of 1 deg. F. temperature.) Since cast iron and brass have such different coefficients of linear expansion, they expand and contract at widely different rates even when subjected to the same temperature. Rods of iron and brass, joined together, will move back and forth as heat is applied or withdrawn. By connecting the rods to a pointer on a dial, through gears and levers, it is possible to indicate temperatures.

The optical pyrometer is a portable instrument used to determine the temperature by comparing the color of the heated object with the color of the filament of an incandescent lamp placed inside a telescope. Fahrenheit temperatures from 1,400 degrees up to about 2,800 degrees are measured with this instrument.

The operator stands back from the heated object or furnace far enough to be comfortable. Around his neck is a strap supporting a control box which contains a battery and a milliammeter with a rheostat. From the control box wires in a cord run to the lamp in the telescope. The operator holds the telescope with one hand and adjusts the control box with the other. He focuses the telescope on the heated object, turns a knob on the control box until the lamp filament in the telescope blends with the color of the heated object, and then reads a scale on the control box which is marked in 18 deg. F. divisions. There are other forms of optical pyrometers, but the one described is one of the most useful.

Seger Cones, sometimes called "Seger's Cones," are slender cones of clay mixtures of different fusibility, that is, different melting points. These cones are supplied in a series, with successive numbers. They are placed where the temperature is to be read. The temperature at the moment of observation lies somewhere between the temperature represented by the cone that has just melted and the next one to melt. That is, if cone number 5 has melted and cone number 6 is still intact, the temperature is somewhere between the temperature represented by number 5 and that represented by number 6. These temperatures are listed in a table supplied by the manufacturer of the cones.

Temperatures indicated by colors.—Hardened steel is too brittle to use without tempering, except for a few special purposes, such as the tips of armor-piercing projectiles. Heating it to about 392 deg. F. (200 deg. C.) removes some of the brittleness and hardness, and renders it fit for tool-making. Beginning at about 400 deg. F. (204.24 deg. C.), temperatures are often estimated by the colors formed on the surface of the steel as the heat increases.

A chart of color ranges and temperatures shows an upward movement through pale yellow, straw, golden yellow, brown, brown purple, purple, bright blue, pale blue, dark blue, dark red, dull red, dark cherry, full cherry, light red, light cherry, orange, light orange, yellow, light yellow, and white.

Plate 22A shows the relationship between Fahrenheit and Centigrade Scales, temperature colors, and hardness tests according to both the Brinell and Rockwell methods.

A portion of the surface of the steel must be polished in advance for the purpose of observing the colors. The steel may be heated by placing it upon a gas-heated plate, a piece of red-hot metal, or in any other manner. (When the part being tempered is small, it is recommended that it be placed in contact with a large piece of steel at a red heat.) The colors must be watched very carefully because they come in rapid succession. One must act promptly when the proper color and shade is reached. The steel is quenched in brine, oil or water, according to the process being followed, and then left to cool.

There is a great deal of guesswork about tempering colors. The reason for this is that no two people see the same thing in the same way. Even if we agreed perfectly as to the correct definitions of such color terms as yellow, straw, brown, purple, etc., we would still disagree as to the separation into such variations of shade as "very faint yellow, very pale yellow, very light yellow, light yellow," etc. Divisions of colors into shades like this series of yellow shades are made in an effort to select temperatures close together. For instance, one method is to start the color-temperature range thus: "420. F., very faint yellow; 430. F., very pale yellow; 440. F., light yellow; 450. F., pale straw yellow; 460. F., deep straw yellow."

The lack of accuracy of the color-range method of observing temperatures makes it extremely advisable to use a thermometer or a pyrometer, depending upon the degree of temperature reached in the work.

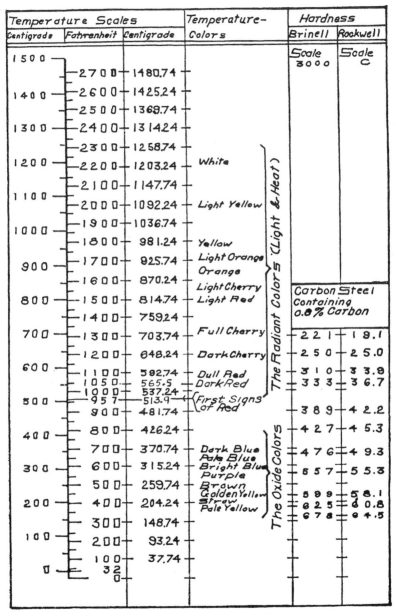

PLATE 22A. TEMPERATURE SCALES, COLORS, AND HARDNESS TESTS.

XV. Bluing and Browning

THE purpose of bluing and browning is to dull the color of the barrel and other metal parts that would otherwise reflect the light and hence frighten the game in hunting, or attract the attention of the enemy in warfare. The appearance is improved and rusting is reduced, but it must be understood that bluing does not render a gun absolutely rust-proof, as most people think. "Browning" is an old English term for treating guns to give them a dark color, but it is almost obsolete and is used synonymously with bluing in the United States. "Parkerizing" is a process that gives an effect similar to bluing; it consists of sandblasting and boiling metal parts in a solution of powdered iron and phosphoric acid.

Bluing can be accomplished by several methods. The quickest and least durable is the application of ready-mixed paints and lacquers with a brush or spray gun. A second method is the treatment of metals with chemicals without heat. A third method is to treat metals with chemicals but to use heat and water; this is the conventional process followed by most gunsmiths. Neither elaborate equipment nor skill is as important as patience in bluing.

Since the bluing process will destroy the finish on the wooden parts of guns, they are separated from the metal parts before the work is started. If any old finish remains, it is removed with emery cloth, fine sandpaper, steel wool, or a soft wire brush on a power wheel, and the entire surface of the metal is brought to a high polish.

Assuming that you are going to blue only a barrel, the first step is to give the bore a light coat of gun grease and plug the ends with

PLATE 23. BARREL BLUING.

pieces of wood about 2 inches long that serve a double purpose as handles and as stoppers to keep the bluing solution from attacking the bore.

The next step is to remove all grease and oil from the outside of the barrel. Wear clean, white cotton gloves from now on. With a clean cotton rag, wash the barrel with benzine or gasoline. The next step is to give the barrel a bath in caustic soda. For this you will need a galvanized tank 6 inches wide, 6 inches deep, and 44 inches long, with handles on the ends. Wash the tank thoroughly with caustic soda, rinse it out with hot water boiled in the tank, and it then should be free from grease and ready to use. Fill the tank about one-half full of water and place it over a stove. When the water boils, add enough caustic soda or lye to make a strong solution. Boil the barrel in this solution for 10 or 15 minutes. At the end of this period, remove the barrel with a pair of steel hooks, still wearing the clean, white cotton gloves. Rinse the barrel in hot running water, or dip it several times in a tank of hot water. A professional gunsmith has three tanks, one for degreasing, one for rinsing, and one for the actual bluing process, but an amateur can do good work with one tank if he keeps it rinsed out between steps in the treatment.

Having degreased the barrel and rinsed out the tank with caustic soda and hot water, fill the tank one-half full with distilled water, or with any water that is free from chemicals that might affect the bluing process. When the water boils, lower the barrel into the tank with the hooks, and let it remain there for about 5 minutes.

In the meantime, prepare the bluing formula. Weigh, by the avoirdupois system, 900 grains potassium nitrate, 750 grains potassium chlorate, and 500 grains bichloride of mercury, and place them in a glass jar. Heat 500 cubic centimeters of water to about 140 degrees F.; pour the chemicals into the glass jar containing the water; stir until the chemicals are dissolved in the water, and then let it cool. About 12 or 14 hours later, add 75 cubic centimeters of spirits of nitre, stir the solution again, and place it in colored bottles bearing poison labels. The solution should not be used for at least 24 hours after it is finally bottled. If you do not have the necessary weighing and measuring equipment, let a druggist prepare it for you.

Returning to the barrel, which was allowed to boil for 5 minutes in a tank of clear water, remove the barrel with the two steel hooks, and swab with the bluing solution just described, using a clean, white cotton swab. There must be no bark, gum, or sap in or on the handle of the swab, and the swab itself must be absolutely free from grease, oil, or dirt. The handle should be long enough to protect your hands from the bluing solution. These details are simple, but failure to observe them causes disappointment when the bluing job is done.

Swab the bluing solution on the barrel as quickly as you can. The heat of the barrel will dry the solution; when this happens, put the barrel back in the tank of boiling water for 5 minutes, take it out again, and remove the rust that has formed with steel wool or with a soft wire wheel on a power wheel. Boil the barrel again for 5 minutes, give it another swabbing with the bluing solution, and repeat this same process from five to ten times. Keep the swab in the solution when it is not in use. When several applications of the bluing solution have given the barrel the desired blue-black color, and the rust has been removed for the last time, coat the barrel with raw linseed oil, or with pure mineral oil, while the barrel is still warm; this stops the action of the bluing solution on the metal. Wait a few minutes, wipe off the oil with a clean, cotton swab, and rub with turpentine and beeswax. Take out the wooden plugs, clean out the bore, and give the entire barrel, inside and out, a light coat of gun oil. It is now ready to be assembled with the rest of the firearm. Other parts of a weapon can be blued in the same manner and at the same time as the barrel.

The equipment and procedure for this bluing process are illustrated on Plate 23. Figure 2 shows a can of gasoline or benzine on a table near the stove; it was placed there merely to remind you that it was one of the materials needed, but everyone realizes that in actual practice inflammable substances should not be placed near heat. Rubber gloves are shown in Figure 2, also, but it is cheaper and better to have several pairs of cotton gloves. Rubber gloves give more protection to the hands from the bluing solution, but they will not last long when exposed to the heat of the barrel, or when used in lifting the tank from the stove.

The temperature of the boiling water is observed by hanging an ordinary deep-fat-frying thermometer in the tank; this can be purchased for a few cents from any "dime" or department store. This type of thermometer is chosen because it has a temperature range as high as 450 degrees F.

A much simpler and cheaper formula consists of 1 part (by weight) commercial sodium nitrate, 2 parts (by weight) ordinary lye, and 2 parts (by volume) water. It is not necessary to remove the grease before this formula is used, since the lye performs that function, but it is necessary to remove any rust spots before the bluing is started. The solution of sodium nitrate, lye, and water is placed in the tank and boiled; water is added if any disappears as steam. When the temperature reaches 280 degrees F., place the parts to be blued in the bath, reduce the heat until the solution barely simmers, and leave them there until the temperature reaches 320 degrees F. for at least 20 minutes. Hold the temperature down to that amount for the required time by adding cold water very slowly in small amounts. At the end of the 20 minutes, remove the metal parts; they should now have a deep, bluish-black color. If there is any rust present, rinse with hot water, remove the rust as described before, lower the temperature and start the process over again. However, if there is no rust, rinse in hot water, polish with fine steel wool (or otherwise, as described in the first process), rinse again in hot water, wipe dry, and give the parts a light coat of gun oil.

This formula may be varied successfully by substituting caustic soda for lye. Another variation is to add slaked lime in the ratio of 1 part (by weight) slaked lime to 8 parts sodium nitrate, 16 parts lye (or caustic soda), and 16 parts (by volume) water. It is apparent that two of the principal advantages of this formula are its low cost and the ease with which the ingredients can be found. However, it is decidedly not in the same class with the first formula if work of a professional quality is to be done.

Returning to our first formula, it will be remembered that the ingredients were corrosive sublimate, potassium chlorate, potassium nitrate, sweet spirits nitre, and distilled water. By adding three more chemicals we can prepare a formula that is a little more expensive and difficult to make but more likely to succeed when applied to gun parts that may not react so favorably to the simpler formula given in the beginning. Here is the formula:

Potassium Nitrate	600 grains (avoirdupois weight)
Bichloride of Mercury	400 grains
Potassium Chlorate	500 grains
Ferric Chlorid	150 grains
Sodium Nitrate	150 grains
Cupric Chlorid	80 grains
Distilled Water	900 c.c.
Spirits of Nitre	90 c.c.

This third formula is prepared just like the first, that is, the chemicals are weighed, the distilled water added, and then the spirits of nitre added; the technique of application is also the same. One detail, however, might be observed in using both the first and the third formulas. If the bluing solution is placed in a wide-mouthed bottle fastened near the top of one of the corners of the tank, the solution will have the same temperature as the water in which the gun parts are boiled. It is necessary to keep only part of the solution hot—just enough for immediate use. The boiling water should not be permitted to get into the solution bottle, and vice versa, the solution should not be spilled into the water.

Common difficulties found in bluing with either the first or the third methods are:

(1) Small parts may not be properly blued unless they are suspended close to the surface of the boiling water in the tank and then quickly coated with the solution while they are still hot. The reason is that small parts cool quicker than large parts.

(2) All parts, whether large or small, must be swabbed with the bluing solution while they are still hot.

(3) Failure of the bluish-black color to appear after the fourth swabbing with the solution may indicate that the parts were not properly cleaned of oil and grease. The only remedy is to start the whole process over again.

(4) If a part is bright red when a part is swabbed the first time, the bluing solution may be too strong. Weaken it with water added very slowly until the volume of the solution is increased from one-fifth to one-half.

(5) When the use of steel wool or a wire wheel removes the bluing, one of two things, or both, may be the trouble. First, the

part was too cold when the bluing solution was applied, or second, the brushing was too violent.

Casehardened or heat-treated gun parts, especially receivers, lock plates, and shotgun actions, may not be receptive to the bluing process, in which event they should be swabbed with nitric acid until they turn black, and rinsed in hot water just before they are placed in the tank of boiling water, using the first and third formulas. The reason for this treatment is that the nitric acid attacks the surface of the parts and permits the bluing solution to work more effectively.

When stainless steel is to be blued, remove grease and oil with alcohol; swab with a coppering solution consisting of 1 part sulphuric acid (by volume) to 100 parts distilled water (by volume) in which copper sulphate has been dissolved until the fluid will not take any more; and then inspect the steel to see if there is a light copper coating. If there is not, place more acid and copper sulphate in the solution and try again. If there is a copper coating, treat the surface with nitric acid until it is black, rinse with warm water, and go ahead with the bluing process, using either the first or the third formula.

CAUTION ON BLUING AND BROWNING

The formulas explained in this chapter are fundamentally those used by many gun-supply houses in preparing solutions which retail for ten or twenty times the cost of the container and ingredients. Each manufacturer may vary the formula slightly, but the chemical action is basically the same.

Some people make a good living by selling through the mail "complete instructions" on how to blue or brown a firearm quickly and inexpensively. Usually, such vendors of information are careful to stay within the federal and state laws, but it is impossible to properly blue any firearm or firearm part easily, quickly, and at a small cost in apparatus and materials unless you already know how and already own the apparatus and materials. It is true that you can do a superficial job easily, quickly, and at small expense, but it will rub off and fool nobody except a slow-witted amateur. Finally, you are handling chemicals, and they are not for children or morons.

XVI. Soldering and Brazing

SOLDERING is the joining of metallic surfaces with a metal or alloy applied in a melted condition. Solders that melt easily are soft solders; those that fuse at a red heat are hard solders. Brazing is soldering with hard solder, especially when an alloy of zinc and copper is used. Sweating is the heating of solder between two metallic surfaces to join them without the use of a soldering iron. Welding is the process of uniting or forming by a fusing heat; it is accomplished either by the process of oxyacetylene or electric arc. Welding also refers to the blacksmith's method of pressing or beating the ends of iron bars into intimate and permanent union while both are softened by heat, but this process is discussed elsewhere under the subject of hand forging.

SOFT SOLDERING

Ordinary soft solders contain tin and lead in varying ratios, to which other metals are sometimes added to lower the melting point, such as bismuth or antimony. Solders with more lead have higher melting points, cost less, and are usually termed "common." An example of common solder is that used by plumbers, which generally contains twice as much lead as tin. As the percentage of lead decreases and the amount of tin increases, the cost increases and the melting point decreases, unless the amount of tin reaches 68 per cent or more, in which case the melting point begins to increase until it reaches the melting point of lead. Solders having a

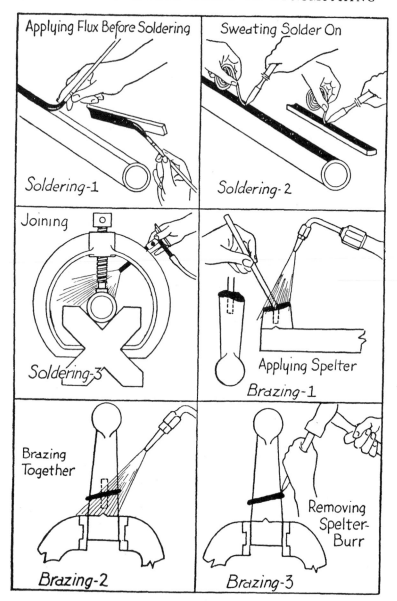

PLATE 24. SOLDERING AND BRAZING.

comparatively large tin content are called "fine," while grades between "common" and "fine" are sometimes classed as "medium." Lead-tin solders made of new or virgin metal are designated as "Class A," while those made of at least one-half virgin metals, the remainder being recovered or "junk" metals, are designated as "Class B."

The melting point of tin is 449.6 deg. F.; this is also the liquefaction point. The melting point of lead is 620.6 deg. F.; this is also the complete liquefaction point. However, the melting point and complete liquefaction point may not be the same when metals are mixed in certain ratios. As an example, for solder made of equal parts tin and lead, with antimony added in an amount equal to .12 per cent of the total, the melting point may be 357.8 deg. F. and the point of complete liquefaction 415.4 deg. F. The solder is completely solid below the lower point, referred to as the "melting point," and completely liquid above the higher point, called the "complete liquefaction point." In the temperature range between the higher and lower points, the solder is partly solid and partly liquid. This explanation is given to enable the reader to interpret technical tables that he may encounter in other texts, since the average person seems to believe that the melting point is the same as the point of complete liquefaction. However, for ordinary purposes of comparison, a table of melting points alone is an adequate guide to solder temperatures.

Disregarding fractions of a degree, the following table of melting points of lead-tin solders is approximately correct:

PER CENT

LEAD	100	90	80	70	60	50	40	30	20	10	0
TIN	0	10	20	30	40	50	60	70	80	90	100

MELTING POINT

| F. deg. | 621 | 564 | 530 | 505 | 465 | 430 | 375 | 365 | 393 | 421 | 450 |

Tables such as this are not exactly the same in all texts because the one preparing the table may base his figures upon materials that are not absolutely pure, he may not read the thermometer closely, or he may conduct his tests at a different altitude than another authority. For ordinary gunsmithing purposes, the temperatures need not be precise in judging solders. The gunsmith wants to know whether the temperature is high enough to damage the bluing or not, and whether it will destroy the temper of the steel or not. Also, it must be remembered that in general, soft solders, melting at low temperatures, are weaker than those melting at higher temperatures. An additional question is whether or not the soldered parts may be subjected to the bluing process later, and if that is probable, whether the solder will melt during the bluing process. Since lead-tin solders have fairly high melting points, a solder with a melting point below the boiling point of water may be desired, such as one composed of 32 per cent lead, 15.5 per cent tin, and 52.5 per cent bismuth, which melts at 205 deg. F.

In addition to the solder, the following equipment is needed: a source of heat, such as a gasoline blowtorch, a bunsen burner, an ordinary gas stove, or a plumber's gasoline furnace; a soldering iron (sometimes called a "copper") weighing from 1 to 2 pounds; a file or scraper or knife for cleaning the surfaces of the parts to be joined; and a "flux" to prevent oxidation of the surfaces of the parts to be joined. Also, it is well to have some method of keeping the parts together while the soldered or sweated joint cools, since even a slight movement of one or both of the parts being joined will cause the solder to crystallize and produce a weak joint.

The soldering iron preferred by the average gunsmith weighs about 1½ pounds, although some insist upon one weighing 2 pounds, because it must hold its heat while it is being used to rub the solder into the surfaces of the parts being joined. The point should be filed very sharp, with square, flat sides, and it should be well "tinned." This simply means coating the point with solder.

One method of tinning is to rub the point of the heated iron over a cake of sal-ammoniac (ammonium chloride) and then on a bar of solder, repeating this until the point of the iron is covered with solder. This should be done where there is a good circulation of air, away from guns and tools, for the fumes from the sal-ammoniac encourage rust.

Another method of tinning the iron is to cut a trough in one surface of a common building brick, melt and pour resin into the trough, melt and pour solder into the trough, and then rub the heated soldering iron against the melted resin and solder in the trough. The iron is rubbed back and forth until the point is completely covered with solder.

Still another tinning method is to drop small pieces of solder on a cake of sal-ammoniac and quickly rub the heated iron against both the solder and the sal-ammoniac until the point is coated with solder.

The iron is hot enough when it produces a warm glow while held about 1 foot from the cheek. It should have a temperature only a few degrees above the melting point of the solder. If overheated, the tinning will be burned off the point, which will then have a dull, corroded-looking surface where the tinning has been ruined. When this happens, heat the iron enough to melt the solder on its point, file the point bright, and dip it in a liquid flux, and retin as before; but this time reduce the temperature.

A flux for soldering is a substance used to promote the fusion of the metals, such as resin, sal-ammoniac, borax, and zinc chloride. The flux is applied to the surface of the parts to be joined with a brush or a swab, the solder is held against the parts, and heat is then applied with the iron. The flux removes any oxide that forms, and allows the solder to flow freely.

Powdered resin is especially good as a flux for soldering ribs to shotgun barrels, because it does not permit corrosion between the barrel and the rib; it is also used in soldering brass, copper, lead, and tin (tinned iron, actually), but other fluxes can be used with results that are at least as good and often better than those obtained from the use of resin.

Zinc chloride is a flux that works well with bismuth, silver, gold, tinned steel, gun metal, copper, and brass. It is prepared by dropping pieces of scrap zinc into a wide-mouthed bottle of hydrochloric acid (sometimes called muriatic acid) until the acid will not consume any more zinc. When the fuming and boiling of the acid have died down, the flux is ready for use, but it is well to add about 1 ounce of sal-ammoniac to each one-half pint of the flux; this tends to prevent any rusting where the objects being joined are iron or steel. Another way to reduce the corrosive danger is to make the flux with zinc and acid, as described above, and then add a mixture of equal parts aqua ammonia and water until this mixture forms one-fifth of the volume of the resulting flux.

Sal-ammoniac (ammonium chloride) can be used by itself as a flux for steel, iron, gun metal, copper, and brass. It is brushed on like powdered resin.

Hydrochloric acid (muriatic acid) is used, full strength, to solder zinc. Other substances that can be used as fluxes are turpentine, beeswax, palm oil, cocoa oil, olive oil, paraffin, vaseline, stearin, and even candles and soap. It is not to be understood that these substances work well with all metals, or as well as the conventional fluxes with any of the metals; they are mentioned only as substitutes for emergency work or experimentation. Where a thin liquid is not desired, the flux can be made into a paste by mixing the liquid flux with starch paste.

Solder at one time was made only in bars, but today it can be obtained in the form of wire, which is much easier to use. This wire solder is usually solid, but it is also made hollow, filled with a flux so that it is ready to apply when the iron is hot.

Sweating is another method of soft soldering, but a soldering iron is not used. Two pieces of steel, for example, are first scraped with a knife, file, or scraper, or gone over with emery cloth, and freed of oil and grease. Second, they are coated with a flux, such as resin or zinc chloride, as described for the previous method of soldering. Third, the surfaces that are to be joined are tinned, as explained before for a soldering iron. Fourth, the surfaces are brought tightly together and clamped in place. Fifth, heat is applied with a blowtorch; this causes the metal to expand, the pores of the metal to open, and the solder on the two surfaces to flow into the pores and make a strong joint. The clamps are kept in place until the metal has cooled. We repeat: any movement of the parts being joined during a soldering process produces a weak joint.

Turning intense heat on a small area of a metal surface without affecting the surrounding metal is a problem that troubles the average amateur gunsmith. The technique is to make a tapered brass tube with one end having a hole about the size of the point of a darning needle, or smaller. A blowtorch or a bunsen burner is held near the metal, with the flame parallel and close to the metal but not touching it. Hold the large end of the tube between the lips and the small end at the side of the flame. Blowing through the tube directs a tiny flame to the spot that is to be heated. Wrapping wet cloths around adjacent parts will also reduce the danger of heating metal outside of the working area.

Sweating is the most general method of joining metal parts in gunsmithing, because soft solder applied with an iron will not hold when subjected to strain. Sweating is used in joining ramps, barrel bands, telescope base blocks, rear sights, sight ramps, swivel bands, forearm screw bands, rear sight bases, ribs, and barrels to one another. Sweating is also used where parts should be held together while they are being machined, to insure a perfect fit when they are assembled with other parts.

A bunsen burner is shown in Figure 3, Plate 4; blocks and clamps are illustrated in Figure 3, Plate 5; and a steel clamp is shown in Figure 4, Plate 7. Figures 1, 2, and 3, Plate 24, show three steps in the sweating process of soft soldering. In Figure 1, the flux is being applied to the barrel of a shotgun and the rib; in Figure 2, an ordinary soldering iron and wire solder are being used to tin the surfaces of the barrel and rib where they are to join; and in Figure 3, a modern, portable blowtorch is being used to direct a flame against the parts being joined. Notice that the parts are held firmly between a block and a clamp. A different block and another clamp are shown in Figure 3, Plate 26. Although Plate 26 pertains to welding, the method of holding the parts together is the same as in the sweating process.

BRAZING AND HARD SOLDERING

Brazing is, strictly speaking, a process of soldering with brass, which is an alloy of copper and zinc with, sometimes, tin. However, it is loosely used as a term to include both the true brazing process and hard soldering, which employs various grades of silver-copper-zinc alloys, commercially known as "silver solders." Hence, when anyone speaks of brazing, it is well to ask whether he means true brazing or hard soldering, since they are different.

True brazing has a limited field of application in gunsmithing because of the high temperatures to which the parts are raised, but the joints thus produced have great mechanical strength. Broken parts can be repaired, lugs are fitted on the bottom of shotgun barrels, drills and reamers are attached to long shanks, and steel parts can be fastened to the bottoms of barrel bands by the brazing process. Parts must not be attached to barrels or receivers by either brazing or hard soldering, because the great heat may put a kink in the barrel or receiver. Also, because of the heat, receivers must be given a new hardening and heat treatment, according to the methods described in the chapter on that subject, to restore their correct properties.

The first step in true brazing is to clean thoroughly the parts to be joined. Second, they are fitted tightly together in clamps, or between a clamp and a block, as in Figure 3, Plate 24. Third, a torch is used to heat the parts red hot. Fourth, powdered borax, as a flux, may be sprinkled over the ends of the parts as their temperature is being raised, just before they are brought tightly together. Fifth, brazing spelter is applied to the joint, either in the form of fine brass filings or in the form of a brass stick.

Another method, which is just as good or better than the one just described, is illustrated in Figures shown as "Brazing-1, Brazing-2, Brazing-3," on Plate 24. Notice that a hole has been drilled in both parts, and a steel rod inserted in one of them; when the parts are clamped together, the steel rod holds them in perfect alignment and also adds strength. The spelter is applied after the parts have been cleaned; a torch melts the spelter over the surfaces; a flux is sprinkled over the surfaces; and then the parts are clamped together. (The clamp is not shown in connection with the brazing process on Plate 24, because it would make the pictures less clear.) When the parts are clamped, the torch is used again; this causes the spelter on the two parts to flow together and enter the pores of the steel (Figure: Brazing-2, Plate 24). Finally, when the metal has cooled, the excess spelter, called a "spelter-burr," is removed with a mallet, as shown in Brazing-3, Plate 24.

Ordinary spelter consists of equal parts copper and zinc; it has a melting point of about 1,616 degrees F., and produces a strong joint on iron and steel parts. Coppersmith's spelter is 3 parts copper to 1 part zinc; it has a melting point of about 1,765 degrees F. The melting point of spelter goes up as the amount of copper is increased; it goes down as the amount of zinc is increased. Tin may be added to the copper and zinc in the spelter in small amounts for the purpose of lightening the color, since brass does not take bluing and contrasts sharply with the surrounding steel when it has a bright yellow appearance. This, of course, is one of the reasons why true brazing is not used more often in repairing fine guns. Tin, however, makes the solder somewhat brittle if too much is used.

Silver solder is a hard solder consisting of silver, copper, and zinc. Gunsmiths sometimes use a silver solder composed of 70 per cent silver and 30 per cent copper. Another proportion popular with gunsmiths is 34.36 per cent copper, 49.24 per cent silver, and 16.4 per cent zinc. When the metals to be joined are alloys containing from 16 to 22 per cent nickel, the solder contains no silver but is composed of 47 per cent copper, 42 per cent zinc, and 11 per cent nickel; this is a "hard solder," although it is not actually a silver solder.

Silver solders are usually grouped in three grades by experts. Grades 1, 2, and 3 are used where a hard solder is required that will flow easier than the usual copper-zinc brazing solder. Their composition and melting points are given as follows:

Grade 1—Silver, 10%; Copper, 52%; Zinc, 38%; Melting point, 1,510 deg. F.

Grade 2—Silver, 20%; Copper, 45%; Zinc, 35%; Melting point, 1,430 deg. F.

Grade 3—Silver, 20%; Copper, 45%; Zinc, 30%; Cadmium, 5%; Melting point, 1,430 deg. F.

When heating to a high temperature, the use of the above three grades would injure the metal; where a strong joint is needed, with hard solders that will flow freely, Grades 4 and 5 are used, as follows:

Grade 4—Silver, 45%; Copper, 30%; Zinc, 25%; Melting point, 1,250 deg. F.

Grade 5—Silver, 50%; Copper, 34%; Zinc, 16%; Melting point, 1,280 deg. F.

When a high degree of malleability and ductility is required, Grades 6, 7, and 8 are used, as follows:

Grade 6—Silver, 65%; Copper, 20%; Zinc, 15%; Melting point, 1,280 deg. F.

Grade 7—Silver, 70%; Copper, 20%; Zinc, 10%; Melting point, 1,335 deg. F.

Grade 8—Silver, 80%; Copper, 16%; Zinc, 4%; Melting point, 1,360 deg. F.

When silver solder is not otherwise available, silver coins can be used successfully, although the gunsmith should keep in mind any Federal laws in existence regarding the destruction or mutilation of currency. In other words, do not make a business of melting down money even if it should prove cheaper than silver solder.

Silver soldering is especially useful in joining small parts that require a strong union. A small blowpipe directs the flame against the limited area of operation, as explained earlier in this chapter. Borax or powdered boracic acid is applied as a flux before heating progresses very far.

Gunsmiths usually purchase their silver solder in the form of thin ribbons, such as those used for joining the ends of band saws. A small piece is cut off to fit the surfaces being joined. Borax is mixed with water to make a paste which is painted over the surfaces. The piece of silver is placed between the two surfaces and they are then clamped together. The torch is directed against the parts until they turn red hot and the solder begins to flow; the clamp is tightened still more, as far as possible. When the joint has cooled, any excess silver can be scraped away. Borax which forms outside the joint is removed by soaking the joint in a pickle bath consisting of 1 part sulphuric acid and 25 parts water. If the parts to be joined rest against a slab of charcoal during exposure to heat, the charcoal will hasten the process by directing the heat back to the joint.

Whenever a part is fastened to a barrel by either true brazing or hard soldering, scale may form in the bore unless it is protected by a thick coating of charcoal paste. The approved formula calls for 1 part by weight, pulverized charred leather; 1½ parts by weight, ordinary flour; and 2 parts by weight, fine table salt. The charred leather is ground very fine, sieved, and mixed with the flour and salt before water is added. When the three ingredients have been thoroughly mixed, water is added slowly while the whole mass is being stirred to avoid lumps. Finally, when the mixture has the consistency of varnish, it is swabbed through the bore in a thin, even coat. The barrel is then exposed to a low, even heat and warmed slowly until the charcoal mixture in the bore is dried. After the hard-soldering or brazing job is done, this charcoal coating in the bore can be removed by the usual cleaning methods, especially if a brass-bristle brush is employed. This process originated in the U.S. Army Ordnance, although the basis for it is centuries old.

SPECIAL PROBLEMS OF SOLDERING AND BRAZING

The above instructions are correct and fundamentally sound for all firearms. However, soldering and brazing are special techniques. Skill is not acquired by reading a book. Furthermore, each firearm and each gun part presents a special problem, depending upon its design, type, make, and model. In case of doubt, practice on a weapon of small value before working on a good gun.

XVII. Hand Forging

FORGING is the forming or shaping of metal by heating and hammering. The metal is not melted, but is worked while hot enough to be in a plastic condition and receive its shape from tools designed to mould by impact. Forging is divided into two broad classes, hand forging and machine forging, according to the tools used, but the principles and results are similar. Hand forging employs the tools of the blacksmith, while machine forging requires heavy, power-driven and automatic equipment. The gunsmith usually confines his forging activities to the hand process, but may rely upon power tools to save muscular effort when he branches out and becomes a manufacturer of gun parts, or even complete firearms.

Hand-forging operations are: First, reducing or drawing down from a larger to a smaller cross section, by fullering and swaging (see Swage and Fuller on Plate 25, mid-section). Second, enlargement of a smaller to a larger cross section by upsetting (see Upsetting process in lower left-hand section of Plate 25). Third, bending to any angle or curve. Fourth, uniting two pieces of metal by hand welding (illustrated in the lower right-hand section of Plate 25). Fifth, the making of holes by punching. Sixth, cutting.

None of the tools for hand forging have sharp edges except the "sets" which are used for cutting. "Hot sets" are keen chisels used to cut hot metal; "cold sets" are less sharp chisels for cutting cold metal. A chisel for cutting hot metal is held in a hole in the anvil face; a chisel for cutting cold metal is handled and hit with a sledge hammer.

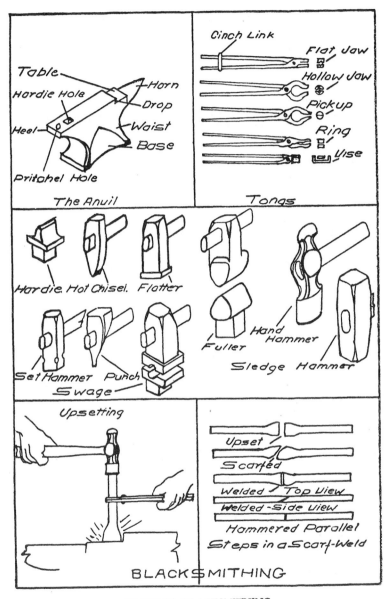

PLATE 25. BLACKSMITHING.

Fullering is roughing-down the metal between tools having convex surfaces; top and bottom fullers are shown in the mid-section of Plate 25. Swaging is a finishing process accomplished by placing the material between top and bottom swages, which are dies of nearly hemispherical shape, as shown in the mid-section of Plate 25.

When a metal bar is to be reduced in cross-sectional size, it is laid upon a bottom fuller which has been set in the anvil. The top fuller is then held over the bar and struck on its head with a sledge hammer (the heads of hand and sledge hammers are shown on Plate 25). The bar is quickly and frequently rotated to bring successive parts of its surface between the top and bottom surfaces until the size is reduced satisfactorily.

Fullering is a preliminary process; it leaves corrugations which must be removed either by the flatter (illustrated in the mid-section, Plate 25) if the surfaces are flat, or by the hollow swages if the cross-sectional shape of the bar is circular. When only a small reduction in size is desired, or when a power hammer is available, work can be saved by eliminating the fullering step and proceeding at once with the swaging process, assuming, of course, that the cross-sectional shape is circular.

Upsetting is the method for enlarging a bar at one end for a short distance, when the increased cross-sectional size is not much more than the original size of the bar. The end to be enlarged is heated, the remainder is left cold, and the end is hammered, as shown in the lower left-hand section of Plate 25. Another method is to lift the bar and drop it heavily on its end on the anvil, so that the heated end becomes both shorter and larger.

Another method for accomplishing the same result as upsetting is to weld a larger bar to a smaller bar. Still another method is to put a ring around the bar, weld the two together, and then work the ring down to the desired shape with swages.

A bar can be bent by either hammering or pulling a heated bar around a fulcrum. This is better than giving the bar a desired curved or angular shape with a hot set or by hand welding, because bending does not injure the fibers of the metal. It is important, however, to avoid bending a bar with a short radius to the bending circle, since that will reduce the cross-sectional area and at the same time it will stretch the fibers on the outside of the bend. Reduction in cross-sectional area in a bend can be counteracted by upsetting when the bend is near the end of the bar.

Punching is done when the hole is small, using a tool such as the one illustrated in the mid-section of Plate 25. When a larger hole is desired, a small hole can be made first and then enlarged by drifting, which is done with tapered punches. When a very large hole is desired, the bar can be bent around and welded to form an "eye." It must be remembered that it is usually easier and better to make holes with a drill than by a forging process, but at the same time a gunsmith cannot know too much about the methods open to him for working metal.

Referring again to the mid-section of Plate 25, the use of the hot chisel, set hammer (for hitting the chisels), punch, swages, flatter, and fullers have been mentioned. The hand hammer, of course, must be much lighter in weight than the sledge hammer, although they appear somewhat similar in the illustration. The "Hardie" is essentially a chisel set in the hardie hole of the anvil face (upper left-hand section of Plate 25), against which a bar is placed and struck with a sledge hammer when it is to be cut off.

Several types of tongs needed for hand forging are shown in the upper right-hand section of Plate 25. These have different shapes for handling various shapes of material. Those shown are called flat jaw (equipped with a cinch link), hollow jaw, pickup, ring, and vise, according to the shape of their jaws. The beginner can get along with one flat jaw and one hollow jaw, and then acquire the others as his work improves in quality.

The steps in making a scarf-weld are shown in the lower right-hand section of Plate 25. From top to bottom, the illustration shows the upsetting of the opposing ends; the scarfing of the opposing ends; top and side views during the welding process; and finally, the ends hammered together.

The success of hand welding depends principally on having perfectly clean surfaces on the parts to be joined, free from any scale or dirt, so that a perfect union of metal can be effected without the presence of foreign substances. Ordinarily, it is safe to say that when metal is to be smoothed without changing its shape, it is brought to a cherry-red heat and hammered lightly, but when its shape is to be changed it is brought to a white heat and pounded heavily but evenly, a hand hammer being used in both cases. However, the degree of heat to which the metal must be brought for hand welding depends upon its chemical contents. This is discussed elsewhere in this book, under "Heat Treatment" and "Metallurgy," but the beginner is advised to practice hand-welding different kinds of iron and steel at various temperatures, until he acquires practical experience before he seriously attempts to make gun parts.

Hand welding must not be confused with oxyacetylene welding, although the types of welds accomplished by the two processes are, in general, the same in shape. Thus, the lap weld, butt weld, corner weld, and flange weld, illustrated on Plate 26 for oxyacetylene welding, can also be made by the hand-welding process. Likewise, the same parts can often be made by either welding process, examples being butt plates, trigger guards, triggers, hammers, tumblers, sears, bolt handles, etc. However, it must be clearly understood that oxyacetylene welding will produce stronger and neater-appearing unions of parts. The gunsmith who wishes to be a master of his profession should learn both hand forging and oxyacetylene welding, since it sometimes happens that a part can be manufactured or repaired easier and better by one process than by the other.

Having discussed the tools of hand forging, we now turn to the anvil, illustrated in the upper left-hand corner of Plate 25. The parts of the anvil shown are the base, waist, drop, horn, table, hardie hole, heel, and pritchel hole. The size of the hardie hole is usually from ⅞ inch to 1 inch in diameter. The size of the pritchel hole is usually from ½ inch to ⅝ inch. The anvil should weigh at least 70 pounds, be made of vanadium alloy steel, properly hardened and tempered, with trued and smooth-polished face and horn. Reliable manufacturers guarantee their anvils against chipping. Professional gunsmiths often prefer an anvil weighing 150 pounds, since it will accommodate heavier work, but it costs about twice as much as the 70-pound anvil and is not necessarily required by the beginner.

The anvil should be mounted on a solid oak block with iron straps. There must be no restriction on the vibration of the hammer, since vibration helps to keep the anvil free from scale. In height, the anvil's top surface should be about halfway between your knees and your waist, when you are standing beside it. Another way of stating this rule is to mount the anvil so that its top surface touches your knuckles. The reason for the rule is that you want the anvil at a height from which you can bend over and use your back muscles to the best advantage in pounding the work. Finally, be sure that the anvil gives a clear, sharp ring when struck; if it gives a dull, flat sound it is of poor quality. When a regular anvil is not available, a short piece of railroad iron, such as a rail, can be used as a substitute.

The only important piece of equipment which we have not yet discussed is the forge. Its selection depends largely upon the kind of fuel available, although the amount and size of the metal to be worked will also be a governing factor. Oil and gas can be used as fuels, as well as coke, hard coal, and soft coal. Most gunsmiths prefer coke, with soft coal as a second choice. When coke or coal is used, it must be free of impurities such as copper, lead, or sulphur.

A handy workman can make his own forge, using one in a neighborhood blacksmith shop as a model, and reducing the dimensions to cut down on fuel consumption, but it is far better to buy the forge from one of the large, reputable mail-order houses, since the cost is little more than the gunsmith would pay for the parts. The smallest practical forge has a 19-inch hearth, 3 inches deep, with a 6-inch fan in an 8-inch case. The tuyère (nozzle through which the air blast is delivered) has plates made of cast iron, since steel may burn out. The legs of the forge should be of tubular steel. The height over-all should be about 39 inches, and the height of the hearth about 31 inches. If heavy work is anticipated, a larger hearth will be found more rigid and it will enable you to bring the work to a higher temperature in less time. Many manufacturers recommend that the hearth be coated with fire clay before use, to protect it from intense heat. When power is not available, an old-fashioned, foot-operated bellows can be rigged to create the necessary draft.

Soft coal is cheap and easy to obtain, hence its use in a forge will be described. Cover the hearth to a depth of about 2 inches, leaving a hollow place in the center over the perforated plate. In this spot, place splinters, shavings, excelsior, or other kindling material, and start the fire. As soon as the kindling begins to burn briskly, gradually cover it with coal while you steadily increase the pressure of the air coming from the bottom. Keep on adding coal to the center until a little cone-shaped mound is built up. The force of the air will convert this mound into a miniature volcano. When the fire is established, extend the center mound until it is high and broad enough to properly heat the metal to be forged.

Next, wet the coal that is away from the mound. Heavy, yellow smoke will rise and carry off any impurities in the coal, such as sulphur, leaving coke which burns with a clean, bright, hot fire that is suitable for heating the metal. Hold the iron or steel in the fire until it is cherry red, at a white-flame heat, or at any other desired temperature, as indicated by the color of the metal, and then work it on the anvil.

As the fuel burns in the center, more coal is added at the edges. When the work is done, let the fire burn out of its own accord, clean out the ashes in the center, retain any coke that is left, prepare kindling wood for the next fire, and you will be ready to start forging again without loss of time.

XVIII. Welding

WELDING is the process of fusing and uniting metals by the application of great heat without pounding or the use of a flux. It is one of the great contributions to the machine age and offers special advantages to the gunsmith. Although an amateur gunsmith may not care to invest in welding equipment, he should understand the process in order to intelligently direct the work of others to whom he may send gun parts for repair or the designs of parts to be manufactured according to his specifications.

Welding permits lighter construction and greater streamlining of gun parts, thus smoothing the operation of firearms and reducing the number of failures at the target range or in the hunting field. Although it is a special trade in itself, welding can be mastered by anyone who is patient and attentive.

The old methods of joining metals—blacksmithing or forge welding, soldering, and brazing—are now seldom used by advanced gunsmiths who possess well-equipped shops. In fact, most modern gunsmiths use welding exclusively in the modern way, because it is cheaper, more efficient, simpler, and can be used on materials which could not be joined by any of the old methods. Welding can be done by either the flame or the electric process. Because the flame process is the one almost universally used by gunsmiths, it will be explained here.

Flame methods all use oxygen in combination with some fuel gas, such as acetylene, city gas, hydrogen, natural gas, liquid gas, Blau gas, thermaline, carbohydrogen, etc., but the easy control and great heat developed by the oxyacetylene flame (about 6,300 deg. F.) and the ease with which dissolved acetylene and carbide can be obtained have combined to establish the greater efficiency, economy, and desirability of the oxyacetylene process.

Another reason for the popularity of the oxyacetylene process with gunsmiths is the comparatively inexpensive apparatus required and the low cost of its operation. Its portability, speed, and simplicity of operation have brought it into use in every crossroads village garage. Extensive disassembly of parts is seldom necessary. Unlike many other craftsmen, the welder need not have any particular mechanical bent, nor does he need much education or training before he can begin to make money.

Oxygen and acetylene are the two gases used in the oxyacetylene process. Oxygen is obtained from air by liquefaction or from water by electrolysis, the former method being the one in general use, because the only impurity present would be nitrogen, which is harmless, whereas oxygen made by electrolysis may contain hydrogen which is dangerous.

The equipment for making your own oxygen is so expensive, and the cost of tanks of compressed gas is so low, that gunsmiths buy oxygen in cylinders containing either 100 or 200 cubic feet of gas reduced to a pressure of about 1,800 pounds per square inch. No charge is made for the steel cylinders if they are returned to the gas manufacturer. Figure 1, Plate 26, shows the gas tanks with the hose and blowpipe.

Acetylene is also obtained in cylinders, holding 100 or 300 cubic feet; it is only generated in the shop when it is needed in very large quantities. The acetylene in cylinders is not actually compressed, as many persons seem to believe; instead, it is dissolved in a solvent which absorbs many times its own volume. This fluid in which acetylene is dissolved does not affect the flow of gas unless the acetylene is taken from the cylinder at a very rapid rate, when it flows with the acetylene and lowers the temperature of the flame. This problem can be met by taking the gas from several cylinders at the same time through a manifold, but ordinarily the gunsmith does not consume the gas fast enough to be worried about this situation.

Oxyacetylene welding torches may be of either the low-pressure

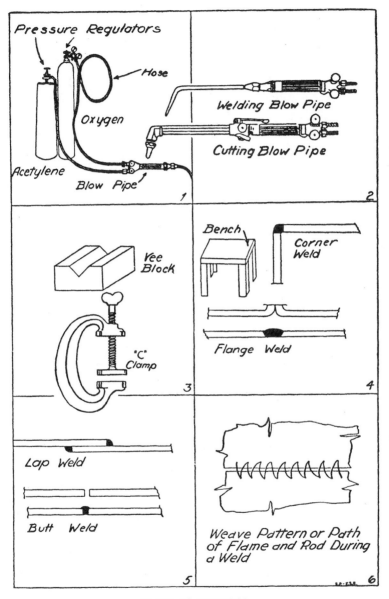

PLATE 26. WELDING.

(injector) type or the equal-pressure type. The acetylene reaches the torch in the low-pressure type at a pressure of only a few ounces; oxygen at a higher pressure goes through the injector and expands in a mixing chamber. There the expansion of the oxygen and its velocity form a suction that draws in the acetylene so that there is an almost half-and-half mixture of oxygen and acetylene. A variation of pressure of either the oxygen or the acetylene is automatically corrected by the injector, keeping a neutral flame without requiring effort from the operator.

In the other type of torch, the oxygen and acetylene come to the torch at a pressure varying from 1 to 10 pounds per square inch, depending upon the size of the tip chosen by the operator. Regulators and torch valves are used to control the pressures. The two gases are mixed in a chamber which may be located either in the tips or the torch handles. Usually oxygen and acetylene are at the same pressure, but sometimes it may be advisable to operate with the oxygen pressure a little higher.

The hose which connects the welding torch to the regulator and the gas supply is usually of high-grade vulcanized rubber and fabric, corrugated to wear longer. It is marked so that the oxygen and acetylene hose will not be confused with each other. This can be done by using different colored hose, moulding the word "oxygen" or "acetylene" into the hose, or by giving one hose a fitting with a right-hand thread and the other a left-hand thread for connecting to the regulator and the torch valve. When new, the hose is protected on the inside by talc powder which is blown out before being used by quickly opening and shutting the valves.

The constant-pressure regulator consists of a regulator valve, a diaphragm, a pressure-adjusting spring, a safety-relief valve, gauges, and a housing. The two-stage regulator for oxygen reduces pressure in two separate stages, using two sets of diaphragms and stem-type valve assemblies, thus assuring a more constant delivery than the constant-pressure regulator having only one step for pressure reduction. An automatic regulator for oxygen delivers oxygen to the blowpipe according to the setting established by the operator; it has a high-pressure gauge to show the pressure in the cylinder, and a low-pressure gauge to indicate the operating pressure of the oxygen at the blowpipe.

The acetylene regulator also delivers gas at a constant pressure to the blowpipe. There is a large gauge to show cylinder pressure and a small gauge to show pressure at the blowpipe when an equal-pressure blowpipe is used, but the small gauge is not needed with the low-pressure (injector) type of blowpipe.

Pressure regulators are indicated at the top of Figure 1, Plate 26. Welding and cutting blowpipes are shown in Figure 2.

We shall next examine the equipment used in welding, learn how to set it up safely, how to adjust it for operation, how to light and adjust the torch, and how to hold the torch while working.

The equipment needed consists of an oxygen cylinder, an acetylene cylinder, a regulator for the oxygen and one for the acetylene, a welding torch (blowpipe), connecting hose (green for oxygen and red for acetylene), goggles to protect the eyes, a spark lighter to ignite the acetylene, a steel and fire-brick bench, and a few adjusting tools. These are fundamental pieces of equipment, subject to slight individual variation according to the place where they are manufactured.

First, remove the oxygen-valve cap, and open and close the tank valve quickly; this blows out any dirt, dust, or grit that might be in the valve. Do not let the stream of oxygen reach a flame or the face of a person. Place the valve cap where it can be found when the tank is to be returned to the manufacturer.

Second, connect the oxygen regulator to the outlet of the oxygen-cylinder valve, using a wrench to tighten the connecting nut but being careful not to put any strain on the regulator.

Third, connect the green hose to the oxygen regulator.

Fourth, connect the acetylene tank, green hose, and regulator. Do not get the acetylene and oxygen equipment confused. The acetylene hose should have a left-hand thread and be tightened counter-clockwise, whereas the oxygen hose goes on clockwise. Check all connections; one test is to place soapsuds on the connections and turn on the gas for a second to see if bubbles come.

Fifth, connect the torch to the oxygen and acetylene hose, again observing that the connections have threads running in opposite directions to avoid confusion.

Sixth, select the correct size of tip, install it in the nozzle, and adjust. A tip that is too small takes more time and gives poor fusion, while one that is too big causes overoxidation which in turn produces poor metal in the weld, as well as a crude appearance. The manufacturer's recommendations should be followed here, for all welding tips of the same size do not have the same numbers.

Seventh, adjust the oxygen regulator. Screw out the adjusting screw to free it from spring tension. Open the oxygen-tank valve all the way and tighten it in the open position. Open the oxygen valve on the torch handle a quarter turn, turn the adjusting screw clockwise until the torch-pressure gauge registers the proper pressure, and then close the oxygen valve on the torch.

Eighth, adjust the acetylene regulator in a similar manner. Release the adjusting valve from spring tension; open the acetylene-tank valve a quarter turn or more until the tank pressure shows on the tank gauge; open the acetylene-torch valve a quarter turn; adjust the acetylene-torch pressure by turning the adjusting screw clockwise until the torch-pressure gauge shows the proper pressure; and then close the torch valve unless you are ready to light the torch.

Ninth, to light the torch, hold a spark lighter in the left hand, open the acetylene valve about one-quarter turn, and spark the lighter at the tip immediately. If you hesitate, there may be an explosion that will burn the left hand. As soon as the gas is lighted, adjust the acetylene valve to let just enough gas to burn to give a flame hot enough for the work. Then, open the oxygen valve very slowly and permit the air in the hose to escape so gradually that it will not extinguish the flame. Gradually open the torch-oxygen valve until the flame changes from the yellow color it previously had to a bluish, cone-shaped flame, commonly called a neutral flame.

The neutral flame has a temperature of about 6,300 deg. F., which is correct for welding. When too much oxygen is delivered, the flame burns with a sharp, hissing sound. If too much of both oxygen and acetylene is delivered, the flame has a harsh, blowing sound. When the pressure is too low, the flame burns inside the tip, overheats the tip, ignites the gases inside the tip, and "pops" or backfires.

Acetylene requires $2\frac{1}{2}$ volumes of pure oxygen for each volume of acetylene if complete combustion is to be obtained. One volume of oxygen comes from the oxygen tank; the remainder of the oxygen is taken from the atmosphere. When acetylene is combined with oxygen in a smaller ratio, the temperature of the flame will be less than that of a neutral flame (6,300 deg. F.) and unburned carbon or oxygen will be released. This release of unburned carbon produces what welders call a "reducing flame"; it carburizes the weld metal, causes slag, brittleness, pores in the metal, and a poor fusion.

Too much oxygen causes a purple flame that welders call an "oxidizing flame," with attending results similar to the defects of the reducing flame. Both the reducing flame and the oxidizing flame are too long, whereas they should be fairly short and cone-shaped. Therefore, we can sum up the facts about the flame by saying that the color, size and shape of the flame, the sound made by combustion, and the appearance of the weld metal all combine to indicate clearly when there is an improper mixture of oxygen and acetylene.

The ragged, reducing, carbonizing flame caused by too much acetylene has some useful functions, even though it is not adapted to general welding. When wear-resisting properties for steel are more important than anything else, a mild casehardening can be accomplished with the reducing flame, since it gives a surface hardness and brittleness. Also, the reducing flame can be used in welding aluminum, monel metal, and stainless steel.

The oxidizing flame caused by too much oxygen can be used to burn or cut steel, which may be an advantage when other cutting methods are not available, but can be a serious disadvantage when it occurs at the wrong time. The appearance of a white-colored slag floating on the surface of the molten metal is a signal for the welder to readjust his torch and reduce the oxygen unless he wants to burn his metal.

Hold the torch firmly in the right hand when you are ready to start welding and have already lighted and adjusted the torch. The head of the torch should form an angle of about 60 degrees to the surface of the work. If the welding head is almost at right angles to the work, the secondary flame will not heat the metal that lies ahead of the spot being welded at that instant; if the welding head is inclined at an angle too much below 60 degrees, molten metal will be forced ahead of the welding spot and it will adhere to the sides of the weld. Of course, the parts must be molten at their edges when the rod is lowered into the weld, and not red hot. Hurrying will do no good; the welder must be patient or he will waste his time and materials.

Move the torch from right to left, away from the body, in order that you may watch the progress of the work. When the welding rod is used, fuse the welding rod and the edges of the parts being joined at the same time. When the parts are comparatively light in weight and thin, and also when material has been removed from each of the parts, give the torch a weaving motion, starting at the right and moving to the left with regular speed. Figure 6, Plate 26, illustrates the weave pattern or path of the flame and rod during the weld. Another way to do the same thing is to move the flame in overlapping circles, letting the diameter of the circles depend upon the size and weight of the parts joined. Gunsmiths who are expert welders prefer the pattern in Figure 6 to the overlapping circle pattern, since the former concentrates the heat better.

In welding steel, it is especially important to remove the oxide that forms on top of the weld. Since it melts at a lower temperature than the other metal, it may be removed like a thin skin when the weld cools, or it may be floated away while the weld is still hot. The oxide must not be permitted to form part of the weld or weakness will result.

Where the parts have been cut away, the resulting groove must be filled from the bottom up to the surface in successive layers, adding filling material slowly, at the same time being careful that each layer is fused not only with the one below but also the layer on top.

Annealing, hammering, and quenching are three treatments that constitute after-treatment for a weld. Annealing is done by heating the work to a bright cherry red with a torch, or in a furnace, and then letting it cool slowly and evenly. Cold air drafts must be avoided. Even cooling can be insured by covering the work with dry sand and letting its temperature fall in a well-regulated furnace.

Hammering is done with quick, light blows of the hand hammer after the weld has been heated to a bright yellow heat, but the hammering must stop as soon as the work drops to a dull red heat.

Quenching consists of plunging the work into water, oil, or brine after heating to the correct temperature. This treatment is used in hardening and tempering small parts that must be very strong, but such parts become hard and brittle, hence quenching is not always advisable.

Figure 3, Plate 26, shows a Vee block and a "C" clamp. Small parts may be held between Vee blocks and kept together by the "C" clamp. If some such method of holding the work is not used, movement may take place during the welding process, or the expansion and contraction of the metal may spoil the weld. Gunsmiths often make jigs and clamps especially designed for holding certain parts that will not remain stationary in the Vee blocks and "C" clamp. This is a problem to be solved according to the requirements of each situation that arises.

A lap weld is shown in the upper part of Figure 5, Plate 26; it is suitable only for small parts and comparatively thin sheets. The butt weld, illustrated in Figure 5, is easy to make and better for most gun work. The flange weld, shown in Figure 4, requires a little preparation. Flange up the edges a fraction of an inch, line up the two parts, and let the metal in the flanges fill the groove, instead of using welding wire. Make the joint flush with the parts and you have a strong, clean weld.

A corner weld, such as the one in Figure 4, Plate 26, is made by first flanging the edges, similar to the flanging of the "flange weld" shown below in the same figure, and then placing the axes of the two parts at right angles to each other. Before the actual weld is attempted, it may be necessary to hold the parts together by "tacking," which means making short welds at intervals; this prevents expansion of the metal. The metal in the flanges may fill the joint, or welding wire can be the filling medium when necessary.

Another way to make a corner weld is to forget about flanging the ends and simply bring them together at right angles, in which case the weld resembles the ordinary butt weld in execution.

Welding stainless steel is rather difficult when it is necessary to retain the stainless property in the weld itself. A perfectly neutral flame is correct, but if it cannot be kept constant, then it is better to have a flame that leans toward carburizing rather than oxidizing. Use a special stainless steel flux, obtainable from any dealer of welding supplies, mix it with water, and paint it along the joint with a brush. When a welding rod is needed, cut a rod from the stainless steel and you will have a weld that closely resembles the joined parts in color and grain.

Choose either a butt or a flanged joint for stainless steel, bring the weld region to a molten heat quickly, insert the rod immediately, and finish the job without allowing it to cool. Be sure to keep the parts stationary during the process.

Professional welders often use a pyrometer to measure the temperature. When this instrument is not available, draw blue chalk marks on the surface of the parts; when they turn white the metal is at the proper temperature for welding. Another substitute for a pyrometer is to rub a dry pine stick over the parts every few seconds; the stick will char and leave a mark when the surface is hot enough for welding to begin.

The welding of aluminum follows the same basic principles as the welding of steel, except that it is necessary to take off the layer of aluminum oxide found on the surface before welding can be started. This can be done by some mechanical means, such as a wire brush or an abrasive, but the best method is to use a special aluminum welding flux, obtainable from dealers in aluminum materials, or directly from the Aluminum Company of America. This flux can be made into a paste with water and painted on the work, or the welding rod can be dipped into the flux before the rod is inserted in the groove. When the flame heats the flux, it carries off the aluminum oxide and leaves a clean area for welding.

Finally, the gunsmith can do many things with the oxyacetylene torch that cannot be accomplished at all by other processes, and even the tasks that can be performed by other methods are better executed by welding. Steel parts, such as bolt handles, can be bent to desired shapes; the torch is a source of heat for sweating sights and other parts into place; and it can be used for the manufacture or repair of actions, hammers, triggers, butt plates, trigger guards, etc.

Only two notes of caution are needed: First, observe the safety precautions regarding the operation of the equipment, as set forth by the manufacturer, and second, proceed with great patience and caution. Practice on scrap metal and old guns before you attempt work on valuable firearms.

XIX. Metallurgy

METALLURGY in the broad sense is the science and art of extracting metals from their ores and preparing them for various uses. The gunsmith must understand the properties of specific metals and alloys, not only to determine whether or not they are suitable for firearms but also for the purpose of changing the mechanical and heat properties of such materials in order to make them fit his particular needs. Modern testing methods enable the gunsmith to take a sample of the material under consideration and predict in general how it will probably perform in service.

Even a slight trace of some element may profoundly influence the mechanical, electrical, and magnetic properties of metals and alloys. Chemical analysis is used to determine their composition, but the methods followed in the various analyses are too long and complicated for the average gunsmith to use himself; instead, he is usually content to be able to understand intelligently the reports on metals made by the chemical engineers employed in factories and laboratories.

Strength and plasticity are two important properties of metals. Strength, from the standpoint of the gunsmith, is the ability of a metal to resist deformation, and plasticity is the ability of a metal to change its shape without breaking. A combination of strength and plasticity is desirable because a tool or a gun part having these properties in the correct ratio can be overloaded in service without danger. For example, if a gun part becomes overloaded in one spot, the property of plasticity permits the load to flow and become distributed to other portions of the part.

Elasticity is that property of an object which causes it to resist deformation when a load is applied and afterward to recover its original size and shape when the load is removed. In theory, the elastic limit is the limit to which a material can be loaded and still recover its original size and shape upon removal of the load. In practice, metals are not perfectly elastic even under small loads, hence some method of arbitrarily determining elastic limits for industrial purposes is adopted and the results are interpreted in regard to the method used.

One of the machines for testing metals measures the load placed upon the sample; this load is divided by the area to obtain the ultimate tensile strength, expressed in pounds per square inch, or in kilograms per square centimeter. A gauge is clamped to the sample, and the elongation of the sample is measured and plotted on cross-sectional paper on horizontal lines against the load which is plotted on vertical lines, the result being a stress-strain curve for that particular specimen.

The point on the stress-strain curve at which the elongation ceases to be in proportion to the load is called the proportional limit, although practically this is the same as the elastic limit. This is important in gun work, because it is usually of more value to know what load will deform a gun part than it is to know what load will cause a rupture.

In testing steel, the load at which the material will continue to elongate, even though the load is not increased, is called the yield point, and is greater than the elastic limit. The plasticity shown by a sample under tension loading is called ductility. It is measured by the amount the sample can permanently elongate, and indicates the extent to which a metal can be drawn from a larger to a smaller size.

Malleability is the quality of deforming permanently under compression without rupture. This property permits the extension or shaping of metal by hammering or rolling.

Toughness is the property of withstanding high unit stress together with great unit deformation before rupture. The difference between ductility and toughness is that ductility involves only the ability to deform, whereas toughness deals with both the ability to deform and the stress developed while the material is being deformed. There is no direct method of measuring the toughness of metals accurately, but the shock resistance may be taken as indicative of toughness. The latter is measured by a machine that indicates the energy consumed in breaking a sample in terms of foot-pounds; the greater the number of foot-pounds needed to break the specimen, the greater is its shock resistance, and hence its approximate toughness.

Fatigue is another important property of metals. All metals are crystalline, with tiny particles that may be stressed beyond their elastic limit under repeated loadings. As the stress is repeated, tiny cracks, sometimes described as "fatigue cracks," appear and continue until failure takes place, this action being termed "progressive failure." Thus, a specimen may fracture under a certain definite load when the load is applied only once, but the same material will fail when a very much smaller load is applied and removed several times. The fatigue limit is the load which may be applied and removed for an infinite number of times without causing failure.

Fatigue limit is usually expressed in pounds per square inch. It is measured on several types of testing machines, hence it is well to compare metals for fatigue purposes according to the results obtained from tests on the same type of machine. For example, one machine rotates a round test bar of steel horizontally with a load applied by means of a weight at one end, the stresses being figured from the dimensions of the specimen bar and the applied loads, the latter varying from a tensile stress to a compressive measurement of the same magnitude. Another type of machine alternately stretches and compresses the specimen.

Hardness is the next characteristic of metals to be considered. Some authorities assume that hardness and ultimate strength are practically the same, and proceed to define hardness as that property which gives metal the ability to resist permanent deformation when a load is applied. However, this treats hardness as though it were a single property, when it is really a combination of properties. A more scientific definition of hardness would show that it is the ability to resist not only plastic deformation but also abrasions and very slight indentations.

The crudest and simplest test for hardness is to see if one material will scratch another. Moh's Scale of Hardness is used in testing rocks and minerals. Hardness is indicated thus: 1, talc; 2, gypsum; 3, calc spar; 4, fluor spar; 5, apatite; 6, feldspar; 7, quartz; 8, topaz; 9, sapphire; 10, diamond. A rule-of-thumb sometimes used for softer minerals is: If it can be scratched by a fingernail, it has hardness up to 2.5; if it can be scratched by a copper coin, it has hardness up to 3; if it can be scratched by a knife blade, it has hardness up to 5.5. Rough surfaces give questionable results. The mineral should be smoothed and the standard testing material moved back and forth several times over a distance of from $\frac{1}{16}$ to $\frac{1}{8}$ inch. If the surface is scratched, it is softer than the material that does the scratching. The only important exception occurs when a mineral breaks off in splinters; this gives a false impression of being softer than it really is.

Gunsmiths, and other metalworkers, often use expressions for hardness which in principle are based upon the Moh's Scale. For example, they will say that steel is "file hard" when it cannot be worked with a file, since the steel is then as hard as the file. Hardened tool steel is likewise called "glass hard" because it will scratch glass. These are rough, rule-of-thumb expressions which have little scientific value. They were useful in the early days of gunsmithing but have no place in the modern world.

Scientific tests are the Brinell, the Rockwell, the Vickers, and the Shore. The Brinell method, named for a Swedish engineer who invented it, employs a hardened-steel ball, 10 mm (0.3937 inch) in diameter, which is forced with a pressure of 3,000 kilograms (for iron and steel), or a pressure of 500 kilograms (for copper and brass), into a flat surface on the specimen to be tested, and permitted to remain there for at least 10 seconds (for iron and steel) or for at least 30 seconds (for soft metals), to make a spherical impression, the diameter of which is measured with a microscope. The hardness is found by dividing the pressure by the area of the surface of the impression made by the ball. The Brinell of annealed tool steel is about 200, and that of hardened tool steel is about 650, while the hardness of annealed copper is only about 40. For steel, there is an approximate relationship between the Brinell numbers and the ultimate strength. Some steels have an ultimate strength which is one-half of the Brinell number, while others have an ultimate strength found by taking $\frac{7}{10}$ of the Brinell number and subtracting 26 from the result.

The Rockwell method uses a steel ball $\frac{1}{16}$ inch in diameter with a load of 100 kilograms in the Rockwell "B" test for soft metals; or a conical diamond point with a load of 150 kilograms in the Rockwell "C" test for hard metals. The load is applied with a weight at the end of a compound lever; this weight is taken off, and the small initial load remains on the penetrating surface. The depth of the impression, rather than its area, is measured by means of a micrometer dial gauge which is part of the apparatus, and it is indicated directly on the dial in an arbitrary system of hardness numbers corresponding inversely to the depth of the penetration. The advantages over the Brinell method are that tests can be made faster, the apparatus leaves only a small mark on the specimen, and extremely hard materials can be tested with a diamond cone. The ultimate strength is found by dividing 3,750 by 130 minus the Rockwell B test number.

The British use the Vickers Pyramid Hardness-testing Machine which is based upon the same principle as the Brinell and Rockwell machines. However, the penetrating device is a pyramid-shaped diamond that is suitable for any degree of hardness. Measurements are taken on the diagonal of the indentation of the diamond by means of a microscope attached to the apparatus.

The Shore method uses an instrument called the Scleroscope. There is a vertical glass tube in which a small cylinder of very hard steel pointed on the end (called the hammer) slides up and down. The instrument is placed over the specimen and the hammer falls about 10 inches onto the surface; the distance it rebounds is indicated on a scale on the tube which is divided into 140 equal parts. Hardness is indicated according to the amount of rebound. Tool steel, having 1 per cent carbon, may be shown as 31; mild steel may read 26 to 30; the hardest steel may measure 110; while wrought iron may read 18. The ultimate tensile strength is found by subtracting 15 from 4 times the Scleroscope reading; this gives ultimate strength in thousands of pounds per square inch.

Brittleness is another term applied to metals. It is relative, since no material is perfectly brittle, for perfect brittleness would mean that no deformation would take place before rupture. Brittleness is the opposite of plasticity. Metals having a high degree of plasticity have no brittleness, and they rupture with a considerable reduction of area, this reduction in area being used as a measure of brittleness or plasticity. Thus, a low or zero reduction of area indicates a high degree of brittleness, while a large reduction of area shows a high degree of plasticity. Brittle metals fail without giving warning.

Ductile metals may fail without giving any visible signs of deformation when they are subjected to concentrated loads. This is especially true if there are sudden and sharp reductions in cross section, sharp corners, notches, and other changes in shape that permit concentrated loading. Such shapes when pulled apart rupture with a brittle fracture, while shapes having gradual reductions in cross section, rounded corners, no notches, etc., behave as plastic materials and rupture only after a noticeable amount of elongation.

Hidden flaws in metal parts of guns can be detected by the "Magna-flux" method which was developed principally by aeronautical engineers. First, the metal is magnetized; this creates magnetic poles in the cracks which are hidden inside the metal. Second, the metal is dipped in a solution of kerosene and powdered iron; this causes the iron particles to climb up the surface of the metal along the lines of the concealed cracks. Third, the metal is examined and compared with other specimens of defective metal if records are to be kept for research purposes, or it may be thrown on the scrap pile without further study.

Corrosion is another characteristic of metals that has been tested frequently, but reports of such tests are of little practical value to the gunsmith because the rate of corrosion varies with the condition of the environment. Tests made with metal left in acid baths will not indicate the amount of corrosion that will take place on a gun part exposed to perspiration. Likewise, metal placed in a tank of rain water will not have the same corrosion rate as that exposed to intermittent rains on hunting trips. Even committees appointed by engineering societies for the study of corrosion admit publicly that relative corrosion should be studied in the field and not in the laboratory.

ALLOY STEELS

Steel is itself an alloy of carbon and iron, but an alloy steel is one to which some element has been added to alter the properties of the steel so that it will be different from ordinary carbon steel. Practically all carbon steels have small amounts of manganese and silicon, and yet they are not classed as alloy steels unless the proportion of manganese or silicon is large enough to change their characteristics noticeably.

The two alloying elements most commonly used are nickel and chromium. When an alloy steel contains one alloying element in addition to the steel, it is termed a "binary" alloy steel. Examples are chromium, tungsten, nickel, silicon, vanadium, manganese, and molybdenum steels. When an alloy steel contains two alloying elements in addition to the steel, it is termed "ternary" alloy steel. Examples are chrome-nickel, chrome-molybdenum, silicon-manganese, and chrome-vanadium steels.

The Society of Automotive Engineers developed a numerical index system for numbering steels, in which the first digit indicates the class to which the steel belongs, that is, whether it is a plain carbon or an alloy steel, and if an alloy steel, the kind of alloy; the second digit indicates the percentage of the predominant alloying element; and the last two digits indicate the average carbon content in "points," or hundredths of 1 per cent. Thus, "SAE 2340" represents a nickel steel of about 3 per cent nickel and .40 per cent carbon. Likewise, "SAE 1020" would be a carbon steel having .20 per cent carbon (the second digit is 0 because no alloy is present).

The basic numerals used as the first digit of the SAE number are as follows:

Carbon steels, 1; Nickel steels, 2; Nickel-chromium steels, 3; Molybdenum steels, 4; Chromium steels, 5; Chromium-vanadium steels, 6; Tungsten steels, 7; Silicon-manganese steels, 9.

Steels for rifle, shotgun, and revolver barrels were at one time either cold-drawn steel, called black-powder barrel steel, or high carbon steel, sometimes called ordnance steel. The development of airplane manufacturing, with its demand for great strength in proportion to weight and size, brought forth two more steels suitable for barrels. These more modern steels are alloy steel, sometimes called 3½ per cent nickel steel; and stainless, or rust-proof, steel.

Cold-drawn, black-powder steel is still used in making some .22 caliber rifle barrels when lead bullets are used in such barrels, and where the breech pressure does not exceed 30,000 pounds per square inch. Since the tensile strength is usually between 45,000 and 65,000 pounds per square inch, there is a reasonably wide margin of safety, provided, of course, nothing happens to build up pressure unexpectedly, such as an obstruction in the bore. However, the introduction of jacketed bullets, and higher pressures for high-velocity cartridges, brought a need for greater elasticity, greater tensile strength, and other properties which could be met only by a steel having more carbon.

The high carbon steel, also called high-power carbon steel or ordnance steel, is sometimes composed of .45 to .55 per cent carbon, with 1 to 1.3 per cent manganese, and not more than .05 per cent phosphorus, and not more than .05 per cent sulphur. Also, steel known as SAE 1350, with .25 per cent silicon added, is used. Such steels have high tensile strength, they wear well, and they are easily worked.

Nickel steel came into use for rifle barrels as pressures increased greatly and jacketed bullets became more common. It is hard, has high tensile strength, wears well, resists corrosion better than ordinary carbon steels, and has more ductility than the increase in strength would seem to indicate. This set of qualities comes largely from the fact that nickel decreases the crystal size of steels.

The full advantage of using nickel as an alloy for steel is received only when this steel is heat-treated for strength in the normal manner, that is: it is heated to the lowest possible temperature to place all the iron and carbon in solid solution, quenched in oil or water to prevent precipitation of iron crystals of large size, and then reheated to restore ductility. Nickel steel having a 3.5 per cent nickel content is not only better than carbon steel which has been heat-treated in this same way, but the nickel steel also has a higher elastic limit.

Stainless steel, the fourth of the steels mentioned as gun-barrel material, is an alloy of iron, chromium, and nickel, having high resistance to corrosion and heat. There is usually a relatively low carbon content and more than 10 per cent chromium. Stainless steel is not absolutely rust-proof, for it will rust if exposed long enough to moisture. It is difficult to bore, ream, rifle, and blue, and is not recommended to the beginner.

The development of metallurgy in aviation has gone far ahead of the farthest points reached in any other industry. For this reason, progressive ordnance experts recommend that steel selected for making barrels in the future be of airplane quality, made in an electric furnace. It should have favorable elongation, tensile strength, yielding point, reduction of area, and hardness, although the latter quality is limited by the tools and machines available for working hard steel.

We have already mentioned SAE 2350, only we called it nickel steel without giving it the technical designation. As explained before, the first digit, 2, shows that it is a nickel steel; the second digit, 3, indicates the approximate percentage of the predominating alloying element (nickel in this case); and the last two digits, 50, show that the average carbon content is approximately .50 per cent. This steel is well adapted to making firearms because it is strong for its weight, it resists wear, it is reasonably easy to machine and heat-treat, and it withstands recoil because its impact and fatigue strengths are good.

An excellent nickel-chromium steel is SAE 3150. It heat-treats well, has high strength, and possesses good fatigue qualities.

A chrome-molybdenum steel which will withstand fatigue and shock is SAE 4150, but it should be heat-treated at the steel mill rather than in the gunsmith's shop.

Manganese, next to carbon, is the most important ingredient in steel, but too great a percentage of manganese makes a rifle barrel difficult to work, just as too much carbon makes it too brittle. The correct proportion for making barrels is to have a carbon content of about .50 per cent, nickel about 1.50 per cent, and manganese about 1.10 per cent. (Where there is a range in the manganese content, the letter "X" may be prefixed before the SAE number.)

Nickel-manganese steel is probably the best possible material for barrels, because it combines all of the desirable characteristics of other steels, and has a few of its own. One of these is the property of penetration hardness. In simple words, this means that when large sections of nickel-manganese steel are heat-treated, the hardness reaches the core instead of remaining on the surface.

Elsewhere in this text, mention is made of "high speed steel." The principal superiority of high speed steels over other steels is that they retain their hardness, and hence their cutting edge, even when heated to a dull red heat (about 1,100 deg. F.). Because of this property they are used for tools that operate at high speeds, such as lathe bits, etc. There is no advantage in this unless the tools turn so fast that they develop temperatures that would soften a cheaper steel. Ordinarily, a barrel would not be made of this material, but when the above-mentioned steels are not available, high speed steel proves very satisfactory.

These high speed steels contain from 12 to 20 per cent tungsten (14 to 18 per cent being the usual range); from 2 to 5 per cent chromium; usually from 1 to 2 per cent vanadium; and sometimes cobalt. The carbon content is ordinarily from .65 to .75 per cent. A typical tool steel is composed of 18 per cent tungsten, 4 per cent chromium, and 1 per cent vanadium. This is referred to as an "18-4-1 steel."

Manufacturers of steel usually have special trade names which are meaningless in themselves to the gunsmith, but the advertising folders issued by the mills give enough details to enable anyone who has read this chapter to select his barrel material intelligently.

NEW DISCOVERIES IN METALLURGY

When aircraft began flying beyond the speed of sound, and especially after the development of jet aircraft, rockets, missiles, and other weapons of the atomic age, scientists developed new metals, new techniques, and new processes; but the information given above is sufficient for the average gunsmith, amateur or professional.

XX. Heat Treatment of Steel

METALSMITHS have long known that they could vary the properties of steel by heating it to a high temperature and quenching it quickly in some liquid, such as water, brine, or oil, but until recently they have regarded the heat treatment of steel as an art with no fixed rules of procedure. The increase in the number of steel alloys has required a close study of the internal structure of steel, which has been accomplished principally by etching the steel and examining it under a microscope. By this means it has been learned that steel is a crystalline structure which changes its form with a change of temperature.

The structure of steel usually changes slowly as the temperature drops. When hot steel is cooled quickly by plunging it into a cold liquid, it keeps the structure that it had when heated even after it has cooled to room temperature, and this structure is entirely different from what it was before the steel was heated. The temperature to which steel is raised before quenching and the speed with which it is quenched are factors which determine its physical properties.

The terms used in describing heat treatment are annealing, normalizing, hardening, and drawing for the usual processes. The special processes are carburizing, cyaniding, and nitriding. The gunsmith uses one or more of these processes in developing the physical characteristics of his steels. The methods of heat-treating and the reasons for such methods constitute the scope of this chapter. Today, heat treatment of steel is an exact science. The results which the gunsmith obtains are in direct ratio to his knowledge, skill, and resourcefulness.

Annealing.—Annealing is the process of subjecting steel to high heat and then cooling. There are three objects in annealing: (1) Any strains put upon the metal while it is cooling, or by mechanical treatment or any other means, are relieved; (2) the grain of the steel is restored to a tiny size that gives it the most favorable qualities; or (3) it is softened after a hardening process. All three objects may be accomplished in one process.

The usual temperatures for annealing are between 1,290 and 1,830 deg. F., which correspond to a range of 700 to 1,000 deg. C. The temperature required is just above the critical point, which is a temperature at which an important structural change takes place, varying according to the chemical contents of the metal. Steel having a low carbon content is annealed at a temperature of about 1,650 deg. F., while steel having a high carbon content is annealed at a temperature somewhere between 1,300 and 1,400 deg. F.

Holding the metal at a required temperature until it is thoroughly heated is called soaking. In annealing, the metal is brought to the required temperature and then soaked at that temperature for a definite time which varies with the nature of the particular steel used. However, a safe general rule is to soak for about one hour for each inch of thickness of the steel to be sure that all of it reaches the required temperature. After soaking, the steel must cool slowly. This is accomplished in either one of two methods: (1) shut off the heat and permit the steel and the furnace to cool together; or (2) bury the heated steel in ashes, sand, or lime.

Gunsmiths commonly pack the steel being heat-treated in a cast-iron pipe or box which contains sand, powdered charcoal, slaked lime, or even ashes. The pipe or box is closed tight with fire clay wherever air can enter and then placed in a furnace heated by electricity, gas, oil, or solid fuel.

Professional gunsmiths sometimes own a small furnace designed especially for heat-treating, but such equipment is not essential. Heating can be done in an ordinary home furnace, a forge, or the fuel box of a kitchen range. Where the use of a pipe or box for packing the steel before heating is not practicable, the steel can be heated directly by one of the means mentioned. Of course, temperature control is difficult when crude equipment is employed.

Under such circumstances, the steel is heated directly to a dull red color, maintained at that heat for the necessary period of time, and then cooled as described before. Since temperature control by the method of visual inspection is inaccurate, annealing is first tried with the metal brought to a dull red; if this fails, try it again with the steel brought to a bright cherry red.

Annealed steel is soft, ductile, fine-grained, and has no internal strains or stresses. It is easily worked and machined, but it is weak, and hence it may be necessary to give it another heat treatment to increase its strength after it has been properly machined and no more mechanical work is required.

The surface of the steel is prone to accumulate iron oxide, called scale, from the annealing process. This can be prevented by placing the part being annealed in a closed pipe or box, as described above, and keeping the receptacle sealed until it has cooled to room temperature. When scale occurs, however, it must be removed by some cleaning or pickling method.

Normalizing.—Normalizing is a form of annealing consisting of heating the steel as described above and then cooling it in still air. This is a quicker form of annealing that softens the steel a little less than true annealing, increases the strength above that of true annealing, relieves internal strains, and makes the steel less ductile than it would be if annealed in the usual manner. Normalizing also refines the grain and makes the steel uniform in structure, just as true annealing does.

Welding steel parts together produces strains and leaves a cast structure adjacent to wrought structures. Normalizing welded parts refines the grain, relieves internal stresses, and hence reduces the probability of cracks and failure from fatigue.

Steel parts of low carbon content are normalized to reduce any distortion that may occur in later heat treatment, and to make it easier to machine them. Medium and high carbon steels are often normalized and then annealed before they are machined or fabricated, in which case the double process is termed double annealing.

Hardening.—Hardening is done by heating the steel above the critical temperature, soaking at that temperature until the material is thoroughly and uniformly heated, and then quenching by plunging it quickly into brine, oil, or water. This produces a fine grain, great hardness, great tensile strength, low ductility, and internal strains. The increase in hardness will not be produced unless the temperature is above the critical temperature so that the most favorable grain structure is obtained. This temperature depends upon the carbon content of the steel.

Heating must be as little above the critical temperature as practical or the steel may warp, or it may crack when it is quenched, but this rule applies principally to small objects. Steel parts of great size and thickness are heated to the upper limit of the hardening temperature range in order to obtain uniform heating throughout the mass.

The hardness of steel increases with the carbon content. Unless steel contains more than .75 per cent carbon it is not suitable for springs, saws, and similar tools. Metal-cutting tools usually contain at least 1 per cent carbon. Files and other very hard tools contain 1.5 per cent or more carbon.

The hardness also depends upon the rate of cooling after the steel has been raised above the critical range. Quenching in oil permits slow cooling because oil absorbs heat slower than water or brine. Quenching in water makes the steel a little harder when the water is at room temperature, but if the water is ice cold the steel becomes still harder. Ice cold brine is even better for hardening. When a greater degree of hardness is desired, an ice-sodium chloride solution can be used, or better yet, mercury near its freezing point, which is —38 deg. F. (—39 deg. C.), will produce about the greatest hardness that can be obtained.

It must be remembered that neither carbon content alone nor the rate of cooling alone will give maximum hardness. A combination of maximum carbon content with maximum speed of cooling is necessary to obtain maximum hardness.

A safe rule-of-thumb followed by many gunsmiths is to quench parts that are subject to great stresses and vibration, such as firing pins and hammers, in oil, and quench parts that are subject only to ordinary surface friction in water. An extension of this rule is to quench thin, weak parts in oil, since water will make them too brittle.

The kind of oil to use for oil-quenching is open to debate. Many gunsmiths recommend sperm oil for steel springs, but prefer raw linseed oil for quenching cutting tools. Lard, kerosene, whale oil, fish oil, cottonseed oil, and other forms of oil and grease have been used successfully where sperm oil or linseed oil were not obtainable.

Returning to the subject of the correct temperature to which the steel must be raised and soaked, we find that temperature varies with the carbon content; the higher the carbon, the lower the temperature at which full hardness is achieved. For steel with .85 per cent or more carbon, the best temperature is just above 1,350 deg. F., while steel with less than .85 per cent carbon may have to be heated to a temperature just above 1,510 deg. F. There is no hard and fast rule that can be applied indiscriminately to several steels.

When no means of measuring the temperature accurately is available, the gunsmith may guess the temperature by observing the color of the steel, but the color varies not only with the heat but also with the chemical composition of the steel. Furthermore, no two men describe the same color in the same terms. For instance, one gunsmith will say that the critical temperature for hardening steel is a "bright cherry red," while another will say that it "varies from dull red to bright red." Still another gunsmith may say that the critical temperature lies "somewhere between a full cherry and a light cherry." Obviously, the best procedure is to either find out from the steel mill the critical temperature for the steel you are using, or determine it experimentally on a sample piece of material.

Drawing or Tempering.—Drawing, sometimes called tempering, is the process of reheating hardened steel to a temperature below the critical range, followed by soaking and then quenching in brine, water, air, or oil. It decreases the brittleness of hardened steel, relieves the strain, restores ductility and somewhat reduces hardness and strength, although the resulting strength, hardness, and ductility depend upon the temperature to which the material was reheated. If the steel was reheated to a high temperature, it will be more ductile but less hard and strong. The object of drawing or tempering is therefore to decrease the brittleness and at the same time keep the steel strong and tough. By heating to about 392 deg. F. (200 deg. C.), steel loses enough brittleness, but not too much hardness, to be used for metal-cutting tools, such as lathe tools and steel engraving tools. Raising the temperature above that amount increases the degree of tempering.

At this point, the reader will doubtless realize that it is impossible to designate the exact temperature for tempering any steel object unless its carbon content is known. However, the approximately correct temperatures in degrees Fahrenheit for tempering certain parts and tools are as follows: Parts subject to friction but not shock, 420 deg.; checking and wood engraving tools, 430 deg.; chamber reamers, 440 deg.; hand reamers, and pins for holding parts together, 450 deg.; machine reamers, milling cutters, and drills for brass, 460 deg.; chisels for woodworking, gauges, and twist drills, 500 deg.; cold chisels, 530 deg.; extractors, flat springs, gun hammers, screwdrivers, and the bodies of firing pins, 550 deg.; thin, flat springs, and the noses of firing pins, 570 deg.

Although it could just as well be brought up under the subject of metallurgy, we may now consider the carbon content of various steel objects that could be worked over and made into gun parts and tools. Since all objects of the same kind, style, make, model, and brand are not necessarily of the same carbon content, the information given here is only general and approximate.

Ordinary gun barrels often have a carbon content ranging from .60 to .70 per cent. Wood augurs, woodworking chisels, screwdrivers, grass hooks, and most blacksmiths' tools have about the same carbon content, except that blacksmiths' hammers may run from .67 to .77 per cent. Band saws have from .68 to .76 per cent carbon.

Mining bits contain about .80 per cent carbon, which is the same carbon content as spring bushing. Lathe chisels contain from .80 to .90 per cent, which is about the same as the carbon content of chipping chisels, circular saws, and wrenches.

Cold chisels contain about .85 per cent carbon and apparently seldom run higher. Drop-forging dies contain from .85 to .90 per cent carbon, which is the same as the carbon content of the facing on an anvil, hoes, chuck jaws, vise jaws, plows made from crucible process steel, and some blacksmiths' punches, although the latter usually have less than .90 per cent carbon.

Blades of pocketknives average about .90 per cent carbon. Machinists' hammers have a carbon content varying from .90 to 1.00 per cent, which is about the same as the carbon content of putty knives, railroad springs, and bricklayers' tools, although some railroad springs have a carbon content as high as 1.10 per cent, and bricklayers' tools may not have more than .95 per cent carbon. Cross-cut saws have from .85 to 1.00 per cent carbon.

A lawn mower has about 1 per cent carbon. Twist drills have from 1.20 to 1.25 per cent carbon, although few run higher than 1.22 per cent. Straight edges (steel rulers) contain from 1.05 to 1.15 per cent carbon. A hatchet has from 1.15 to 1.25 per cent carbon. Paper knives (letter openers) have from 1.05 to 1.10 per cent carbon. Axes average about 1.20 per cent, and ball bearings have about the same content. Reamer blades average from 1.20 to 1.25 per cent carbon. Most files contain between 1.25 and 1.30 per cent carbon, although cheap ones often contain less. Woodworking knives contain from 1.15 to 1.20 per cent carbon, and garden rakes contain about the same amount, although they sometimes have as much as 1.25 per cent carbon. Taps contain from 1.20 to 1.25 per cent carbon, although they often contain less than 1.22 per cent. Magnets contain from 1.23 to 1.25 per cent, although they may contain as little as 1.20 per cent carbon. Skates have about 1.15 per cent carbon. Steel-cutting saws contain about 1.60 per cent carbon.

SAE (Society of Automotive Engineers) Steel No. 1030, has from .25 to .35 per cent carbon, .50 to .80 per cent manganese, .045 per cent phosphorus at the most, and .05 per cent surphur. It is essentially a structural steel used a great deal in making automobiles, and in rifle parts such as barrel bands, ramps, and sight bases.

SAE Steel No. 2015 is a nickel steel especially suitable for case-hardened gun parts, such as receivers, where both strength and hardness are needed. The carbon range is .10 to .20 per cent; the manganese range is .30 to .60 per cent; there is a maximum phosphorus content of .04 per cent; the maximum sulphur content is .045 per cent; and the nickel range is .40 to .60 per cent.

SAE Steel No. 2330 is a nickel steel primarily used for axles, crank shafts, driving shafts, transmission shafts, and similar structural parts needed in both the automotive and aeronautical industries, but it can also be used for making rifle and pistol barrels. The carbon range is .25 to .35 per cent; the manganese range is from .50 to .80 per cent; the maximum phosphorus content is .04 per cent; the maximum sulphur content is .045 per cent; and the nickel range is from 3.25 to 3.75 per cent.

The heat-treatment method for SAE Steel No. 2330 will now be described in considerable detail, since it illustrates the procedure sequence suitable for one type of barrel steel:

1. The temperature of the furnace must not be more than 1,100 deg. F. when the steel is inserted.

2. The temperature is then increased gradually to 1,450 to 1,500 deg. F. and held there for about 20 or 25 minutes.

3. The steel part or parts are removed from the furnace and quenched in oil.

4. When hardness-testing equipment is available, the parts are tested to see if they are about 500 on the Brinell hardness scale. If they are more than 500, the tempering temperatures should be increased; if less than 500 the tempering temperatures should be reduced. The increase or decrease of tempering temperatures is in direct proportion to the increase or decrease of Brinell hardness.

5. If an ultimate tensile strength of 125,000 is satisfactory, the tempering temperature for SAE Steel No. 2330 is 950 deg. F., but if an ultimate tensile strength of 150,000 is needed, then the tempering temperature should be 800 deg. F. In either case, the gun parts should normally be left at the tempering temperature for about one-half hour.

6. The gun parts are next removed from the furnace and permitted to cool in still air.

7. If the ultimate tensile strength is 125,000, the Rockwell test will read C-25 to C-32, and the Brinell test will show from 250 to 300. If the ultimate tensile strength is 150,000, the Rockwell test will show a hardness of C-33 to C-37, and the Brinell will be from 310 to 360.

A steel extensively used for such automobile parts as axles, gears, springs, and drive shafts SAE 6135, a chrome-vanadium, medium carbon steel. It is also suitable for gun springs.

Another chrome-vanadium steel which is suitable for making gun springs is SAE 6150, which is extensively used in both the automobile and aviation industries. The heat treatment of this steel for making springs follows:

1. Have the furnace temperature below 1,100 deg. F. when the parts are inserted.

2. Increase the temperature gradually to 1,525-1500 deg. F. and hold it there for at least 15 minutes, depending upon the thickness of the parts.

3. Remove the gun parts and quench them in oil.

4. Insert the hardened parts in a furnace having a temperature below 700 deg. F.

5. Raise the furnace temperature to 700-850 deg. F. and hold it there for between 30 minutes and one hour, depending upon the thickness of the parts.

6. Allow the parts to cool in still air.

7. Test for hardness. The Brinell test should show 400 to 444; the Rockwell should be from C-42 to C-47. The ultimate strength is about 200,000 pounds per square inch.

Heating small, irregular-shaped parts uniformly is made easier when a lead bath is used. A plumber's melting pot is filled with chemically pure lead which is brought to a bright red heat. The steel parts are suspended in the lead until they acquire the same heat. If the parts are large, they are preheated by any reasonable process to prevent cooling the lead too much when they are immersed in the bath. By bringing the lead to the proper heat, the parts can be heated without the anxiety that accompanies the usual furnace method. An old plumber's pot is better than a new one, for the sulphur is then burned out of the cast iron. Another caution is to cover the surface of the lead with powdered charcoal to prevent oxidation.

The problem of scale forming on heated steel, especially when the steel is exposed to the air, has been mentioned. By coating the steel with a mixture of boneblack and sperm oil, or boneblack and linseed oil, scale formation is prevented. The boneblack comes off when the work is placed in the quenching bath. When this mixture cannot be made, coat the steel with melted boracic acid; this will often come off in the quenching bath, but if it does not, dipping the steel in boiling water will remove the boracic acid.

The special heat treatments called carburizing, cyaniding, and nitriding are explained in Chapter XXI, *Surface Hardening*. The chapters on Temperature, Metallurgy, Heat Treatment, and Surface Hardening, are all closely related and should be studied as a unit. Furthermore, all material on metals and the handling and treatment of metals is of importance to the gunsmith.

XXI. Surface Hardening

FOR some gun purposes it is desirable to have a hard surface that resists wear, and a tough, strong core. These qualities can be obtained in steel in various ways. Heat-treating by itself will produce either a very hard and strong steel, or it will produce one that is tough and fairly hard all through the metal. If the surface, often called the "case," is to be harder than the highest degree of hardness obtainable by heat treatment, and if at the same time it is to have a tough core, we must resort to methods of surface hardening described in this chapter.

A hard surface or case resists abrasion and wear, while a soft core resists shock stresses. Any desired depth of casehardening can be obtained, from a thin film to over ⅛ inch, thus making it possible to vary the surface hardening to conform to gun design and construction requirements. Soft machinery steel that has been casehardened may prove more satisfactory than tempered steel from the mechanical viewpoint and also it is much less expensive and difficult to obtain.

Carburizing.—There are three methods for accomplishing surface hardening: carburizing, cyaniding, and nitriding. Carburizing, when followed by a special form of heat treatment, is called casehardening, and it is the most important of the three surface-hardening methods. A piece of steel is carburized, quenched, reheated to refine the core, quenched quickly, reheated again to refine and harden the surface, quenched quickly, tempered at a low temperature, and then slowly cooled. One or more of these steps may be eliminated, depending upon the particular ends in view for the job at hand.

Steels for carburizing may be either plain carbon steels or alloy steels. The carbon content should not be more than .18 per cent for light parts which should have tough cores. The carbon content for heavy parts which must have strong cores may be between .15 and .25 per cent, although sometimes steel having as much as .55 per cent carbon can be successfully carburized. The latter is the exception to the rule.

Carburizing is the heating of low carbon steels with some material rich in carbon, whether it is liquid, solid, or gaseous. When the material containing carbon is heated, a gas is given off which carries carbon to the steel that in turn absorbs the carbon because it is, itself, poor in carbon content. The nature of the material rich in carbon, the temperature to which that material is raised, and the time during which the process takes place all determine the depth to which the carbon will enter the steel and hence it ultimately determines the degree of casehardening.

The surface of the steel will absorb carbon until the carbon content of the steel reaches an amount somewhere between .80 and 1.25 per cent, but the carbon content of the steel is less and less from the surface into the core where there is no more carbon than there was before the carburizing process began. The heat treatment following the carburizing will toughen the core and harden the case in accordance with the principles of heat treatment explained in the previous chapters, where it was shown that hardness is associated in steel with a high carbon content.

Carburizing With Solids.—The older gunsmiths favor carburizing with some carbon-rich solid material, such as bone, charred leather, wood charcoal, or coke. Any one of these materials may be used exclusively, or they may be used in combination with one another. The addition of 40 parts barium carbonate to 60 parts wood charcoal is one of the formulas used; the purpose of the barium carbonate is to give off its own carbon and at the same time hasten the formation of carburizing gas from the charcoal.

The parts to be carburized are packed in a cast-iron or mild steel box big enough to hold them all and equipped with legs 2 or 3 inches high to permit the furnace gases to circulate freely over the entire surface of the box. The surface of each of the gun parts is covered with the carburizing material to a depth of at least ½ inch, the lid is tightly closed, and all places where air might enter are sealed with moist fire clay containing a little salt that is added to prevent cracking. The hardening box is now ready for the furnace.

The furnace is heated to between 1,600 and 1,700 degrees F. as quickly as your facilities will permit. Some carburizing steels need a furnace heated to a temperature between 1,600 and 1,650 degrees, some should have a range of 1,625 and 1,675 degrees, and still others require a range of 1,650 and 1,700 degrees, but in no instance is the temperature greater than 1,700 degrees.

The carbon will enter the steel faster at higher temperatures, but the grains of steel increase in size with the increase in temperature, hence the temperature is kept within the critical range for the particular steel being hardened to avoid lowering the quality.

The size of the parts, the hardening box, and the packing all affect the process because they cause the carburizing temperature to fall behind the temperature of the furnace anywhere from a few degrees to as much as 100 deg. F. For this reason the furnace is held at the carburizing temperature long enough for the gun parts to acquire the necessary depth of carbon penetration.

SAE 1020 carbon steel is a typical steel used in making parts to be casehardened. A case depth of $\frac{1}{64}$ inch is reached in one hour and it requires about twice as long to harden to a depth of $\frac{1}{32}$ inch. Either of these depths is great enough to resist shock stresses and take care of ordinary abrasion. If the box of parts is left in the furnace too long, the casehardening deepens and produces a steel that may crack when shock loads are impressed.

When the time period has been reached, the box is removed and cooled naturally in air if warpage is feared, but where there is no danger of warpage the gun parts are taken from the box and quenched in oil. When the parts have been cooled by either means, they are now carburized and ready for refining the grain, hardening, and tempering.

Carburizing With a Liquid Salt Bath.—Carburizing in a liquid salt bath is a method unknown to most gunsmiths because it is a comparatively recent development of the aircraft industry, and has its principal application to small parts where a case depth of .04 inch is sufficient. This method produces more uniformity of carbon penetration and carbon content, it is faster, and it is easier than the solid carbon method.

The salt used to give the liquid heat must have a melting point several hundred degrees below the temperature of the carburizing process. The necessary carbon is furnished by adding amorphous carbon (that is, carbon that will not crystallize) to the salt at the beginning and then adding more salt as the process progresses. To conserve the materials, the salt and carbon bath is covered with a layer of carbon that keeps the liquid from disappearing in the form of a vapor. After bringing the bath to a temperature between 1,600 and 1,675 deg. F., it is kept there for as long as 4 hours if a depth of .04 inch is desired in carburizing SAE 1020 steel. Shorter periods will give smaller carbon contents. After carburizing, the gun parts are quenched in either oil or water and prepared for refinement, hardening, and tempering.

Carbonizing With Gas.—There are several methods of carburizing with gas, but none of them seem to work as well in gunsmithing as they do in other trades. The best method, which is the most recent, is to heat the parts in an electric furnace which constantly receives carbon vapor generated by "cracking" an oil in another furnace. This carbonizing is too complicated and difficult for a small gunsmithing shop to handle.

Core Refinement.—The carburizing temperature is above the critical range and it is maintained for a considerable period of time, thus increasing the grain size of steel and reducing ductility. To restore a small grain size and the proper ductility, the steel is reheated slightly above the upper critical point, held there until it is uniformly heated at that temperature, and then quenched in oil.

SAE 1020 steel parts are first heated to 1,200 deg. F., placed in the furnace quickly and gradually brought to a temperature of 1,600 deg. F. during a period of between 30 and 60 minutes, depending upon the size of the parts, although 30 minutes is long enough for most small parts, while large parts may require at least 45 minutes. The parts are then held at that temperature (soaked) for about 10 minutes, and then quenched in oil.

Hardening the Case.—The temperature required to refine the core is above the critical range of the case and causes the case to have larger grains and increased brittleness. To refine the grain and harden the case, the steel is reheated slightly above the critical range of the case and quenched in oil.

Using SAE 1020 steel as an example again, the furnace is brought to a temperature of 1,000 deg. F., the parts are placed in the furnace, and the temperature is quickly brought to at least 1,400 and not more than 1,430 deg. F. The parts are soaked for 10 minutes and then quenched in oil without delay.

Tempering Carburized Parts.—The previous process of hardening the case produces strains which must be relieved. The furnace or oil bath, whichever is being used, is brought to a temperature somewhere between 300 and 400 deg. F., the parts are inserted and held there long enough to be uniformly heated at that temperature, and then they are taken out and cooled naturally in still air. If the parts are to be very hard, the tempering temperature is 300 deg. F., or very slightly more, but if only mild hardness is desired, the desirable temperature is close to 400 deg. F.

Caution Regarding Threaded Parts.—Do not cut threads if they are to be subjected to carburizing and hardening. Instead, leave extra steel where the part is to be threaded; carburize; turn off, on a lathe, part of the steel on the part to be threaded; use heat treatment to refine the core and harden the case, followed by tempering to remove strains caused by hardening; turn the steel part to the size for threading, and then thread where needed.

Cyaniding.—Cyaniding is a method of giving steel a surface hardness by heating the steel in contact with a cyanide salt and then quenching. Small gun parts and tools are hardened by heating them red hot in a blowtorch or gas burner, dipping in powdered cyanide, and heating again, repeating the process several times, if necessary, before quenching. The resulting hardness is due to nitrogen in the form of iron nitride in the case; it is not the result of increased carbon content, since the latter is quite low.

The method used where extensive hardening is performed by a shop is as follows: Bring the sodium cyanide or potassium cyanide bath to a temperature between 1,550 and 1,600 deg. F. Bring the parts to a temperature of 750 deg. F. and place them in the bath for at least 10 and not more than 20 minutes. Follow this with quenching in water. The entire surface of each part must be cooled, because lack of uniformity in cooling causes soft spots in the case. Leaving the parts in the bath for more than 20 minutes makes them too brittle and full of spots having more carbon than the surrounding area.

CAUTION: Cyaniding is a simple but dangerous process. The pot in which the parts are bathed in cyanide must be covered and there must be some controlled means of ventilation which carries the cyanide fumes away from the worker. Cyanide is a deadly poison. One whiff of cyanide fumes or exposure to cyanide in any form is extremely apt to cause immediate death. Cyanide must not be left where people or animals can get it, or where it will contaminate eating or drinking utensils. Even a minute amount on the end of a pencil will cause death if the pencil is touched to the lips or the eyes.

Nitriding.—Nitriding is a comparatively new process of hardening the surface of special alloy steels by heating in contact with ammonia gas or some other material containing nitrogen. This method is superior to casehardening accomplished by carburizing, since it gives greater hardness without the cracking or distortion that accompany the older casehardening process in many instances. However, nitriding is possible only with steels which contain from .90 to 1.50 per cent aluminum, and even then the desired aluminum content seems to be between 1 and 1.5 per cent.

The special steel (known as nitralloy) is heated to 950 deg. F. and exposed to ammonia gas for not less than 48 hours nor more than 72 hours. Quenching is not necessary. This is why cracking and distortion of steel parts hardened by this process is nonexistent.

One of the properties of nitralloy of interest to gunsmiths is that it is supposed to resist corrosion caused by exposure to fresh or salt water, the atmosphere, or perspiration. However, even the most ardent boosters of this new steel are hesitant about staking their reputations on its corrosion-resisting characteristic.

Previous heat-treating processes seriously affect the hardening of this steel, and they must be corrected where they would otherwise lead to brittleness, large grains, or nonuniform hardening. Gas welding is not successful because it burns away most of the aluminum and leaves material that will not nitride satisfactorily. There are several other disadvantages, but they are regarded by some experts as outweighing the unfavorable characteristics of this steel for certain purposes. Generally, nitralloy is not regarded as a steel ordinarily used or even considered by gunsmiths making or repairing small arms.

XXII. Drilling, Reaming, and Chambering the Barrel

STANDARD factory rifle barrels, completely finished in and outside, rifled, chambered, blued, threaded and polished, ready to be attached to the receiver, can be purchased from most factories in normal times, or from the larger dealers in gunsmith supplies, especially for Remington, Winchester, and Savage rifles. The purchaser, obviously, must specify the make, model, caliber, barrel length, barrel cross-sectional shape (round or octagon), and action, and sometimes he must give other details, or else he must deliver the rifle to the factory or dealers and let them attach the new barrel, if they are willing to do this work.

Rifle-Barrel Blanks.—Barrel blanks are usually stocked by a few of the larger dealers and supply houses. These blanks are machined carefully to obtain a perfect balance and rifled accurately. They are gauged about as precisely as are the barrels at the government arsenals, which are designated as "star gauge." However, these blanks are not finished, chambered, blued, threaded, or polished. These operations, plus head-spacing and fitting, are left to the gunsmith. Descriptions of such rifle-barrel blanks are given here as a guide to gunsmiths who may wish to consider the purchase of blanks, or make their own barrels.

Barrel blanks for calibers .25, .30, .32, .35, .25 Roberts, 7 mm., and .30-06, weigh about 4 pounds 7 ounces; they are 24 inches long; the shoulder length is .765 inch, the cylindrical length (distance between barrel shoulder and start of chamber) is 1.110 inches, the diameter at the muzzle is .700 inch, the diameter at barrel (just ahead of the sharp taper) is .895 inch, the diameter at the chamber is 1.125 inches, the diameter at the barrel shoulder is 1.125 inches, the diameter at the start of the chamber is the same as that at the barrel shoulder, and the length of the sharp taper is 2.500 inches.

Barrel blanks for calibers .30/30, .300 Savage, .303 Savage, and .30-06, are made of the best grade smokeless steel, and have the following dimensions: bore diameter, .300 inch; depth of rifling, .004 inch; 6 grooves; one turn in 12 inches; right-hand twist; weight about $5\frac{1}{2}$ pounds. They have a chamber diameter of $1\frac{1}{32}$ inches; shoulder length, $\frac{3}{4}$ inch; diameter at muzzle, $1\frac{1}{16}$ inches; total length, $24\frac{1}{4}$ inches. There is no sharp taper from the start of the chamber to the muzzle, as there is on the previously described barrel blank. The shoulder is rough turned and the barrel is given a hot rolled finish.

Barrel blanks for experimental purposes in caliber .32-20 are made of the best smokeless steel, the shoulder is rough turned, and the barrel has a hot rolled finish. The length is 31 inches, the shoulder length is $1\frac{1}{8}$ inches, the diameter at the chamber is 1 inch, the diameter at the muzzle is $1\frac{1}{32}$ inches, and there is no sharp taper. The bore diameter is .3045 inch; depth of rifling, .003 inch; 6 grooves; one turn in 20 inches; right-hand twist; weight about $6\frac{1}{2}$ pounds. For experimental purposes in caliber .25-20, the above dimensions remain the same except that the bore diameter is .250 inch; depth of rifling .003 inch; 6 grooves; one turn in 14 inches; right-hand twist; weight about $6\frac{1}{2}$ pounds.

Barrel blanks for experimental purposes in caliber .250-3000 are $22\frac{1}{4}$ inches long, with a rough turned shoulder and a hot rolled finish. The other dimensions are: shoulder length, $\frac{3}{4}$ inch; muzzle diameter, $1\frac{1}{16}$ inches; chamber diameter, $1\frac{1}{32}$ inches; bore diameter, .250 inch; depth of rifling, .0035 inch; 6 grooves; one turn in 14 inches; right-hand twist; weight about $5\frac{1}{4}$ pounds.

Barrel blanks for small-bore standard rifles using the .22 Long Rifle cartridge are usually made of low carbon barrel steel, with a rough turned shoulder, and a hot rolled finish on the barrel. The dimensions are: length, 31 inches; shoulder length, $1\frac{1}{8}$ inches; diameter at muzzle, $1\frac{1}{32}$ inches; diameter at chamber, 1 inch; bore diameter, .217 inch; depth of rifling, .0025 inch; 4 grooves;

one turn in 16 inches; right-hand twist; weight about 6½ pounds.

Barrel blanks for small-bore, super-accurate, match-grade rifles, especially for single-shot rifles with Ballard, Luna, Martini, and similar actions, are usually made up only on special order and cannot be delivered by dealers for at least a month from the time the order is received. (As we have indicated already, these dimensions are given as a guide to barrel design, as well as for the purposes of selecting blanks.) The dimensions of such top-grade small-bore barrels are: length, 30 inches; shoulder length, .765 inch; diameter at rifling, 1 inch; diameter at muzzle, ¾ inch; diameter at chamber, ⅞ inch. The cost of super-quality small-bore blanks is usually about twice that of standard quality blanks.

Barrel blanks for Winchester rifles to handle calibers .22 Long Rifle, .22 Hornet, and .22-3000 Lovell cartridges have the following dimensions: diameter at breech, 1.16 inches; cylindrical length 3 inches with a straight taper from there to the muzzle of .01 inch per inch of length; finish ground; total length, 28⅜ inches; muzzle diameter, .906 inch; finished bore, .217 inch (minus tolerance, .001 inch); rifled, .222 inch; 6 grooves.

Barrel blanks for Winchester rifles to handle calibers .220 Swift, .257 Roberts, .270 Winchester, 250-3000 Savage, .30-06, and 7 mm., are obtainable in the following dimensions: total length, 30 inches; diameter at breech, 1.25 inches; cylindrical length, 3 inches; straight taper .014 inch per inch of length from termination of cylindrical length to the muzzle; finish ground; diameter at muzzle, .875 inch.

Barrel Length.—The barrel must be long enough to permit the complete combustion of the powder in the discharged cartridge, to give the bullet a sufficient spin and to provide sufficient distance between the front and rear sights for accurate aiming. High-power hunting rifles average between 24 inches and 28 inches long, when accuracy is desired. The barrel length should never be less than 22 inches for caliber .375, 20 inches for caliber .30, and 18 inches for caliber .25. These are minimum lengths, excusable when barrels are shortened for use on horseback or at close quarters, but it must be remembered that reduction in barrel length below that needed for the complete consumption of the powder on discharge causes increased recoil, increased flash, increased report, decreased range, and decreased accuracy. At the other extreme, high-power rifles intended for match firing may be made between 28 and 30 inches long because of the increased sight radius and the greater ease in holding and swinging at the offhand position.

A .22 caliber barrel can be as short as 10 inches and still give fairly accurate results in a machine-rest; an experienced marksman can obtain reasonably good scores with a barrel as short as 18 inches, but to obtain maximum velocity the barrel should be between 18 and 22 inches long, and it may be desirable to make the barrel 28 or 30 inches long to obtain balance, improve its swinging qualities at the offhand position, and to better the appearance. The addition of barrel length increases the weight, which is desirable in rifles of this caliber.

Other Dimensions and Weight.—The barrel must be heavy enough to hold steady, avoid the effect of body tremors on aim, and impart a stiffness to the weapon that eliminates vibrations as much as possible, since the "whipping" of a lightweight barrel reduces accuracy. Weight, in itself, does not necessarily mean strength, but the high pressures of modern cartridges have increased the need for thickness which in turn means more weight.

Increased weight brings less shock from recoil. This is explained by Newton's third law of motion which is: to every action there is an equal and opposite reaction. On firing, the weight of the gun multiplied by the velocity of recoil will equal the weight of the projectile times its velocity. By increasing the weight of the barrel, and hence the weight of the gun, the shooter receives less discomfort. This is unimportant in the case of small-bore rifles, but it is a major item in the design of high-calibre rifles.

At the other extreme, too much weight means that the rifle cannot be swung into the aiming position quickly, and it also tires the hunter or marksman who carries it for a considerable period of time. Therefore, modern rifles are made heavy at the breech, where the powder pressure is the greatest, and the balance is thus located a short distance forward of the trigger.

In describing rifle-barrel blanks, we spoke of the shoulder length, which is the distance from the rear end of the blank to the shoulder, along the main horizontal axis of the barrel. From the shoulder forward to the point where the taper begins, there is the largest diameter of the barrel, and the horizontal distance along the main axis of the barrel is known as the cylindrical length. Then, there may be one long straight taper to the muzzle; or there may be two tapers, the first being a sharp one, and the second a long straight taper to the muzzle. Sometimes there are three tapers, but this is an unusual feature. A target rifle may have no taper, or it may have one straight taper, resulting in greater barrel thickness, and hence increased weight, whereas the use of two or three tapers results in a decrease in thickness and a decrease in weight.

Turning Down the Barrel.—After a barrel is bored, but before it is reamed and rifled, it should be turned down to the desired size and shape on the lathe, being careful not to reduce its diameters so much that it vibrates greatly when fired. Plugs are made of hardened steel for the chamber and muzzle ends of the barrel; these are pushed into the barrel tightly, but without hammering. The outer ends of the plugs are drilled in their centers, countersunk, and fitted in the lathe. Excess metal is removed with the turning tool; a rough finish is given with a mill file moved back and forth along the revolving barrel; a fine file is used in a like manner for a further finish; and then emery cloth and crocus cloth may be used in turn for a final, mirror-like finish. Be careful that the barrel does not become very warm from friction, or expansion will take place. A slight rise in temperature is unavoidable and the danger of the barrel being sprung from expansion is taken care of by loosening the dead center of the lathe.

Barrel Drilling.—When the rough steel has been turned to the exterior shape of the barrel, a hole is drilled along the long axle. This can be done on a regular factory barrel-drilling machine; on a lathe; with a pull-through contrivance, like that explained in the chapter on rifling the barrel; or entirely by hand, although the latter method is primitive and extremely crude unless performed by a person who has ruined many pieces of steel in acquiring experience.

A barrel drill is made of high speed steel, usually about 2 inches long, with a single cutting edge and a single V-shaped groove extending straight back from the point. On the side opposite from the V-groove, a small hole runs the length of the drill to carry oil from the oil tube to which the drill is brazed. At the drill point, the included angle is the same as that of an ordinary twist drill, but the V-groove has an included angle of about 90 degrees, and is cut almost to the center of the drill. The diameter of the drill is reduced at its rear for a little more than ¼ inch of its length to permit brazing on the oil tube, which also functions as a driving tube.

The oil and drive tube is made of high carbon steel, slightly smaller in diameter than the drill, and longer than the barrel. On one side a V-shaped groove is pressed into the tube to provide a passage out of the rifle bore for oil and the steel chips cut away by the drill. Oil, such as lard oil or black sulphur oil compound, but not machine oil, is pumped under pressure through a flexible hose into the tube from its rear end; it passes through the hole provided for this purpose in the drill; lubricates the point of the drill; and flows back through the V-shaped groove pressed into its side, carrying with it the chips. The barrel revolves rapidly on the lathe (where a lathe is used) but the drill is fed into the steel slowly, since there is only one cutting edge and the hole through the barrel must be made gradually.

Reaming the barrel.—Having drilled a rough hole through the solid steel to form a barrel, this hole must be reamed to size before the rifling is cut. Three reamers are used: first, a roughing reamer, which may have either 4 or 6 grooves; second, a finishing reamer, which has 6 grooves; and third, a burnishing reamer, sometimes called a final finishing reamer, which also has 6 grooves. The roughing reamer removes from .005 inch to .006 inch from the hole through the barrel cut by the drill; the finishing reamer takes out from .003 inch to .004 inch more; and the burnishing reamer cuts the hole to a diameter equal to the distance between the lands after the grooves are cut in the rifling process. In practice, the whole process is sometimes accomplished with a single reamer by careful gunsmiths who wish to save time.

Barrel reamers are drawn through the barrel by an oil tube attached to the lathe carriage while the barrel blank revolves slowly. This combined draw and oil tube is brazed· to the front of the reamer, where there is also located a pilot, which is a raised portion of the reamer slightly smaller in diameter than the bore of the barrel. From the oil tube, oil flows through a hole in the pilot and out through tiny holes around the circumference of the tool, just in front of the cutting edges of the flutes. Steel chips are thrown to the rear by the flutes of the reamer as they eat their way through the barrel; no return device is needed on a barrel reamer like the one on the barrel drill.

Chambering Reamers.—Chamber reamers are also made for roughing, finishing, and burnishing, but most gun-supply houses sell only what they call first cut and finishing rifle chamber reamers. These are ready-made for the following cartridges: .219 Zipper, .220 Swift, .256 Newton, .25-20 Winchester, .25-35 Winchester, .257 Roberts, .270 Winchester, .280 Dubiel, 6.5 x 53 Mannlicher, 6.5 x 58 Mauser, 7 x 57 Mauser, 7 x 64 Magnum, .300 Magnum, .30 Newton, .30-30 Winchester, .300 Savage, .30-06 U.S., .30-40 Krag, .303 Savage, .32-20 Winchester, 8 x 57 Mauser, 8 x 60 Magnum, 8.15 x 46 Target, .33 Winchester, .35 Winchester, .35 Remington, .35 Newton, .375 Magnum, and .38-55 Winchester.

There is also a .22 caliber chamber reamer available as a combination first cut and finishing reamer, which cuts not only the chamber but the recess for the rim as well. This is made with either a long or a short shank, and for the .22 short, .22 long, .22 long rifle, and .22 extra long cartridges. In addition, there is a special extra long shank reamer for use in Mauser type actions without removing the receiver from the barrel, available in all regular-make rifle calibers.

The process of chambering consists of reaming out the breech of the barrel with chambering reamers to form the hole or chamber into which the cartridge fits. Just before the final reaming is done, the barrel is threaded to fit the receiver, and then the finishing reamer is used to make the size and shape of the chamber correspond with the head space, as well as with the face of the bolt or the breech block of the rifle.

The chamber reamers have pilots for the purpose of riding the tops of the lands and keeping the flutes of the reamer cutting where they belong instead of gouging the rifling; also, there are stop guides at the rear of the reamers to indicate when each one has been driven far enough into the chamber, so that it will not make the chamber too long.

Chamber reamers, like barrel reamers and barrel drills, are driven by hand or in a lathe. For some strange reason, most men think that lathes are beyond their means, and yet excellent lathes can be purchased in normal times for about fifty dollars new, and for less than one-half that amount in secondhand condition. When it is remembered that many sportsmen think nothing of spending one hundred dollars on dolling up a rifle, it is easy to see that a lathe will soon pay for itself if a gunsmith wants to solicit some work from his friends.

The homemade "pull-through" described in the chapter on rifling is a good substitute for a lathe, but blacksmiths in remote villages of China, India, and North Africa turn out rifles drilled and chambered with tools that look like long corkscrews turned with a hand windlass.

MOST GUNSMITHS BUY BARRELS READY-MADE

Most gunsmiths, both professional and amateur, buy barrels for all types, makes, and models of firearms from a firearms factory, a distributor, or a man who specializes in producing custom-made barrels; hence most readers of this book will never make a barrel. Furthermore, all barrel makers do not necessarily follow the procedures in this chapter. All good gunsmiths, and certainly all good manufacturers of barrels, are individualists who pride themselves on developing their own processes and procedures. Nevertheless, a knowledge of drilling, reaming, and chambering a barrel is an essential part of the mental equipment of a good gunsmith, or even of a person who will never do any gunsmithing work but wants a fundamental understanding of firearms.

XXIII. Rifling

RIFLING is the system of spiral grooves cut into the bore of rifles, pistols, and revolvers, for the purpose of giving a spin to the bullet that will insure its steady flight, point forward, to the target. Between the grooves are "lands," which are the raised surfaces of the bore that remain after the grooves are cut. These lands dig into the bullet as it passes through the barrel and rotate it about its longer axis.

The number of grooves which constitute the rifling may vary in number from 2 to 8. They are cut into the bore to depths varying from .002 inch to .006 inch, depending upon the caliber, the relative widths of the lands and grooves, and other factors. The direction in which the rifling twists may be either left or right. American arms, in general, have rifling that twists to the right, as viewed from the breech, except that Colt pistols and revolvers twist to the left, as shown in "C" of Plate 27.

The amount that the rifling advances for each complete turn is called the pitch, that is, a rifle may have one complete turn in each 10 inches of barrel length, for example, or a revolver may have one turn in 20 inches. The pitch varies from as little as one complete turn in 6½ inches to one turn in 60 inches. Bullets long in proportion to their diameter usually require a faster pitch than those which are short in proportion to their diameter, since this increased pitch causes a greater spin and hence improves accuracy.

The lower part of "B," Plate 27, shows cross-sectional views of two barrels. The one on the left has 5 lands and 5 grooves. The one on the right has 6 lands and 6 grooves. The arrow in each picture indicates that the caliber is usually designated by the bore size before the grooves are cut. Rifles, pistols, and revolvers vary in caliber from .218 to .50 inch. Theoretically, a caliber designates the diameter of the bore between the lands in hundredths of an inch, but practically, manufacturers are not always careful about this measurement. Thus, .38 Smith & Wesson Special is actually .357 caliber.

Cartridges are designated according to various systems. Many years ago, center-fire cartridges of .45 caliber, having a 70-grain powder charge and a bullet weighing 500 grains, were described as 45-70-500. Gradually the use of three hyphenated numbers was dropped and only two were given; thus, the caliber .32 cartridge having a 40-grain powder charge was called a 32-40.

Later the name of the maker or inventor was included. Thus we have the .30 Newton, the .22 W.R.F. (Winchester Rim-Fire), and others where only the caliber and the name were given. A variation from this idea is the practice of designating United States Government cartridges. For example, the .30 caliber cartridge for the United States Rifle, Caliber .30, Model of 1903, is called a ".30-06 Govt.," because an improved bullet design was adopted in 1906. Designations in thousandths instead of hundredths of an inch are also found, such as the .405 Winchester, the .303 Savage, etc. A variation of the latter method is to give the muzzle velocity after the caliber, such as the .250-3000 Savage. Recently we have seen the introduction of advertising words after the caliber, such as the .220 Winchester Swift, and the .22 Savage High Power.

Another designation is the "Mark" method. After the First World War, the United States Government adopted a boat-tailed bullet; cartridges loaded with this projectile became known as the .30 M-1. The letter "M" stands for "Mark," or possibly for "Modification," although the British and the United States Navy have always referred to it as "Mark" in designating successive modifications of arms and ammunition, as "Mark 1," "Mark 2," etc.

A word of warning at this point is worth while to gunsmiths. Calling the U. S. Rifle a ".30-30" is a gross display of ignorance. If it were a ".30-30" it would use a cartridge with a .30 caliber bullet, true enough, but it would be loaded with 30 grains of black

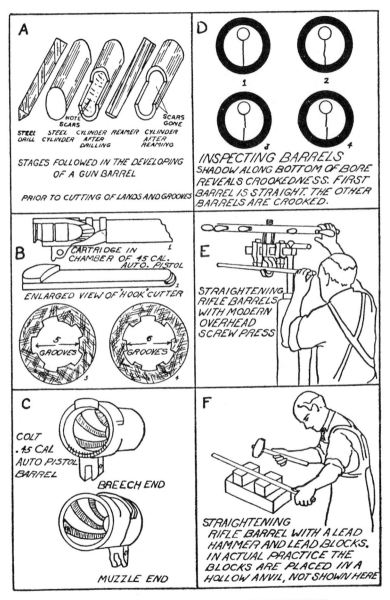

A STEEL DRILL · STEEL CYLINDER · CYLINDER AFTER DRILLING · REAMER · CYLINDER AFTER REAMING

NOTE SCARS

SCARS GONE

STAGES FOLLOWED IN THE DEVELOPING OF A GUN BARREL

PRIOR TO CUTTING OF LANDS AND GROOVES

D INSPECTING BARRELS
SHADOW ALONG BOTTOM OF BORE REVEALS CROOKEDNESS. FIRST BARREL IS STRAIGHT. THE OTHER BARRELS ARE CROOKED.

B CARTRIDGE IN CHAMBER OF 45 CAL. AUTO. PISTOL

ENLARGED VIEW OF 'HOOK' CUTTER

5 GROOVES

6 GROOVES

E STRAIGHTENING RIFLE BARRELS WITH MODERN OVERHEAD SCREW PRESS

C COLT .45 CAL AUTO PISTOL BARREL

BREECH END

MUZZLE END

F STRAIGHTENING RIFLE BARREL WITH A LEAD HAMMER AND LEAD BLOCKS. IN ACTUAL PRACTICE THE BLOCKS ARE PLACED IN A HOLLOW ANVIL, NOT SHOWN HERE

PLATE 27. BARREL MAKING AND STRAIGHTENING.

powder, which is a load that is as out of date as the muskets carried up San Juan Hill in the Spanish-American War.

Having discussed some of the technical terms associated with rifling, we can now examine the actual process. The upper left-hand section of Plate 27, marked "A," shows a steel drill, a solid steel cylinder before being drilled, a cylinder with a rough hole drilled through its long axis, a reamer, and the same cylinder after the reamer has enlarged the hole to the true bore size and removed the scars left by the drill.

The grooves are cut by either of two tools, the scrape cutter or the hook cutter. Scrape cutters work in pairs, one on each side of a rifling rod, cutting two sets of grooves at a time, each on an opposite side of the barrel from the other. At the end of each stroke, the rifling rod is turned through an arc of a circle the required number of degrees (depending upon how many grooves are to be cut), and another pair of grooves is cut. Each of these strokes is quite shallow; it sometimes requires as many as one hundred strokes to cut the grooves deep enough, hence the scrape cutters go around and around the bore, over and over again in the same grooves.

The scrape cutter is used for an even number of grooves, such as 4, 6, or 8, but where an odd number of grooves is to be cut a hook cutter (illustrated in section "B," Plate 27) is employed. This will cut 5 or 7 grooves, and it can be used for cutting an even number of grooves, since it cuts only one groove at a time, and not a pair of grooves, as does the scrape cutter. The hook cutter does the job faster but not so well as the scrape cutter.

The small drawing in the upper part of "B," Plate 27, shows that the cartridge in the Colt .45 Caliber Automatic Pistol is seated in the bore of the barrel, with the bullet bearing against the rifling, just as the bullet does in a rifle. This is contrasted with the way a revolver is loaded, since the cartridge in the latter is loaded in a cylinder chamber and hence the bullet gains velocity before it is given any rotation by the rifling.

The upper right-hand corner of Plate 27, marked "D," shows how rifled barrels look to an inspector, when viewed from the breech, pointed toward a window having a vertical line on its surface. The shadow along the bottom of the bore reveals any crookedness. The one near the letter "D" is straight; the other three are crooked.

The right middle section of Plate 27, marked "E," shows the comparatively modern overhead screw press used to straighten a barrel. The inspector sights through the barrel on a vertical line, as explained before. Wherever there is any break, curve, bend or bead to the shadow along the bottom of the bore, a curve exists that must be straightened. The barrel is slowly rotated so that all of the bore is examined carefully. Adjusting the barrel with one hand, the operator uses the other to exert pressure with the overhead screw press, bending the barrel in the opposite direction from the curve he finds, but just enough so that when pressure is released the barrel will spring back to a straight line. Too much pressure will merely curve the barrel opposite from the first defect; too little will not permanently remove the fault.

The lower right-hand section of Plate 27, marked "F," shows a gunsmith straightening a barrel with a lead hammer and lead blocks. In actual practice the lead blocks are placed in a hollow anvil, or in a vise. The veteran gunsmiths sometimes claim that this old-fashioned method is far better than the use of the overhead screw press because the blows from the hammer break some of the steel fibers in the barrel and lessen the tendency to spring back into its former crooked condition. They argue that the real danger does not lie in the barrel springing back immediately after it is straightened so much as it does in the springing back that occurs when the barrel becomes hot from prolonged firing on the rifle range or in the field.

This argument is countered by those who logically point out that the gunsmith cannot look through the barrel and at the same time strike it with the hammer, that he must guess at what he is doing. They compromise by admitting that if the barrel is sighted on a horizontal line painted on a window and the blows are struck one at a time, with inspections of the bore after each blow, it is possible for a man to straighten barrels by this method after acquiring some experience. Only a few experts can straighten barrels.

Plate 28 shows the rifling of a barrel by a method that is adapted to the equipment of anyone who has a lathe and a few simple tools. This procedure was actually followed by Mr. William Fadda, while he was Machine Shop Instructor, Polytechnic College of Engineering, Oakland, California. He manufactured rifle, pistol, and revolver

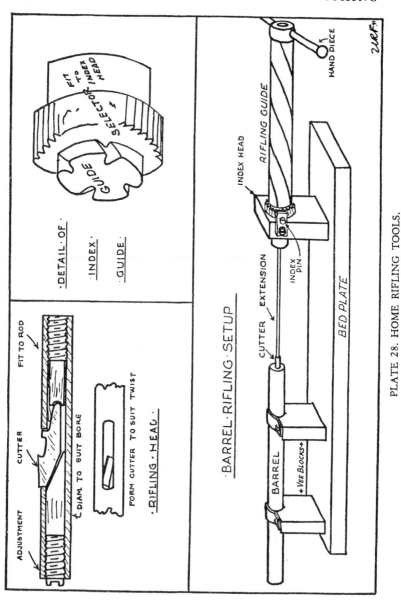

PLATE 28. HOME RIFLING TOOLS.

barrels that were tested by the author of this text and found to be the equal of any of American or English manufacture, and superior to many of those barrels made on the Continent of Europe.

The Rifling Head is shown in the upper left-hand corner of Plate 28. The design is a basic one that can be varied to meet any particular set of specifications. The head is made from a steel tube of a suitable diameter to fit the bore, about 4 inches long (long enough to guide well without tipping), and about .04 inch thick. One end is threaded to fit the extension rod which carries the rifling head through the barrel. The other end is threaded for a screw adjustment to raise the cutter for successive cuts. This is accomplished by a tapered wedge acting on the tapered base of the cutter, as shown in the lower part of the upper left-hand picture.

The cutter itself is of a conventional design, being hook-shaped and having plenty of clearance to gather the chips. The forward shoulder of the recess in the upper edge of the cutter should be rounded to prevent chips from piling up and scoring the barrel. The cutter is given a suitable twist to conform with the pitch of the rifling. The cutter should be made of high speed steel so that it will stand up under repeated use without requiring resharpening. The average professional gunsmith with a metal lathe can make this rifling head in about 4 hours; an amateur may require from 6 to 8 hours, depending upon his ability.

The Index Guide, shown in the upper right-hand corner of Plate 28, can be made from an ordinary steel gear, such as those sold in auto-supply houses, or it can be taken from some junked piece of machinery, such as a lathe or an automobile. The outside diameter of the gear should be about 3 inches, and it should have a number of teeth equally divisible by the number of lands and grooves. For example, if there are to be 4 lands and grooves, then the gear should have exactly 16, 20, 24, 28 (or some other exact multiple of 4), or 32 teeth.

The rifling guide is machined with a twist equal to the pitch desired for the barrel. The pins fit into the helical grooves cut into the guide. Pins are made of tool steel. They are cut out of stock and fitted to grooves. The gear is mounted on a sleeve in which the pins are inserted. The unit, consisting of sleeve and rifling guide, is mounted in a rest, preferably a steel block. On the block there is mounted an index pin which determines the number of lands and grooves on the bore of the barrel. This is accomplished by removing the pin, turning the index guide the required number of teeth for the number of lands desired. The rifling guide proper is fitted with a ball-bearing handle (labeled "hand piece" in the illustration). This enables the operator to move the rifling guide back and forth smoothly, without friction, thus assuring a smooth and accurate cut.

The extension rod with the rifling head on one end is fitted to the rifling guide. The extension rod is just long enough to pass through the barrel, thus avoiding any "whipping" effect. The barrel is mounted on Vee blocks, clamped rigidly to prevent vibration. The Vee blocks and also the index head are mounted on a substantial wooden plank or metal plate, called a "bed plate."

A metal lathe with a bed 6 feet long is necessary for the best work. The barrel can be held in the chuck of the lathe, and the index head can be mounted on the bed of the lathe, similar to the mounting of a "steady rest" with which most lathe operators are familiar. In this way, special apparatus, such as the Vee blocks and clamps, bed plate, and the block for holding the index head can be eliminated.

After a steel bar of the proper length and thickness has been drilled and reamed, it is put into the barrel rifling setup illustrated. The gunsmith pulls the rifling guide; this, in turn, pulls the cutter through the bore and cuts one groove, but the depth of the cut should be about .0005 inch, slightly more or less. There is not enough clearance to cut a groove to the full depth and do it accurately in one operation, for the chips of metal accumulate and interfere with the movement of the cutter.

Some gunsmiths try to keep on cutting shallow paths until one groove is finished and then go on to the next groove, but the better practice is to take a shallow cut on one groove, go to the next groove, and so on, around and around until all of the grooves have been completed. In this manner, grooves are cut more evenly and smoothly, and there is less chance for some grooves to be deeper than others.

Hand Rifling, Using Another Barrel As a Guide.—An easy rifling guide to use is another barrel of the same twist as the one you wish to cut. It need not have the same number of grooves, although this is preferable. Mount the barrel blank that is to be rifled on the left of the workbench, using two clamps bolted to the bench, with the muzzle of the barrel blank to the left. A few inches to the right of the rear end of the barrel blank is the spot where the muzzle of the guide barrel will be located; about 4 inches to the right of this spot support the front part of the guide barrel, being sure that the guide barrel has its longitudinal center line in line with what will be the corresponding center line of the future barrel. Then mount a fourth clamp near the right end of the guide barrel.

The fourth clamp not only holds the guide barrel in place at the right end, but it also tightly holds a flanged sleeve which is itself clamped to the guide barrel. (This sleeve flange prevents the guide barrel from moving longitudinally.) A number of holes corresponding to the number of grooves to be cut in the new rifle are drilled around the circumference of the sleeve in a straight line.

At a point in line with one of the sleeve holes, a pin is driven through the fourth clamp. When the guide barrel is loosened by releasing the tension of the clamps, the guide barrel and the sleeve are turned together to bring one of the holes in the sleeve in line with the pin hole through the fourth clamp.

A rod several inches longer than the distance between the breech of the guide barrel and the muzzle of the new barrel blank is attached to the rifling head, and also to a guide block which follows the grooves in the guide barrel.

This guide block is made as follows: Stuff a ball of cotton waste down the bore of the guide barrel until it is about 6 inches below the muzzle when the guide barrel is held vertical, muzzle uppermost. Insert the rod mentioned above until what will later be its right end rests on the cotton waste. Hold the rod in the center of the bore, direct a torch or the flame from a bunsen burner against the upper walls of the barrel, melt nickel-babbitt, and pour the molten metal into the muzzle until it fills the space in the barrel above the cotton waste. When the nickel-babbitt has cooled, withdraw it from the guide barrel and trim off any excess metal. Remove the cotton waste, clean the barrel, and put the guide rod and the guide block back in the bore. Place little marks with a punch on both the guide block and the guide barrel at a point where one of the grooves in the guide barrel reaches the muzzle.

A wooden or steel handle is now mounted at right angles to the rod, at the right end of the guide barrel. Clamps are tightened, and the rifling cutter is in place. Force the rifling cutter through the new barrel blank, thus making the first rifling cut.

To make the second cut, proceed as follows: Drop the cutter down. (If it is a shimmed up hook-type cutter, take it off the rifling head and push the head back through the bore.) Replace the cutter. Loosen the clamps on the guide barrel. Withdraw the index pin, revolve the guide barrel in the clamps until the next pin hole is reached, replace the pin, tighten the clamps, and for the second time force the cutter through the bore. Repeat the process until one cut has been made for each grove.

Raise the cutter, make a second cut in the first groove, and continue until all grooves are cut to the required depth. The barrel being rifled is kept supplied with liberal quantities of lard oil or black sulphur oil compound where the latter is obtainable. These cutting oils are fed into the new barrel under pressure through a tube, like a little garden hose.

For this reason it seems better to use a tube for the cutting rod, with oil pumped into the tube at one end and coming out the other through perforations in the rifling head. The oil is forced through the tube with an ordinary automobile oil pump driven by an electric motor. Another method is to force the oil into and through the new barrel with air pressure, using a compressor. Oil flows out of the barrel and through a screen which retains metal chips, dirt, etc.; finally it is returned to the source from which it was pumped.

When a hook cutter is used, the chips resemble the shavings removed from wood by a plane if all is going well, but if the chips are broken or come off in the form of short wires, the cutter must be removed and its face ground to a sharp edge. On the other hand, a scrape cutter usually gives little trouble, although it, too, must be kept well stoned. Keep a continuous flow of cutting oil during the rifling process. When the cutter comes out of the new barrel after each run, remove all chips with an old toothbrush before it starts through again.

LAPPING

Lapping is the process of polishing the bore of a firearm with a lead plug coated with abrasives. It may be applied either to a newly rifled barrel, to remove the fine wire burrs raised by the rifling cutter, or to an old weapon which has a rough, pitted bore. It works well with rifles, revolvers, pistols and shotguns.

Select a steel rod having a diameter less than that of the bore. A steel cleaning rod with a jag tip or a slotted tip will do. A few inches from the tip of the rod, wrap it with string. Place the rod in the bore, with the tip of the rod a fraction of an inch below the muzzle. Place the barrel, with the rod in it, in a vise, muzzle up. Heat the barrel with a blow torch and pour melted lead into the bore at the muzzle to form a solid slug around the tip of the rod. When the lead cools and hardens, push the slug part way out of the muzzle, remove the string, and cut off any lead that has overflowed around the muzzle. Then, oil the slug and pull the rod from the breech until the bottom part of the slug can be inspected and freed from any string that could not be removed before. Be sure that you do not actually remove the slug from the bore at any time before lapping is completed.

Leaving the rod in the barrel, place the barrel horizontally in the vise. Now work the slug back and forth through the barrel, not forgetting that it must never completely leave the bore during the process. At each end of a stroke, apply a light machine oil and a coat of valve-grinding compound. Continue to stroke back and forth until you believe that the bore is sufficiently smooth. Remove the plug, wipe out and inspect the bore, and, if necessary, cast a new slug and repeat the treatment.

In lapping pistol and revolver barrels, an ordinary straight handle is sufficient for the rod, but a rod for lapping rifle or shotgun barrels should have a hardwood cross-bar handle bolted on a ballbearing bicycle pedal which, in turn, is welded to the lapping rod, thus making it possible to rotate the rod easily in the bore. A rotating handle will do no harm on a lapping bar for handguns, but it requires so little strength to lap them that it hardly seems worth while to use anything but a simple handle.

Gunsmiths do not agree that lapping should be attempted by beginners. The equipment and process are easy but therein lies the danger. An amateur may enjoy lapping a barrel so much that he overdoes it and wears down the rifling. Furthermore, a skilled gunsmith who has had long experience in lapping barrels can tell by the "feel" of the lapping rod if the job is done, while a tyro must remove the rod, wipe out the bore, inspect it, and decide whether or not he must repeat the operation.

Lapping is the final polishing process for the bore in the opinions of many experts, while others insist that it be followed with the use of emery, crocus cloth, and rouge. In any event, at the completion of any bore-polishing operation, the bore must be cleaned with hot water and soap, as described elsewhere in this text, and then thoroughly dried and oiled.

ULTRAMODERN METHODS OF RIFLING

Most readers of this book may never rifle a barrel. Those who do may prefer to use ultramodern equipment and methods, if they are comparatively wealthy; but the instructions in this and other chapters on barrels are for the man of limited means and they are so simple that if you were on a desert island, with a few simple tools and a limited access to iron or steel, you could make a firearm.

XXIV. Striking and Polishing Barrels and Parts

STRIKING and polishing are operations performed upon barrels and parts for the purpose of removing exterior defects such as scratches, scars, and tool marks before bluing or heat-treating. Striking is practically the same as draw-filing, which was explained in the chapter on general gunsmith tools and equipment and illustrated in Figure 4 of Plate 9. The reader is urged to refer back to the rather detailed discussion of files in that chapter before proceeding further. Polishing includes the use of both abrasives and soft buffing wheels.

A striking file for most barrel work should be flat, at least 1 inch wide and about 10 inches long, and have a fine cut. A striking file for working around parts attached to a barrel may be shorter and it may have a convex surface where it is necessary to work a concave surface on a gun part. Special striking files are stocked by the larger dealers in supplies for gunsmiths, but the ordinary pillar files obtainable through any hardware dealer are entirely satisfactory.

Striking in the strict sense of the term is a hand operation. Factories use a lathe-like grinding machine that gives a barrel its required taper and at the same time leaves a very bright, smooth surface, but the machine leaves a fine grain around the circumference of the barrel for its entire length. This grain may or may not be removed by striking; when it is removed, the work is customarily done by a special section of mechanics who are experts with the file.

A beginner who does not expect to strike many barrels or parts may dispense with the use of a handle, but a professional may find it advisable to fit handles at both ends of a striking file so that he can have a firmer and steadier grip on the tool and at the same time avoid wear on his hands, since the file is properly grasped at both ends and worked back and forth at right angles to the barrel or part being "struck."

The barrel or part is held between soft jaws (lead, felt, etc.) in the vise. Chalk is frequently rubbed over the cutting surface of the file to prevent the filings from filling the recesses between the file teeth. A file card or brush is used to clean the file every few strokes, and another coating of chalk is applied after each cleaning.

Barrel-striking should be done with firm, even strokes for the whole length of the barrel, taking one stroke forward and the next one backward. It is not sufficient merely to scratch the barrel; neither should you exert so much pressure that you spring the barrel in any spot. Instead, the steel of the barrel should come off in fine wires, some being short and straight, while others are long and curly, but all of them very fine. At the rear end of the barrel near the chamber the surface is rounded and requires the use of a convex striking file if you are to avoid cutting down the radius of the barrel.

If you have performed the striking operation correctly, there should be no flat surfaces, but even professional gunsmiths find that they have taken cuts that are too deep, resulting in flat surfaces here and there on the barrel. These must be removed by polishing.

The first step in polishing is to take a strip of either emery cloth or carborundum cloth about 1 inch wide and 1 foot long and rub it briskly from one end of the barrel to the other, at right angles to the bore, holding one end of the cloth strip in each hand, just as though you were shining a shoe. Polish once with abrasive cloth numbered 1/0, then with 2/0, and finally with 3/0, but if you have only one grit size, it will be sufficient for quite satisfactory work. This step is called "cross-polishing."

The next step is draw-polishing, or draw-finishing, as it is sometimes called. Make a wooden holder for emery cloth by cutting semicircular troughs at right angles to the long dimension of a hardwood block about 1 foot long. The radius of each of these troughs or grooves should be such that you can select a size that fits the part of the barrel which is being polished, using a small size for the forward end of the barrel, a larger size for the middle portion, and a still larger size for the rear. Line each trough with leather glued to the wood, and then fasten abrasive cloth to the leather with rubber cement. Be sure that the radius of each trough is such that it will still be big enough to fit the barrel after the leather lining and the abrasive cloth have been added. Abrasive cloth having a grit size of 1/o is satisfactory, although some gunsmiths start with that size and then finish with an abrasive cloth numbered oo. Where two sizes are used, you can have either extra troughs cut in the wooden holder, or have two holders, one for each size of abrasive cloth.

The finish should now be smooth but fairly dull in color. If you desire a bright finish, especially when an excellent job of bluing is to follow, further polishing is necessary. This can be done by rubbing the barrel with a felt pad dipped into a mixture composed of equal parts powdered rouge and optical emery with just enough light oil added to form a paste. If you are very particular, follow with another job of draw-polishing, and then apply the emery powder and rouge paste again.

The use of any oil in polishing or buffing fills the pores of the metal to such an extent that the bluing process will be unsuccessful unless the oil has been previously removed. The removal of grease and oil is explained in the chapter on bluing; it is mentioned here because it is of the utmost importance.

When a Springfield rifle is converted from its original military condition into a sporter, the removal of the fore-end, hand guard and rear sight base will leave the barrel bare for most of its length and it will be found to have a rough finish. If you have a lathe, it is comparatively easy to grind the barrel smooth, turning it to a satisfactory taper and giving it a correct radius at the rear, but if you do not have a lathe, the barrel must be worked down by hand.

The striking file for this purpose should be a vixen file at least an inch wide. The correct length is a matter of argument among gunsmiths. Some use a vixen file 10 or 12 inches long, while others claim that a full length file may leave a wavy surface and insist upon breaking the file into pieces 2 or 3 inches long which are held in the palm of the hand during the striking process. Since the teeth of the vixen file are large and deep individual teeth cut on a curve, the metal is removed from the barrel easily and rapidly.

Since a vixen file cuts deeper than the regular striking file, flat surfaces are usually left and they must be removed.

This is accomplished by striking the barrel with a mill file at least 1 inch wide and 1 foot long, crossing-polishing with an abrasive cloth as explained before, draw-polishing with an abrasive cloth, cross-polishing again, and finally striking and polishing the barrel as explained at the beginning of the chapter. A great deal of labor is required, but anyone who wants to change a Springfield from a military arm to a sporter must expect to pay the price.

When the sight base is removed from the Springfield barrel, the spline cut can be filled in by drilling a series of holes, inserting screws in the holes, hammering the screw heads flush, and then striking and polishing them at the same time that the rest of the barrel is "struck" and polished. This, however, is just another example of the amount of hand labor required in converting the Springfield to a sporter.

Personally, the author has never been convinced that anything was gained by materially altering the Springfield other than the creation of employment. Of course, the military sights are not well adapted to match-firing, and they are open to criticism by anyone who wishes to hunt big game at long ranges, but the substitution of improved sights does not require the removal of the fore-end and hand guard.

Parts attached to the barrel but easily removed, such as the sights, sight bases, bands, etc., may be removed and polished separately. Parts such as the Springfield fixed stud that are left on the barrel should be polished before the barrel is struck and polished, but in striking and polishing the barrel, approach such parts carefully with the file or the abrasive cloth to avoid damaging their edges. If a very fine job is desired, polish parts attached to the barrel so that the "grain" left in the final polishing process runs in the same direction as the long axis of the barrel.

Parts that are joined to the barrel by solder must be polished before the solder is applied and then polished again after soldering. Excess solder must be scraped off before the barrel is blued because solder cannot be blued and it will contrast sharply with the remaining surface.

Surfaces that are not straight can be struck with a wide file having a convex or concave cutting face, according to the shape of the surface being worked, or it is possible to use a narrower flat file if you proceed with extreme caution. Polishing can be done on such surfaces by wrapping the abrasive cloth around the same file used for striking, or, better yet, cut pieces of softwood to the desired shape and wrap them in the abrasive cloth. Try to copy the direction of the factory polishing, but if this is not apparent work in the direction of the factory milling cuts, smoothly following the shape of the part being polished. For example, in polishing the trigger guard, follow its curve; do not move the abrasive at right angles to the main fore-and-aft axis.

The hardness of the abrasive should be appropriate to the hardness of the metal being polished. Thus, a very fine emery cloth should be used on the brass trigger guards found on old guns, while a coarse abrasive is needed on a hardened receiver, such as a No. 1 carborundum cloth.

The shape of small parts must not be varied during the polishing process. One method of avoiding this danger is to hold the part being polished in a pin vise (Figure 9, Plate 5), a sight spanner (Figure 1, Plate 7), or a spring spanner (Figure 2, Plate 7). The pin vise or spanner is then inserted in the machinist's vise. If the part is held directly between the jaws of the regular vise it may be damaged, while if lead or felt is placed over the jaws of the machinist's vise the gun part may not be held firmly.

An alternate method is to stretch the abrasive cloth over some smooth surface and rub the gun part against the cloth instead of rubbing the cloth against the part. Still another method is to drill and tap a hole in a piece of soft steel or scrap brass and temporarily fasten the small part to the piece of scrap metal, which is, itself, held in the vise while the small gun part is being worked, or you can use the piece of scrap metal as a handle while the attached part is rubbed over the abrasive cloth.

Polishing rifle bolts is something of a problem to most beginners until they learn that the extractor and extractor collar should be removed before placing the bolt in the vise. Coarse carborundum cloth, such as No. 0 or No. ½, is needed. Wrap the cloth around a stick or around the index finger to reach out-of-the-way corners. Be sure that you do not remove any metal from the lugs, for then you may have trouble in extracting and ejecting fired cartridges, opening the bolt after firing, etc. If there is any question about the danger of removing metal from the bolt, be content to give it a good polish with jeweler's rouge and forget about abrasives.

Polishing labor can be greatly reduced by using a buffing wheel mounted on almost any of the usual power tools. The surface of the removable buffing wheel may be coated with an abrasive powder, or it may be covered with some soft material for the final phase of polishing, such as felt or muslin. When an abrasive wheel is not immediately available, roughen the surface of the wheel, paint it with glue, and sprinkle it with an appropriate abrasive powder before the glue dries; or roll the bolt on a surface covered with emery.

Elsewhere in this text it has been mentioned that shotgun barrels have thin walls which may be destroyed by too much compression in a vise. For striking and polishing, the barrel of a shotgun can be held firmly but safely in a wooden cradle or jig designed especially for this purpose. The interiors of shotguns, or any firearms for that matter, can be protected with appropriately carved wooden blocks, but it is unwise to place anything inside a barrel, since it may be very difficult to remove.

XXV. Barrel Removing and Changing

BARREL removing and changing is a simple operation when you know a few "tricks of the trade." First, the finish of the firearm must be protected. Second, enough leverage must be applied to remove a barrel that has been rusted in place. Third, a new or a repaired barrel must be properly adjusted in the frame or the receiver, as the case may be.

The finish is protected by means of either felt-faced (or leather-faced) wooden blocks; or with lead sheets bent to fit, as illustrated in Figure 1, Plate 29. These blocks or sheets are then inserted between the jaws of a vise that holds the gun, as shown in Figure 2, Plate 29. A variation of the same principle is the use of grooved wooden blocks to hold the barrel of a pistol or revolver, as represented in Figure 3. When it is not desirable to use an ordinary vise, a special contrivance, known as a barrel vise or clamp block, portrayed in Figure 6, may be employed. These objects have been mentioned elsewhere in this text, but they have many uses, not the least of which is barrel clamping.

Figure 4 shows an octagon barrel held in a vise while the receiver is unscrewed with a monkey wrench. The drawing does not reveal the means of protecting the finish, but this is done by wrapping the barrel with a lead sheet, or by wrapping it with felt. A similar protective covering may be chosen when a barrel is held in the barrel vice of Figure 6. Likewise, the surface of the gun where a monkey wrench is applied should be covered with some material that shields the finish.

A barrel that cannot be restored to firing condition can be handled much more roughly than one that is still good for thousands of rounds. One of the several varieties of pipe wrenches stocked by most hardware and plumbing supply houses, such as the Billings-type chain pipe wrench, marked "A" in Figure 5, Plate 29, will prove effective in removing a bad barrel.

When the rifling is intact but the finish must be restored, an ordinary pipe wrench having soft jaws, such as the one marked "B" in Figure 5, will remove the barrel without setting up internal stresses that would occur if a pipe wrench were chosen.

The wrench marked "C" in Figure 5 has a piece of tool steel brazed or welded to its upper jaw, with a 90-degree notch cut into the auxiliary jaw, but the angle of this jaw can be varied to fit any job, its purpose being to bear against the upper surface of the forward end of a receiver.

Sometimes it is found that felt or lead protects the finish but does not permit a strong grip on the gun while it is held in the vise or a wrench. When this occurs, emery cloth should be sprinkled with powdered resin on the cloth side and wrapped around the part that is to be held fast, being sure that the emery side is on the outside. Thus, a barrel held in a vise or clamp block may be protected with emery cloth, and also the receiver or frame may be covered with another piece of the same material.

If the handle of the monkey wrench is not long enough to provide the required leverage, remove the wooden handle and bolt, clamp or weld a steel rod, a piece of pipe, or even an old gun barrel to the steel handle of the wrench. This will make it possible to remove the barrel with a minimum of strength, unless the jaws of the monkey wrench slip. When this happens, something should be done to anchor the lower jaw of the monkey wrench after it has been fully tightened against the barrel. One method is to drill several small holes in the set-screw of the wrench and tighten it with a piece of drill rod of suitable diameter. Another way is to drill a hole in the lower, movable jaw of the wrench, and then drill several holes in the main shaft of the wrench, so placed that a steel rod ("pin") can be passed through both the jaw and the shaft. Of course, the "pin" must be strong enough to resist the tendency to shear off when the wrench is moved, but fortunately most barrels can be removed without resort to such drastic measures.

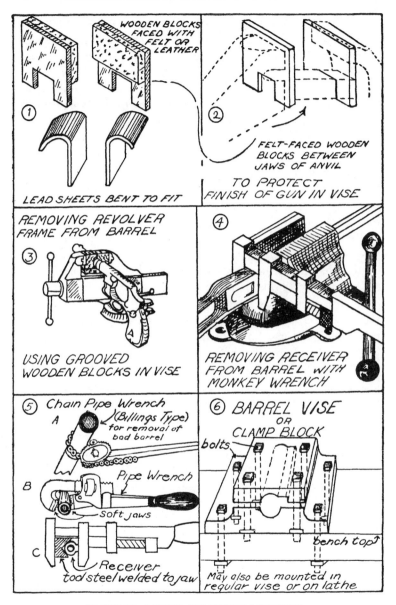

① WOODEN BLOCKS FACED WITH FELT OR LEATHER

LEAD SHEETS BENT TO FIT

② FELT-FACED WOODEN BLOCKS BETWEEN JAWS OF ANVIL

TO PROTECT FINISH OF GUN IN VISE

③ REMOVING REVOLVER FRAME FROM BARREL

USING GROOVED WOODEN BLOCKS IN VISE

④ REMOVING RECEIVER FROM BARREL WITH MONKEY WRENCH

⑤ Chain Pipe Wrench (Billings Type) for removal of bad barrel

A

Pipe Wrench

B

Soft jaws

C

Receiver tool steel welded to jaw

⑥ BARREL VISE OR CLAMP BLOCK

bolts

bench top

May also be mounted in regular vise or on lathe

PLATE 29. BARREL REMOVING METHODS.

The barrel vise or clamp block (Figure 6) can be made of cast iron but tool steel is better. The upper and lower parts can be made from separate blocks, or one solid block may be drilled, reamed, and cut into two blocks. In either event, the blocks are drilled to receive draw-bolts, four being used to mount the lower block, and four more for holding down the upper block when the barrel is inside.

The lower block may be bolted to the top of the workbench or to a lathe. It can also be held in a machinist's vise, in which case the mounting bolts are not needed.

The barrel is usually held fast while the receiver or frame is turned. This is done because it is easier to get a grip on the receiver of a rifle or the frame of a revolver than it is to turn the barrel. Special care must be observed in handling a shotgun barrel, since its walls are thinner than those of a rifle. If too much pressure is applied by the vise or clamp block, the shotgun barrel may be bent or crushed beyond repair. However, shotgun barrels seldom need to be held as tightly as rifle barrels because they are easier to unscrew.

An old backwoods method of removing a rifle barrel dispenses with the need for a monkey wrench. The rifle is held with its receiver in a vise, the finish being protected by blocks of soft wood, gunny sacks, strips of felt from old hats, or anything else that is both soft and handy. A piece of manila rope is doubled in the middle and wrapped tightly around the barrel, the loose ends turned under near the receiver and the loop end left free near the muzzle. Usually the rope is wound around the barrel in a counter-clockwise direction, as viewed from the muzzle, since that is the direction in which a rifle barrel normally unscrews. A strong stick is placed inside the loop and turned in the direction that the rope is wound until the barrel unscrews.

Soaking the junction of the barrel and the receiver with ordinary "penetrating oil," such as that sold by garages for use on automobile springs, or kerosene, may make removal easier. Another source of help is heat. Warm the receiver just enough to cause expansion without affecting its heat-treated properties, and the barrel should come out without difficulty. If every method of removing the barrel fails, saw it off near the receiver, drill what is left of the barrel out of the receiver (being careful not to damage the threads of the re-ceiver) and take out any remaining pieces with a prick punch.

Some gunsmiths insist upon removing the bolt or breech mechanism before they try to take out the barrel in order to avoid any damage to the working parts. This is all right if a wooden plug is inserted to take the place of the mechanism removed, but otherwise the receiver may be crushed between the jaws of the vise. In the case of a bolt-action rifle, it seems better to leave the bolt in place but not locked.

Screwing a barrel into the receiver is fairly easy if the index lines are watched. They are two short, shallow lines, one on the receiver and one on the barrel, which exactly line up and meet when the barrel is screwed all the way into the receiver. Usually, it is possible to screw the barrel within about a quarter turn of the meeting place of the index lines; a wrench is needed to complete the job, such as one of those illustrated on Plate 29.

The shoulder of the barrel should fit snugly against the receiver ring, the pressure between them being the same at all points of contact. A test for fit is made by lightly coating the end of the receiver with some coloring substance, such as lampblack or Prussian blue, screwing in the barrel tightly and noting any inequality of pressure as shown by the coloring on the receiver. File down any high spots with a fine file and repeat the process until you are satisfied that the contact is even at all points.

Fitting the barrel is especially important for revolvers. The barrel must line up perfectly with the cylinder. If the cylinder is out of line the bullet strikes more on one side of the rifling than the other and it will be deformed. Another trouble is that the place where the bullet strikes the rifling causes shavings of metal to be left in the bore; these shavings decrease accuracy and safety.

You can test the alignment of the barrel and cylinder by making a testing plug called a "range rod" from tool steel. Design it to fit the barrel snugly. Hold the trigger back and with one of the chambers of the cylinder lined up with the barrel, push the range rod through the barrel from the muzzle and into the chamber. If it does not pass smoothly into the chamber, the revolver was not properly designed, it was poorly built, or the cylinder lock may be worn.

The range rod test is not infallible. Sometimes the rod will enter the chamber smoothly but the cylinder still does not line up with the barrel. The fault may be that the notches on the cylinder and the hand that engages these notches are both worn so that the cylinder cannot turn far enough for the latch to drop into place. The test for this condition is to hold back the cylinder with one hand and cock the revolver with the other hand, watching for any slippage of operation. Next, cock the hammer and pull the trigger (with the gun empty, of course) but hold the trigger all the way back; while the trigger is held back, rock the cylinder from side to side to see if there is lost motion. If there is any play in the cylinder under this condition it may be on one side or the other and thus indicate the reason why metal is shaved from the bullets. The condition is serious enough to call for a replacement of worn parts. We describe this problem at this point because amateurs sometimes think the barrel alignment is at fault when it is really a case of other parts being out of order.

Returning to our subject of barrel changing, we find that the threads where the barrel screws into a frame or a receiver may need cleaning. Rust may be removed by an acid solution or the use of an abrasive. After the rust is removed, wipe the threads with an old toothbrush dipped in gasoline to remove oil and grease. However, grease and oil should be removed before an acid solution is used to take away rust, and then again after the rust has disappeared, just to be safe. A light coat of oil should be placed on the threads immediately before the barrel is screwed into the receiver or frame.

We have seen how the use of a fine file can remedy a condition where a barrel will not screw all the way into the receiver or frame. When the opposite condition exists, that is, when the barrel goes in a little too far for proper alignment, another remedy is needed. This consists in using a lathe to face-off the end of the barrel and the barrel shoulder enough for the barrel to make another complete turn, minus enough of a turn to let the barrel and receiver or frame meet properly.

The amount of material to be removed in facing-off the end of the barrel and the barrel shoulder is easily calculated. Count the number of threads to the inch; this will show how many thousandths of an inch the barrel must enter the receiver to complete one turn of the threaded portion. Next, decide whether it is necessary to make one complete turn of the barrel or not. Usually less than a complete turn is needed. Multiply the distance in thousandths of an inch that the barrel makes in one complete turn by the fraction that shows what part of a complete turn is required to line up the barrel. The product is the distance that the micrometer carriage stop on a lathe must be withdrawn from the lathe carriage in order to control the facing-off process.

For example, when it is only necessary to make one more complete turn minus one-quarter turn, in order to fit the barrel, this shows that ¾ turn, or ¾ of 360 degrees (which, of course, is 270 degrees) is the amount needed. Multiply the number of thousandths of an inch that the barrel moves forward with one complete turn in the threads by ¾ and you have the amount that the barrel and barrel shoulder must be faced-off on the lathe.

Having shortened the barrel at the breech in order to remedy a condition of the barrel screwing past the index mark, the breech end of the chamber must be deepened. This forces you to return the weapon to the factory unless you have a rechambering reamer.

Since chambering is an exacting operation and any inaccuracy will create a dangerous condition in the gun, many barrel experts resort to another method of getting the barrel to screw up to the index mark and not go past it. They insert a ring-shaped steel shim of the proper thickness between the shoulder of the barrel and the bearing surface of the receiver, lubricating it to reduce any tendency for it to shear under the twisting force that develops as the barrel is screwed into place.

When the threads on a new barrel are a little too big for the receiver or frame, coat them with valve-grinding compound and screw the barrel inward by hand as far as you can progress without force; then back up a short distance and start forward again. Keep this up, adding more valve-grinding compound as it is needed, going back and forth but all the time advancing steadily. When the barrel has been screwed in the full distance, unscrew it, swab the valve-grinding compound from the barrel and the receiver or frame, dry the threads, oil the threads, and now screw the barrel into place without the compound. This time you may tap lightly with a mallet, but strong, heavy blows are ruinous.

Rifle barrels often have an extractor groove at the breech. If the barrel is shortened at the breech, it may be necessary to restore the groove. This can be done by hand-filing, on a milling machine, or with a portable grinding tool.

XXVI. Head Space

HEAD SPACE, in simple language, is the distance from the face of the breech block, or the breech bolt, to the base of the cartridge when the action is closed. Another way to express the same idea is to say that head space is the clearance between the face of the breech and the base of the cartridge when the breech is closed.

Another definition of head space is the distance from the surface in the rifle chamber which halts the forward movement of the cartridge to the face of the breech. The surface in the rifle chamber which stops the forward movement of a rimmed cartridge is the bottom of the rim recess. The front stop for a rimless cartridge is the shoulder of the chamber. Head space distance for a rimmed cartridge is the maximum cartridge rim thickness plus a small clearance. Head space distance for a rimless cartridge is comparatively long because it is necessary to measure it to the shoulder in the "bottleneck" chamber, which is sloping and not at an angle of 90 degrees to the face of the breech. Since the slope exists, a definite point on the shoulder is selected by the rifle manufacturer, and from this point head space is measured to the face of the breech.

The shortest factory-made rifle cartridge must not be too short even in the longest chamber of a rifle which will receive a cartridge which might seem to fit, even though the rifle caliber and the cartridge caliber are the same. In a similar manner, the longest factory-made rifle cartridge must fit into the shortest chamber of a rifle having the same caliber as the rifle. The net result is that there is a narrow range for the dimensions of both the chamber of the rifle and the cartridge which is fired in that particular rifle.

Head space is generally inspected by means of a *Go-Gauge* and also a *No-Go-Gauge*. When a bolt-action rifle is examined, the *Go-Gauge* is placed in the chamber of the rifle. The bolt should close without unreasonable effort. If it does so, the chamber of the rifle is not less than the minimum allowable length. Next, the *No-Go-Gauge* is placed in the chamber. If the bolt can be closed without unreasonable effort, the chamber does not exceed the maximum allowable length.

If too much force is used in closing the bolt after the *No-Go-Gauge* has been placed in the chamber—that is, if the bolt handle is forced down more than it would be in the normal loading and firing of a cartridge—the person inspecting the rifle may erroneously believe that the rifle has too much head space.

Some riflemen and gunsmiths make the mistake of testing head space in a bolt-action rifle by using factory-made cartridges instead of the *Go-Gauge* and the *No-Go-Gauge*. They load live cartridges into the rifle, one at a time, and place *shims* at the base of each cartridge as it is loaded into the rifle. A *shim* for this purpose is merely a round piece of paper, fiber, or metal (brass or copper usually), cut to the same diameter as the base of the cartridge.

In the first edition of this book, three methods were given for determining the approximate head space of a bolt-action rifle when the proper gauges were not available. In all three methods, factory-made live cartridges were used. In one method, the cartridges were used without shims and in the other two methods shims were used. All three methods were used by many gunsmiths and rifle experts who did not necessarily claim to be gunsmiths; but the author has learned that there is no substitute for the use of the proper gauges and cautions the reader against using cartridges instead of gauges.

There are at least two good reasons for not using live cartridges instead of the *Go-Gauge* and the *No-Go-Gauge*. One is that the brass of which a cartridge case is made is springy in nature—that is, it is not rigid but fairly flexible. The other reason is that in spite of all efforts of cartridge manufacturers to make cartridges uniform no two are identical in the strict scientific sense. They appear and measure identical even to most experts, but in the dictionary sense of the term, they are not identical.

Dies are used in manufacturing cartridge cases. The dies are made of heat-treated hardened steel to resist wear, but the forcing of brass into the dies gradually wears down the dies until they become larger and larger; hence the brass cartridge cases gradually increase in size, although this increase is so small that it is not apparent to the casual observer and only an experienced man with the proper measuring devices can detect the variation in size among cartridges from the same factory, made in the same lot. Cartridge manufacturers may not publicize this, but they have told the author the facts, and it is in the best interests of the firearms fraternity in general and the national defense in particular that the truth be known.

The *Go-Gauge* and the *No-Go Gauge* are made of steel. They are principally used by ordnance technicians and ordnance officers of the armed forces of the United States at U.S. Arsenals and Armories and in the field. In addition, firearms manufacturers, dealers, and gunsmiths who want accurate results use these gauges. In civilian life, they are obtainable from any well-stocked dealer in firearm supplies. In ordering, specify the make, model, type, caliber, and other important characteristics of the rifle for which the gauges will be used.

Some textbooks on ordnance and gunsmithing simply say that "the bolt should be stripped" before using the gauges. In the author's experience, this means removing the firing-pin assembly from the bolt.

If the bolt closes on the *No-Go Gauge,* a conscientious inspector may regard the bolt, and even the rifle, as unsafe for service and send one or both to an ordnance technician for repair or consignment to the ordnance salvage dump. However, this is the strict procedure.

Damage to the bolt-action rifle may result from firing it when too much head space exists, and it is possible for the shooter to be injured. However, these are possibilities and not necessarily probabilities. Authors of books and magazine articles have blown up the dangers of excessive head space for bolt-action rifles to the point where it gives some shooters nightmares. The author has fired U.S. Rifle, Model 1903, commonly called the "Springfield," using the caliber .30-06 cartridge, in marksmanship practice, in competitive matches, and in the field, even when it had excessive head space, and nothing happened to either the rifle or the shooter.

Head space must be considered not only for bolt-action rifles but also for other weapons. The author has fired shotguns having a chamber-rim recess deep enough for the loaded shotgun cartridges (popularly called "shells" or "shotshells") to rattle back and forth in the chamber when the shotgun was shaken. These shotguns had too much head space, but neither the shotguns nor the author blew up when the guns were fired. The author also has fired lever-action rifles with head space so excessive that his shooting companions would not stand within twenty yards of him while he was shooting, and yet no damage resulted.

At this point, the reader may rightfully say that the author's philosophy is this: "Now I have warned you in great detail about the dangers of improper head space. Do not do as I do but as I tell you to do, and you will live to march at the funerals of those who disregarded my warnings."

The bolts for bolt-action rifles are theoretically interchangeable. The bolt of one rifle will fit any other rifle of the same make, type, model, and caliber in the ordinary mechanical sense of the term, but the head space may be correct, too much, or too little. A safe precaution is to lightly etch the barrel serial number on the bolt which is known to fit that particular rifle with the correct head space. Then, when a bolt is removed for cleaning or any other purpose, there is less opportunity for inserting the wrong bolt in the rifle. Also, if it is necessary to replace an original bolt with a new bolt, head space must be checked.

When a new barrel is placed on a rifle, head space must be checked. This is true for both bolt-action and lever-action rifles.

When either the breech block or the barrel, or both, are changed on a lever-action rifle, head space must be inspected.

Headspace gauges are used for the accurate inspection of head space in a shotgun. These are available from dealers in firearms equipment and are made in different forms; but the author prefers to use a *Go-Gauge* and a *No-Go-Gauge,* similar in principle and application to such gauges provided for bolt-action rifles. But again it is necessary to emphasize that in buying head-space gauges the purchaser must specify the make, model, type, and other characteristics of the weapon for which the gauges will be used. Obviously, for a shotgun the gauge is specified among the other characteristics.

Shotgun cartridges ("shells") rattle back and forth in the chamber when the shotgun is shaken, even when the gun is a high-quality weapon, if there is too much head space. This is especially noticeable in a double-barrel shotgun with extractors that move straight forward and backward. In a magazine (repeating) shotgun manufactured with an extractor that exerts a slight degree of pressure on the side of the loaded shotgun cartridge ("shell"), the rattle indicating excessive head space may not be heard by the owner; hence he does not suspect the existence of excessive head space and learns about it for the first time when the gun is examined by an experienced gunsmith.

Head space is not as critical in a shotgun as it is in a rifle, but there are upper and lower limits in the dimensions of the chamber of a shotgun closely observed and maintained by the manufacturer at the factory.

Excessive head space is sometimes caused by defective cartridges. This is rarely caused by factory-loaded cartridges. Hand-loaded cartridges can be just as good or even better than factory-loaded cartridges, but if the hand-loader is inexperienced or careless his cartridges may vary enough from the dimensions of the cartridge designed for a particular weapon to cause excessive head space. This is easily understood by referring back to the definition and explanation of head space at the beginning of this chapter.

Cartridge cases which have been reloaded repeatedly become brittle and rupture easily. This is especially true if the primer is of the mercuric type, either corrosive or noncorrosive, since mercury changes the crystalline structure of brass, makes it very brittle, and robs it of tensile strength.

Altering the shape of the taper of the neck of a rimless cartridge case during the resizing process in hand loading affects the head space, because the neck or shoulder of the case arrests the forward movement of the cartridge itself. This danger is not so pronounced in resizing a rimmed cartridge, since the neck does not serve the same purpose as the neck of the rimless cartridge. However, the rim of the rimmed cartridge is battered in the resizing dies, it becomes thin, and the head space is changed. For the above reasons, when a gunsmith's customer complains that a rifle was not properly head-spaced, the gunsmith should examine some of the customer's fired cases to see if any of them are partially ruptured, have cracked necks, or stretched bases; if they have, a new lot of ammunition should be fired. A second examination of fired cases will probably show that the cartridges rather than the rifle were at fault.

Primers are clues to excessive head space. At the time of the explosion, the cartridge case may stretch where the base meets the walls, or the primer may be driven out. If there is too much head space, the breech pressure causes the walls of the case to press against the walls of the chamber, and the primer is driven backward and out of the case until it strikes the face of the breech and flattens. The cartridge case, meanwhile, has started to travel back and in so doing it slides along the primer, with the result that normally the primer does not materially project from the base. If you can feel the primer protruding from the surface, this does not necessarily indicate excessive pressure, but it certainly indicates too much head space.

Insufficient Head Space.—If the head space is insufficient, the bolt or the breech block will not close properly on the cartridge, because the chamber is too short. There are two remedies: First, lengthen the chamber with a finishing reamer; or second, use a shorter bolt or a shorter breech block. However, it must be remembered that cartridges of one make may not give any trouble in this respect, while those of another make will be a small fraction of an inch too long and combine with the shortness of the chamber to produce insufficient head space.

Reloaded or hand-loaded cartridges sometimes have stretched cases that cause insufficient head space. This is particularly true when cartridges having high breech pressures are fired in lever-action rifles. The breech actions of such weapons have no provision for locking at the front, the steel is not hard enough to resist the expansion of the cartridge case on explosion, and the result is that the case is stretched too long for the chamber. Cases stretched in this manner should be junked.

Everything in this chapter applies to almost all firearms which either the amateur or professional gunsmith will work on, and also it is of great importance to all shooters, whether they are target shooters, hunters, soldiers, sailors, or marines.

Furthermore, a book or magazine article may carry the word "simplified." These two deceptive words, "complete" and "simplified," are forced on ethical publishers and authors by competitors who have been rushing into the booming market for anything written on firearms.

The inspection of head space and the correction of incorrect head space is "simplified" in this chapter if you read the text very carefully and then apply the instructions to one make, type, and model at a time. It is "complete" only when you have inspected and corrected head space (when necessary) on every firearm on the market, which is impossible in the lifetime even of the best of gunsmiths.

Finally, head space is not an isolated subject. It is related to many other gunsmithing problems. If you are a beginner, read this whole book carefully before you start inspecting or correcting head space.

XXVII. Sights

SIGHTS are divided into two general types—metallic and telescopic. Metallic sights are further divided into two kinds, front and rear, and each of these subdivide as to detailed types. Telescopic sights are low-power telescopes containing some means of sighting on the target and adjusting for elevation and windage.

The three most popular types of metallic front sights are the (1) Bead, or barleycorn, which is a round bead mounted on a very thin blade; (2) Blade, which is a straight blade of metal with square sides and a flat top, mounted near the muzzle; (3) Aperture, or peep, which is a disc pierced through the center so that the target can be seen through and centered in the hole instead of being brought to rest on top of the front sight.

The two types of metallic rear sights are (1) the Open Sight, which is mounted on top of the barrel, somewhere near the breech; it is a notch, having either a V-shape or a flat bottom and straight sides; (2) the Aperture, or peep, rear sights; it has a hole through which the target is viewed and centered, and is usually mounted well to the rear on the receiver, although it can be mounted behind the firing pin on the tang of a rifle. A sight mounted on the receiver is called a "receiver sight"; likewise, one mounted on a tang is called a "tang sight."

An old type of metallic sight, called a "tube sight," has front and rear sights mounted inside the tube. It is mounted over the barrel or along the side of the barrel, and is usually adjusted by moving the whole tube, since the sights within the tube are customarily fixed.

Generally it has no lenses and is more of a curiosity than a practical sighting system.

Plate 30 shows the fundamentals of making sights in the home workshop. The upper left-hand section illustrates blade-type front sights, made of bar stock, or thin flat material, preferably cold rolled steel, although softer metals such as bronze and brass can be used. Actual design of the sights depends upon the purpose for which the gun will be used and upon the whims of the maker. The sights shown here were cut out with a jeweler's saw when soft metal was used, and with a hacksaw when cold rolled steel was chosen. They were finished by filing to shape and smoothing down with abrasives. Plain sights, such as these, can be blued easily by merely heating to the proper color in oil, but sights with inserts must be blued before the inserts are added.

The upper right-hand corner of Plate 30 shows how ivory, plastic, bone, gold, or other materials can be made into beads that are either pressed or screwed into holes drilled in a front sight blade. These must not be confused with the true bead-type sight which has a bead standing upright as the principal part of the front sight, whereas the beads mentioned here are part of a blade-type sight.

The left-hand middle section of Plate 30 shows a simple ramp sight, with two methods of fitting to the barrel. It can be cut out of bar stock and either screwed or fitted to the barrel. The sight proper can be fitted by means of a slot; a dovetail can be cut to take a conventional front sight as supplied by the manufacturer of the firearms.

The right-hand middle section of Plate 30 illustrates a much neater ramp-type front sight that is made by sweating or brazing the ramp to a tube of streamline proportions that is, in turn, pressed or slid onto the barrel.

The bottom section of Plate 30 shows how to make a simple receiver sight. The base block is made first from a piece of cold rolled steel which is slotted with a hacksaw and file to receive the sight arm (marked "angle iron arm" in the illustration). If the steel is taken from an angle iron it saves shaping. Notice that the arm is slotted along its center on the vertical surface to receive the lock screw and cover plate. The eyepiece can be made of a piece of small bar stock filed to shape, as shown in the drawing. It may be slotted on either side for the hold-down screws. The slots allow adjustment

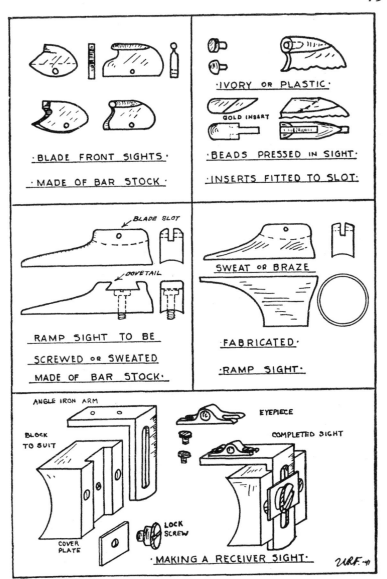

· BLADE FRONT SIGHTS ·

· MADE OF BAR STOCK ·

· IVORY OR PLASTIC ·

GOLD INSERT

· BEADS PRESSED IN SIGHT ·

· INSERTS FITTED TO SLOT ·

BLADE SLOT

DOVETAIL

RAMP SIGHT TO BE
SCREWED OR SWEATED
MADE OF BAR STOCK.

SWEAT OR BRAZE

· FABRICATED ·

· RAMP SIGHT ·

ANGLE IRON ARM

BLOCK
TO SUIT

EYEPIECE

COMPLETED SIGHT

COVER
PLATE

LOCK
SCREW

· MAKING A RECEIVER SIGHT ·

PLATE 30. HOMEMADE SIGHTS.

for windage. The aperture should be threaded and a commercial aperture disc inserted. The base block is then drilled for the screws which hold it on the receiver. The parts are then blued to match the finish of the rifle.

With this introduction to the subject of making sights, we can now take up the various detailed problems, one at a time. Examining manufacturers' catalogs of sights and sight parts will broaden your knowledge and suggest designs of your own. Many of the outstanding sights sold commercially today originated in the minds of amateur gunsmiths, and almost all of the manufacturers started as home craftsmen.

The front sight can be made of cold rolled steel, as we have already suggested. Cold-drawn steel may bend or break. Either tool or alloy steel is better than cold-drawn steel. Screws are the best fastening medium, but the front sight can also be mounted with pins, or placed in a dovetailed slot.

For the purpose of explaining the assembly, design, and manufacture of both front and rear sights, we may well examine the illustrations, starting with Figure 57, Plate 37, and ending with Figure 83, Plate 38, wherein the parts of United States Rifle, Caliber .30, Model of 1903, are shown. We have chosen this particular rifle because it is typical of military-type, bolt-action rifles, and also because it is brought to the gunsmith for remodeling and repair more than any other rifle.

The front sight of the United States Rifle, Caliber .30, Model of 1903, Figure 57, Plate 37, is secured in its slot in the movable stud by the front sight pin, Figure 58; the pin is tapering, and its small end is driven in from the right and the ends are upset to prevent accidental removal. The fixed stud and movable stud, with front sight in place, are shown assembled, Figure 59, right side view, and Figure 60, front view. The fixed stud "A" has a slot "B" which, bearing on a lug on the upper side of the barrel, prevents lateral displacement of the stud; and a hole "C" for the stud pin, which prevents longitudinal displacement of the stud. The movable stud "D" has the front sight pin hole "E." It is held by the undercut slot in the fixed stud and secured from lateral displacement by the front sight screw "F." The recess for this screw is not drilled in the movable stud until the correct position of the movable stud has been determined. The rear face "G", of both the fixed stud and movable stud, is serrated to prevent any reflection of the light from this surface interfering with the aiming. The fixed base, Figure 61, rear end view, and Figure 62, right-side view, has the holes "A" and "B" for the base pin and base spline, respectively, by which it is firmly secured to the barrel and lateral and longitudinal movement prevented; the undercut "D" for the tenon of the hand guard; the lightening cuts "E"; the barrel hole "F"; the pivot lug "G" for the movable base; the undercut "H" for the lip on the rear end of the movable base; the undercut "I" for the windage screw and the lip on the front end of the movable base; the lug "J" on the top of which are two zero marks for the wind-gauge graduations, and the chamfer "K", the seat for the windage screw collar. This chamfer is carried to the rear to permit the assembling of the fixed base and the windage screw. On the left side of the front lug the chamfer corresponding to "K" is merely a conical recess for the head of the windage screw. The base spline locates and prevents the base from turning on the barrel. The base pin, similar to the base spline, prevents longitudinal movement of the base on the barrel.

We now turn to Plate 38 to continue our examination of the sight assembly of the Springfield Rifle. The movable base, Figure 63, top view, and Figure 64, right-side view, has the ears "A" in which are the holes "B" for the joint pin, which serves as a hinge for the leaf; the wind-gauge graduations "C", each point of which corresponds to a lateral deviation of 4 inches for each 100 yards (on this particular design); the lip "D" which fits in the undercut in the rear end of the fixed base; the spring opening "E"; the spring seat "F" which is undercut to admit the lip on the front end of the base spring; the lip "G" in which is a worm gear for the engagement of the windage screw; the pivot hole "H" for the pivot lug on the fixed base, and the shoulders "I" on which the front end of the leaf rests when down. The hole "K" is made for convenience in manufacture.

The windage screw consists of the screw, collar, spring, knob, and pin, Figures 65, 66, 67, 68, and 69, respectively. The taper head of the screw fits into the conical recess in the left side, and the taper of the collar into the chamfer in the right side of the fixed base; the thread on the screw engages the worm gear in the lip of the movable base. Under the action of the spring, lost motion due to wear is prevented between the windage screw and the movable base, and between the windage screw and the front lug of the fixed base.

The base spring, Figure 70, top view, and Figure 71, side view, has the lip "A" which fits into the undercut in its seat in the movable base; the free end "B", and the hole "C", by which, with the aid of a drift made for the purpose, the spring is assembled or dismounted by driving it into or out of its seat in the movable base.

The joint pin, on which the leaf hinges, is shown in Figure 72. It is cylindrical, with rounded ends, and fits tightly in the ears of the base.

The leaf, Figure 73, top view (when down), and Figure 74, right-side view, has the joint "A" in which is the joint pin hole; the rib "B"; the undercut "C" for the drift slide (not shown in the drawing, but located to the left of the cut-out part of the leaf), and the sighting notch "D." The free end of the base spring bears against the lower end of the leaf and maintains it in either its lowered or raised position. The leaf is graduated for various ranges; the one illustrated is graduated from 100 to 2,850 yards. The lines extending across one or both branches of the leaf illustrated are 100-yard divisions, the longer of the short lines are 50-yard and the shorter lines 25-yard divisions.

The drift slide, .05 peep, Figure 75, top view (leaf down), has the peephole "A", .05-inch diameter; the field view "B" (triangular-shaped hole); the drift slide pin "C", riveted to the slide in manufacture, and the notches "D." The lines on either side of the peephole and lower notch enable the drift slide to be accurately set at any desired graduation on the leaf.

As the slide is moved up or down on the leaf the drift slide moves with it and at the same time has a lateral movement in the undercut between the branches of the leaf, thus automatically correcting for drift. This movement corrects for all drift up to 600 yards on the design illustrated, but for only part of the drift beyond that range.

With the leaf up, on the design illustrated, ranges from 100 to 2,350 yards can be obtained through the peephole; from 100 to 2,450 yards through the lower notch at the bottom of the field view; and from 1,400 to 2,750 yards through the upper notch in the upper edge of the drift slide.

The 2,850 range, on the design illustrated, is obtained through the sighting notch in the upper end of the leaf.

With the leaf down and using the battle sight notch in slide cap, the sights are set for 547 yards or battleline firing for the down position of the slide, in the design illustrated.

The slide, Figure 76, top view (leaf down), Figure 77, front view (leaf down), and Figure 78, right-end view, has the leaf slot "A"; the clearance "B" for the open notch in the drift slide; the slide cap screw hole "C"; slide binding screw hole "D"; slide cap pin hole "E", and the dovetailed groove "F" for the slide cap.

The slide cap, Figure 79, top view (leaf down), and Figure 80, cross section, has the battle sight notch "A", slide cap screw hole "B", slide cap pin hole "C", the groove "D" for the drift slide pin; and the clearance "E" for the upper notch in the drift slide.

The cap is attached to the slide by entering the dovetailed groove at the right, and by the slide cap screw at the left, thus securing the slide to the leaf.

The slide cap screw is shown in Figure 81.

The slide cap pin, Figure 82, is inserted in the pin hole "E" in the slide, Figure 76, and fitting into a groove in the slide binding screw, Figure 83, prevents the accidental removal of the latter.

The size and shape of the sight parts presented here are those of the United States Rifle, Caliber .30, Model of 1903, as issued to the United States Army during the First World War. Both the size and the shape have been modified at various times by the United States armed forces, for various reasons. The parts described and illustrated in this text were chosen because they are the ones usually found on the older rifles which come to the attention of the gunsmith. The principles of design, construction, assembly, and repair apply to similar sight parts on later models.

SIGHT CONSTRUCTION PROBLEMS

Having explained the classification of sights, the construction of simple sights in the home workshop, and the assembly of Springfield sights, we are now ready for a more detailed discussion of sight construction problems.

Gold-Bead Front Sights.—The gold-bead front sight is an excellent one for daytime use, but many hunters prefer an ivory bead for hunting during the day when the light is poor, and especially favor it for night hunting, bearing in mind, of course, that night hunting is generally prohibited in the United States as a game-conservation measure.

The gold bead can be removed and replaced by an ivory bead, but a simpler expedient is to paint the gold bead with white lacquer applied with a toothpick or a matchstick. The lacquer dries quickly and can be scraped off in the morning with a knife.

The manufacture of the gold-bead sight has already been discussed very briefly. Details of construction are as follows:

First, obtain gold wire, from $\frac{3}{32}$ inch to $\frac{1}{8}$ inch in diameter, and between 16 and 22 carat in gold content; a piece of this wire less than 1 inch long is enough to make several gold beads. When gold wire is not commercially available, a dentist may be willing to cast a small piece that will meet your needs. Upset the end to fit the slot.

Second, prepare the hole to receive the gold. Let us assume that the upper rear end of the front sight has a square corner when seen from the side. Measure down a little more than $\frac{1}{8}$ inch from the top surface and the same distance forward from the rear surface. At the intersection of lines drawn at right angles to these points, drill a hole through the sight about $\frac{1}{16}$ inch in diameter. The purpose of this hole is to act as an anchorage for the gold pounded into the sight.

Third, using a thin jeweler's hacksaw, saw a slot from the upper rear corner of the sight down to this hole, being sure that the width of this slot is at least $\frac{1}{32}$ inch narrower than the diameter of the gold wire that you intend to use. This insures a tight fit for the wire.

Fourth, at the upper rear corner of the sight, saw out a rectangle. The vertical dimension of this rectangle should be equal to the height you want the gold to be in the back of the front sight. The horizontal, side-view dimension of this rectangle should be about equal to the vertical dimension. The horizontal dimension at right angles to the barrel is determined by the width of the front sight blade.

Fifth, drill a very small hole forward and downward through the slot cut in the third step, above. This hole should have a diameter very slightly more than the width of the slot; its purpose is to assist in holding the gold in place. Extend this hole a little deeper than the bottom of the slot, so that it crosses the hole drilled from the side.

Sixth, place the front sight blade in a vise between lead jaws and hammer the gold wire into place, working from both sides as well as the top of the slot. File away any surplus gold on the sides. At the rear upper corner of the sight blade, you can file the gold so that it is flush with the rectangular slot cut at right angles to the axis of the barrel, or, if you wish, you can give the gold a curve on its upper and rear surfaces.

Ordinary Hunting Rifle Front Sights.—Straight, square, steel-blade front sights, sometimes called "Marine Corps type" front sights, are excellent for hunting, and are usually used in conjunction with a very wide, square notch in the rear sight. The blade may be as narrow as .070 inch for indoor practice, and as wide as .100 inch for hunting, although .090 inch is probably as wide as the blade should be for most hunters, and .050 inch is considered correct for military purposes. The more narrow sight blade looks sharp and clean to the shooter, and enables him to see the front sight more distinctly than he can when the blade is wide.

The height of the front sight can be determined experimentally in the following manner:

Cut out a "dummy" front sight blade from scrap brass or soft steel or iron, making it a little higher than the expected correct height. Mount this dummy front sight blade on the rifle. Bore-sight the rifle, that is, make sure that the fore-and-aft axis of the front sight corresponds to the fore-and-aft axes of both the barrel and the rear sight. Then, aim the rifle at a target. If you are using a military peep sight, bring the tip of the front sight to the exact center of the peep sight, and align the sights with the bull's-eye so that the bottom edge of the bull's-eye sits on the top edge of the front sight. The eye should be focused on the target; if this is done, the target appears sharp and clear. If possible, fire a few shots at a target at the range at which most hunting will be done.

If the dummy front sight is too high, as it may be at first, file it down to the correct height for accurate and easy aiming. You now have the correct height. The dummy can be used as a pattern, or if you wish to order a new front sight from a manufacturer, you can mail him the dummy, especially if you have made it to the desired width, height, and shape.

In ordering hunting rifle sights from a manufacturer or a supply house, it is not necessary to send a dummy if you want standard sights for common weapons such as the Springfield, Krag, Winchester Model 54, although it is necessary to specify the height, and it is well to give the desired width. Likewise, it is advisable to give the desired diameter of the hole for a peep sight. Fortunately, the directions for ordering given in catalogs usually include such advice.

In ordering sights for rifles not in general use, a complete technical description and a drawing should be sent. Better yet, send the old sights if you want them duplicated, or send a dummy in ordering a front sight blade.

A variation of the ordinary hunting-rifle front sight is the tapered shape, that is, the side view is the same, but the sight is tapered in thickness and appears to the shooter as being spear-shaped, with a sharp point at the top. This works well with an aperture rear, when the light is good, but it is not satisfactory with an open rear sight, especially when the light is poor.

Another variation of front sight shape may take the form of a square sitting on the top of a dull spear head, or a circle in the same position, as seen from the rear by the shooter. This design is mechanically unsound because the metal cut away in tapering the blade below the square or circle weakens the blade and permits bending. Of course, much the same thing can be said against the tapered shape described above.

Aperture Front Sights.—There are several forms of aperture front sights. No matter which form is chosen, the finish should be jet black inside and out; the use of a bright finish defeats the main purpose of the aperture sight, which is the control of the light. Of greater importance is the size of the aperture, which may be as small as $\frac{1}{16}$ inch (technically expressed as .0625 inch), or as great as .136 inch (slightly more than $\frac{1}{8}$ inch). If the aperture is too small, the light is diminished and it is difficult to see the target. If the aperture is too big, too much light is admitted, the orthoptic principle is reduced, and it is hard to line up the sights with the target. In general, a small aperture is adapted to indoor target practice, while a large aperture works better outdoors. No matter how large the aperture may be, this type of sight is a handicap if the target must be picked up quickly, as in hunting.

A simple tubular front sight can be made from a half-inch length of quarter-inch steel tubing. The tube is grooved on one side, and brazed to the base of the old front sight. A smaller tube is fitted inside, and this smaller tube is drilled through to give a hole of the correct aperture diameter. By having several smaller tubes with various diameter holes, the aperture size may be changed without mounting a new sight each time the firing conditions are different than they were before. Obviously, the larger tube should be of steel, while a softer metal, such as copper or brass, can be used for the inner tube. A short section cut from a discarded rifle barrel can be used for the larger tube after the rifling is reamed out.

An ordinary post front sight may be mounted inside the tubular front sight, or it may be mounted a short distance in front of the tube. A variation of this idea is to have a post front sight in the usual position and mount behind it a very short tube, which is really nothing more than a ring to give definition to the post. Still another form of aperture front sight consists of two rings, one behind the other, both of which may also be described as very short tubes.

Wherever a tubular front sight is used, whether it is a ring or actually a tube, the rear of the hole may be made larger than the front, thus providing a taper, or bevel, from front to rear. This feature is preferred by many shooters, but it is by no means a standard design practice.

Rear Sights.—Rear sights, such as the Springfield folding leaf sight, are difficult for the average gunsmith to make unless he has special form cutters and special milling-machine fixtures, as well as equipment for making springs. When the shooter wants a rear sight made to his individual specifications, it is customary for the gunsmith to order the sights from a factory or supply house, complete except for the notch or the aperture.

A plain flat bar with no notch is one form of rear sight preferred by those who believe that they can naturally find the center, but it is usual for this type of rear sight to be provided with some centering device. This may be a fine gold, platinum, or ivory vertical line inlaid in the sight bar, or it may be a triangle made of such material and inlaid so that it points like an arrow to the center of the bar. Of course, with this sight, the tip of the front sight is brought above the upper edge of the rear sight, and it is well to have a bead for the front sight so that the shooter can always raise the front sight the same amount.

Rear sights with notches are in the majority. The notch may be rectangular, circular, or V-shaped. It may be either wide or narrow along the top of the bar; it may be either deep or shallow; and if it is shallow it may have a vertical notch extending from its bottom to a point near the bottom of the bar. No arbitrary rules can be given for selecting the shape, width, or depth of the notch; these matters depend upon the circumstances of shooting, such as the amount of light that can be expected, the time available for lining up the sights with the target, and the personal peculiarities of the shooter.

XXVIII. Trigger-pull Adjustments

THERE are two principal objects of trigger-pull adjustment. First, the amount of pull necessary to discharge the cartridge must not be so great that unnecessary time and energy are consumed in firing; and the pull must not be so light that there is danger of premature or accidental discharge. Second, the pull must be smooth and even. Adjustments are necessary because firearms usually come from the factory with too much pull for accuracy and comfort. For example, a shotgun may have as much as 15 pounds pull when only 4 pounds is sufficient.

Trigger-pull adjustments are explained according to the type of firearm from the viewpoints of mechanical design and operation. Triggers may be divided into three broad classes: the plain trigger, the bolt-action trigger, and the set trigger. The set trigger may be further divided into single and double set triggers. Two more classes can be added for the sake of clarity: shotgun triggers and automatic pistol triggers, but these classifications are purely arbitrary. The principles of trigger-pull adjustment apply to all types and classes; only the rules for handling tools in making the adjustments are subject to variation.

Disregarding the springs, there are three essential parts in a trigger mechanism: the object that strikes the primer in the cartridge, which may be called a hammer, striker, firing pin or some other name; the sear, which holds the hammer in the cocked position, and may be a separate part or may be integral with the hammer; and the trigger itself. The trigger, of course, is a lever, pivoted on a pin or screw, with one end serving to release the sear at the moment of firing, while the other end receives the force exerted by the shooter's finger.

Triggers may be better understood if we treat them as levers. In Figure 1, Plate 31, at the top of the figure, the force applied is at the left end, the little arrowhead under the bar is the fulcrum, located between the force and the weight, and the weight is at the right end. Since the fulcrum is between the force and the weight, this is a lever of the first class.

The next lower lever belongs to the second class because the fulcrum is at one end, the weight is in between, and the force applied is at the other end.

The third-class lever has the fulcrum at one end, the force is between the fulcrum and the weight, and the weight is at the other end.

The distance from the force to the fulcrum is called the power arm and the distance from the weight to the fulcrum is called the weight arm. According to the principle of moments, if these distances are measured perpendicular to the lines of action of the force and the weight, respectively, then the product of the force multiplied by the power arm is equal to the product of the weight multiplied by the weight arm. In other words, the moments of the two forces about the fulcrum must be equal and opposite. The mechanical advantage of the lever is the ratio of the power arm to the weight arm.

In the illustrations of the three classes of levers in Figure 1, Plate 31, "a" is the distance from the force to the fulcrum, and "b" is the distance from the weight to the fulcrum.

The combination of two classes of levers results in a compound lever, such as the one shown at the bottom of Figure 1, Plate 31, where the upper right-hand lever is a first-class lever and the lower left-hand lever is a second-class lever. In this illustration, the force of the left-hand lever is equal to the weight of the right-hand lever. The dimensions indicated are given merely to show that actual dimensions are indicated in practice, instead of using the letters "a" and "b."

A plain trigger is a lever of the first class. Since the sear and trigger form one part pivoted with a pin or screw, the pressure of

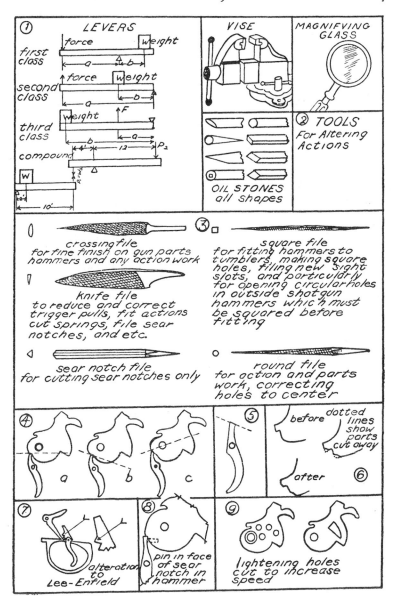

PLATE 31. TRIGGER AND HAMMER ALTERATIONS.

the hammer notch on the sear is the weight, the pressure of the finger on the trigger is the force, and the pin or screw is the fulcrum located between the weight and the force.

Where the trigger and sear are not one part, but are separate parts, the pressure of the hammer notch is the weight, the sear is the lever, and the trigger transmits the force. If the sear is pivoted between the force and the weight, it forms a lever of the first class, while if it is pivoted so that the weight lies between it and the force, it is a lever of the second class. A similar comparison can be made between the third-class lever and an arrangement where the pivot is at one end, the pressure of the hammer notch is at the other end, and the trigger operates between the two.

Returning to the first-class lever, which is easier to discuss, it is apparent that if the distance from the force to the fulcrum is great in proportion to the distance of the weight from the fulcrum, less force is needed but such force must travel farther. Translating this into trigger terms, we find that the length of the pull of the finger (the force) on the trigger represents the "creep" or "slack" in the trigger pull, while the weight represents the pressure exerted between the sear point and the hammer notch. Therefore, we attack the problem of trigger adjustment by reshaping the hammer notch.

The tools required for adjusting trigger pulls and for generally altering actions are a vise, a magnifying glass, a supply of oilstones of various shapes, and a variety of files. The beginner can get along with one 6-inch American-Swiss Pillar file, ⅛ inch wide, with super-smooth teeth; and a ¼ inch, three-cornered, hard, fine, knife-edge Arkansas slip-stone, but as he progresses into the professional class he will gradually add to his equipment. These tools are shown in Figures 2 and 3 of Plate 31.

Figure 3 of Plate 31 shows the assortment of files favored by most professional gunsmiths; the profiles at the ends of the drawings of the files are their cross-sectional shapes. These files have many uses; they are by no means limited to trigger-pull adjustment although they are presented here with that idea in mind.

The crossing file is used for giving a fine finish to gun parts in general, especially to hammers and other action work. The knife file is used to reduce and correct trigger pulls, to fit actions, to cut springs, to file sear notches, and for similar cutting work. The sear notch file is principally used to cut sear notches. The square file is used for fitting hammers to tumblers, making square holes, filing new sight slots, and particularly for opening circular holes in outside shotgun hammers which must be squared before fitting. The round file is generally used for working down the action and various gun parts, for correcting holes to center, and similar purposes.

Figure 4 of Plate 31 illustrates how the trigger pull can be reduced in the "hammer-action" type of trigger and at the same time the "creep" (length of the pull) can be eliminated almost entirely. In "a" of Figure 4, the hammer notch is reshaped so that the sear point and the surface of the notch bearing against it are parallel to each other and at right angles to a line drawn from the trigger pivot to the sear point. This adjustment makes it possible to squeeze the trigger without increasing the pressure of the hammer.

A common mistake made by beginners is shown in "b", where the hammer notch is beveled so that it permits the hammer to cam the sear forward until it is free, thus lightening the trigger pull so much that the slightest jar will fire the weapon.

When most rifles leave the factory the hammer notch is at an angle shown in "c", which requires a heavy trigger pull because when the trigger is squeezed, the sear has to cam back the hammer and operate against the whole force of the mainspring under tension before the sear is free.

Reshaping the hammer notch does not reduce the length of the pull. To take out the "creep," use the hard Arkansas stone to polish the point of the sear and the hammer notch. Do this under the magnifying glass to be sure that the shape of the hammer notch is not changed at this step in the work. Squeeze the trigger; if the sear forces back the hammer a little as you squeeze, you can see the movement of the hammer as well as feel it. This shows that it is necessary to alter the angle of the hammer notch.

Working under the magnifying glass, use the Arkansas stone to bevel the hammer notch very slightly. Test the trigger pull again. It may be necessary now to use the small file to change the notch. Do not bevel back the point of the sear at a sharp angle, such as that shown in Figure 5, Plate 31, because this will cause the hammer to fall if the sear moves the least bit, the sear cams forward, the trigger flies away from the finger, and the aim is spoiled. This is bad because the trigger finger should be in contact with the trigger and control it before the fall of the hammer, during the fall, and after the fall. To use a golfing expression, the trigger finger should "follow through."

The sear point should press against the hammer notch with equal pressure along the entire width of the notch. Test this by snapping the trigger suddenly while the hammer is pressed forward with the thumb. A narrow bright streak on the hammer notch which contrasts with a darker band shows unequal pressure exerted by the sear point. This difference is made more apparent by placing lampblack on the notch. When this fault is found, stroke the sear point over an oilstone, working in one direction only, with a constant angle between the sear point and the stone.

Beginners are prone to become impatient with the oilstone and turn to a file as a tool that works faster. They often grind off the front edge of the hammer notch to make it shallower. This eliminates creep and makes the pull of the trigger lighter, but the sear will not move far enough forward to clear the half-cock notch or the safety while the hammer is falling, with the result that the notch and sear point strike together and break one of them.

Another mistake is to file the sear thinner. This is useless because the rear edge of the sear point will travel to the front edge of the hammer notch with the same speed as before. Instead of making the sear thinner, the rear edge of the sear point should be very slightly beveled, as we have already indicated.

Figure 8, Plate 31, shows how excessive creep is eliminated by "pinning" when it is caused by too much depth to the hammer notch. Drill a $\frac{1}{16}$ inch hole in the hammer below the notch. Drive a pin made from drill rod into this hole. File off the pin until the sear can engage the hammer notch deep enough to give a clean trigger pull without letting the hammer slip off. The danger of premature discharge can be tested by cocking the weapon and holding it in one hand, while the other hand strikes the gun from various angles, or by bouncing the cocked gun on a soft board. If the hammer jars off, file down the pin until jarring does not discharge the weapon.

Figure 6, Plate 31, shows how the hammer of a .38 caliber Officer's Model revolver can be altered. The three views show the notch in the hammer before alteration, dotted lines indicating the parts cut away, and the shape after the work is completed. When performed by an expert, this alteration will produce a clean, smooth pull, but when done by a beginner, the result may be a ruined hammer.

Conservative ordnance engineers and gunsmiths insist that in adjusting the trigger pull, the notch should not be touched; instead, all work is done on the trigger point. They also insist that in stoning the point, it must never be stoned across but always in the direction of the motion of the trigger point.

Figure 7, Plate 31, illustrates an alteration to a Lee-Enfield Rifle. The same method can be applied to other bolt-action rifles. The tooth-like protrusion indicated by an arrow, both in the assembled drawing and in the enlarged view to the right, is ground down. Hold it against an emery wheel for part of a second, round off the corners with a carborundum stone, assemble the mechanism, and test for trigger pull. Repeat this process until you have the desired amount of pull, but do not remove too much metal or the rifle will fire prematurely.

Open-hammer type actions, such as those found on some of the Winchester and Stevens arms, may be speeded up by cutting lightening holes in the web below the hammer spur, or by cutting out a triangular piece, as shown in Figure 9, Plate 31. Since the hammers are hardened in manufacture, it is necessary to anneal them before cutting the lightening holes and then reharden them after the holes are cut.

Figures 1, 2, 3, and 5, Plate 32, show parts of the United States Rifle, Caliber .30, Model 1903, popularly called the Springfield. Figure 1 shows the contact between the sear nose and the sear notch. Figure 2 shows top and side views of the sear, and also views of the sear pin and the sear spring. Figure 3 shows the trigger, right view and front view, with views of the trigger pin. Figure 5 shows the firing pin, with the names of its parts: head, neck, firing pin rod, locking shoulder, groove, cocking piece, knob, lug, sear notch, cocking cam, and nose.

The firing pin consists of the firing pin rod and the cocking piece, which are made separately, the former being screwed into the latter and riveted in assembling; the length of the rod is adjusted so that when the front end of the cocking piece bears against the interior shoulder of the sleeve the striker point will project the proper distance beyond the face of the bolt.

The sear has the sear nose, pin hole, trigger slot, trigger pin hole, and the sear spring seat, which is occupied by the sear spring, its upper end bearing against the receiver. The sear pin hinges the sear in the receiver.

The trigger is hinged in its slot in the sear by the trigger pin. It has a finger piece which is knurled to prevent slipping of the finger in firing; a bearing, which is the central curved surface at the top of the right view in the drawing; a trigger pin hole; a heel, which is the left curved surface at the top of the right view in the drawing; and a "stop," which is the little nose that projects to the right, just to the right of and below the trigger pin hole in the drawing.

Refer again to Figure 1, Plate 32. The arrow indicates the contact surfaces between the sear nose and the sear notch; these are the surfaces which must be worked in order to obtain the desired trigger pull. The principles of operation followed here will apply to other bolt-action rifles. The contact surfaces are carefully stoned and then the nose of the sear is given a slight radius on the end. The face of the sear notch on the cocking piece is stoned back at a slight angle from the vertical, with the result that the rear face of the sear only bears for a short distance at the bottom edge of the sear notch. These two contact surfaces must be highly polished, and they must bear evenly against each other. Uneven surfaces can be detected by using lampblack before assembly and then examining the surfaces for unequal pressure.

Generally, the sear spring should not be altered, but on some bolt-action rifles the sear spring is too stiff. A small part can be cut off, the trigger pull tried, and the process repeated until the sear spring loses its stiffness, but too much must not be removed. The test here is to give the trigger a preliminary squeeze and then release it without squeezing it far enough to release the firing pin. The spring should permit the sear to engage completely with the cocking-piece under these circumstances.

Figure 4, Plate 32, illustrates three other methods of reducing

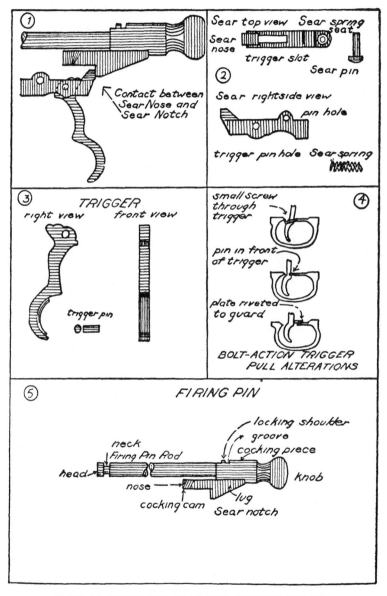

PLATE 32. FIRING PIN, SEAR AND TRIGGER DETAILS.

trigger pull in bolt-action rifles. In the top drawing, a small hole is drilled and tapped through the trigger, and a screw is passed through the trigger from the rear to the front to bear against the front edge of the trigger slot in the trigger guard. This prevents the trigger from traveling forward its full distance. The screw may work loose from firing and require tightening.

In the middle drawing of Figure 4, a small hole is drilled part way through the trigger from front to rear, and a pin is driven into this hole and filed off to a length that will reduce the movement of the trigger forward.

The bottom drawing of Figure 4 shows a small steel plate riveted to the trigger guard, or fastened with screws, so that the rear end of the plate limits the forward movement of the trigger.

Needless to say, the suggestions for trigger-pull adjustment given here are for general application. A member of the armed services who makes any unauthorized alteration to his weapons is subject to discipline and may be required to reimburse the government for any "damage," even though such alteration actually improves the shooting qualities of the firearms. Similarly, a gunsmith should have the permission of the owner before he makes any radical alterations.

Set triggers, both single and double, sometimes called "hair triggers," seldom call for the attention of the gunsmith because they are ordinarily found only on better grade weapons which are carefully adjusted before being placed on sale. A set trigger consists of a trigger with a small hammer that rises and strikes the sear in the action a sharp blow that releases the true hammer when the trigger is squeezed. A small screw is used to lighten or increase the pull; this is not hardened and may work loose as its threads are worn. One remedy is to dismount the set-trigger mechanism, and reduce the size of the screw hole by lightly pounding around its edges with a small ball-peen hammer. There is a risk of battering the edges, so it is better to find a new screw with a size that is a little too big, thus ensuring a tight fit.

When the parts of a set trigger have not been properly hardened, .the mechanism should be disassembled and all parts except the springs casehardened, as explained in another chapter of this book.

Then, the wear on screw threads and other bearing surfaces will be reduced.

The ordinary set-trigger mechanism has a rear trigger that sets the front trigger; squeezing the front trigger discharges the piece, but squeezing the rear trigger has no effect on firing. Instead of the rear trigger, there may be either a button or a lever, or there may be a single trigger that is set by pushing it forward. Some European set-trigger weapons may have as many as five levers, each of which is released in its turn. Such guns can be fired by a force hardly stronger than that exerted by breathing on the trigger. The gunsmith must be very careful if he test fires set-trigger guns, for even experts accustomed to their peculiarities encounter accidental discharges.

Turning to automatic pistols, we find that their care and repair follow the same principles as other firearms, but there are a few points to observe that are peculiar to this type. It is almost impossible, for instance, to eliminate all of the creep because of the distance from the trigger to the hammer, and the number of connecting links and bars. Honing the sear point and hammer notch will reduce the pull about as much as safety will permit. Eliminating all of the creep may cause the automatic pistol to fire "full automatic" and empty itself at the first squeeze of the trigger, whereas it should be fired semi-automatic, that is, one shot for one pull.

When the Colt .45 caliber automatic pistol is being adjusted, first remove the hammer, sear, trigger, and similar parts from the receiver. Next, smooth the groove in which the trigger slides, using a narrow pillar file and finishing with a fine grade of emery cloth wrapped around the file. Spread the sides of the trigger where they touch the grooves to remove any side play, and give them a good polish to reduce friction.

With the receiver of the pistol in a vise, squeeze the guard close to the frame; this removes vertical trigger play. Polish all the contact points of the sear, hammer, pins, sear spring, etc., and try to take out any excess motion when the parts are assembled. You may find that the rounded end of the disconnector and the milled slot in the slide in which the disconnector engages are not operating with a smooth contact; this may be caused by roughness of the milled slot and it can be corrected by polishing.

Sear and hammer adjustment for the Colt .45 caliber automatic pistol is no different from similar work on other types except that it is more difficult to perform. The trigger pull desired is just about 4 pounds—a few ounces too much is better than too little. Also, there is often excessive back slap when the hammer falls. This can be prevented by welding a trigger stop to the grip safety, by constructing a stop that operates against the magazine catch, by mounting a screw in the trigger, or by mounting a screw in the trigger guard, as previously explained and illustrated.

Shotgun trigger adjustment offers a few special problems. First, there should not be too much pressure by the triggers against the sears. Second, both triggers of a double-barrel shotgun should have the same pull. By disassembling the gun and observing the bearing surfaces, you may find that the sears need to be stoned until they are equal in size, shape, and operation, especially on the angles at each end where they disengage from the tumblers. Each angle is stoned back until it is free of the top of the notch in the tumbler and then a slight radius is given to the end. Where there is a shallow cut in the tumbler, the sear may require an angle rather than a radius. This can be determined by observation and experiment.

It is not necessary to place the action back in the stock for each of the successive tests usually found necessary for adjusting trigger pull. Simply assemble the trigger guard and place a piece of pipe between the trigger guard and the upper tang. Tighten the rear screw against this pipe, just as though the trigger guard were in the stock. Mount the barrels in the action with the forearm in position. You can then test for trigger pull without causing the guard to spring.

We have previously explained and illustrated the speeding up of action time by removing metal from the hammers. Other methods of accomplishing the same thing are: substituting heavier and stiffer main springs; shortening the fall of the striker or hammer; substituting lighter firing pins or hammers; and changing the location of sear notches in tumblers or hammers. The method chosen depends, of course, upon the design of the action.

Coil springs are used in most American shotguns, particularly those sold on a price basis, but they are far inferior to flat or V-type springs if the latter are made from good quality steel that has been properly heat-treated. You can make your own springs by following instructions in forging, heat treatment, etc., given elsewhere in this book, but use the old spring as a model for size and shape. A makeshift step that sometimes works well is to wind a small-gauge copper wire around an old spring near its bottom; this increases the tension and gives more life and speed.

The fall of the hammer may be shortened by changing the sear notch or the trigger notch. However, before sear notches are cut in a hammer, you must be sure that there is enough distance between the old notch and the new one to permit a clean cut; otherwise you may spoil the hammer entirely. If the hammer is of an obsolete design and cannot be replaced by the factory, you must then make a new one.

In all cases where casehardened parts are cut by a file, a stone, an emery wheel, or by any other process, they must be rehardened. This is an important general rule that applies throughout gun-smithing, not merely to trigger and action adjustment.

The lock-time on bolt-action rifles can be speeded up by cutting off the end of the cocking piece and then rounding it over on the end, especially if it is shaped like the old-style cocking piece on the Springfield, but this is an objectionable practice. The firing pin rod will then come unscrewed because it was threaded into the cocking piece at the factory, and then held fast by riveting. This is broken when the end of the cocking piece is sawed off. If you insist upon removing the end of the cocking piece, drill a hole through the new end, insert a short length of drill rod as a pin and rivet this pin over on each side to hold the firing pin rod in place.

Lock time can also be speeded up by increasing the length of a striker, thus reducing the distance it must travel before hitting the primer in the cartridge. However, the striker must not project, as a firing pin, more than .065 inch beyond the face of the bolt or it will pierce the primer and cause gas to leak to the rear, with results that are sometimes dangerous. A longer striker requires a heavier and stronger spring or it defeats the purpose for which it was designed.

Finally, a set of trigger weights is absolutely necessary if you wish to eliminate guess work in adjusting trigger pulls. These can be purchased, ready-made, from any dealer in shooting supplies, or you can make your own. They weigh exactly 2 pounds, 1 pound, ½ pound, and 4 ounces, respectively. You need one of each except that two of the half-pound weights should be available.

Make the weights by pouring melted lead into empty tubes or cans in which a bent wire is inserted. This wire should be strong and stiff and have a nut, bolt, or a bent-over end at the bottom, so that it will not pull out of the lead in use. When the lead cools, check each of the weights on scales that are absolutely accurate. The trigger pull may vary 2 ounces one way or the other in testing guns, but the weights themselves must be correct.

XXIX. The Springfield Rifle

THE United States Rifle, Caliber .30, Model 1903, is a breech-loading magazine rifle of the bolt type. It is commonly called the "Springfield Rifle." It was the principal infantry weapon of the First World War. It was used in action by the United States Marine Corps during World Wars I and II, to some extent during the Korean War, and in all the small wars the Marine Corps fought overseas from World War I to the Korean War. It was used by landing forces of the Navy when they went ashore with Marines. Officially, this rifle is now obsolete, but it is one of the "Guns of Glory" and is used by thousands of civilian hunters and marksmen. It is described and illustrated in this chapter as it existed in 1917, because this is the original, fundamental form from which later modifications were developed. See Plate 33.

The principal dimensions, weight, and technical facts are: Weight without bayonet, 8.69 pounds. Weight with bayonet, 9.69 pounds. Length without bayonet, 43 inches plus. Length with bayonet, 59 inches plus. Diameter of bore, .30 inch. Minimum trigger pull, 3 pounds. Facts about rifling are: Number of grooves, 4. Twist, uniform, right, one turn in 10 inches. Magazine capacity, 5 rounds.

The illustrations of the Springfield shown on Plates 32 to 39, inclusive, are taken from ordnance drawings of the United States Rifle, Caliber .30, Model 1903, as it existed in 1917, because the older drawings more accurately portray the parts as they are usually found in the possession of civilians. However, there are very few modifications in the later designs, the nomenclature is the same, and a person having the latest Springfield will have no trouble in following instructions. Dimensions, weights, and ballistic data given here are correct for modifications of the Springfield as issued in 1942.

The rear sight of the Springfield is adjustable for windage, and the drift of the bullet to the right is offset automatically by the construction of the rear sight leaf. The leaf is graduated from 100 to 2,850 yards. The lines extending across one or both branches of the leaf are 100-yard divisions, the longer of the short lines 50-yard and the shorter lines 25-yard divisions. The drift slide, which may be moved up or down the leaf, has notches called open sights and a circular hole called the peep sight. With the leaf raised to the vertical position the lines on either side of the peep sight, and the lower notch, enabled the drift slide to be set accurately at any desired graduation on the leaf. With the leaf down and using the "battle-sight" notch in the slide cap, the sights are set for 547 yards for the down position of the slide. The rear end of the rear-sight movable base is marked with wind-gauge graduations, each point of which corresponds to a lateral deviation in the point of impact of the bullet of 4 inches for each 100 yards of range to the target.

The maximum rate of accurate fire with this weapon depends upon the skill and position of the operator and the visibility of the target. It varies from 10 to 15 shots per minute. The effectiveness of rifle fire during combat decreases as the range to the target increases. Its use in battle at ranges greater than 600 yards is considered "unusual" by the United States Army, but riflemen of the United States Marine Corps have often brought down the enemies of the United States at ranges greater than 600 yards. This statement is not intended as a reflection on the Army, but merely as an indication of what can be done with a rifle when the soldier has received training in marksmanship at long ranges. It is true, however, that most men who are killed in battle by rifle fire are shot at close ranges.

Some of the names of the parts of the Springfield which a gunsmith will learn first are: Cocking Piece, Bolt Handle, Bolt, Breech, Rear Sight, Windage Screw, Hand Guard, Upper Band, Front Sight, Muzzle, Barrel, Front Sight Cover, Bore, Stacking Swivel, Lower Band Swivel, Balance, Floor Plate, Trigger, Trigger Guard,

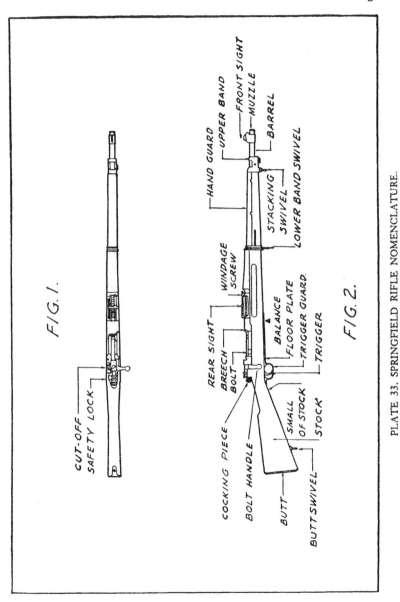

FIG. 1.

CUT-OFF
SAFETY LOCK

HAND GUARD
UPPER BAND
FRONT SIGHT
MUZZLE
BARREL
STACKING SWIVEL
LOWER BAND SWIVEL

REAR SIGHT
WINDAGE SCREW
BREECH
BOLT
BALANCE
FLOOR PLATE
TRIGGER GUARD
TRIGGER

COCKING PIECE
BOLT HANDLE
SMALL OF STOCK
STOCK
BUTT
BUTT SWIVEL

FIG. 2.

PLATE 33. SPRINGFIELD RIFLE NOMENCLATURE.

Small of Stock, Stock, Butt Swivel, Butt, Safety Lock, and Cut-Off. Names referring to the Rear Sight are: Sight Leaf, Sight Graduations, Drift Slide, Peep Sight, and Wind Gauge. Names referring to parts mentioned in removing the Bolt are: Receiver, Bolt, Bolt Handle, Safety Lug, Safety Lock, Cut-Off, and Grasping Groove. Names of parts of the Bolt include: Sleeve, Sleeve Lock, Striker, Firing Pin Rod, Firing Pin Sleeve, Mainspring, Safety Lock, and Cocking Piece. Other parts of the bolt are: Tongue, Groove, Extractor, Extractor Collar, Safety Lug and Right Lug. All of these parts are illustrated and labeled on the plates accompanying this chapter. A gunsmith can "get by" with calling parts "gadgets" but it is more professional and it makes work easier to call parts by their correct names. Plates 32 to 39, inclusive, should be studied carefully.

Gunsmiths would like to receive all rifles properly cleaned, but if everyone cleaned his rifle properly there would be less work for gunsmiths, since the majority of rifles become unserviceable not through shooting but through the lack of intelligent and proper care. Needless to say, at military inspections, unless otherwise ordered, rifles must be clean, the bore protected with a thin film of medium rust-preventive compound, the mechanism lubricated with thin oil, such as sperm oil, and the oiler in the butt of the rifle filled with oil.

The parts to be removed for cleaning the rifle are the front sight cover, floor plate and follower, gun sling, oiler and thong case, and the bolt.

To remove the floor plate and follower, insert the point of a cartridge through the hole in the floor plate and press on the floor plate catch. This releases the floor plate which may then be removed together with the magazine spring and follower. Raise the rear end of the magazine spring high enough to clear the lug on the floor plate and draw it out of its mortise; in the same manner separate the magazine spring from the follower. To assemble, proceed in reverse order.

To remove and disassemble the bolt.—First, place the cut-off at the center notch; cock the piece by raising and lowering the bolt handle; turn the safety lock to the vertical position; raise the bolt handle and draw out the bolt to the rear. Second, press the sleeve lock in with the thumb to unlock the sleeve from the bolt; unscrew the sleeve by turning to the left and remove it. Third, hold the sleeve between the forefinger and thumb of the left hand; draw the cocking piece back slightly with the middle finger and thumb of the right hand; turn the safety lock down to the left with the forefinger of the right hand and allow the cocking piece to move forward in the sleeve. This partially relieves the tension of the

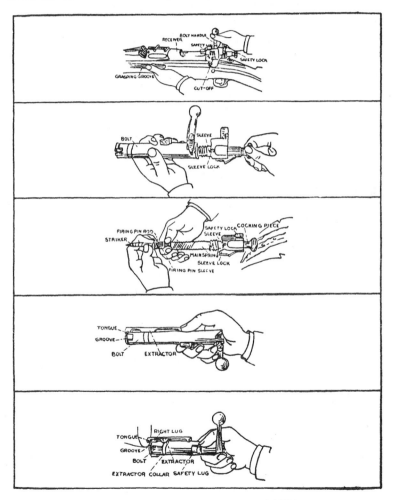

PLATE 34. SPRINGFIELD BOLT DETAILS.

mainspring. With the cocking piece against the chest, draw back the firing pin sleeve with the forefinger and thumb of the right hand and hold it in this position while removing the striker with the left hand. Fourth, remove the firing pin sleeve and mainspring; pull the firing pin out of the sleeve. Turn the extractor to the right, forcing its tongue out of its groove in the front of the bolt; and force the extractor forward and off the bolt. See Plate 34.

To assemble and replace the bolt mechanism.—Turn the extractor collar until its lug is on line with the safety lug on the bolt; insert the lug on the collar in the undercuts in the extractor by pushing the extractor to the rear until its tongue comes in contact with the face of the bolt; turn the extractor to the right until it is over the right lug; press the hook of the extractor against some rigid object until the tongue on the extractor enters its groove in the bolt. (This is illustrated in the bottom figure of Plate 34.)

With the safety lock turned down to the left, assemble the sleeve and firing pin; place the cocking piece against the chest and put on mainspring, firing pin sleeve, and striker. (This is illustrated in the figure next to the bottom of Plate 34.)

Hold the cocking piece between the thumb and forefinger of the left hand, and by pressing the striker against some object, not hard enough to injure it, force the cocking piece back until the safety lock can be turned to the vertical position with the right hand; insert the firing pin in the bolt and screw up the sleeve until the sleeve lock enters its notch on the bolt. Pull the cocking piece back and turn the safety lock to the vertical position. Place the cut-off at the center notch; hold the piece under the floor plate in the fingers of the left hand, the thumb extending over the left side of the receiver; take the bolt in the right hand with the safety lock in a vertical position and safety lug up; press the rear end of the follower down with the left thumb and push the bolt into the receiver; lower the bolt handle; turn the safety lock and the cut-off down to the left.

Care of the Springfield Rifle during periods when no firing is done, in garrisons, posts, camps and around a home, is more important than many people seem to think. This is especially true in damp or dusty regions, and when the rifle has been exposed to the elements in any way. Even an ordinary inspection of a rifle leaves sweaty marks that induce rust. Instructions for cleaning are given in another chapter, with separate sections devoted to care and cleaning when no firing is done, after firing, in the field, and on the target range.

FUNCTIONING

To load the magazine, turn the cut-off up, showing "on"; draw the bolt fully to the rear and insert the cartridges from a clip, or singly from the hand. To load from a clip, place one end of a loaded clip in its seat in the receiver, and with the fingers of the right hand under the rifle against the floor plate, and the base of the thumb on the powder space of the top cartridge near the clip, press the cartridges down with the thumb into the magazine with a firm, steady push until the top cartridge is caught by the right edge of the receiver. The empty clip is removed with the right hand. After loading the magazine, to place a round in the chamber, close the bolt. As the bolt is closed the top cartridge in the magazine is pushed forward into the chamber. When the rifle is used as a single loader, cartridges are inserted directly into the chamber with the hand, the cut-off being turned down.

Extraction of the empty case from the chamber by the extractor is started during the rotation of the bolt and is completed as the bolt is drawn to the rear.

When the bolt is drawn fully to the rear the head of the case strikes against the ejector point and the case is ejected from the receiver.

When the cut-off is up and the bolt fully to the rear, the top cartridge in the magazine is forced up into the path of the bolt by the magazine spring. When the cut-off is turned down the magazine is "off." The bolt cannot be drawn fully back, and its front end, projecting over the rear end of the upper cartridge, holds the latter down in the magazine below the action of the bolt. The magazine mechanism then remains inoperative, and the rifle can be used as a single loader with the cartridges in the magazine held in reserve.

In magazine fire, after the last cartridge has been fired and the bolt drawn fully to the rear, the follower rises and blocks the path of the bolt, thus showing that the magazine is empty. A new clip may then be inserted and the magazine refilled, or the bolt may be closed without reloading by first forcing the follower down until it is below the path of the bolt.

To unload.—With the cut-off up, move the bolt forward and back until no cartridges remain in the magazine or chamber.

To set at safe, which can only be done when the piece is cocked, turn the safety lock to the right. This locks the firing pin in position and the piece cannot be fired. To set at ready, turn the safety lock to the left.

Cocking can be done either by raising the bolt handle until it strikes the left side of the receiver and then turning it down, or by pulling the cocking piece directly to the rear.

CARTRIDGES FOR THE SPRINGFIELD

The principal classification of ammunition for the Springfield, based upon use, is: Ball, for use against personnel and light matériel; Tracer, for observation of fire and incendiary purposes; and Armor-piercing, for use against armored vehicles, concrete shelters, and other bullet-resisting targets.

Armor-piercing, tracer, and range dummy cartridges resemble ball cartridges with the following exceptions: armor-piercing is painted black for ¼ inch from the point; tracer is painted red for ¼ inch from the point; and range dummy has a short narrow slot cut in the side of the cartridge case near the base.

Other types for special purposes are: Guard, for guard purposes; Blank, for simulated fire, signaling, and salutes; Dummy, for training (they will not fire); and Range Dummy.

An ammunition lot number which becomes an essential part of the marking is assigned when ammunition is manufactured. This number is marked on all packing containers and on an identification card inclosed in each packing box. It is required for all purposes of record including grading and use, reports on condition, functioning, and accidents, in which the ammunition might be involved.

The various types of ammunition are further identified by color bands, painted on the sides and ends of the packing boxes, as follows: cartridge, armor-piercing, Blue on yellow; cartridge, ball, Red; cartridge, blank, Blue; cartridge, dummy, Green; cartridge, gallery

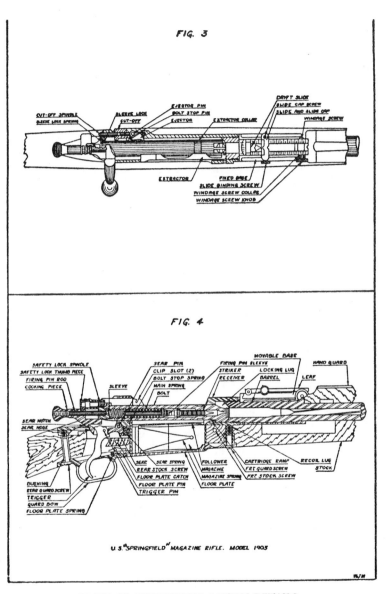

FIG. 3

FIG. 4

U. S. "SPRINGFIELD" MAGAZINE RIFLE. MODEL 1903

PLATE 35. SPRINGFIELD ACTION DETAILS.

practice, Brown; cartridge, guard, Orange; cartridge, tracer, Green on yellow. There is also a special packing for the Air Corps, not for use with the M1903 Rifle, consisting of cartridge, ball, and cartridge, tracer, in metallic link belts, marked with a composite band of yellow, red, and green stripes (yellow on left, red in center, green on right).

The care, handling, and preservation of small-arms ammunition is a comparatively safe and simple matter, as compared with other types of ammunition. However, the boxes must not become broken or damaged. All broken boxes must be repaired immediately and careful attention should be given to the correct transfer of the markings to the new parts of the box. When suitable equipment is available, the metal liner of each box should be air-tested and sealed.

Ammunition boxes should not be opened until the ammunition is to be used. When removed from the airtight container, especially in a damp climate, the ammunition corrodes and eventually becomes useless. Likewise, protect the ammunition from mud, dirt, sand, dust and water. If it gets dirty or wet, wipe it off with clean, dry rags. Light corrosion on cartridges should be wiped off. However, cartridges must not be polished for the purpose of making them look pretty.

In the military service, ammunition is graded in accordance with orders issued by the Ordnance Department. This is in addition to the lot number. Where the lot number has been lost, the ammunition is arbitrarily placed in grade 3. The purpose of grading is to assign suitable ammunition to each type of weapon. Aircraft machine guns, for instance, would normally receive the best grade. No ammunition of caliber .30 is fired by the Army until it has been positively identified by ammunition lot number and grade as shown in the latest information released by the Ordnance Department.

The maximum range for the Cartridge, Ball, Caliber .30, M1, was approximately 5,500 yards, but the manufacture of this Mark 1 has been discontinued. The maximum range for the Cartridge, Ball, Caliber .30, M2, is approximately 3,450 yards.

Blank cartridges must not be fired in the direction of personnel at distances less than 20 yards because the wad or paper cup in a cartridge may fail to break up and be shot through the air.

In firing blank cartridges there are sometimes misfires in which the primer explodes but fails to ignite the powder charge. When this occurs, some of the powder is blown into the bore of the weapon. A series of such misfires where the powder fails to ignite will cause an accumulation of powder and then, when a normal cartridge is fired, a tremendous explosion may result. When misfires occur in more than 5 per cent of the blank cartridges in any lot, the firing of that lot is suspended.

DESCRIPTION AND NOMENCLATURE OF THE RIFLE

Figure numbers used on the plates to illustrate the nomenclature of the Springfield Rifle are for convenience in reference and have no relationship to figure numbers on other plates, necessarily. The Rifle is shown in Figures 1 and 2, Plate 33. The Barrel with the Fixed Stud and Fixed Base attached is shown in Figure 3, Plate 36. The Receiver, Figure 4, top view, and Figure 5, right-side view, has a hole marked "A", called the well, which receives the bolt; a magazine opening marked "B"; a channel for the top locking lug; a cut-off seat "D"; a cut-off thumbpiece recess; ejector pin hole "F"; clip slots "G"; cocking piece groove "H"; sear nose slot; extracting cam "J"; sear pin hole "K"; gas escape hole "L"; recoil lug "M" (in which is the hole for the front guard screw); the recess for the bolt locking lugs; the locking cams; the locking shoulders; the safety shoulders; and the cartridge ramp.

On the upper surface of the front end is stamped the serial number of the rifle and the place of manufacture.

The Bolt, Figure 7, Plate 36, top view, Figure 8, rear view, and Figure 9, front view, has the handle "A"; the locking lugs "BB", which sustains the shock of the discharge, the one on top being slotted to allow the passage of the point of the ejector; the safety lug "C", which comes into play only in the event of the locking lugs yielding under powder pressure; the extractor collar groove "D"; extracting cam "E"; sleeve clearance "F"; safety lock spindle notch "G"; sleeve lock notch "H"; firing pin hold "I"; cocking cam "J"; cock notch "K"; extractor tongue groove "L"; gas escape hole, not shown, between the locking lugs; the rim "M"; and two small circular notches, not shown, on the left side of the slotted locking lug; this side of the lug rotates 90 degrees when the bolt is drawn

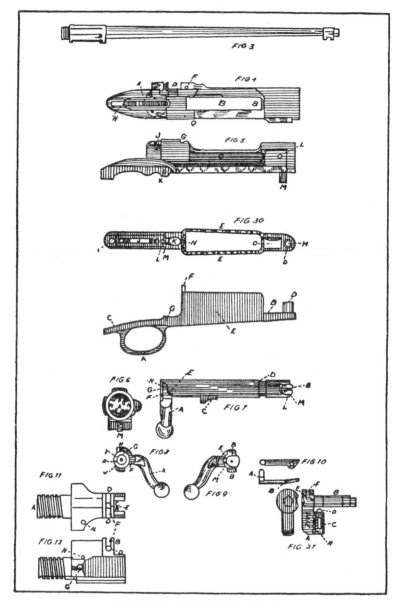

PLATE 36. SPRINGFIELD PARTS.

back for loading, and one of the notches engages with the bolt stop pin "A", Figure 10, in either single or magazine loading, retaining the bolt in place in the open position.

The Bolt Stop, Figure 10, consists of the pin "A", and the flat spring "B", riveted together in manufacture. The pin projects through its hole in the receiver just in front of the cut-off opening, and is held in place and operated by the spring which fits into a slot in the receiver in the rear of the magazine.

The Sleeve, Figure 11, top view, and Figure 12, left-side view, has the barrel "A", which is threaded for the purpose of securing the sleeve to the bolt; the safety lock seat "B"; the safety lock plunger groove "C"; the recesses "D", for retaining the safety lock when turned to the right or left; the recess "E" for retaining safety lock in dismounting bolt mechanism; the bevel "F", for dismounting the safety lock from the sleeve; the sleeve lock recess "G"; and the sleeve lock pin hole "H." There are also the safety lock spindle and firing pin holes, the cocking piece groove and the undercut for the rear end of the bolt. None of the last four is shown in the illustration.

The Sleeve Lock, Figure 13, Plate 37, left-end view, and Figure 14, under-side view, has the spindle "A", which is bored out to receive the sleeve lock spring; the latch "B", and the sleeve lock pin groove "C." It is designed to prevent accidental turning of the sleeve when the bolt is drawn back.

The Sleeve Lock Spring and Pin are shown in Figure 15.

The Firing Pin, Figure 5, Plate 32, consists of the firing pin rod and the cocking piece, which are made separately, the former being screwed into the latter and riveted in assembling; the length of the rod is so adjusted that when the front end of the cocking piece bears against the interior shoulder of the sleeve the striker point will project the proper distance beyond the face of the bolt. Other parts are the knob, lug, cocking cam, nose, sear notch, locking shoulder, locking groove, neck, and head.

The Firing Pin Sleeve, Figure 17, Plate 37, sectional view, fits over the front end of the firing pin and the rear end of the striker, covering the joint hole, and preventing accidental separation of the firing pin and striker; its rear end forms the front bearing for the mainspring.

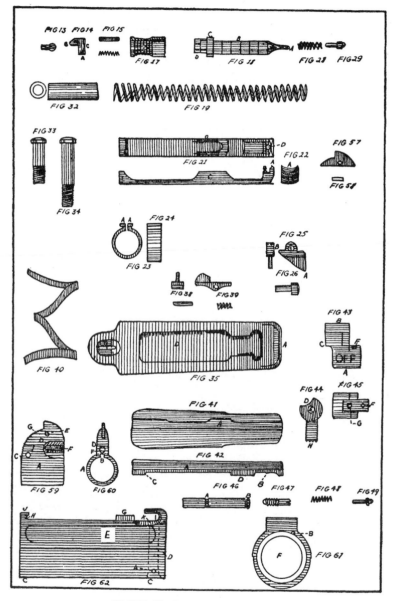

PLATE 37. SPRINGFIELD PARTS.

The Striker, Figure 18, Plate 37, has the point "A", the body "B", the shoulder "C", and the joint hole "D", by which it is secured to the firing pin. The annular grooves on the striker retain the lubricating oil and prevent the accumulation of rust thereon.

The Mainspring is shown in Figure 19, Plate 37.

The Extractor, Figure 21, Plate 37, top and side views, and Figure 22, front-end view, has the hook "A" by which the cartridge case is extracted from the chamber; the tongue "B" which rides in its groove at the front end of the bolt; the lug "C" which is undercut to receive the ears on the lugs of the extractor collar; the gas escape hole "D", and a back rest, which is curved to fit the circle of the bolt.

The Extractor Collar, Figure 23, Plate 37, end view, and Figure 24, side view, has the ears "AA", which fit in the undercuts on the inside of the extractor, by which means and with the assistance of the extractor tongue and groove the extractor is held in place. The collar is bent into position on the bolt in manufacture, and should not be removed unless proper tools are at hand to replace it.

The Ejector, Figure 25, Plate 37, has the point "A", the heel "B", and the ejector pin hole "C." It is hinged on the ejector pin in its recess in the left side of the receiver, ejection being accomplished by the slotted lug on the bolt coming in contact with the heel when the bolt is drawn to the rear.

The head of the Ejector Pin, Figure 26, Plate 37, is slotted for the purpose of providing sufficient tension to hold the pin in its place during the process of assembling.

The Safety Lock, Figure 27, Plate 36, rear and side views, consists of thumbpiece "A", the spindle "B", spring "C", and plunger "D", assembled in manufacture. It has the cam "E", the locking groove "F", the cocking piece groove "G", the plunger hole "H", and a bolt clearance. The spring and plunger are shown in Figures 28 and 29, Plate 37. The plunger, projecting into its groove in the sleeve, under the action of the spring, prevents any movement of the safety lock to the rear, and when in the recesses in the groove retains the safety lock turned either to the right or left or in the vertical position for dismounting bolt mechanism. The words "Safe" and "Ready" impressed on opposite sides of the thumbpiece indicate that the firing mechanism is locked or ready for firing.

The Guard, of which the body of the magazine forms a part, is shown in Figure 30, Plate 36, right-side and top views, respectively. Its parts are the guard bow "A", front tang "B", rear tang "C", front guard screw stud "D", magazine walls "E", rear end of the magazine "F", floor plate pin hole "G", front guard screw hole "H", rear guard screw hole "I", trigger slot "J", floor plate lug slot "K", floor plate spring hole "L", floor plate catch slot "M", ramp "N". and the lightening cut "O."

The Guard Screw Bushing, Figure 32, Plate 37, fits tightly into the stock between the receiver and the rear tang of the guard, and serves as a stop for the screw, preventing its being screwed down tight enough to bend the guard.

The Guard Screws, front and rear, Figures 33 and 34, Plate 37, secure the guard to the receiver.

The Floor Plate, Figure 36, Plate 37, sectional view, has the tenon "A", which fits into a groove at the front end of the magazine and with the assistance of the floor plate catch retains the floor plate securely in its place at the bottom of the magazine; the lug "B". which is slotted to receive the floor plate catch and has a tenon on its front end which fits into a slot in the magazine; the cavity "C", through which the floor plate catch is released by means of the end of a bullet; the magazine spring recess "D", and the magazine spring seat "E."

The Floor Plate Catch, indicated in Figure 4, Plate 35, hinges on the Floor Plate Pin, Figure 38, Plate 37, and is operated by the Floor Plate Spring, Figure 39, Plate 37. Its function is to retain the floor plate in its seat.

The Magazine Spring is shown in Figure 40, Plate 37; the smaller end slides into the undercuts on the follower, and the larger end fits in the same way into the undercuts in the floor plate.

The Follower, Figure 41, Plate 37, top view, and Figure 42, right-side view, has the rib "A", which serves to locate the cartridges in the magazine and guides the last cartridge into the chamber; the front stop for the magazine spring "B"; the rear stop for magazine spring "C"; and the lugs "D", in which are the undercuts for the magazine spring.

The Cut-Off, Figure 43, Plate 37, side view, Figure 44, rear view, and Figure 45, outer edge, has the thumbpiece "A", body "B",

magazine fire groove "C", dismounting groove "D", cut-off spindle
hole "E", cut-off plunger hole "F", cut-off screw hole "G", and the
serrature "H." The words on opposite sides of the thumbpiece indicate to the firer whether the magazine is "on" or "off." When the
cut-off thumbpiece is turned down, indicating "off," and the bolt is
drawn to the rear, the rear end of the slotted locking lug stops
against the projecting front end of the cut-off body. The piece is
then ready for single loading. When the cut-off thumbpiece is turned
up, indicating "on," and the bolt is drawn to the rear, the rear end
of the slotted locking lug stops against the shoulder at the rear end
of the magazine fire groove. The piece is then ready for loading
from the magazine. When the cut-off thumbpiece is in the intermediate position, the dismounting groove "D" permits the bolt to be
drawn entirely out of the receiver.

The Cut-Off Spindle, Figure 46, Plate 37, has the cut-off screw
groove "A" and the dismounting groove "B." The Cut-Off Screw,
Figure 47, Plate 37, goes through the cut-off from the outer edge
of the thumbpiece, its end fitting into the groove in the cut-off
spindle. The Cut-Off Spring, Figure 48, and the Plunger, Figure 49,
both of Plate 37, retain the cut-off in its seat in the receiver with the
thumbpiece turned up for loading from the magazine, down for
single loading, or in the intermediate position for permitting the
removal of the bolt. The spindle head works in a groove in the left
side of the receiver, having three small notches corresponding to
the above positions of the cut-off.

The Sear and the Trigger are shown in detail in Figures 1, 2,
and 3 of Plate 32, and described in the chapter on Trigger-Pull Adjustments. Otherwise, they would appear as figures 50 to 56 inclusive (not presented here) of the ordnance drawings of this series.

The Front and Rear Sights, with their various attaching and
adjusting parts, are shown in Figures 59 to 83, inclusive, of Plates 37
and 38. The various parts and assemblies are described in detail
in the chapter on Sights.

The Stock, and the parts pertaining principally to the stock, are
shown in Figures 84 to 108, inclusive, and described in the chapter
on Inletting the Action.

The reader is reminded that Plates 32 to 39, inclusive, are to be
examined as a group for the purpose of understanding not only the

Springfield but also bolt-action rifles in general. Furthermore, the fundamental principles of design, construction, assembly, and repair which apply to the Springfield apply broadly to all rifles, and to a great extent to shotguns. Plates 34, 36, 37, 38, and 39 show details. Plates 33 and 35 show the relationship of the parts to one another when the rifle is assembled.

TO COMPLETE DISMOUNTING

Special Note: In the armed services of the United States the following dismounting is not done by the enlisted man unless he has received direct authority to do so. Those unfamiliar with the Springfield should be very careful to lay out the parts in order, from left to right, as they are removed, to be sure that they can be reassembled correctly.

Having dismounted the bolt and magazine mechanism, as explained in the earlier part of this chapter, proceed as follows:

1. Turn the safety lock to dismounting bevel on sleeve and remove it by striking the thumbpiece a light blow.

2. To dismount the sleeve lock, drive out the sleeve lock pin from the top and remove lock and spring, being careful not to lose the spring.

3. Remove the front sight pin (see directions for replacing broken parts, given later) and remove front sight.

4. Press in rear end of lower band spring and drive forward the lower band by a few sharp blows on the lug and then on top with a hardwood block.

5. Remove upper band screw and drive upper band forward, in the same manner prescribed for the lower band.

6. Move upper band forward on barrel until stopped by movable stud, and then remove lower band by slipping it over upper band and movable stud. To remove upper band entirely from barrel requires the removal of the front sight screw and the movable stud.

7. Draw hand guard forward until free from the fixed base and remove.

8. Remove guard screws and guard. It may be necessary to tap gently on the front and rear of the guard bow to loosen.

9. Remove barrel and receiver from stock.

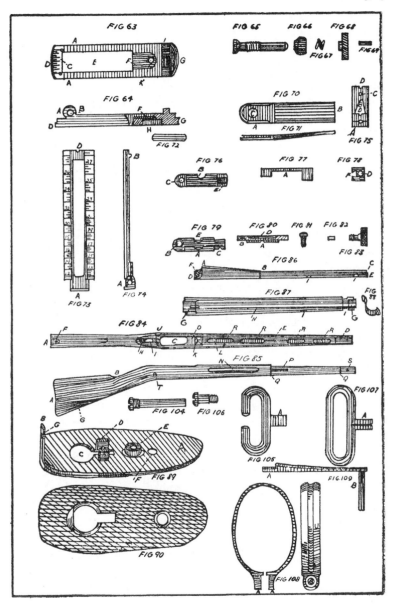

PLATE 38. SPRINGFIELD PARTS.

10. To remove the lower band spring, drive its spindle out of its hole in the stock from the left.

11. Unscrew the butt swivel screws and remove the butt swivel plate from stock. The butt swivel, consisting of the plate, swivel, and pin, permanently assembled, is issued complete.

12. Unscrew butt plate screws and remove butt plate from stock.

13. Unscrew butt plate spring screw and remove the butt plate spring; drive out butt plate pin (explained later) and remove butt plate cap.

14. Remove cut-off by loosening the screw in the end of the thumbpiece until it disengages the groove in the cut-off spindle; insert the blade of a screwdriver in the notch in the rear end of the spindle and force it out. Remove the spring and the plunger, being careful not to lose them.

15. Remove the ejector by driving out the ejector pin from the upper side.

16. Remove sear and trigger by driving out the sear pin from the right, being careful not to lose the sear spring.

17. Remove trigger from sear by driving out the trigger pin from either side.

18. Remove floor plate catch and spring by driving out the pin from either side.

19. Remove bolt stop by inserting a small punch or end of striker in the hole on the left end and forcing it from its pocket.

Special Note: The leaf should never be removed from the movable base except for the purpose of making repairs. The fixed base and the fixed stud ordinarily should never be removed from the barrel. The barrel ordinarily should never be unscrewed from the receiver. The barrel and receiver may be asembled only at establishments properly fitted for this work, for which reason gunsmiths and dealers order barrels and receivers assembled and not barrels alone, whenever this is possible. However, the gunsmith who carefully studies the sections of this book dealing with the removal of barrels can accomplish this task.

To Assemble After Dismounting.—Reverse the process and follow in inverse order the operations of dismounting. In assembling the sleeve lock to the sleeve, be careful to compress the lock and spring while driving in the pin from the bottom of the sleeve. To assemble

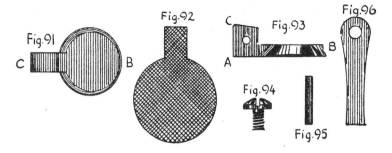

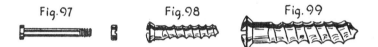

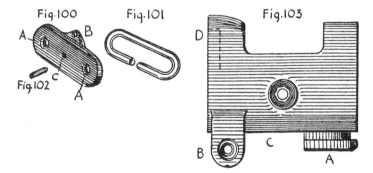

PLATE 39. SPRINGFIELD PARTS.

the safety lock and sleeve, insert the safety lock spindle in its hole in the sleeve as far as it will go; then, with the thumbpiece vertical and pressed against some rigid object, introduce the point of the tool provided for this purpose between the safety lock spindle and the safety lock plunger, forcing the latter into the thumbpiece until it slips over the edge of the sleeve. Further pressure on the safety lock thumbpiece, together with the gradual withdrawal of the tool, will complete the assembling. In assembling pins and screws, follow the directions given later for replacing broken parts. The floor plate spring and the cut-off spring are alike, except in length. The latter being the longer, care should be taken not to substitute one for the other.

PARTS WHICH ARE MOST LIABLE TO REQUIRE REPAIR

Bolt Stop.—This is worn by continual contact with the bolt.

Cocking Piece.—The nose is worn from neglect to keep it lubricated.

Lower Band Swivel And Screw.—Screw, if not riveted in place, works loose and, with swivel, is lost.

Safety Lock.—Thumbpiece knocked off by a blow.

Stacking Swivel And Screw.—Screw, if not riveted, works loose and, with swivel, is lost.

Stock.—Bruises, cuts, pieces chipped from different points, broken at small.

Striker.—Point burned by defective cartridge, or broken at the joint hole by snapping with chamber empty.

REPLACING BROKEN PARTS

Butt Plate Pin.—This pin has both ends upset; the burr on one end must be filed off and the pin driven out with a drift; when a new pin is put in, its ends must be upset with light blows of a hammer.

Front Sight.—The burr on the left side must be filed off and the pin driven out from the left with a drift; when the new front sight is in place, a new pin is driven in from the right and its left end upset with light blows of a hammer.

Lower Band Screw.—This screw, when in place, has its end upset and riveted over the band ear. It should never work loose, if properly assembled, and when it has to be removed to replace an injured swivel the burr on the end should be filed off and the screw taken out, the end being again upset when the screw has been returned to its place.

Stacking Swivel Screw.—As the screw is made long and its end upset, it should be kept well screwed up at all times. It is removed to replace a broken swivel and replaced as explained above, care being taken to upset the end only.

Trigger Pin.—This is a straight pin and can be driven in or out from either side.

INJURIES WHICH DO NOT RENDER PARTS UNSERVICEABLE

Bolt.—The entire flange at front end may be broken off, except a small portion on the opposite side from the extractor hook, which is required to hold, in connection with the extractor hook, the empty case while it is being drawn to the rear for ejection. If automatic ejection is not desired, the entire flange may be dispensed with.

Butt Plate.—Bruises, cuts, or wearing.

Butt Swivel.—Bent.

Cocking Piece.—Moderate wearing of nose. The nose can wear until raising and lowering the bolt handle fails to cock the piece.

Extractor.—Moderate wear or break of edge of hook.

Floor Plate.—Bent or bruised.

Guard.—Bent, bruised, or cut.

USING THE RIFLE WHEN CERTAIN PARTS ARE MISSING

The parts which are not absolutely essential are the ejector, safety lock, cut-off, bolt stop, sleeve lock, floor plate, magazine spring, and follower.

When the ejector is missing, the empty cartridge cases drawn to the rear by the extractor can be removed from the receiver by the finger.

The safety lock does not affect the usefulness of the rifle if it is missing; it is merely a precautionary device.

The cut-off may be missing, but the rifle can be loaded from the magazine, although the magazine cannot be held full in reserve; single loading with the cut-off missing and the magazine empty requires that the shooter load directly into the magazine, as otherwise the forward motion of the bolt will be stopped by coming in contact with the follower. If this happens, care should be taken in drawing back the bolt not to withdraw it from the receiver.

The absence of the bolt stop and sleeve lock does not affect the usefulness of the rifle. The absence of the floor plate, follower, and magazine spring only prevents the use of the magazine, but does not prohibit the use of the arm as a single-loader.

Finally, the gunsmith should caution the average shooter that except when repairs are needed, the following parts will constantly be injured if allowed to be dismounted for cleaning; and when repairs are necessary, they should be removed only by a gunsmith, or someone skillful in the use of tools on delicate mechanisms, viz: bolt stop, cut-off, safety lock, sleeve lock, front sight, movable stud, lower band, upper band, and stacking swivel screws. It is emphasized particularly that unless the screwdriver is handled carefully, and with skill, the screws may be injured at either the head or the thread.

TAPS BUT NOT SURRENDER

The buglers and the trumpeters of the Army, the Navy, the Air Force, and the Coast Guard, together with the field musics of the Marine Corps, have allegorically sounded "Taps" over the United States Rifle, Caliber .30, Model 1903, and all its later modifications. Officially, it is archaic, inadequate, and obsolete. It has been supplanted by U.S. Rifle, Model 14, 7.62 Millimeters, which the author of this book regards as the greatest shoulder weapon ever issued to the armed forces of any nation in the world.

Nevertheless, most amateur and professional gunsmiths will be working on one form or another of the "Springfield" during our lives and the lives of generations of Americans yet unborn. For centuries to come it can be fired in target practice, in hunting, and if necessary in the defense of our Republic. Eventually it will become a gun collector's choice possession, because, as the author said at the beginning of this chapter, it is one of the "Guns of Glory"!

XXX. Remodeling Military Rifles

MILITARY rifles are preferred by an overwhelming majority of hunters for several reasons: they can be bought at low prices from the United States government in times of peace; the ammunition is readily available in all parts of the United States and Canada; they have a high velocity and a flat trajectory; both the arms and the ammunition are highly accurate; they are of rugged construction and require a minimum amount of repair work; they are designed and built to fit the average man's body; gunsmiths and gun-supply houses are well acquainted with their characteristics and keep a good stock of replacement parts on hand; and finally, a great number of men and boys become familiar with them from carrying them in the various high schools and private academies, the National Guard, the state guards and state militias, the Naval Reserve, the Naval Militia, and the regular armed services. For these reasons we shall concentrate this discussion upon the military rifles of the United States in general use today, but our remarks will apply with considerable force to other military arms.

However, before beginning the technical instructions, the author wishes to introduce a few personal remarks for whatever they may be worth to the reader. First, he has fired the Springfield, Enfield, and Krag rifles in various armed services of the United States since he was fifteen years old. Second, he has fired these three rifles at different kinds of big game in the United States and in several foreign countries during the same period of time. Third, it is his belief that U.S. Rifles, Models 1903 and 1917, are adapted to the hunting and marksmanship needs of the average man or woman and that it is by no means necessary to remodel or alter it in any way. This statement will raise a howl of protest from manufacturers, jobbers, retail dealers, gunsmiths, and gun editors, all of whom have the same vested interest in making the rifle owner dissatisfied with the condition of his rifle as the automobile people have in making the car owner ashamed of last year's model, even though it gets him back and forth cheaply, easily, and in comfort.

In making this statement, the author wishes to "hedge" or compromise in only one respect: Note that we based our statement upon the needs of the average citizen and not the outstanding marksmen. The reason for this is that the service rifle as issued, particularly the Springfield, will shoot closer to the target than the average shooter can hold his shots. If a man cannot keep his shots within a 3-inch circle at a certain range, he does not require a rifle accurate enough to keep all shots within a 2-inch circle at the same range. Furthermore, aside from accuracy, much of the remodeling of military arms is nothing more than beauty-parlor work—manicuring, spit-curling, and permanent waving. Why spend thirty dollars for parts and materials and then knock away all the prettiness the first time you hit the brush?

Having fired a shot on the side of freedom from doodads, we shall now proceed to remodel a rifle the way we do the job for our friends, not necessarily the way we treat the faithful old Springfield that we take into the field.

The U. S. Rifle, Model 1903 (Springfield).—Disassemble the rifle, laying the parts out on a long table in the order in which they are removed. Work on the stock first. Remove grease and oil with gasoline. Saw off the forearm (fore-end) about 2½ inches in front of the lower band and fill in the channel with a piece of matching walnut. Shape a forearm tip to your ideas. Build up the comb of the butt stock. Cut the hand guard even with the front edge of the lower band. Add a pistol grip if you prefer this type of grip. Lengthen the stock by adding wood, or by means of a rubber recoil pad. Place a cap on the pistol grip.

The remodeling of the stock should follow the principles and rules explained in the chapters on Stock Design, Stock Repairs and Alterations, Checkering and Carving Stocks, and Stock Finishing.

If the old stock is too badly cracked, marred, or chipped to be made over to the satisfaction of the owner, it should be set aside and a new one bought or made. Do not throw away the old stock because it can be used to practice upon, and it can be cut up into pieces for making repairs, inserts, and additions.

The next step is to strike and polish the barrel, and polish the magazine, floor plate, receiver, and other metal parts. Review the chapters on Striking and Polishing Barrels and Parts, and Barrel Removing and Changing. Note that it is sometimes possible to buy from the United States government a bolt assembly for the Springfield Rifle that is already polished, and the same thing applies to a number of jobbers and dealers in gun parts.

Remove the military front sight from the movable stud, insert an ivory or gold bead and replace the movable stud; or make and attach a front sight ramp to which a temporary brass sight is fitted, to be removed and replaced later by a permanent sight of the correct dimensions.

Remove the drift slide from the rear sight movable base by knocking out the pin; replace with a commercially made folding leaf sight of better design; or replace with any of the commercially made rear sights that meet your individual requirements. Obviously, if the rifle is already equipped with a good rear sight, these remarks do not apply. The chapters on Sights and Fitting Sights should be reviewed.

Before fitting the front sight to the barrel permanently, a swivel band is made and fitted. The rifle should now be assembled, whether the oiling process for finishing the stock is completed or not, and the rifle should be sighted in on a target. Disassemble, continue oiling the stock if necessary, repolish the barrel to remove any discolorations left by altering the sights, blue all metal parts, check the wooden parts, put the last touches on the oil finish of the stock, and assemble the rifle, keeping in mind the principles explained in the chapter on Inletting the Action and Bedding the Barrel.

Some gunsmiths use two turned steel collars to keep the hand guard in place when they do not intend to polish or reblue the barrel and action. In this case, the hand guard covers the rough portion of the barrel at its rear, and tenon-shaped ends fit tightly under the collars. The lower half of each of the collars is reduced in thickness by filing until it is little more than a thin band.

When these collars are used, one is designed to fit the barrel at the place where the forearm swivel is mounted, the other fits the barrel at the breech just in front of the receiver ring. The front sight movable stud is removed, the forward collar is notched to slip over the fixed stud, and a hole is drilled and tapped in the bottom of the collar to receive the swivel screw. The fixed base of the rear sight is removed before mounting the rear collar. Finally, the thin, lower half of each collar is inletted into the forearm.

The U. S. Rifle, Model 1917 (Enfield).—The U. S. Rifle, Model 1917, commonly called the Enfield although it is caliber .30, and not the British caliber .303, was issued to and used by United States troops in the First World War; after that war it was sold by the government to individuals, but at the beginning of the Second World War the sale of arms by the government to individuals was discontinued, government-owned rifles issued to clubs were re-called, and those government models owned by individuals and still serviceable were bought back by the government when the owners were willing to dispose of them. Since this arm frequently comes into the hands of gunsmiths for remodeling, the detailed processes to be followed are important.

When a target rifle is desired, the rear sight wings are ground off and a full micrometer sight, having ½ inch adjustments, made for fine adjustment and close shooting, is installed. The regular issue front sight is left in place and shaped to more uniform lines by grinding off the wings and tapering the sides gently downward. Altering the stock follows the principles and rules previously explained in this and other chapters.

When a sporting rifle is desired, the issue stock may be retained, the comb is raised and a well-shaped pistol grip is attached. The forearm is shortened and the hand guard is removed. The issue front sight is retained and reshaped as explained above. A micrometer rear sight is installed.

Since the stock of the Enfield rifle has too much drop for most shooters, some of the bottom is cut off and wood is added to the top, as explained in the chapter on Stock Repairs and Alterations. Reshaping, checkering, and polishing the stock are operations that add considerable beauty and some utility to the rifle, but they are luxury expenditures.

Disassembling the U. S. Rifle, Model 1917 gives considerable trouble to beginners. It is done as follows: Draw the bolt to the rear; pull back the safety; close the bolt, thus creating a clearance between the cocking piece and the bolt sleeve; insert a screwdriver in the clearance, withdraw the bolt, and unscrew the firing pin.

The Krag Rifle.—The Krag Rifle, more properly called the Krag-Jorgensen, is the term applied to the U. S. Rifles, Models 1892, 1896, 1898, and 1899, issued as Rifles, Cadet Rifles, and Carbines. Authorities differ as to the proper model designations, but it is sufficient to point out that as far as the gunsmith is concerned the fundamental principles of design are common to all models, and such differences as exist are of little practical consequence.

This rifle has been sold by the United States government to individuals in the past at low prices; there are many such rifles still in the hands of the people; and there are also many civilian-made rifles constructed upon the Krag-Jorgensen system. Whether it is worth while to remodel one of these rifles depends entirely upon its condition and its owner's willingness to pay for the work, but it should be remembered that the Krags are inferior to both the Springfields and the Enfields for modern hunting and marksmanship. The remodeling procedure follows:

1. The barrel may be too long for the customer, unless it was made short for cadet use, or for a carbine. Saw it off behind the front sight base to the desired length, and crown the muzzle. Strike and polish the barrel. Prepare the barrel to receive a front sight. Buy or make the desired type of front sight and fit to the barrel. When the barrel is polished is a good time to polish the receiver and all other metal parts.

2. Decide what you wish to do with the barrel bands. The original front military barrel band and swivel may be retained, in which case they are set aside until final assembly. If an inside front barrel band is desired, fit it to the barrel now. If a leaf rear sight is desired, fit a band for holding it over the rear sight screw hole and fill the other screw hole with a short plug made from a drill rod, or fill it with a shortened screw; file down the plug or screw and polish flush with the barrel surface. If a leaf sight is not selected,

prepare the receiver to take the type preferred, but avoid the cocking-piece type of rear sight; it does not work well on the Krag.

3. Attach the rear sight.

4. Saw off the forearm a few inches ahead of the forward band, fill in the cavity under the barrel, and shape the tip. Heighten the comb and attach a pistol grip. Fill in the grooves in the hand guard. Remove the old finish from all wooden parts, and take out dents and scratches. Check the stock and give it an oil finish.

5. Reblue all metal parts.

6. Assemble the rifle, and put on a new sling.

Some of these steps can be omitted, and others may be added in accordance with suggestions made elsewhere in this book. In general, Krags usually offer an opportunity for practice, but few of them are worth an extensive outlay of time and money in an expectation that a de luxe target or hunting rifle will be produced by remodeling.

Bending the Bolt Handle.—The bolt handle can be bent, but it is not advisable except where it is necessary to permit it to clear a telescopic sight. Wrap the bolt in soaking wet rags and place it in a vise. Heat the bolt handle to a cherry red with an acetylene torch, or some other source of heat that can be confined to a small area. Have two bars of cold rolled steel handy, each of them notched to fit the bolt. With one lever, hold the handle so that it will not move at the junction of the bolt and handle, since that point will be dangerously weakened by twisting or bending. With the other lever, bend the handle to the desired position. Keep the rags wet and the handle at a cherry-red color, let the handle and bolt cool gradually for a few minutes with the rags in place, and then remove the rags and dip the bolt and handle into water at room temperature.

The bolt and handle are now soft and can be filed, blued, or checked; the shape of the metal may be changed slightly, but do not reduce the size materially or you will weaken the bolt and handle beyond their safety limit. Do not attempt to harden the bolt and handle unless you are an expert at heat treatment, for there is a serious danger of breakage.

Some gunsmiths wrap the bolt in wet rags, bring it to a cherry-red heat to soften it, remove the rags and saw off the handle on a diagonal line between the junction of the bolt and handle and the point where the handle was bent originally. The handle is then turned upside down and welded to the part of the handle left projecting from the bolt. New metal is filled in with welding rods, rough projections are ground away, and the handle is then smoothed and polished. This is no job for an amateur to attempt on a good rifle, and there are few experts who will risk the chance of ruining the bolt and handle by this method.

Those who want detailed instructions for remodeling military rifles beyond the scope of this chapter can obtain a variety of excellently written and illustrated pamphlets at nominal cost from The National Rifle Association of America, 1600 Rhode Island Avenue, N.W., Washington, D.C. This is a nonprofit organization supported by the membership fees of public-spirited citizens. Membership is available to any reputable citizen of the United States of America, but it is not necessary to become a member to buy its publications.

XXXI. U.S. Rifle, 7.62-MM, M14

MODEL DESIGNATION

THE *U.S. Rifle, 7.62-MM, M14,* also is officially known as *7.62-MM Rifle, M14, and Rifle Bipod M2.* Unofficially, it is often called the "Model 14" or the "M-14." The arabic numerals in official publications are written after the capital letter "M" without a space or a dash, thus: M14. There are technical and historical reasons for referring to this rifle as "Model 14," but they are boresome to most people and not important enough to include in this text.

The "7.62-MM" refers to the fact that this rifle is chambered for the "NATO 7.62-MM" cartridge. "NATO" is the abbreviation for North Atlantic Treaty Organization. It includes the United States of America and foreign nations in alliance with the United States under the North Atlantic Treaty, signed on April 4, 1949, in Washington, D.C., by the representatives of twelve free and independent nations. The signatory nations, in alphabetical order, were Belgium, Canada, Denmark, France, Iceland, Italy, Luxembourg, the Netherlands, Norway, Portugal, the United Kingdom, and the United States of America.

This alliance was increased to fourteen during the Korean War, when, on October 22, 1951, in accordance with the provisions of Article No. 10 of the Treaty, Greece and Turkey signed the Treaty. Three years later, in December, 1954, the Republic of Germany, commonly called "West Germany," became a member of the alliance. Other nations can join and any nation can withdraw, but the nations listed above have figuratively written their names in letters of gold in the pages of what may be the history of mankind's last clear effort to save the world for freedom.

There is no standard NATO rifle. Each of the nations belonging to NATO is free to select its own rifle, but there is a common agreement that all NATO nations select rifles which will fire the standard 7.62 millimeter cartridge. Obviously, when troops of different nations are serving together, the use of a standard cartridge eliminates one of the most ancient of military problems.

The "7.62 millimeter" designation is based upon the metric system, which is the international decimal system of weights and measures based on the metre and the kilogram. Under the metric system, names for multiples of the several units are formed by using Greek prefixes, and the names of the subdivisions are formed by using Latin prefixes.

The spelling of the metric prefixes and the basic units is not uniform throughout the world. For example, in the United Kingdom and France, the word "metre" is used, whereas in the United States of America it is spelled "meter."

One millimeter (also spelled "millimetre") is one one-thousandth's part of a meter ("metre"). It can be written as a fraction, thus: 1/1,000 meter (or "metre"). This equals 0.03937-inch. Multiplying 7.62 times 0.03937-inch, the product is 0.2999994-inch. Therefore, for practical purposes, the 7.62-millimeter rifles are chambered for firing what is otherwise known as a caliber .30 cartridge, but this statement must be taken with a few reservations.

Although the 7.62-mm. cartridge is essentially the old familiar caliber .30-06 cartridge, used for generations by the armed forces of the United States of America, the NATO cartridge is about one-half inch shorter and has a different shape and ballistic characteristics. It is not possible to fire the NATO cartridge in weapons chambered for the caliber .30-06 cartridge. Likewise, it is not possible to fire the caliber .30-06 cartridge in weapons chambered for the NATO cartridge.

When the rifle is referred to as 7.62-*MM Rifle, M14, and Rifle Bipod M2*, the phrase "and Rifle Bipod M2" pertains to a light, portable, folding mount which clamps onto the gas cylinder and gas-cylinder lock of the rifle. It is primarily composed of three main groups: (1) The yoke assembly; (2) the right leg assembly; and

(3) the left leg assembly. A self-locking bolt locks the jaws of the yoke assembly when clamped on the rifle. Actuation of pivot-plunger buttons controls the extending of the leg assemblies or permits rotating them to the carrying position parallel with the rifle barrel. The rifle is shown with the bipod attached in Plate 40.

DESCRIPTION

The 7.62-mm rifle, M14, is a light-weight, air-cooled, gas-operated, magazine-fed, shoulder weapon, designed primarily for either semi-automatic fire or full automatic fire at the cyclic rate of 750 rounds per minute. The rifle is chambered for the 7.62-mm NATO cartridge, as mentioned before, and is designed to accommodate a 20-round cartridge magazine and the M2 rifle bipod already described. In addition, it is designed to accommodate the M76 grenade launcher and the M6 bayonet. For training purposes, a M12 blank-firing attachment and a M3 breech shield are used.

The rifle can be fired from the shoulder, the hip, or the M2 bipod. Each cartridge in the magazine is stripped from the magazine during the counterrecoil of the bolt.

The weight of the basic rifle with empty magazine and without a sling is 9.1 pounds. The weight of the rifle with sling attached and ready to fire, fully loaded, is 11.0 pounds. The length of the rifle with the flash suppressor attached is 41.31 inches. The barrel itself is 22.0 inches long. Technically, the type of firing is known as the *rotating bolt type.*

The *average muzzle velocity* of the M14 rifle using M-59 ball cartridges is 2,800 feet per second. Translated into the metric system this is 853 meters per second.

The *maximum range* for the M-59 ball cartridge having an average muzzle velocity of 2,800 feet per second (853 meters per second) is sometimes given as 3,200 *meters.* Since one meter equals about 39.37 inches, multiply 3,200 by 39.37 and the product is 125,984 inches, which equals 10,498.6 feet. The English *statute mile* used in the United Kingdom, the United States of America, and in several other English-speaking nations is 5,280 feet, or 1,609.3 meters. By dividing 10,498.6 feet by 5,280, we arrive at 1.988 miles; hence the maximum range is almost two statute miles.

The length of the rifling is 19.91 inches, although the barrel is

22.0 inches long, as stated above. The barrel is rifled with four grooves, with one right-hand twist for each 12.0 inches of rifling. The maximum trigger pull is 7.5 pounds and the minimum trigger pull is 5.5 pounds. The maximum chamber pressure generated within the rifle is 50,000 pounds per square inch.

The over-all height of the bipod when closed is 9.75 inches; when extended it is 13.25 inches; and when folded it is 11.25 inches. The weight of the bipod is 1.25 pounds.

All of these statements are subject to change. The M14, like all weapons, will undergo constant improvements, and this is also true of the bipod, the ammunition, and everything connected with it. Furthermore, there is no reason for revealing the full capabilities of this splendid weapon in a book intended for general circulation.

Plate 40, drawn by Ordnance Corps, U.S. Army, shows the *M14 Rifle with its M2 Bipod, and with the hinged door of the butt-plate assembly in the open position for access to the storage compartment inside the stock.*

PLATE 40. M14 RIFLE WITH M2 BIPOD, AND WITH HINGED DOOR OF THE BUTT-PLATE ASSEMBLY IN THE OPEN POSITION FOR ACCESS TO THE STORAGE COMPARTMENT INSIDE THE STOCK. (Courtesy Ordnance Corps, U.S. Army.)

The M2 Bipod is a major item because it is used in conjunction with the rifle when the rifle is fired automatically, that is, with the trigger held back by the shooter. The bipod is lightweight, folds into a convenient load, and is composed of a yoke assembly and two adjustable legs. These legs are folded for ease in carrying and have a locking device to maintain a rigid position during firing. The yoke assembly includes a quick-disconnect feature which makes it possible to connect or disconnect the yoke to the gas cylinder of the rifle in a hurry.

Accessories include the Grenade Launcher M76 and Grenade Sight M15; together with the Bayonet Knife M6 and its Scabbard M8A1. The bayonet knife M6 is secured to the rifle on the bayonet lug of the flash suppressor by a latching lever within the handle and by a loop on the guard which encircles the flash suppressor. The M8A1 scabbard is provided with the M6 bayonet, for carrying purposes when the bayonet is not attached to the rifle.

AMMUNITION

Ammunition for this rifle is classified as small arms ammunition and is produced in five types: (1) Armor Piercing; (2) Ball; (3) Dummy; (4) Tracer, and (5) Blank.

Armor-piercing bullets are fired against vehicles, weapons, and armored targets in general. The *M61 armor piercing cartridge* for the M-14 Rifle has a boat-tailed bullet, and is composed of a gilding metal-clad jacket, a hardened steel core, a lead antimony base, and a point filler. The tip of the bullet is painted black for identification.

Ball cartridges have bullets with comparatively soft cores and are used against people only. The *M59 ball cartridge* for the M-14 Rifle has a boat-tailed bullet (the rear of the bullet is tapered). The bullet is composed of a gilding metal jacket, a soft steel core, a lead antimony base, and a point filler. The tip of the bullet is not colored. There is no necessity for an identification coloring because the ball cartridge is the one used most of the time.

Tracer cartridges for the Model-14 Rifle are referred to as "M62 Tracer Cartridges." The cartridge has a boat-tailed bullet that weighs less than the bullets in the armor-piercing and ball cartridges described above. The bullet is composed of a gilding metal or gilding metal-clad steel jacket, a lead antimony core, a tracer, sub-igniter and igniter composition, and a closure cap. The tip of the bullet is painted orange for identification. The armed forces usually do not go into details about tracer cartridges in their modern instructions, but it is the personal experience of the author that tracer cartridges have several valuable uses if fired by a man with average intelligence, as follows: (1) They can be fired to spot (indicate) the target for heavier weapons, including artillery, thus giving the range and deflection; (2) They can be used to spot the target for shoulder weapons, including the M-14 Rifle itself; (3) They can be used for the general observation of the effect of any shoulder rifle from which they are fired, including the M-14 Rifle, but they have a lower muzzle velocity than either ball cartridges or armor-piercing cartridges; hence the tracers may fall short of the true range and give a false impression of the range; (4) Under certain conditions they have a slight incendiary effect and may set fire to inflammable property of the enemy; and (5) They tend to frighten the enemy because it is bad enough for a soldier to hear bullets coming at him but when the bullets not only whine but throw off fire and light, he wants to leave the battle line in order to help his wounded comrades to the rear immediately. Needless to say, these comments on tracer bullets present the views of the author only and do not necessarily reflect the official opinions of the armed forces of the United States. (Required by U.S. Navy Regulations.)

In addition to all the above uses, tracer bullets can be used in signaling according to a prearranged code; or in an emergency they can be fired in short and long bursts representing the dots and dashes of the International Morse Code used in radio communications. Under such circumstances the words signaled should not be clear to the enemy. For example, the slang, jargon, or argot of various occupations or sports could be used.

Dummy cartridges are used for training in the operation of loading and unloading. They are completely harmless. They contain neither a real bullet nor powder. *The M63 Dummy Cartridge* for the M14 rifle has six longitudinal corrugations in the body of the cartridge case and no markings on the dummy bullet.

Blank cartridges for the M14 rifle are used for simulated fire, in maneuvers, and in firing salutes. There is a one-piece cartridge case with a hollow bullet-like nose which is closed with a disk sealed in the mouth, but there is no bullet. Blank cartridges in general have been used for at least thirty years by the armed forces of the United States of America in machine guns and automatic shoulder arms for instructional purposes, on maneuvers, etc., but only when the weapons were equipped with special blank-firing attachments. When blank cartridges are loaded into any automatic or semiautomatic weapon which is not equipped with a special blank-firing attachment, malfunctions ("jams," etc.) occur very soon after firing starts.

Blank cartridges are dangerous at short ranges because the wad which seals the mouth of the cartridge is shot into space. A man can easily lose his eyesight if shot in the face with the wad from a blank cartridge.

CARTRIDGE PACKING

Ammunition for the M14 is prepacked in *5-pound magazine chargers.* Twelve chargers are packed in a cloth bandolier. The *Magazine Filler* is an adapter which fits over the top of an empty magazine (when the magazine is not in the rifle) and makes it easier to load cartridges into the magazine. One magazine filler is normally packed in each case of ammunition.

CARTRIDGE NOMENCLATURE AND TERMINOLOGY

Plate 41 is a *side-view drawing of a cartridge* prepared by the Ordnance Corps, U.S. Army. This drawing is valuable not only to those interested in the M-14 Rifle but to all gunsmiths and shooters. In addition to naming and pointing out the principal parts of a cartridge, it includes dimension lines that show how measurements are taken. These are the horizontal lines with arrows at both ends.

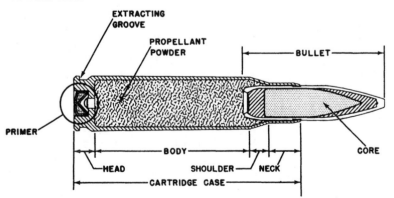

PLATE 41. SIDE-VIEW DRAWING OF A CARTRIDGE, NAMING AND DESIGNATING PRINCIPAL PARTS. THE HORIZONTAL LINES WITH ARROWS AT EACH END ARE DIMENSION LINES THAT SHOW HOW MEASUREMENTS ARE TAKEN FOR VARIOUS PURPOSES. (Courtesy Ordnance Corps, U.S. Army.)

CARE AND HANDLING OF AMMUNITION

The following instructions apply not only to cartridges for the M-14 Rifle, but to ammunition in general:

(1) Avoid breaking or damaging ammunition boxes.

(2) Keep ammunition clean and free from mud, sand, and water. If dirty, wipe it off with a clean, dry rag that is free from grease, oil, dust, or any abrasive substance. Wipe off corrosion as soon as it is found. When a weapon is loaded with unclean ammunition the operating parts can be damaged and malfunctions will occur.

(3) Never expose ammunition to the direct rays of the sun. Heat causes the powder in the cartridges to produce excessive pressure and affects ballistic characteristics.

(4) In addition to sunlight, heat from any source, such as hot water pipes, radiators, stoves, etc., is not only detrimental to the ballistic characteristics of ammunition but can, under extreme conditions, cause an explosion.

Small arms ammunition is not dangerous to handle if you follow the above rules.

TACTICAL USE

The U.S. Rifle, Model 14; the M2 Bipod; the M76 Grenade Launcher; and the M6 Bayonet do not duplicate other items now in the supply system of the armed forces of the United States. These items are now replacing, and eventually will replace, several weapons now part of the equipment of the armed forces of the United States and its allies. Throughout this text, the term "U.S. Rifle, Model 14" (which is the author's own personal preference as a name for the new rifle and its closely associated items), the term "Model 14," and the term "M-14" refer to what the armed forces refer to as 7.62-*MM Rifle M 14 and Rifle Bipod M 2*. However, the armed forces, with no regard for typography, usually leave no space and insert no dash between the capital letter "M" and the digit following it; hence the official communications usually read "M14," "M2," etc.

With this boresome but necessary prelude, we shall now call the roll, thus:

The Model 14 Rifle replaces:

(1) U.S. Rifle, Caliber .30, Model 1903, commonly called "the Springfield Rifle," the principal infantry weapon of World War I; a secondary shoulder weapon of World War II and the Korean War; the darling of the United States Marine Corps from World War I until today. This so-called Model 1903 Rifle fires the so-called .30-06 cartridge; but both the Rifle and the cartridge have been improved several times since originally issued. The official policy reads that the Model 14 Rifle replaces *Rifle US Caliber .30, M1, M1C and M1D*. Notice that the numeral 1 is jammed between the letters without a space or a dash.

(2) the policy also dictates that the Model 14 Rifle also replaces *Carbine, US Caliber .30, M1, M2, and M3*. This is the semiautomatic rifle which on January 9, 1936, was adopted by the U.S. Army to replace the U.S. Rifle, caliber .30, Model 1903, commonly called the "Springfield." Shortly after adoption by the Army, the U.S. Navy and U.S. Marine Corps adopted the same weapon. One of its several names is *U.S. Rifle, Caliber .30, M1*, but it is popularly called the "Garand Rifle" in honor of its inventor and developer, John C. Garand, a civilian employee of the U.S. Armory, Springfield, Massachusetts.

In the first edition of *Gun Care and Repair—A Manual of Gunsmithing* the author devoted an entire chapter of twenty-nine pages of text and illustrations to the Garand Rifle, which was and is an excellent rifle but which has now been displaced for several reasons, the most important of which is that the NATO nations agreed upon an interchangeable 7.62 millimeter cartridge.

When this agreement was reached, it was necessary for the United States to have a rifle chambered to take the 7.62 cartridge. The experts decided that while they were solving this problem they would design, develop, and manufacture a rifle that would combine all the advantages of several infantry shoulder arms without any of the disadvantages of the weapons to be displaced. The result is the U.S. Rifle, Model 14.

(3) The Model 14 Rifle with its M2 Bipod replaces "Rifle, Automatic, Caliber .30, M1918A2." In other words, when the Model 14 Rifle is mounted on its bipod it replaces Browning Automatic Rifle, Caliber .30, Model 1918, and all of its modifications. This is an air-

cooled, gas-operated, magazine-fed shoulder rifle, fully automatic and highly effective as an infantry weapon. In its original form it was fired either from the shoulder or the hip, but later it was provided with a bipod. The official phrase in the order replacing this weapon refers to "M1918A2," with all the letters and numerals jammed together. The "A2" means the latest version which has the bipod. Although this will not be an item for collectors or hunters, it has passed into the pages of history along with our other "Guns of Glory," because it, too, served well the cause of freedom.

(4) The Model 14 Rifle with its M2 Bipod also replaces what the official edict describes as "Gun, Submachine, Caliber .45, M3 and M3A1." This is the famous Thompson Submachine Gun, Caliber .45, The author devoted all the Chapter 32 in the original edition of *Gun Care and Repair—A Manual of Gunsmithing,* sixteen pages in all, to the Model 1928 A-1 version, but long before the official adoption of U.S. Rifle, Model 14, the author decided to delete the chapter on the "Tommy Gun" on the advice of officers of the Army, Navy, Marine Corps, and Coast Guard, and the recommendation of sheriffs, police officers, and other law-enforcement officials, simply because it never was effective at anything except very short ranges, malfunctions were comparatively common, and at close quarters it was possible to accidentally kill or injure more friends than enemies. Sheriffs and police departments have the "Tommy Guns" locked up in glass cases. Periodically, they open the cases; clean, oil, and inspect the guns, and then lock them up again. The gun has only one great value today. School children ask policemen to let them see "the Tommy Gun the Chicago gangsters used." Sometimes they refer to it as "Al Capone's Tommy Gun." This is one of the products of the educational programs developed by American television stations. Therefore shed no tear for this weapon. It does not belong with the "Guns of Glory."

(5) The Model 14 Rifle with its M76 Grenade Launcher replaces Grenade Launcher M7A1.

(6) The Model 14 Rifle obviously is not fired from its bipod with a bayonet attached and it is equally apparent that there is no point in attaching a bayonet while launching grenades. However, it has its own especially designed bayonet, designated as M6 Bayonet, which replaces Bayonets M1, M4, M5, and obviously all other bayonets.

MARK, MODIFICATION, AND MODEL

Throughout the history of modern warfare, the English-speaking people have designated any important change, whether or not it actually was an improvement, by adding to the official designation of the firearm or other piece of equipment such words as "Model," "Mark," or "Modification." In the lexicon of the armed forces these words have been abbreviated to the letter "M." Then when there was some change not important enough to merit a new "Mark," "Model," or "Modification" designation, arabic numerals have been added. It does not require a fortuneteller to prophesy that this will happen in the case of any martial firearm development. Nevertheless, the information in this text is fundamentally complete. The latest information about minor changes is supplied to armed forces by their own organizations. Civilians can purchase publications on the latest developments from their own government. In the United States, the Superintendent of Documents, Washington 25, D.C., supplies a free price list of publications on martial arms, which are sold at a nominal price.

THE GREATEST SHOULDER WEAPON OF ALL TIME

It is the fixed opinion of the author that the 7.62-*MM Rifle M14 and Rifle Bipod M2,* which the author refers to as U.S. Rifle, Model 14 (and frequently to save space calls the Model 14), is the greatest shoulder weapon ever issued to the armed forces of any nation; that it possesses the major advantages and few, if any, of the disadvantages of the several weapons it displaces; and that it will continue to fire effectively under the most rugged of combat conditions.

ECHELONS OF MAINTENANCE OF THE MODEL 14

The word *echelon* is derived from the French word *échelle,* which means a ladder. In English, echelon has many different meanings, but the word always suggests steps, levels of command, levels of arrangement, levels of responsibility, etc.

The first and second echelons of Model 14 maintenance are together known as *organizational maintenance* because the rifle is maintained in good firing condition by members of the combat organization armed with this valuable weapon. All men armed with the Model 14 are in the first echelon of maintenance, which means they are trained in and are responsible for the proper inspection, cleaning, and replacement of a few parts.

The second echelon of maintenance of the Model 14 is the *company armorer*. He must have above average skill in the inspection, cleaning, and replacement of certain parts, but in addition he is expected to perform comparatively minor repair work, such, for example, as the repair of the bolt assembly. He is a member of the combat organization.

Field maintenance is the collective term for the third and fourth echelons of Model 14 maintenance. Normally, those responsible for field maintenance of the Model 14 in the United States Army are personnel of the Ordnance Corps. Although they are combat troops within the strict meaning of the term, they rely upon the front-line organizations to perform the organizational maintenance described above.

Field maintenance is performed by mobile and semimobile Ordnance Maintenance Units and also by Post Ordnance Shops. *Third echelon maintenance and supply support* is provided by Ordnance Direct Support Companies that send forward *contact teams* to provide "on site" maintenance and supply support for the Model 14 Rifles of the front-line organizations. Obviously, the fourth echelon is responsible for the major overhaul and supply, together with other important duties.

The reader is again reminded that the author's explanations are his personal statements and do not necessarily reflect the opinions or policies of the armed forces of the United States of America.

NOMENCLATURE

Plate 42 shows *eleven major assemblies, sub-assemblies, and parts manufactured for the United States of America by Thompson Ramo Woolridge, Inc., together with a drawing of the Rifle without its bipod, and with its cartridge magazine in place. This drawing was prepared by Thompson Ramo Woolridge, Inc., and is used with their permission.*

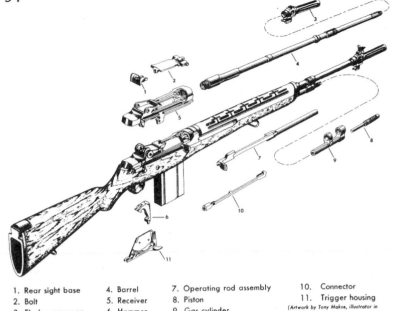

1. Rear sight base   4. Barrel   7. Operating rod assembly   10. Connector
2. Bolt   5. Receiver   8. Piston   11. Trigger housing
3. Flash suppressor   6. Hammer   9. Gas cylinder   *(Artwork by Tony Makse, illustrator in Technical Publications and Presentations.)*

PLATE 42. ELEVEN MAJOR ASSEMBLIES, SUB-ASSEMBLIES, AND PARTS OF THE M14 RIFLE MANUFACTURED BY THOMPSON RAMO WOOLRIDGE, INC., TOGETHER WITH A DRAWING OF THE RIFLE WITHOUT ITS BIPOD AND WITH ITS CARTRIDGE MAGAZINE IN PLACE. (Courtesy Thompson Ramo Woolridge, Inc.)

Plate 43 shows the *Stock with the Butt-Plate Assembly and the Hand-guard Assembly,* as drawn by the Ordnance Corps, U.S. Army. The stock, stock liner, butt-plate assembly, butt swivel, front-swivel assembly, stock ferrule, rear hand-guard band, and the hand-guard assembly (of which the rear hand-guard band is a part) are labeled. The scale in the lower, left-hand corner of the drawing provides a

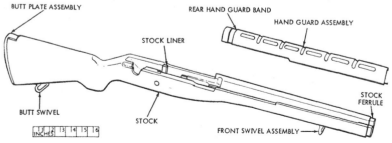

PLATE 43. M14 STOCK WITH BUTT-PLATE ASSEMBLY AND HAND-GUARD ASSEMBLY. (Courtesy Ordnance Corps, U.S. Army.)

means of determining the dimensions of the parts illustrated.

For convenience of maintenance and repair, the rifle is divided into groups composed of magazine (cartridge), firing mechanism, stock with butt-plate assembly, hand-guard assembly, operating rod and connector group, bolt assembly, and barrel and receiver group.

DISASSEMBLY AND ASSEMBLY

Field stripping is the disassembly (taking apart) of the major components of any artillery piece, machine gun, shoulder weapon, or hand gun for cleaning, inspection, and general maintenance. A soldier armed with the M14 Rifle is authorized to disassemble his rifle to the extent defined by the term *field stripping*. The amount of disassembly he is authorized to perform without supervision is adequate for normal maintenance.

The frequency of disassembly and assembly should be kept to the minimum consistent with maintenance and instruction requirements, because too much disassembly and assembly wears out the parts, eventually makes them unserviceable, and causes inaccurate fire. When excessive disassembly and assembly has reduced the mechanical effectivness and fire accuracy of the rifle, the soldier loses confidence in himself and his rifle. A simple thing like this can lose a skirmish, a poor skirmish can lose a battle, and defeat in one battle may lose a whole war! Victory begins with the soldier and his rifle.

The M14 can be taken apart and put together again without using force. All parts of any M14 can be interchanged with the parts of another M14 except the bolt. For reasons of safety, operating efficiency, and accuracy of fire, bolts should not be interchanged.

While any firearm is being disassembled, including the M14, the parts should be laid out on a clean, smooth surface, from left to right. In the beginning, the soldier names each part as he lays it on the table or floor during disassembly. This is called "learning nomenclature." Then, when the rifle is disassembled, the soldier assembles it in reverse order, working from right to left and naming each part. He eventually memorizes the names of the parts and is no longer required to name them as he disassembles them.

Main Groups of the M14.—The individual soldier can disassemble the following: (1) barrel and receiver group except certain specified parts; (2) magazine group; and (3) firing-mechanism assembly.

A trained noncommissioned officer or a company armorer can disassemble the above three groups, plus the bolt group, except that he cannot disassemble the bolt roller from the bolt stud. Under the supervision of a noncommissioned officer or the company armorer, the individual soldier can perform the disassembly of the four groups mentioned above. However, there are certain parts that none of the above-mentioned persons can disassemble without orders from higher authority. Those parts which cannot be disassembled except under these conditions are listed and described later in this text.

In addition to the barrel and receiver group, the magazine group, the firing-mechanism assembly, and the bolt group, already mentioned, there is the stock group. Without further discussion of the separation of the M14 into groups for disassembly, we shall proceed to the actual disassembly.

Beginning Disassembly.—Pull the operating rod handle to the rear and inspect the chamber to be sure it is clear. Hold the operating rod to the rear with the edge of the right hand and at the same time depress the magazine follower with the right thumb, so that the bolt can move forward over the follower. As the bolt moves forward over the rear of the follower, remove the right thumb, regrasp the rifle with the left hand, and release the operating rod handle. Place the safety in the safe position. Next, place the butt of the rifle on your left hip or thigh, with the sights to the left, and loosen the sling. Grasp the magazine with your right hand so that the thumb is against the magazine latch and the fingers are around the front of the magazine. Push the magazine latch with the thumb, then pull the magazine out of the receiver.

To remove the firing-mechanism assembly, grasp the rear of the trigger guard with the thumb and forefinger of your right hand and pull downward and outward as far as the guard will go. Lift out the firing mechanism assembly.

Next, lay the rifle on a flat, clean, dry surface, with the sights up and the muzzle to the left. Grasp the receiver with the left hand over the bolt and raise the rifle a few inches. With the right hand, strike down on and grasp the small of the stock, separating the stock group from the barrel and receiver group. You now have the rifle disassembled into three main groups: (1) *barrel and re-*

ceiver group; (2) *firing-mechanism assembly;* and (3) *stock group.*

Assembly of the Three Main Groups.—You are only beginning to learn disassembly and assembly, but before learning detailed disassembly, reassemble the three main groups. First, find a clean, dry, smooth surface. Previously, we suggested a table or a floor, but this is for training. In the field, you may have to do this work on the ground; but spread out your blanket or some large piece of cloth, such as your half of a "pup tent," if you are fortunate enough to have one with you.

Place the barrel and receiver group on your clean, dry, smooth surface, sights down. Pick up the stock group and engage the stock ferrule in the front band. Then lower the stock group onto the barrel and receiver group.

Unlatch and open the trigger guard. Place the firing-mechanism assembly straight down into the receiver, making certain that the guide rib on the assembly enters the recess in the receiver. Close and latch the trigger guard. You have now assembled the three main groups, and you are ready to learn how to disassemble and assemble the M14 more completely.

Disassembly of the Barrel and Receiver Group.—*The barrel and receiver group* is illustrated in Plate 44, which is a cutaway view prepared by the Ordnance Corps, U.S. Army.

(1) *Remove the connector assembly.* Turn the barrel and receiver group on its left side with the operating rod handle up and the muzzle pointing away from you. If the rifle has been modified for *selective firing* (explained later in this text), press in and turn the selector until the face marked with the capital letter "A" is toward the windage knob. With the bolt closed, place the right thumb on the rear of the connector assembly and the first finger (or the first

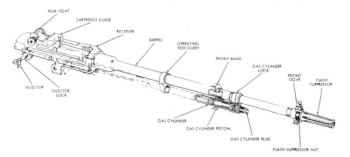

PLATE 44. BARREL AND RECEIVER GROUP, CUT-AWAY VIEW. (Courtesy Ordnance Corps, U.S. Army.)

and second fingers) of the right hand inside the rear of the receiver. Push forward with the thumb until the forward end of the assembly can be lifted off the connector lock. Turn the connector assembly clockwise (around to your right, as the hands of a clock move) until the slot in the rear end is aligned with the elongated stud of the sear release. Slowly lower the front end of the connector assembly a short distance and lift the rear end off the elongated stud of the sear release.

Caution: Do not bend the connector assembly or damage the overhang of the sear release when removing the connector assembly.

(2) *Remove the operating rod spring and operating rod spring guide.* Place the barrel and receiver group on that clean, dry, flat surface mentioned before, sights down, muzzle to the left. Using your left hand, pull toward the muzzle on the operating rod spring to relieve the pressure (tension) on the connector lock. With the forefinger of your right hand, pull the connector lock toward your body and disconnect and remove the operating rod spring and guide.

(3) *Remove the operating rod.* Turn the barrel and receiver group so that the sights are up and the muzzle is pointing away from you. Pull back the operating rod handle until the guide lug on its inside surface is aligned with the disassembly notch on the right side of the receiver. Rotate the operating rod downward and outward; then pull it to the rear, disengaging it from the operating rod guide.

Plate 45 is an operational view of the operating rod and connector group. Plate 46 is an exploded view of the operating rod and connector group, with the parts numbered and designated thus: (1) connector assembly; (2) operating rod spring guide; (3) operating rod spring; and (4) operating rod assembly.

(4) *Remove the bolt.* Grasp the bolt by the roller and, while sliding it forward, lift it upward and outward to the right front with a slight rotating motion. Plates illustrating the bolt and its parts accompany the explanation of bolt disassembly and assembly.

Field Stripping of the M14 Accomplished.—When you have performed the operations described above, you have *field stripped* the M14 Rifle. Just as a check on your own work, if you have laid out assemblies, subassemblies, and parts in the correct order as you removed them, you will find that the following are laid out, more or

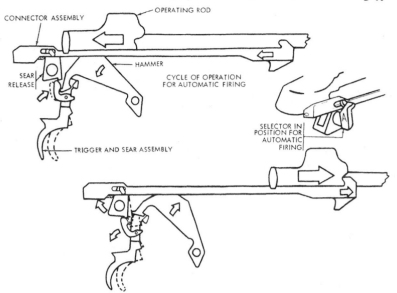

PLATE 45. OPERATIONAL VIEW OF OPERATING ROD AND CONNECTOR GROUP. (Courtesy Ordnance Corps, U.S. Army.)

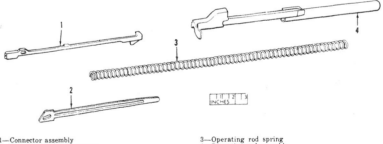

1—Connector assembly
2—Operating rod spring guide

3—Operating rod spring
4—Operating rod assembly

PLATE 46. EXPLODED VIEW OF OPERATING ROD AND CONNECTOR GROUP. (Courtesy Ordnance Corps, U.S. Army.)

less parallel to each other, from left to right in this order: connector assembly; operating rod spring guide; operating rod spring; operating rod; bolt; and barrel and receiver. Having field stripped the MI4, you are now ready to learn the details of assembly and disassembly, but you must remember that some of these operations must not be performed unless you are qualified, authorized, and ordered to do this work.

Assembly of the Barrel and Receiver Group.—(1) *Replace the Bolt.* Lay the barrel and receiver on the clean, dry, flat surface mentioned before, sights up, muzzle pointing away from you. Hold the bolt by the roller and locking lug and place the rear end on the bridge of the receiver, with the firing-pin tang pointed down. Turn the bolt counterclockwise (that is, to the left instead of to the right) as far as necessary to let the tang of the firing pin clear the bridge. Guide the left locking lug of the bolt into its groove on the left side of the receiver. Lower the right locking lug on its bearing surface and slide the bolt halfway to the rear.

(2) *Replace the Operating Rod.* Hold the operating rod at the handle, insert the front end into the operating rod guide, and position (locate) the rod so that the recess in the hump fits over the bolt roller. Turn the operating rod to the left until the guide lug will fit in the disassembly notch on the receiver. Then move the operating rod forward until the bolt is closed.

(3) *Replace the Operating Rod Spring and Operating Rod Spring Guide.* Turn the barrel and receiver over so that the sights are down and the muzzle is to the left. Place the operating rod spring guide into the operating rod spring, hump end up, and place the spring and guide inside the operating rod. Grasp the spring and guide with the left hand and compress the spring until the hole in the guide can be aligned with the connector lock. Lower the guide and push the connector lock in with the right thumb.

(4) *Replace the Connector Assembly.* Turn the barrel and receiver on its side with the operating rod handle up, muzzle pointing away from you. Place the hole in the rear end of the connector assembly on the elongated stud of the sear release. Place the right thumb on the rear of the connector assembly, place the index finger (forefinger) of your right hand on the sear release bracket, and place the middle finger in the rear of the receiver. Push toward the muzzle with your right thumb and, at the same time, turn the front of the assembly counterclockwise until it can be lowered onto the connector lock.

Disassembly of Bolt.—Plate 47 is an exploded view of the bolt assembly. The numbered parts are: (1) extractor; (2) cartridge

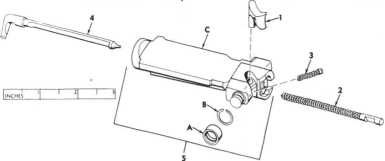

PLATE 47. EXPLODED VIEW OF BOLT ASSEMBLY. (Courtesy Ordnance Corps, U.S. Army.)

ejector; (3) extractor spring plunger; (4) firing pin; and (5) bolt and roller assembly. The lettered parts are: (A) roller; (B) retainer; and (C) bolt.

Plate 48 is another exploded view of the bolt assembly, which is merely a simplified form of Plate 47 with fewer details. The parts numbered are: (1) extractor; (2) cartridge ejector; (3) extractor spring plunger; and (4) firing pin. The large object in the center of the group which has no number is the bolt. We now proceed to disassemble the bolt, first with the bolt out of the rifle, and then with the bolt in the rifle.

(1) *Bolt Out of Rifle.* If authorized to disassemble and assemble the bolt, whether it is in or out of the rifle, you are supplied with a *combination tool* which has a *wrench head* and also a *screwdriver blade.* Hold the combination tool in your right hand and the bolt in your left hand. Push the combination tool into the face of the bolt with the screwdriver blade beneath the extractor. Turn the combination tool clockwise with your right hand, maintaining pressure against the ejector and spring. Then lift the extractor from the bolt. When the extractor is clear, allow the ejector (which is under pressure) to slowly push the combination tool away from the face of the bolt until it is no longer under spring pressure. Remove the ejector and spring. Lift out the extractor spring and plunger.

Do not separate the ejector from its spring and do not separate the extractor spring from its plunger. Remove the firing pin from the rear of the bolt. Do not disassemble the bolt roller from the stud.

If you have disassembled the bolt in accordance with the above explanations, the subassemblies and parts have been laid out on the flat surface (mentioned repeatedly for emphasis) approximately parallel to each other, from left to right as follows: extractor; extractor spring and plunger; ejector and spring; firing pin; and bolt.

(2) *Bolt in Rifle.* The *combination tool* is used, but when the bolt is in the rifle the *wrench head* portion of the combination tool is used to remove the extractor, extractor spring and plunger, and the ejector and spring. In order to do this, insert the *wrench head* into the chamber with the *screwdriver blade* of the combination tool beneath the extractor. Slowly and gently close the bolt against the *wrench head.* Insert one cleaning rod section into the socket and turn the rod section counterclockwise with the left hand until the extractor is free. Sometimes it is necessary to hold the bolt forward during this operation so that the screwdriver blade will engage properly with the extractor, but this presents no problem if you proceed slowly. Next, lift out the extractor. Permit the bolt to move to the rear and then remove the ejector and spring, and also remove the extractor spring and plunger.

Having learned to disassemble the bolt whether it is in or out of the rifle, you are now ready to assemble the bolt, whether it is in or out of the rifle.

Assembly of the Bolt.—Having disassembled the bolt, its assembly is comparatively simple if you proceed slowly. First, the assembly is explained when the bolt is out of the rifle, and then when the bolt is in the rifle.

(1) *Bolt Out of Rifle.* Insert the firing pin, being careful that the tang fits into the recess on the rear of the bolt. Hold the bolt in the left hand with the bolt roller in the "up" position and to the right. Replace the ejector and ejector spring so that the cut on the ejector is toward the bolt roller. Replace the extractor spring and plunger. Engage the ejector with the combination tool held in your right hand, being careful to push the ejector into position with the combination tool. When the combination tool is against the face of the bolt, push the extractor into position and allow the combination tool to turn as the extractor pushes on the *screwdriver blade* portion of the combination tool.

(2) *Bolt in Rifle.* When the bolt is in the rifle, before you begin

the assembly make certain that the tang of the firing pin is seated in the recess in the rear of the bolt. Install the ejector and ejector spring so that the cut on the ejector is toward the bolt roller. Replace the extractor spring and plunger. Insert the extractor in its position and insert the *wrench head* of the combination tool in the chamber with the *screwdriver blade* portion of the combination tool in position beneath the extractor. Slowly close the bolt on the wrench until the wrench is fully seated. During the closing of the bolt, the ejector contacts the wrench first, but be extremely careful to prevent the ejector from slipping off the wrench. While holding the bolt forward, push the extractor downward into its position. If necessary, use a rod section to push the extractor until it is completely seated in the bolt.

During the disassembly and assembly of the bolt, when this work is done with the bolt in the rifle, the rifle must be held with the muzzle lowered sufficiently to keep the firing pin in the bolt. However, if the firing pin must be replaced, remove the bolt from the rifle and disassemble the bolt according to the previously described procedure for *Disassembly of Bolt—(1) Bolt Out of Rifle.*

Disassembly of Rear Sight.—The disassembly of the rear sight should be supervised by a commissioned officer. This is the official policy. The author believes that in practice the commissioned officer will delegate his authority to a competent noncommissioned officer, although if anything goes wrong the officer is responsible.

Place the barrel and receiver group on that clean, smooth surface that we continue to mention. The sights must be up and the muzzle pointing away from your body. Lower the *aperture (hole) part of the rear sight as far as it will go.*

If the rifle has been *zeroed*, the sights have been adjusted so that under normal conditions a bullet will strike dead center at the base range from which all variable calculations will be made. Therefore, you must examine the reading on the *elevating knob* of the rear-sight assembly and write in a notebook the elevation reading, because you will need this when you replace the elevating knob.

The rear sight is visible in Plate 40; the rear sight base is Item No. 1 in Plate 42; the rear sight is clearly indicated in Plate 44; and its construction is so simple that it presents no problem to anyone who has any aptitude for the use of simple tools.

Having examined and recorded the reading on the elevating knob, the next step is to unscrew the nut in the center of the *windage knob,* using *the screwdriver blade of the combination tool;* but in doing this the slot in the nut must not be damaged. The nut will become loose but it cannot be removed and no attempt should be made to remove it. Unscrew the windage knob counterclockwise until the *windage-knob assembly* can be removed without force. Push forward very lightly on the right side of the *rear-sight base* and remove the *rear-sight elevating pinion assembly* by pulling it to the left without force.

Finally, pull the *aperture* part of the rear sight upward about one-half inch and put your right thumb under it. Then push forward and upward, thus removing the *aperture* part of the rear sight, the *rear-sight cover,* and the *rear-sight base.*

In arranging the subassemblies and parts of the rear sight on the clean, smooth, dry surface we have mentioned so often, the most efficient layout is not from left to right, with all items parallel to each other. Instead, place the *windage-knob assembly* on the extreme right. Place the *rear-sight base* to the left of the *windage-knob assembly,* and lay the *rear-sight elevating pinion assembly (including the elevating knob)* to the left of the *rear-sight base.* Place the *rear-sight cover* above the *rear-sight base,* and lay the *aperture* part of the rear sight below the *rear-sight base.* With this layout you can assemble the rear sight easily and comparatively quickly. However, if you can find a more efficient arrangement, by all means use it.

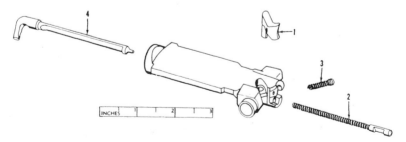

PLATE 48. SIMPLIFIED EXPLODED VIEW OF BOLT ASSEMBLY. (Courtesy Ordnance Corps, U.S. Army.)

Assembly of the Rear Sight.—The *rear sight cover* and the *rear sight base* are assembled to form a single unit. Place the front lip of the sight cover in the slot at the forward end of the sight housing.

Raise the base slightly and push forward and downward with the *screwdriver blade of the combination tool* against the rear part of the sight cover, seating it in its slot in the rear of the sight housing.

Replace the *windage-knob assembly* and screw it in until it draws the base to the center position on the windage gage. Push lightly forward on the right rear of the base while inserting the *elevating pinion assembly* from the left, meshing the pinion with the teeth on the *aperture* until the threaded end of the pinion contacts the *windage knob.* Tighten the nut in the center of the windage knob until you encounter a pronounced resistance. When the nut is tight, back it off one complete turn to obtain the correct tension.

Refer to your notebook in which you recorded the reading you found on the elevating knob before disassembly. This reading must be opposite the index mark on the receiver when the aperture part of the rear sight is at its lowest position. When this is correct, tighten the elevating knob screw.

The tension of the rear sight is of vital importance because if it is not adjusted correctly the rear sight will not keep its adjustment in elevation during fire, the bullets will not strike the target accurately, the shooter will lose confidence in his rifle, and he will lose confidence in himself as a soldier.

Two symptoms of incorrect tension are: (1) the aperture part of the rear sight drops when the rifle is fired; and (2) when you turn the elevating knob you fail to hear clear, sharp clicks.

If either or both of the above symptoms are present, examine tension as follows: (1) run the aperture up about twenty clicks; (2) press downward on the top of the aperture with your thumb; and (3) if the aperture drops, the tension is incorrect and must be adjusted.

Tension is adjusted as follows: (1) be certain that the elevating knob screw is tight; (2) tighten the windage-knob nut one click at a time; (3) after each click in tightening the windage nut, examine the tension according to the procedure in the preceding paragraph; and (4) continue the procedure until the aperture no longer drops. If you follow these procedures carefully and cannot set the proper tension, the rear sight must be replaced or repaired.

The sight tension may be correct and yet the windage knob may seem hard to turn. This is a very minor problem. The solution is to press inward on the *elevating pinion assembly* with the thumb of the left hand while turning the windage knob with the right hand.

FIRING MECHANISM

Nomenclature of Firing Mechanism.—Plate 49 is an exploded view of the firing mechanism. The parts illustrated and numbered are: (1) trigger pin; (2) trigger and sear assembly; (3) hammer-spring housing; (4) hammer spring; (5) hammer-spring plunger; (6) hammer pin; (7) hammer; (8) safety; (9) safety spring; (10) trigger guard; and (11) housing assembly.

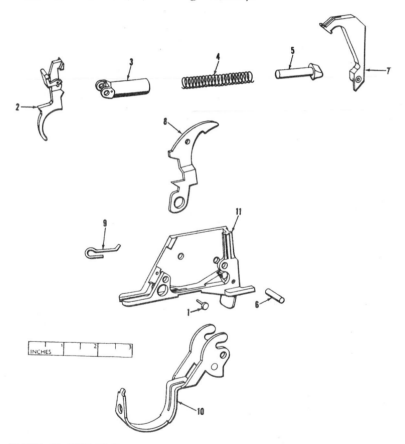

PLATE 49. EXPLODED VIEW OF FIRING MECHANISM. (Courtesy Ordnance Corps, U.S. Army.)

Disassembly of the Firing Mechanism Assembly.—During the disassembly of the firing-mechanism assembly, the parts should be arranged on a flat, clean, dry surface and laid out so that they are approximately parallel to each other, from left to right, in the following order: (1) trigger pin; (2) trigger and sear assembly; (3) hammer-spring housing; (4) hammer spring; (5) hammer-spring plunger; (6) hammer pin; (7) hammer; (8) safety; (9) safety spring; (10) trigger guard; and (11) trigger housing, referred to in Plate 49 as "housing assembly." The parts illustrated in Plate 49 are the same as those listed here for a left-to-right arrangement, but in Plate 49 the pictures of the individual parts are not drawn as they appear when laid out during disassembly—hence the necessity for what otherwise would be unnecessary repetition.

Disassembly can be performed efficiently and easily in six easy steps or stages, as follows:

(1) Close and latch the trigger guard. Place the safety in the "off" position and press the trigger, permitting the hammer to go forward. Hold the firing-mechanism assembly in your left hand with its vertical face to the left, resting against your left thumb and with the open face resting against the palm of your left hand. With the tip of a cartridge, apply pressure on the trigger pin until its head is unseated.

Next, hold the firing mechanism assembly with your right hand, open face up, trigger guard to the left, right forefinger (index finger of right hand) over the sear, right thumb on the vertical face of the firing-mechanism assembly. With the left thumb and left forefinger (left index finger) apply pressure to the trigger pin, pinching it between your left thumb and left forefinger, and remove the trigger pin. Slowly release the pressure, permitting the hammer spring to expand.

(2) Move the firing mechanism assembly from your right hand to your left hand and hold it with the vertical face toward your body, just as it was toward your body before when it was being held in the right hand. The open face is still up. With your right hand, remove the trigger and sear assembly, hammer-spring housing, hammer spring, and hammer-spring plunger.

(3) Unlatch and open the trigger guard. Hold the firing mechanism in your left hand with the vertical face away from your body

and the open face down. Push out the hammer pin with the tip of a cartridge. Turn the trigger housing over. Move the hammer slightly to the rear and lift it out.

(4) Leave the trigger guard unlatched. Turn the trigger guard housing over so that the open face is down and push the stud of the safety from its hole with the tip of a cartridge. Remove the safety and the safety spring by lifting them out of the trigger housing.

(5) Hold the rear end of the trigger housing between the thumb and forefinger of your left hand. With your right hand, grasp the trigger guard and slide it to the rear until the hammer-pin holes in the wings of the trigger guard are slightly forward of the safety-stud hole. Cant (tilt) the trigger guard to the right; push it forward and upward; and remove it from the trigger housing (housing assembly).

(6) Do not remove the magazine latch from the trigger housing (housing assembly). You have now completed the disassembly of the firing mechanism assembly.

Assembly of the Firing Mechanism Assembly.—Assuming that you laid out the parts from right to left as explained above, the assembly is relatively easy. Like the disassembly, the assembly is performed efficiently in six stages or steps, as follows:

(1) Hold the rear of the trigger housing in your left hand. The open face of the trigger housing is to the right and the vertical face is away from you. The trigger guard extends above your left hand and looks something like an inverted capital letter "U," with the unattached end of the trigger guard pointing downward toward your left hand. You now have the rear of the trigger housing in a convenient position. Place the hammer stop on the trigger guard on the floor of the trigger housing, slightly forward of the safety slot. Next, rotate the trigger guard down and to the left.

(2) Continue to hold the trigger housing in your left hand, but now hold it so that the vertical face is to the left and the open face is up. Place the loop of the safety spring on its stud in the trigger housing with your right hand and rotate it clockwise into position. The short arm of the safety spring should be along the base of the trigger housing.

(3) Place the right forefinger over the safety spring stud to hold the safety spring in place. Insert the finger piece of the safety through its slot in the base of the trigger housing and turn the trigger housing over so that the open face is down. Seat the safety stud in its hold in the trigger housing with the left hand by forcing the safety down against the pressure of the safety spring.

(4) Hold the trigger housing in your left hand, the vertical face away from you and the open face up. Place the safety in the "off" position. Place the hammer in position, holding it halfway between the cocked and fired positions. Be sure that the hammer toe is in front of the hammer stop on the right wing of the trigger guard. Align the hammer-pin hole in the hammer with the holes in the trigger housing and trigger guard. The trigger guard must not be latched. Replace the hammer pin from the top and seat it.

(5) Assemble the hammer-spring plunger, hammer spring, and hammer-spring housing into one unit. Hold the trigger housing in your left hand with the vertical face toward you and the open face up. Place the plunger in its seat on the hammer. Make sure that the cut-away portion of the hammer-spring housing is toward the safety. Hold these parts in place with your left thumb and insert the trigger in the trigger slot so that the notch at the curved rear surface of the finger piece bears against the rear of the slot in the trigger housing. Place the wings of the hammer spring housing astride the sear pin. With your right forefinger hooked over the sear and your right thumb on the vertical face, apply pressure to compress the hammer spring and align the holes for the trigger pin. Insert the trigger pin as far as its head, but *at this step the trigger pin is not fully seated.*

(6) Hold the firing-mechanism assembly with your right hand, open face up, trigger guard to the left, right forefinger over the sear, thumb on the vertical face, and apply a squeezing pressure between your right thumb and the remainder of your right hand, although the principal pressure is exerted by the right thumb and the right forefinger. Then seat the head of the trigger pin by pressing on it with your left thumb. You now have completed the assembly of the firing mechanism assembly.

Review of Illustrations for Firing Mechanism Assembly.—Refer to Plate 42, where Item No. 11 is the trigger housing, drawn with its right side toward the reader. Plate 49, an exploded view of the firing-mechanism subassemblies and parts, contains Item No. 11, which is a larger drawing of the trigger housing, with its right side toward the reader. In both Plate 42 and Plate 49, the trigger housing is drawn so that its forward surface is to the reader's right and its rear portion to the reader's left.

Plate 50 *is an operational view of the firing mecahnism*—that is, it is drawn primarily to illustrate operation and functioning, but it is extremely helpful in explaining disassembly and assembly. Actually, it is two views. *The upper view shows the mechanism with the safety off. The lower view shows the mechanism with the safety on.* However, the important feature of these two drawings on Plate 50 is their large, clear portrayal of important parts which must be accurately identified not only during the study of operation and functioning but especially during the disassembly and assembly of the firing mechanism.

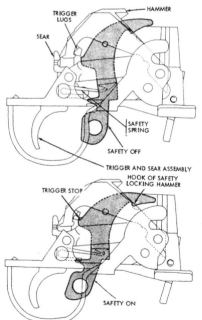

PLATE 50. OPERATIONAL VIEW OF FIRING MECHANISM. (Courtesy Ordnance Corps, U.S. Army.)

You are urged to observe carefully the shape, location, and relationship to other parts of the hammer, trigger lugs, sear, safety spring, trigger and sear assembly, hook of safety locking hammer, and trigger stop; also the relationship of the parts to each other with the safety off in the upper drawing of Plate 50, and the relationship of the parts to each other with the safety on in the lower drawing. Actually, you are not expected to fully understand operation and functioning of the rifle in order to disassemble and assemble the

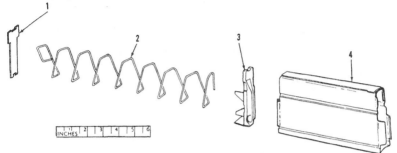

PLATE 51. EXPLODED VIEW OF CARTRIDGE MAGAZINE. (Courtesy Ordnance Corps, U.S. Army.)

firing mechanism, but the facts presented here will make your work easier and more interesting.

Disassembly of the Magazine.—Plate 51 is an exploded view of the cartridge magazine. The numbered parts are: (1) base; (2) spring; (3) follower; and (4) tube. These same parts are also referred to as the magazine base; the magazine spring; the magazine follower; and the magazine. During disassembly, the parts should be laid out from left to right, approximately parallel to each other, in the order of the numbers given above, but not as they are illustrated in Plate 51.

Use the point (tip) of a cartridge to raise the front of the magazine base until its indention (notch or recess) is clear of the magazine. Grasp the magazine with either hand, using one finger of that hand to cover the base. Remove the base with the other hand while the finger of the grasping hand controls the expanding spring. If you do not keep control of the spring while you remove the base, the spring will fly out of the magazine (tube) with sufficient force to injure a person. Remove the magazine spring and the magazine follower, and then separate them. This completes disassembly of the magazine.

Assembly of the Magazine.—Refer to Plate 51. The spring (Item No. 2) as it appears in Plate 51 has its rectangular-shaped end at the left of the drawing. This is satisfactory for illustrating nomenclature, but it gives the wrong idea about assembly. Grasp the spring and reposition it inside the follower (Item No. 3 of Plate 51) with the rectangular-shaped end of the spring against the rear of the follower. Replace the follower and the spring inside the magazine (Item No. 4 of Plate 51, also called a "tube"). Be sure that the follower is fully seated. The next step is to replace the base (Item No. 1 of Plate 51).

Place the top of the magazine down on a flat surface and compress the spring with both hands. Holding the spring with the left hand, replace the magazine base with the right hand. You now have completed the assembly of the magazine.

When handling any spring that is compressed (under tension), always remember that if you lose control of the spring while it is still compressed it may fly through the air and injure someone. Also, if this happens under field conditions, you may lose the spring and the rifle will not function until you obtain a new spring. These comments apply not only to the magazine spring but to any and all springs found in firearms.

CONVERSION FOR SEMI-AUTOMATIC
AND AUTOMATIC FIRE

Conversion to Fire Selectively.—The M14 is normally issued with a *selector* so that it can be fired either semiautomatically or automatically; but when it is equipped with a *selector lock* it can be fired semiautomatically but not automatically. The procedure for changing the rifle, so that it can be fired either semiautomatically or automatically, is called *conversion to fire selectively.*

Plates 52 and 53 show the *selector* installed. Plate 52 shows the selector positioned for automatic fire. Plate 53 shows the selector positioned for semiautomatic fire. *These plates show the normal, standard equipment of the rifle as regularly issued.*

When the M14 is issued in a form equipped to fire only semiautomatically, and not both semiautomatically and automatically, it can be converted to fire *selectively.* This is done by removing the *selector lock* and replacing it with a *selector and selector spring, thereby providing the features illustrated by Plates 52 and 53.*

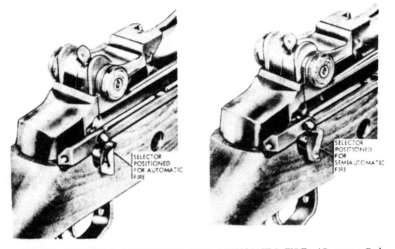

SELECTOR POSITIONED FOR AUTOMATIC FIRE

SELECTOR POSITIONED FOR SEMI-AUTOMATIC FIRE

PLATE 52. SELECTOR POSITIONED FOR AUTOMATIC FIRE. (Courtesy Ordnance Corps, U.S. Army.)

PLATE 53. SELECTOR POSITIONED FOR SEMI-AUTOMATIC FIRE. (Courtesy Ordnance Corps, U.S. Army.)

The conversion is begun by separating the rifle into the three main groups and removing the connector assembly. Lay the barrel and receiver group on a clean, dry, flat surface. The sights must be up and the muzzle pointing away from your body. With either a drift punch or a flat-faced punch of appropriate size and shape, drive out the selector shaft pin which secures the selector lock. Remove the selector shaft lock. Hold the selector shaft in place and turn the rifle over, so that the sights are down. *Do not remove the shaft.*

Next, place the selector spring and selector on the selector shaft, compress the spring on the shaft, while rotating the selector until the point of the selector shaft engages in the recess in the selector. In this position, the holes in the selector and shaft are in alignment. Replace (insert) the selector shaft pin. Replace the connector assembly and assemble the rifle. The rifle now can be fired either semi-automatically or automatically by turning the selector to the desired setting, as illustrated in Plates 52 and 53. When the capital letter "A," shown on Place 52, faces the shooter as he holds the rifle in the firing position, the rifle will fire automatically—that is, it will continue to fire as long as the shooter keeps the trigger pulled back and the ammunition loaded into the rifle is not exhausted. The position of the selector can be determined in darkness by touch. When set for automatic fire, the lug end of the selector is up.

Conversion to Fire Semiautomatically Only.—Assuming that you have converted the rifle to fire selectively, or it has been issued to you with the equipment for selective fire already installed, you may be ordered to convert the rifle to fire semiautomatically only.

Separate the rifle into the three main groups and remove the connector assembly. Lay the barrel and receiver group on a flat, clean, dry surface. The sights must be up and the muzzle pointing away from your body. Use a suitable drift or flat-faced punch to drift out the selector shaft pin. Hold the selector shaft in place and turn the rifle over so that the sights are down. Remove the selector and the selector spring. Remember that the selector spring is not used when the selector shaft lock is installed.

Hold the selector shaft in place with the right hand and place the selector shaft lock on the shaft. Press the selector shaft lock and the shaft together while rotating the lock until the point on the selector shaft engages in the recess of the lock. Replace the pin. Replace the connector assembly and assemble the rifle. The rifle will now fire semiautomatically only. As explained several times before, this means that the shooter must squeeze the trigger for each shot, release the trigger and then squeeze it again for a second shot, and so on, continuing this procedure until the load of ammunition in the rifle is exhausted.

XXXII. U.S. Rifle, 7.62-MM, M14, Operation, Functioning and Maintenance

BASIC INSTRUCTIONS

What to Do When New Rifles Are Received.—When new rifles are received they are sealed in water and vaporproof, volatile corrosion inhibitor bags, packed two in a carton and five cartons in a box, making a total of ten rifles in a box. Each carton is removed from the box and each rifle is removed from its carton and bag. The bore of the rifle must be cleaned with a cleaning patch. *A light coat of oil should be applied to all metal parts except the chamber and other parts which come into contact with the ammunition.*

When time permits, disassemble, clean, and lubricate the locking lugs of the bolt, bolt roller, bolt guides, cocking cam on bolt, operating-rod guide groove, camming surfaces of operating rod, and operating-rod spring. When new bipods are received they are sealed in bags of the same material as the rifles. Each bipod is removed from its carton and bag and then a light coat of oil is applied to the leg assemblies and the yoke assembly.

The M14 rifle may be equipped with a selector lock and also have a selector and spring in a package fastened to the rifle. The organization commander determines from which rifles the selector locks are to be removed and replaced with selectors; but, regardless of the decision on this subject, selectors and locks not installed on the rifles are retained. The combat unit is responsible for any installation or removal of either the selector or the selector lock. As explained elsewhere in this text, a punch can be used to drive out a spring pin, but this should be a 1/16-inch punch with a straight shank and should have a flat point to avoid spreading the pin.

NORMAL OPERATION

Preparation for Firing.—Be sure the bore is clear. The ammunition must be clean and of the correct type and grade. Place the safety in the safe position by pressing it to the rear, as illustrated in Plate 54, to prevent firing.

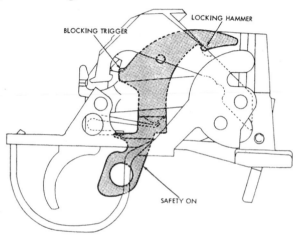

PLATE 54. FUNCTIONING OF SAFETY WITH SAFETY IN "ON" POSITION. (Courtesy Ordnance Corps, U.S. Army.)

Service Before Firing.—Examine the rifle and bipod in accordance with the *Chart of Preventive Maintenance Service performed by Rifleman,* Plate 78

Loading the Rifle.—Insert the front end of a loaded magazine into the magazine well until the front catch snaps into engagement. Then pull to the rear and upward until the magazine latch locks the magazine into position, as illustrated in Plate 55, which shows both the installation and the removal of the magazine. The left view of Plate 55 shows the installation and the right view shows the removal of the magazine, referred to by the artist as "magazine cartridge," although the author believes it more logical to call it a "cartridge magazine."

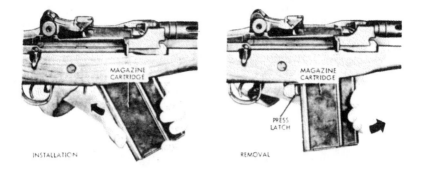

PLATE 55. INSTALLATION AND REMOVAL OF MAGAZINE. (Courtesy Ordnance Corps, U.S. Army.)

If the magazine is empty, the rifle can be loaded by means of a 5-round clip, but it is important to first push the safety to the safe position, as illustrated in Plate 55. To load from a clip to the magazine while the magazine is in the rifle, draw the bolt assembly all the way to the rear, compress the bolt lock and ease the bolt forward until the movement of the bolt is restricted by the bolt lock. Place the loaded clip into the slot of the cartridge-clip guide and push down until the bottom of the clip touches the top of the magazine follower, as shown in Plate 56.

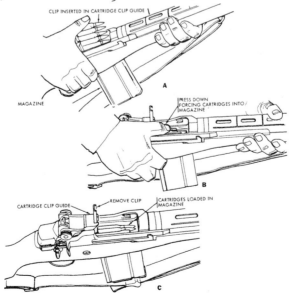

PLATE 56. LOADING THE RIFLE. (Courtesy Ordnance Corps, U.S. Army.)

With the fingers of the right hand under the housing of the firing mechanism and the ball of the right thumb on the powder space of the top cartridge, near the clip, press the cartridges straight downward until all cartridges are emptied from the clip into the magazine. To fully load the magazine, it must be charged in this manner with four clips, one at a time. After the five cartridges from each clip are loaded into the magazine, the clip is removed and placed in some receptacle which will be sent to the supply room or salvage dump later.

An alternate method of loading requires the use of the *combination tool* mentioned in the previous chapter. Plate 57 shows how this

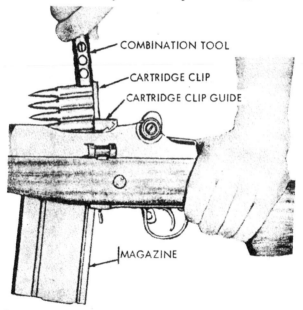

COMBINATION TOOL

CARTRIDGE CLIP

CARTRIDGE CLIP GUIDE

MAGAZINE

PLATE 57. LOADING MAGAZINE, USING COMBINATION TOOL. (Courtesy Ordnance Corps, U.S. Army.)

is done. Insert a cartridge clip in the cartridge clip guide. Place the open end of the combination tool on the base of the cartridge at the top of the clip. Push downward, forcing the cartridges into the magazine. Remove the clip from the guide. Release the bolt lock by drawing the bolt to the rear, and then close the bolt. As the bolt assembly is closed, the top cartridge in the magazine is pushed forward into the chamber. Now release the safety in order to be able to fire the rifle. The safety in the "off" position is illustrated in Plate 58.

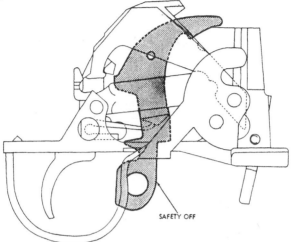

SAFETY OFF

PLATE 58. FUNCTIONING OF SAFETY WITH SAFETY IN "OFF" POSITION. (Courtesy Ordnance Corps, U.S. Army.)

Loading Magazine When Out of Rifle.—Plate 59 shows how to load the magazine when it is not in the rifle. The top view, marked "A," shows how to load the magazine with the *combination tool.* The middle view, marked "B," shows how to load the magazine by hand. The lower view, marked "C," shows how to force cartridges into the magazine by placing the base of the end cartridge of a clip against the butt-plate assembly.

In loading the magazine by hand when the magazine is out of the rifle, hold the magazine in your left hand with the open end pointing toward your right hand. Insert the cartridges with the ends (tips) of the bullets toward the front of the magazine, which is the portion with the square recess.

To load the magazine with the *magazine filler,* described in the previous chapter, slide the filler over the top rear portion of the magazine. Insert a 5-round magazine charger in the filler. Place the thumb of either hand on the top round (cartridge) and push the five rounds into the magazine. Remove the magazine charger and repeat the process until 20 rounds have been loaded into the magazine.

Then remove the magazine filler. Place the clips as they are removed from the cartridges in some receptacle provided for that purpose.

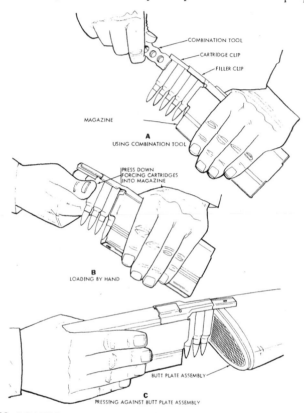

PLATE 59. LOADING MAGAZINE WHEN IT IS NOT IN RIFLE. (Courtesy Ordnance Corps, U.S. Army.)

CONTROLS FOR OPERATION AND MAINTENANCE

Rifle Controls.—The *selector* is on the right side of the receiver, slightly below the rear sight. Its function is to regulate the firing of the rifle either as a semiautomatic rifle or as an automatic rifle. Plate 52 of the previous chapter shows the selector positioned for automatic fire and Plate 53 of the same chapter shows it positioned for semi-automatic fire. When the selector is in position with its blank face toward the rear and its projection downward, the rifle will fire semiautomatically. When the selector is in position with its face marked "A" toward the rear and the projection is upward, the rifle will fire automatically.

The *trigger and sear assembly,* illustrated in Plate 45 of the previous chapter, is located inside the trigger-guard assembly and is part of the firing mechanism. Its function is to control the firing of the rifle for both semiautomatic and automatic fire. In firing semiautomatically, squeeze the trigger for each round fired. In automatic fire, squeeze the trigger and hold it back until the ammunition load of the rifle is exhausted or until you want to cease automatic fire temporarily.

The *safety* is located on the firing mechanism near the trigger-guard assembly. Its function is to lock the trigger, sear, and hammer, thus preventing the firing of the rifle. Plates 54 and 58 illustrate the functioning of the safety in both the "on" and "off" positions. In Plate 54, the *blocking trigger* and the *locking hammer* are labeled, but the same parts in Plate 58 are not labeled. As explained before, when the safety is in the rear position the rifle will not fire. When the safety is pressed to the forward position the rifle will fire.

A *gas spindle valve* is located at the front end of the stock and is connected to the gas cylinder. Its function is to control the gases used in firing the rifle, and also to control the gases used in firing the rifle grenade. The upper drawing of Plate 60 shows the slot of the spindle valve in the vertical or "on" position. In this position, the spindle valve is open and releases gases needed for the functioning of the rifle. The lower drawing of Plate 60 shows the slot of the spindle valve in the horizontal or "off" position, with the spindle valve closed. This permits the full pressure of the gases generated by the combustion of the powder in the cartridge case to be used in propelling a rifle grenade and prevents the by-pass of the gases into the gas chamber.

Rear sight controls consist of the *windage knob,* located at the right rear side of the receiver; and the *pinion assembly,* located at the left rear side of the receiver and calibrated in meters. The function of the windage knob is to adjust the lateral movement of the rear sight. To move the rear sight to the right, the windage knob is turned clockwise. To move the rear sight to the left, the windage knob is turned counterclockwise. The function of the pinion assem-

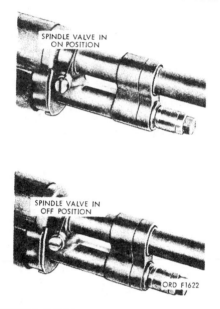

PLATE 60. GAS SPINDLE VALVE IN "ON" AND "OFF" POSITIONS. (Courtesy Ordnance Corps, U.S. Army.)

bly is to adjust the elevation of the aperture (rear sight hole). Turning the pinion clockwise raises the elevation. Turning the pinion counterclockwise lowers the elevation.

The *operating-rod handle* is located at the right-hand side of the receiver. The rifle can be operated manually by means of this handle. This is done by moving the operating handle to the rear position and then releasing it. This permits the force of the magazine spring to position the top round in the path of the bolt after the operating rod has moved the bolt to its rearward position. As the operating rod moves the bolt forward, the bottom face of the bolt engages the base of the cartridge, ramming it forward and feeding, chambering, and locking the cartridge in the barrel.

Bipod Controls.—The combination tool is used to tighten the self-locking bolt in the right jaw, securing both the right and left jaws to the gas chamber. This is the installation procedure. For removal, the combination tool is used to loosen the self-locking bolt in the right jaw. Spread both the right and left jaws apart and remove the bipod from the rifle.

The pivot-plunger buttons are located on the leg assemblies. Press the top button of the right- or left-leg assembly to permit rotating the legs to a nopen or a closed position. Press the bottom button of the right- and left-leg assemblies to permit extending or closing the leg assemblies.

How to Zero or Target the Rifle.—As explained in the previous chapter, the *zero* of a rifle is the adjustment of the sights, which under normal conditions will cause the bullet to shoot dead center at the base range from which all variable condition calculations will be made. The word *zero,* also is used as a verb. For example, you may be told to "zero" your rifle. Also, you may be told to "target" your rifle, which means the same thing.

The following is the procedure for zeroing the M14 rifle at a distance of 100 meters, with no wind blowing:

(1) Raise aperture from lowest position to eight clicks elevation.

(2) Align windage center index line on sight base with center index line on the receiver.

(3) Fire three "warm-up" rounds. Then fire four more rounds, adjusting the sights after each round to move the impact of the bullet to the center of the target. Then fire five consecutive rounds semiautomatically. The impact of the 5-round shot group should be inside a circle having a diameter of 6.1 inches.

(4) Adjust the sights to bring the point of impact of round to the center of the target by correcting with one click of elevation or windage for each 28 millimeters (about 1.125 inches) of movement required.

(5) Maximum adjustments which are permitted are: (a) six clicks elevation or depression; and (b) three clicks windage in either direction. You can make adjustments in elevation or depression alone, windage alone, or both, according to the results you need to obtain.

After the rifle has been zeroed, loosen the locking screw on the pinion assembly which secures the elevation knob. Be sure that you do not move the aperture. Turn the elevation knob until the 100-meter mark (between 2 and 12) is aligned with the mark on the side of the receiver. Tighten the screw to lock the knob.

If the rifle cannot be zeroed according to the above instructions, it must be sent to the ordnance personnel in the third or fourth echelons of maintenance for further inspection, and possibly for repair.

Firing the Rifle.—Firing can be semiautomatic with the selector lock; semiautomatic with the selector; or automatic with the selector, explained as follows:

(1) *Semiautomatic fire with selector lock.* The cycle of operation for semiautomatic fire with selector lock, and also with the selector, is illustrated in Plate 61. To fire semiautomatic with the selector

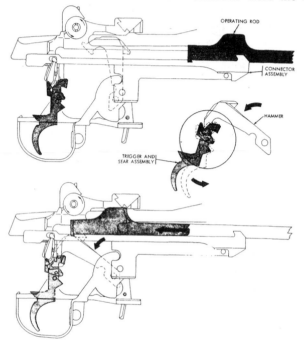

PLATE 61. CYCLE OF OPERATION FOR SEMI-AUTOMATIC FIRE WITH SELECTOR OR WITH SELECTOR LOCK. (Courtesy Ordnance Corps, U.S. Army.)

lock, push the safety forward. Squeeze the trigger to fire one round, release the trigger, then squeeze it again for a second shot, release the trigger, then squeeze it again for a second shot, release the trigger, and continue the procedure for successive shots. See Plate 62 for feeding, chambering, and locking action.

(2) *Semiautomatic fire with selector.* Refer to Plate 61 for the cycle of operation for semiautomatic fire with selector or with selector lock. After removing the selector lock, as explained elsewhere in this book, and installing a selector (assuming that it is necessary to perform this procedure), position the selector for semi-

automatic fire, with its blank face toward the rear and its projection downward. Push the safety forward and the rifle is ready to fire semiautomatically. With each squeeze of the trigger the rifle will fire one round. See Plate 62 for feeding, chambering, and locking action.

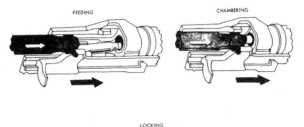

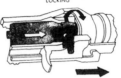

PLATE 62. FEEDING, CHAMBERING, AND LOCKING ACTION. (Courtesy Ordnance Corps, U.S. Army.)

(3) *Automatic fire with selector.* Plate 45 of Chapter 31 consists of three drawings which illustrate the cycle of operation for fire with the selector. The upper drawing shows the cycle of operation for automatic firing. The small drawing near the upper right-hand corner of the plate shows the selector in position for automatic firing. The large lower drawing shows that the operating rod has moved forward, whereas the large upper drawing shows the travel to the rear of the operating rod. The arrows on the parts in both the large upper drawing and the large lower drawing indicate the direction of movement of important parts.

The procedure for automatic fire with selector is as follows: (a) Position the selector for automatic fire with the face of the selector marked "A" toward the rear and projection upward. (b) Push the safety forward, and the rifle is ready to fire automatically. (c) The rifle will fire automatically as long as the trigger is squeezed (held all the way back) and as long as there is ammunition in the magazine. Release the trigger to cease firing.

Misfire.—A misfire is a failure to fire. A misfire is not dangerous in itself but, since it cannot be distinguished immediately from a delay in the functioning of the firing mechanism or from a *hangfire* (explained below), a misfire should be considered as a possible delay in firing until such a possibility has been eliminated beyond any doubt. This is extremely important, because men have lost their lives by not realizing the potential danger accompanying a misfire.

A delay in the functioning of the firing mechanism can result from the presence of foreign matter, such as sand, gravel, grit, frost, ice, oil, or grease. These can create a partial mechanical restraint which, after some delay, is overcome as a result of the continued force applied by the spring and by the firing pin striking the primer. In this connection, no cartridge should be left in a hot weapon any longer than circumstances require because of the possibility of a *cook-off*, explained below.

Hangfire.—A hangfire is a delay in the functioning of a propelling charge at the time of firing. The amount of delay is unpredictable but in most cases it will fall within the range extending from a small fraction of a second to several minutes. For this reason, a hangfire cannot be distinguished immediately from a misfire and therefore there is always great danger in assuming that a failure of a weapon to fire is a misfire whereas, in reality, it may prove to be a hangfire.

Warning: During the prescribed time intervals, the rifle must be kept trained on (aimed toward) the target and all personnel must stand clear of the muzzle.

Cook-Off.—A cook-off is a functioning of a cartridge chambered in a very hot weapon, brought about by the heat of the weapon. If the primer in the cartridge or the propelling charge (powder) in the cartridge should cook-off, the projectile (bullet) will be propelled from the weapon with normal velocity, even though no attempt has been made to fire the primer by actuating the firing mechanism.

In the event of an overheated weapon there may be doubt about whether or not the cartridge will fire, or when it will fire. The same precautions must be taken when a cook-off occurs as when a *hangfire* exists.

A cook-off can be prevented. A cartridge which has been loaded into a very hot weapon should be fired immediately. If not fired immediately, remove it not more than five seconds after it has been loaded into the weapon.

Safety Procedures for Removing a Cartridge in Case of Failure to Fire.—After a misfire, the following *general safety precautions,* as applicable, must be observed until the cartridge has been removed from the rifle and the cause of the failure to fire determined:

(1) Keep the rifle trained (aimed) on the target and keep all personnel clear of the muzzle.

(2) All personnel not required for handling the weapon must be ordered to stay clear of the vicinity of the weapon before the bolt is retracted and the cartridge removed.

(3) When the cartridge is removed from the rifle it must be kept separate from all other cartridges until it has been determined whether the cartridge or the firing mechanism of the rifle was at fault. If the rifle is found to be the cause of the misfire, the cartridge can be reloaded and fired after the cause of the failure to fire is corrected.

(4) *The time intervals* for waiting, after the failure of the rifle to fire, are as follows:

(a) Always keep the cartridge in the chamber for five seconds from the time a misfire occurs, to protect yourself against an explosion outside of the rifle if a hangfire develops.

(b) If the barrel is hot and a misfire stops operation of the rifle, wait five seconds with the cartridge locked in the chamber to insure against danger from a hangfire. Having waited five seconds, extract the cartridge immediately to prevent a cook-off.

(c) If the cartridge cannot be extracted within ten seconds, it must remain locked in the chamber for at least five minutes because of the possibility of a cook-off.

(d) If the barrel is hot and a misfire occurs when attempting to resume firing after an intentional cessation of firing, the cartridge should remain locked in the chamber for five minutes because of the possibility of a cook-off.

Warning: Do not retract the bolt when a hangfire or a cook-off is suspected. A hangfire will normally occur within five seconds from the time the primer is struck, and a cook-off will normally occur after ten seconds of contact with the chamber in a hot barrel. If 150 cartridges are fired within a 2-minute period, the barrel will become hot enough to cause a cook-off.

Service During Firing.—The *Chart of Preventive Maintenance*

Services Performed by Rifleman, Plate 78, previously mentioned under "Service Before Firing," includes maintenance instructions for service during firing.

Unloading the Rifle.—The rifle is unloaded in the following manner:

(1) Push the safety to the rear position, which prevents firing.

(2) Grasp the magazine, placing the thumb on the magazine latch, and squeeze the latch. Push the magazine forward and downward to disengage it from the front catch and remove the magazine from the magazine well.

(3) Pull the operating-rod handle to the rear to extract and eject the cartridge in the chamber. Inspect the chamber to be sure the rifle is clear. In other words, be sure there is no cartridge in the rifle.

Another expression that has come down through generations since the invention of breech-loading firearms is *"bore clear."* Artillerymen of the Army and Marine Corps and Naval gunners have shouted this phrase for more than a century. The *bore* is the inside of any rifle, revolver, pistol, shotgun, or artillery piece. When the rifle is unloaded, the bore must be clear. This is only part of the condition of an unloaded automatic or semiautomatic weapon, because not only must the bore be clear but the magazine must be removed from the magazine well.

OPERATION UNDER UNUSUAL CONDITIONS

Atmospheric Conditions Affect Operation.—Temperature, humidity, atmospheric pressure, and other environmental conditions affect the efficient operation of all firearms, including the M14. In addition to the normal preventive-maintenance service, special attention must be paid to cleaning and lubrication in extremely cold or hot climates, damp or dry conditions, a salty atmosphere, and when there is an unusual amount of sand, mud, or dust in the firing area.

Cold Climate Operation.—The centigrade thermometer is graduated so that Zero is freezing and 100 degrees is the boiling point of water at a barometric pressure of 760 mm. The Fahrenheit thermometer, under standard atmospheric pressure, is marked so that the freezing point of water is 32 degrees above the zero of its scale and the boiling point is 212 degrees.

When the temperature is consistently below Zero Fahrenheit (which is equivalent to -17.77 centigrade), prepare all materiel for cold-weather operation. Extreme cold causes lubricants to congeal. Therefore, the rifle and bipod must be thoroughly cleaned, using what the armed forces call "CR, rifle bore cleaner," and all lubricants and grease removed. They should then be lubricated with a special low-temperature type lubricating oil.

Having done this, work the various controls throughout their entire range, at intervals frequent enough to keep them from freezing in place. This also reduces the physical effort required to operate the various controls.

When materiel is not in use, if it is stored outside buildings it must be protected with a covering from snow, ice, and moisture and the covering must be secured (anchored or tied) so that the wind, rain, and snow will not reach the operating parts.

These comments apply merely to the kind of cold weather found in the northern part of the United States of America and the southern portion of Canada. Special preparations must be made for operations in arctic lands.

Hot Climate Operation.—In hot climates, the film of oil necessary for operation and preservation dries out quickly. Inspect the rifle daily, paying particular attention to all hidden surfaces, such as bolt and roller, operating rod and recess, cam surface and bolt-locking recess in receiver, and the yoke assembly and leg assemblies of the bipod. Corrosion may occur on hidden surfaces and not be detected soon enough to prevent malfunctioning caused by lack of oil.

Perspiration from the body contains acids and salts which cause rust. After handling firearms and other materiel with metal parts clean, wipe dry, and restore the oil film, using the prescribed special lubricating oil, designated as "PL."

Hot-and-Dry Climate Operation.—When operating in hot, dry climates, clean and oil the bore of the rifle more frequently than usual. Rapid and extreme changes of temperature and humidity cause moisture to condense in a light film on unpainted metal and produce rust. When this film of condensed moisture forms on unpainted metal, immediately wipe briskly until entirely dry, and then coat with the prescribed special lubricating oil, designated as "PL."

Hot, Damp and Salty Atmosphere.—When the area in which you are serving is hot, damp, and salty, inspect all materiel frequently; clean and lubricate the bore and exposed metal surfaces of weapons much more frequently than required for normal use. Moisture and salt in the atmosphere tend to emulsify oils and greases and destroy their rust-preventive qualities. Inspect frequently for corrosion. When materiel is not in active use, cover unpainted surfaces of metal parts with a film of the special lubricating oil designated as "PL."

Sandy Operating Conditions.—When operating in a sandy area, clean and lubricate everything more often. Keep sand out of mechanisms, especially when inspecting and lubricating them. Protect all parts from flying sand during disassembly and assembly by *paulins,* also called *tarpaulins,* which are merely sheets of heavy canvas with grommets, for tying.

When getting ready for action in a sandy area, remove the lubricant from the bolt, barrel and receiver, connector assembly, operating rod, firing mechanism, and bipod, because they will be covered with sand, which acts as an abrasive and rapidly wears out metal parts. After action, clean and lubricate all exposed parts, but, unless otherwise ordered, do not proceed to clean and lubricate all rifles at the same time after a skirmish or battle. The enemy might come back and catch you with your bolt out.

A sandstorm is much more dangerous to metal parts than most people realize. The author has seen automobiles after a sandstorm in the desert regions of California. All the finish was removed as neatly and completely as though an automobile-body shop were preparing an automobile for a new paint job.

Muddy Operating Conditions.—Remove all mud, clean and dry, and then lubricate all materiel as soon as possible after it has been exposed to mud, paying attention not only to exposed parts but also operating mechanisms of the rifle and bipod.

Landing and Fording Operations.—Before going ashore from a vessel or before fording a stream, river, or lake, whenever you must carry the rifle by hand and not in a landing craft or vehicle, the following procedure applies:

(1) Lubricate locking lugs of the bolt, operating lug, and recesses. Also lubricate the bolt guide, the antifriction roller on the bolt, and

the operating-rod guide groove on the side of the receiver. Use a light coat of rifle grease (called lubriplate 130A).

(2) Protect the rifle, bipod, and other materiel from waves and sudden splashes of water.

(3) If your rifle and other metal equipment is accidentally partially or completely submerged in water, particularly salt water, carry out the following procedure, consistent with the tactical situation: (a) After submersion in salt water, wash in clear water to remove the corrosive salts; (b) as soon as the tactical situation permits, disassemble all assemblies which require disassembly for proper lubrication, dry them, and lubricate as soon as the situation permits; and (c) perform a complete cleaning and lubrication job, being sure that you drain or wipe dry all trapped moisture, clean all exposed parts, and coat with a film of the special lubricating oil designated as "PL."

HOW TO CLEAN THE RIFLE

General Cleaning Procedure.—(1) Immediately after firing the rifle, thoroughly clean the bore with the rifle bore cleaner (designated "CR"), being sure that all surfaces, including the rifling, are well coated. Wipe dry and apply a light coat of the special lubricating oil designated as "PL."

(2) The bore should be swabbed with a flannel cleaning patch, saturated with either the rifle bore cleaner ("CR") or with hot water and soap. Clean the bore carefully. Do not leave any trace of burned powder or other foreign substance in the bore. Then apply a light coat of the special lubricating oil ("PL").

Cleaning Procedure When Rifle Is Assembled.—The chamber should be cleaned with a cleaning brush, using the following procedures *when the rifle is assembled:*

(1) Screw the threaded end of the cleaning rod section into the ratchet base of the brush, as illustrated in Plate 63. Be sure all threaded areas are clean, undamaged, and not cross-threaded when assembled.

(2) Remove the magazine.

(3) Apply a light coating of rifle-bore cleaner to the chamber.

(4) Insert the brush in the chamber with the thumb pushing against the base of the brush, as illustrated in Plate 64.

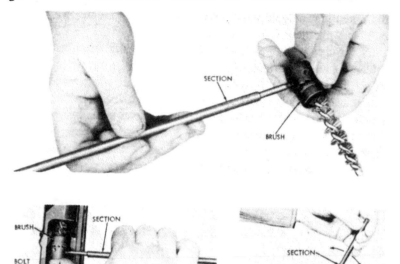

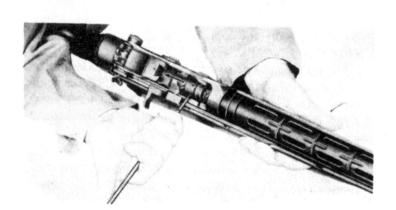

PLATE 63. SCREW THE THREADED END OF CLEANING-ROD SECTION INTO THE RATCHET BASE OF THE CHAMBER-CLEANING BRUSH. (Courtesy Ordnance Corps, U.S. Army.)

PLATE 64. INSERT THE BRUSH IN THE CHAMBER. (Courtesy of Ordnance Corps, U.S. Army.)

PLATE 65. MOVE THE CLEANING-ROD SECTION FROM SIDE TO SIDE. (Courtesy Ordnance Corps, U.S. Army.)

PLATE 66. REMOVE BRUSH FROM CHAMBER. (Courtesy Ordnance Corps, U.S. Army.)

(5) Pull operating rod rearward, release the bolt lock, and *ease*

the operating rod and bolt fully forward, seating the brush in the chamber.

(6) Move the cleaning-rod section from side to side several times, as illustrated in Plate 65.

(7) Grasp the cleaning-rod section as close to the receiver as possible, with the fingers pulling rearward and the thumb exerting a forward pressure on the end of the rod, as illustrated in Plate 66. (*Caution:* Grip the stock of the rifle during cleaning to prevent damaging the hand guard.) Continue to pull the cleaning-rod section rearward until the brush clears the chamber. Grasp the operating-rod handle, relieving the tension on the brush, and remove the cleaning-rod section and the brush from the receiver.

Cleaning Procedure When Rifle is Disassembled.—(1) Insert the brush in the chamber, with the thumb exerting pressure on the base of the brush.

(2) Move the cleaning-rod section from side to side several times.

(3) Remove the brush and the cleaning-rod section from the chamber.

(4) Clean other metal parts of the rifle and bipod with a dry cloth to remove moisture, dirt, perspiration, etc.; and then oil lightly with the special lubricating oil ("PL").

General Safety Precautions for Cleaning.—(1) Do not dilute the rifle-bore-cleaner solvent, the cleaning compound. Do not add anti-freeze solutions to it. Store the cleaning solvent in a warm but not hot place. Shake the solvent or cleaning compound vigorously before using.

(2) Do not use Diesel fuel oil, gasoline, benzene (benzol), or high-pressure water, steam, or air for cleaning the rifle.

(3) Dry-cleaning solvents and mineral-spirits paint thinners are flammable and must not be used near an open fire. Have fire extinguishers handy when these liquids are used. They evaporate quickly, dry the skin, and, if used without rubber gloves, they can caues cracks in the skin and inflammation. Finally, any room where such liquids are used should be well ventilated and no smoking permitted.

FUNCTIONING OF THE M14

Cycle of Operation.—The *cycle of operation* is the order in which the many parts inside the rifle work each time a cartridge is fired. The cycle for the M14 is fundamentally similar to that of all small arms, including rifles, revolvers, semiautomatic pistols, and shotguns.

Of course, the cycle of operation of the M14 has its own individual characteristics, but they are not difficult to learn and a knowledge of what happens inside the rifle makes it easier to understand the cause of and remedy for various stoppages.

Cycle of Operation for Semi-Automatic Fire.—The cycle of operation for semiautomatic fire can be broken down into eight steps for the M14. These are: (1) feeding; (2) chambering; (3) locking; (4) firing; (5) unlocking; (6) extracting; (7) ejecting; and (8) cocking.

Set the selector for semiautomatic fire with the blank face of the selector facing your body, and assume that a fully loaded magazine has been loaded in the rifle and that the first round has been fired already. Hence the bolt is to the rear, as illustrated in Plate 67, which

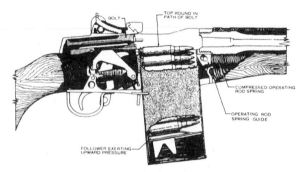

PLATE 67. POSITION OF PARTS WHEN THE BOLT IS TO THE REAR. (Courtesy Ordance Corps, U.S. Army.)

is labeled to emphasize the bolt, the top round in the path of the bolt, the follower exerting upward pressure against cartridges in the magazine, the compressed operating-rod spring, and the operating-rod spring guide.

Feeding.—Feeding occurs when a cartridge is forced into the path of the bolt. The top cartridge is forced into the path of the bolt by the magazine follower, which is under the pressure of the magazine spring.

Chambering.—Chambering takes place when a cartridge is moved into the chamber. This occurs as the bolt goes forward under the pressure of the expanding operating-rod spring. The bolt picks up the top cartridge in the magazine and drives it forward into the chamber, as illustrated in Plate 68, which is labeled to show the bolt driving the top round into the chamber, and is also labeled to indicate the ejector. Chambering is complete when the extractor snaps into the extracting groove on the cartridge and the ejector is forced into the face of the bolt.

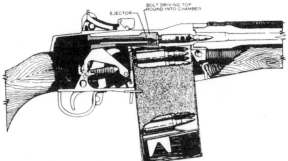

PLATE 68. CHAMBERING THE CARTRIDGE. (Courtesy Ordnance Corps, U.S. Army.)

Locking.—Locking takes place when the bolt is fully closed. This prevents the loss of gas pressure until the bullet has left the muzzle. The bolt is locked by the rear camming surface in the hump of the operating rod forcing the bolt roller down. This engages the locking lugs on the bolt with the locking recesses in the receiver, as illustrated by Plate 69, which is labeled to show the locking recesses in the receiver, the locking lugs, the rear camming surface in the recess in the hump of the operating rod, and the bolt roller.

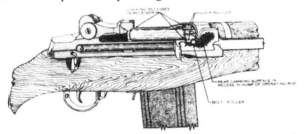

PLATE 69. LOCKING. (Courtesy Ordnance Corps, U.S. Army.)

Firing.—Firing takes place when the firing pin strikes the primer. When the trigger is squeezed the trigger lugs are disengaged from the hammer hooks and the hammer is released. The hammer moves forward under the pressure of the hammer spring and strikes the tang of the firing pin, driving the firing pin against the primer, activating it, and thus firing the round, as illustrated in Plate 70, which is labeled to emphasize the hammer hooks, the hammer, the bolt, the firing pin, the primer, the trigger, and the trigger lugs.

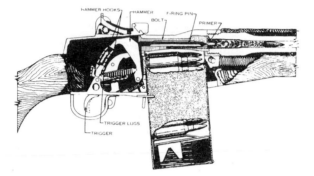

PLATE 70. FIRING. (Courtesy Ordnance Corps, U.S. Army.)

Unlocking.—Unlocking takes place after the cartridge has been fired. As the bullet is forced through the rifling of the barrel by the expanding gases, a small amount of gas enters through the gas port into the hollow gas piston and the inside of the gas-cylinder plug. The gas inside the piston and plug expands and, when the gas builds up enough pressure to overcome the tension of the operating-rod spring, the piston begins its travel to the rear, driving the operating rod and the bolt with it. When the piston has traveled slightly less than 5/32-inch, the gas ports are no longer aligned, hence no more gas can enter the piston. This is illustrated in Plate 71, which is labeled to emphasize the operating rod, the lower gas port, the gas piston, other gas ports, and the gas-cylinder plug.

The remainder of the gas in the barrel follows the bullet out of the muzzle. There is about ⅜-inch rearward movement of the operating rod before unlocking begins. This is a safety feature to insure that all gas not needed for other purposes has left the barrel before unlocking starts. After the operating rod has moved the very short distance of about ⅜-inch, the camming surface inside its hump forces the bolt roller upward, disengaging the locking lugs on the bolt from the locking recesses in the receiver. The bolt is thus

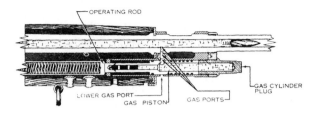

PLATE 71. ACTION OF THE GAS. (Courtesy Ordnance Corps, U.S. Army.)

unlocked and is ready to be moved to the rear, as illustrated in Plate 72, which is labeled to emphasize the bolt, bolt-locking recess, right locking lug on the bolt, the bolt roller, the camming surface in the hump of the operating rod, and the operating rod. Any gas left in the gas cylinder or the piston after the bolt is all the way to the rear escapes through the lower gas port in the cylinder.

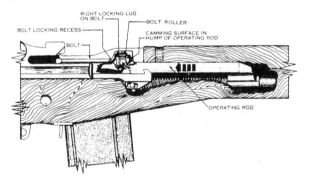

PLATE 72. UNLOCKING. (Courtesy Ordnance Corps, U.S. Army.)

Extracting.—Extracting is the act of pulling the empty cartridge case from the chamber. As the bolt begins to unlock extraction begins to take place. When the bolt is moved to the rear it pulls the empty cartridge case with it, as illustrated in Plate 73, in which the bolt, the extractor engaged in the extractor groove on the empty cartridge case, and the empty cartridge case, are all emphasized.

Ejecting.—Ejecting is the act of throwing the empty cartridge case out of and away from the receiver. As soon as the bolt has withdrawn the empty cartridge case clear of the chamber the force of the ejector spring and plunger pushes the bottom edge of the

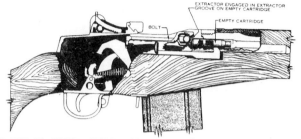

PLATE 73. EXTRACTING. (Courtesy Ordnance Corps, U.S. Army.)

cartridge base away from the bolt face. This causes the front (neck) of the cartridge case to move upward and to the right. The rapid rearward movement of the bolt causes the cartridge case to strike the angle on the lower-right corner of the magazine charger guide as the cartridge case is turned sideways. The rapid forward movement of the operating-rod handle causes the leading edge of the "camming hump" to strike the cartridge case with the angle on the outer edge of this "hump," continuing the movement of the empty case to the right front. When the last round has been fired and the bolt is held in the rearward position by the bolt lock is held in the rearward position by the bolt lock, the ejector propels the last round out and away from the receiver, as illustrated in Plate 74.

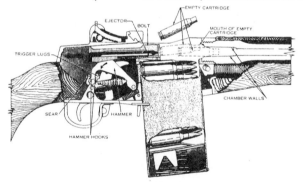

PLATE 74. EJECTING AND COCKING. (Courtesy Ordnance Corps, U.S. Army.)

In Plate 74, the trigger lugs, ejector, bolt, empty cartridge case, mouth of empty cartridge case, chamber walls, sear, hammer hooks, and hammer are all labeled for emphasis in explaining not only ejection but also cocking.

Cocking.—Cocking takes place when the hammer is forced into the correct position for firing the next round. This happens as the bolt continues to the rear. The rear end of the bolt forces the hammer back and rides over it. The hammer is caught by the sear if the trigger is still held to the rear, but by the trigger lugs if the trigger pressure has been released, as illustrated in Plate 74.

Additional Illustrations Explaining Parts and Subassemblies Involved in Cycle of Operation.—Plate 75 is a partial exploded view of the barrel and receiver group, with parts labeled and numbered. Although other plates have included most of the parts and subassemblies found on Plate 75, this particular plate is more complete and is extremely helpful in obtaining a clear understanding of the cycle of operation, as well as other subjects covered in this and the preceding chapter.

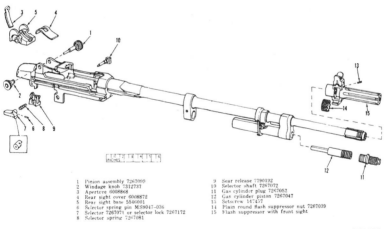

1 Pinion assembly 7267099	9 Sear release 7790192
2 Windage knob 7312737	10 Selector shaft 7267072
3 Aperture 6008868	11 Gas cylinder plug 7267052
4 Rear sight cover 6008872	12 Gas cylinder piston 7267047
5 Rear sight base 5546001	13 Setscrew 147457
6 Selector spring pin MS9047-036	14 Plain round flash suppressor nut 7267039
7 Selector 7267071 or selector lock 7267172	15 Flash suppressor with front sight
8 Selector spring 7267081	

PLATE 75. PARTIALLY EXPLODED VIEW OF BARREL AND RECEIVER GROUP, WITH PARTS LABELED AND NUMBERED. (Courtesy Ordnance Corps, U.S. Army.)

Plate 76 illustrates the cycle of gas operation during firing, recoil, and counterrecoil. It presents a more complete pictorial presentation of the action of the gas than Plate 71, but both are essential to a proper knowledge of the functioning of the rifle.

Plate 77 consists of two drawings which illustrate extraction and ejection. The upper drawing shows the empty cartridge case after it has been ejected. The lower drawing shows the extraction process.

In both drawings, arrows indicate the direction of movement. The ejection drawing has two arrows to clarify the direction of travel of the ejected fired-cartridge case. The extraction drawing has arrows indicating the direction of movements during this step or phase of the cycle of operation.

Cycle of Operation for Automatic Fire.—The following steps or phases constitute the sequence of the cycle of operation for *automatic fire,* sometimes called "full automatic":

(1) The selector must be set for automatic fire (the capital letter "A" faces the shooter). Turning the selector to automatic fire rotates the sear release until it is in a position to make contact with the sear.

(2) After the first cartridge has been fired (and with the trigger held to the rear), the operating rod starts its rearward movement under pressure of the expanding gases. As it moves to the rear, the connector assembly moves rearward one-eighth of an inch under pressure of the connector-assembly spring. The movement of the connector assembly rotates the sear release on the selector shaft so that the flange on the sear release allows the sear to move forward into a position where it can engage the rear hammer hooks. Then, when the bolt drives the hammer to the rear, the sear engages the rear hammer hooks and holds the hammer in the cocked position.

(3) After the bolt moves forward and locks, the shoulder on the operating rod engages the hook of the connector assembly and forces it forward one-eighth inch. This rotates the sear release on the selector shaft, causing the flange on the sear release to push the sear to the rear, disengaging it from the rear hammer hooks. The hammer will then go forward if the trigger is held to the rear. If the trigger is released at any time prior to the firing of the last round, the hammer will be held in the cocked position by the trigger lugs, and automatic actuation of the sear release by the connector assembly will not release the hammer to fire the chambered cartridge.

PREVENTIVE MAINTENANCE

Preventive Maintenance by the Rifleman.—Preventive maintenance means exactly what the phrase indicates. It is the performance of many precautions which will avoid malfunctions, stoppages, and

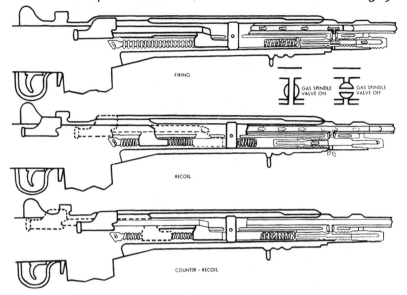

PLATE 76. CYCLE OF GAS OPERATION DURING FIRING, RECOIL, AND COUNTER-RECOIL. (Courtesy Ordnance Corps, U.S. Army.)

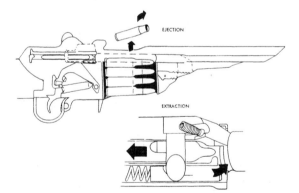

PLATE 77. EXTRACTION AND EJECTION, SHOWING MOVEMENT OF PARTS AND CARTRIDGE CASE. (Courtesy Ordnance Corps, U.S. Army.)

other handicaps to the efficient firing of the rifle. Plate 78, is a chart showing the preventive-maintenance services performed by the rifleman armed with the M14.

Preventive Maintenance by the Armorer.—The *armorer* is a member of the same combat organization as the riflemen armed with

Before firing	During firing	After firing	Daily	Weekly	Procedure
		Intervals			
					USUAL CONDITIONS
		X	---	---	*Bipod.* Check for secure installation.
X	---	X	---	---	*Rifle.* Clean chamber and bore
		X	---	---	Clean bore of weapon and all component parts which came in contact with expelled gases.
				X	Examine bore for powder fouling or corrosion.
					Apply lubriplate grease to all friction surfaces during damp weather and before amphibious operations.
		X	---	---	Wipe outside finished surfaces of rifle and oil lightly
		X	---	---	Check gas cylinder plug for secure installation.
				X	*Bipod.* Clean and lubricate yoke and leg assemblies.
					UNUSUAL CONDITIONS
					Preventive-maintenance services for usual conditions will apply, with emphasis on servicing by the operator to combat the effects of extreme cold and extreme heat The special services described below are required to assure optimum results under unusual conditions.
					Extreme Cold
		X	X	---	*Clean.* Remove ice, snow or moisture from all parts.
				X	*Lubricate.* Lubricate items sparingly
				X	*Inspect.* Inspect flash supressor for cracks.
		X	---	---	Check gas cylinder plug for secure installation.
					Extreme Heat
				X	*Bore.* Clean and lubricate bore
X	---	X	---	X	*Clean.* Remove mud and sand from all parts.
X	---	---	X	X	*Lubricate.* Check for fouled lubricants and lubricate as necessary
				---	*Barrel, Receiver Group, and Bipod.* On dusty and sandy terrain, clean but do not oil exposed finishes.
					Before Immersion
					Lubricate. Before amphibious action, lubricate parts listed with lubriplate.
					After Immersion
					Clean. Remove water and sludge from all parts. If immersed in salt water, wash with fresh water, dry thoroughly and lubricate.
					Lubricate. Lubricate as necessary

PLATE 78. CHART OF PREVENTIVE MAINTENANCE SERVICES PERFORMED BY RIFLEMAN. (Courtesy Ordnance Corps, U.S. Army.)

the M14. He is expected to have had more training and experience in preventive maintenance than the average rifleman, and he generally is a man with above-average mechanical aptitude. For these reasons, he is given the responsibility of performing certain tasks which are not assigned normally to the rifleman. Plate 79 is a chart showing the preventive maintenance services he performs.

Caution: These charts are the best available at the time this text was published, but they are only guides intended to simplify and systematize the work of riflemen and armorers. Such charts are always subject to change when new and better methods are discovered.

TROUBLE SHOOTING

Trouble Shooting for the Rifle.—Plate 80 is a chart showing the

Intervals			Procedure
Weekly	Bi-monthly (60 days)	Semi-annually (6 months)	

			USUAL CONDITIONS
X	---	---	*Barrel and Receiver Group.* Check for unusual wear, erosion, and damage to bore. Check rear sight group for functioning; check operating rod assembly and guide for proper fitting.
X	---	---	*Stock, w Butt Plate Assembly, and Hand Guard.* Check for cracks, proper fitting, and condition of wood
X	---	---	*Bolt Group.* Check for damaged firing pin and function. Check bolt roller, extractor, and ejector for proper functioning.
X	---	---	*Firing Mechanism.* Check for proper functioning of safety. Magazine latch must hold magazine in rifle.
X	---	---	*Bipod.* Check for functioning of controls and secure installation on rifle.
X	---	---	*Lubricate.* See that all items have been lubricated as prescribed.
X	---	---	*Equipment.* See that equipment and tools are complete, serviceable, cleaned, and properly stored.
X	---	---	*Publications.* See that all publications are available, legible, and properly stored.
			UNUSUAL CONDITIONS
			Maintenance operations, as prescribed under usual conditions, will apply under unusual conditions except for extreme-cold weather. Intervals are shortened in extreme-cold weather.

PLATE 79. CHART OF PREVENTIVE MAINTENANCE SERVICES PERFORMED BY ARMORER. (Courtesy Ordnance Corps, U.S. Army.)

troubles sometimes encountered with the M14, and their causes and probable remedies. All men armed with the M14 must be familiar with these details if they expect to become efficient, and eligible for promotion. Evrything cannot be mastered at one swoop. A child must crawl before he can walk. Even the most intelligent men must learn one step at a time although later they wonder why they found anything mysterious or difficult in the operations involved.

Trouble Shooting for the Bipod.—Plate 81 is a comparatively short and simple chart showing trouble shooting for the M14 bipod.

HEAD SPACE

Preliminary Recommendations.—Chapter XXVI of this book is entirely devoted to head space, and it should be reviewed by anyone who fires, maintains, or repairs any type, make, model, or caliber of firearm. Plate 82 illustrates the method of gaging head space for the M14.

Procedure for Gauging Head Space of M14.—(1) When gauging the head space of the M14, have the operating-rod assembly and connector assembly positioned on or removed from the receiver, to avoid interference with the free movement of the bolt.

Malfunction	Probable cause	Corrective action
	Rifle M14	
Magazine inserts with difficulty	Bent or deformed magazine cartridge.	Replace magazine cartridge
	Damage to or restricted movement of magazine latch.	Repair or replace
Short recoil	Undersize or damaged piston	Repair or replace
	Gas cylinder oversize	Replace
	Bent operating rod	Replace
	Damaged operating rod guide	Replace
	Defective operating rod spring	Replace
	Damaged operating rod spring guide.	Replace
	Bolt binding	Clean or repair bolt and/or receiver as required.
	Burs, foreign matter, and improper lubrication.	Clean, repair, and oil as required.
	Restricted movement of operating rod.	Repair or replace component interfering with movement of operating rod.
	Cartridge clip guide pin restricting bolt movement.	Drive pin up into receiver.
	Distorted or damaged receiver	Repair.
Bolt fails to close tightly	Extractor does not open enough to pass over rim of cartridge.	Clean, repair, or replace extractor.
	Operating rod binding	Clean, repair, or replace component interfering with movement of operating rod.
	Weak or broken operating rod spring.	Replace
	Damaged or blocked ejector	Repair or replace. Inspect bolt face for damage.
Bolt fails to close tightly—	Damaged or deformed bolt and/or receiver.	Repair or replace.
	Insufficient headspace	Replace bolt
Failure to feed	Short recoil	See "Short recoil."
	Round improperly placed in magazine cartridge.	Reseat round in magazine.
Failure to extract cartridge case	Excessive headspace or ruptured cartridge.	Check headspace
	Spindle valve closed	Open valve.
	Broken extractor	Replace extractor.
	Sheared rim on cartridge	Use cleaning rod to remove cartridge. Then clean chamber and ammunition.
Failure to eject cartridge case	Weak, missing, or frozen ejector spring.	Replace
	Short recoil	See "Short recoil."
Failure of bolt to open after fire	Gas cylinder spindle valve closed, gas cylinder plug missing, gas piston seized or improperly installed in cylinder.	Open spindle valve. Install gas cylinder plug. Repair and/or install gas piston.
Failure to fire	Lower tang on hammer strikes stud on trigger guard.	Install hammer properly.
	Inadequate firing pin protrusion ...	Gage protrusion and replace as required
	Hammer spring housing damaged ..	Replace.
Failure to hold bolt rearward	Damaged or deformed bolt lock	Repair or replace
	Bolt lock movement restricted	Clean spring and recess and/or replace spring.
	Weak or damaged magazine spring and/or magazine.	Replace magazine.
	Short recoil	See "Short recoil".

PLATE 80. CHART OF TROUBLE SHOOTING, MALFUNCTIONS, PROBABLE CAUSES, AND CORRECTIVE ACTION FOR THE RIFLE. (Courtesy Ordnance Corps, U.S. Army.)

(2) Clean the barrel chamber, head-space gauge, bolt, and receiver. Be sure that there are no foreign substances which can detract from a correct reading. Insert the head-space gauge provided for the M14 in the face of the bolt assembly and position it so that the cartridge ejector enters the clearance cut on the base of the head-space gauge. Place the gauge against the face of the bolt.

(3) In testing for head space, the bolt must not be forced. Instead, it should be "felt," using only the slightest finger-tip pressure. Move

Rifle Bipod M2		
Fails to stay on rifle	Jaw securing bolt loose	Tighten.
	Jaw securing bolt stripped	Replace defective components.
	Plunger worn or damaged	Replace as required. Clean as required
Legs fail to stay in up or down position.	Yoke does not retain plunger in -position.	Replace as required.
	Plunger spring frozen or damaged.	Replace spring. Clean as required
Leg cannot be extended or retracted.	Plunger immobile	Clean and lubricate as required. Replace plunger spring or plunger as required
	Leg damaged	Straighten or replace as required.

PLATE 81. CHART OF TROUBLE SHOOTING, MALFUNCTIONS, PROBABLE CAUSES, AND CORRECTIVE ACTION FOR THE BIPOD. (Courtesy Ordnance Corps, U.S. Army.)

the bolt forward. *The bolt should not close.* If the bolt does close, it will be necessary to test the rifle with a *field-test bolt,* as explained below. Remove the bolt assembly and insert the field-test bolt into the receiver.

(4) Insert the head-space gauge into the face of the field-test bolt. Move the bolt forward. If the field-test bolt does not close, the *original rifle bolt* is worn and must be replaced. If the field-test bolt does close on the head-space gauge, *the rifle must be withdrawn from service and the barrel and receiver sent to the salvage yard.*

(5) Head space is important, both for operation and safety, because it is measured in the M14 as the distance between the shoulder of the chamber and the face of the bolt when the bolt is in the locked position. Excessive head space will cause a ruptured cartridge, thus allowing gas to enter the receiver, which can damage the rifle and may injure the shooter and anyone near him if an accident occurs.

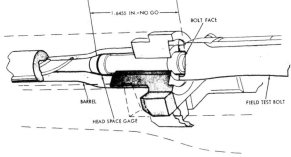

PLATE 82. GAGING HEAD SPACE. (Courtesy Ordnance Corps, U.S. Army.)

Removal of Ruptured Cartridge Case.—Plate 83 illustrates the removal of a ruptured cartridge case. This is a cut-away drawing. Arrows point to the M3 cleaning rod, the ruptured cartridge-case extractor, and the ruptured cartridge case. Plate 78 was especially drawn for the M14. There are various types of ruptured cartridge-case extractors on the civilian market for use with other weapons.

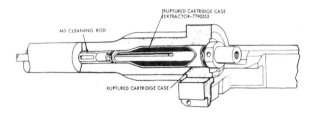

PLATE 83. REMOVAL OF RUPTURED CARTRIDGE CASE FROM M14 RIFLE. (Courtesy Ordnance Corps, U.S. Army.)

XXXIII. Automatic Pistol, Caliber .45, M 1911 and M 1911 A-1

THE automatic pistols, caliber .45, M 1911 and M 1911 A-1, are recoil-operated, magazine-fed, self-loading hand weapons. The recoil developed in firing the cartridge is utilized to perform the functions of extracting and ejecting the empty cartridge case, cocking the hammer and forcing the slide to the rearmost position, thereby compressing the recoil spring. The action of the recoil spring forces the slide forward, feeding a live cartridge from the magazine into the chamber, leaving the weapon ready to fire again.

The M 1911 A-1 pistol is a modification of the M 1911 pistol. The operation of both models of pistols is exactly the same. The changes consist of the following:

1. The tang of the grip safety is extended better to protect the hand.

2. A clearance cut is made on the receiver for the trigger finger.

3. The face of the trigger is cut back and knurled.

4. The mainspring housing is raised in the form of a curve to fit the palm of the hand and is knurled.

5. The top of the front sight is widened.

6. The notch in the rear sight is widened to correspond with the widening of the front sight.

The first .45 caliber military automatic pistol was made by Colt's Patent Fire Arms Manufacturing Company in 1905. From 1908 to 1911, it was made with a spur-type hammer; a few experimental models were made with a short-grip safety. It was superseded by the Government Model 1911.

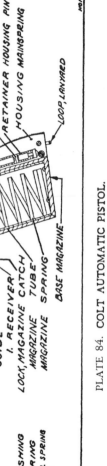

PLATE 84. COLT AUTOMATIC PISTOL.

Since the United States adopted this pistol for all of its armed forces in 1911, it has been made continuously with no material changes except those enumerated above.

The pistol is designed to fire cartridge, ball, caliber .45, M 1911. The magazine holds 7 cartridges. The upper cartridge is stripped from the magazine and forced into the chamber by the forward motion of the slide. The pistol fires but once at each squeeze of the trigger. When the last cartridge in the magazine has been fired the slide remains open. The magazine catch is then depressed and the empty magazine falls out. A loaded magazine is then inserted, making seven more shots available. The rate of fire is limited by the dexterity of the operator in inserting magazines into the pistol and the ability of the firer to aim and squeeze.

General Technical Information.—The barrel has a bore caliber of .45 inch; the number of grooves is 6; the twist in rifling is uniform left hand, one turn in 16 inches; and the barrel is 5.03 inches long. The over-all length of the pistol is 8.593 inches; the height of the front sight above the axis of the bore is .5597. The weight of the pistol with the magazine is 2.437 pounds; the weight of a loaded magazine is about .481 pound when 7 rounds are loaded; the weight of the empty magazine is .156 pound. The trigger pull of new or repaired pistols is 5½ to 6½ pounds; the trigger pull of pistols carried in action by troops is from 5 to 6½ pounds.

DISASSEMBLING AND ASSEMBLING

Disassembling.—To disassemble the pistol, proceed as follows, noting the numbers of the parts which refer to the accompanying illustration, Plate 84, such numbers being from the original ordnance drawings:

(a) Remove the magazine by pressing the magazine catch which is at the outside end of the "lock, magazine catch" shown on Plate 84.

(b) Press the recoil spring plug (16) inward and turn the barrel bushing (13) to the right until the recoil spring plug (16) and the end of the recoil spring (14) protrude from their seat, releasing the tension of the recoil spring (14). As the recoil spring plug (16) is allowed to protrude from its seat, the finger or thumb should be kept over it so that it will not jump away and be lost or strike the operator. Draw the slide (3) rearward until the smaller rear recess in its lower left edge stands above the projection on the thumbpiece of the slide stop (8); press gently against the end of the pin of the slide stop (8) which protrudes from the right side of the receiver (1) above the trigger guard and remove the slide stop (8).

(c) This releases the barrel link (11), allowing the barrel (2), with the barrel link (11) and the slide (3), to be drawn forward together from the receiver (1), carrying with them the barrel bushing (13), recoil spring (14), recoil spring plug (16), and recoil-spring guide (15).

(d) Remove these parts from the slide (3) by withdrawing the recoil spring guide (15) from the rear of the recoil spring (14) and drawing the recoil spring plug (16) and the recoil spring (14) forward from the slide (3). Turn recoil spring plug (16) to the right to remove from recoil spring. Turn the barrel bushing to the left, until it may be drawn forward from the slide (3). This releases the barrel (2) which with the barrel link (11) may be drawn forward from the slide (3), and by pushing out the barrel link pin (12) the barrel link (11) is released from the barrel (2).

(e) Press the rear end of the firing pin forward until it clears the firing pin stop which is then drawn downward from its seat in the slide; the firing pin, firing pin spring, and extractor are then removed from the rear of the slide.

(f) The safety lock is readily withdrawn from the receiver by cocking the hammer and pushing from the right on the pin part or pulling outward on the thumbpiece of the safety lock when it is midway between its upper and lower positions. The cocked hammer is then lowered and removed after removing the hammer pin from the left side of the receiver. The mainspring housing pin is then pushed out from the right side of the receiver which allows the mainspring housing to be withdrawn downward and the grip safety rearward from the handle. The sear spring may then be removed. By pushing out the sear pin from the right to the left side of the receiver, the sear and disconnector are released.

(g) To remove the mainspring, mainspring cap, and housing pin retainer from the mainspring housing, compress the mainspring and push out the small mainspring cap pin.

(h) To remove the magazine catch from the receiver, its checkered left end must be pressed inward, when the right end of the magazine catch will project so far from the right side of the receiver that it may be rotated one-half turn. This movement will release the magazine catch lock from its seat in the receiver, when the magazine catch, the magazine catch lock, and the magazine catch spring may be removed.

(i) With the improved design of magazine catch lock the operation of dismounting the magazine catch is simplified. When the magazine catch has been pressed inward the magazine catch lock is turned a quarter turn to the left by means of a screwdriver, or the short leaf of the sear spring. The magazine catch with its contents can then be removed. The improved design will be recognized from the fact that the head of the magazine catch lock is slotted.

(j) The trigger can then be removed rearward from the receiver.

(k) The hammer strut or the long arm of the screwdriver can be used to push out all the pins except the mainspring cap pin, lanyard loop pin, and ejector pin.

(l) The slide stop plunger, the safety lock plunger, and the plunger spring may be pushed to the rear out of the plunger tube.

(m) The magazine should not be disassembled except for cleaning or to replace the magazine follower or magazine spring. To disassemble proceed as follows: Push the magazine follower downward about ¼ inch; this compresses the magazine spring. Insert the end of a drift through one of the small holes in the side of the magazine to hold the magazine spring, then slide out the magazine follower. Hold hand over end of the magazine before removing drift from hole to prevent magazine spring from jumping away.

Assembling.—(a) Proceed in the reverse order.

(b) It should be noted that the disconnector and sear are assembled as follows: Place the cylindrical part of the disconnector in its hole in the receiver with the flat face of the lower part of the disconnector resting against the yoke of the trigger. Then place the sear, lugs downward, so that it straddles the disconnector. The sear pin is then inserted in place so that it passes through both the disconnector and the sear.

(c) The sear, disconnector, and hammer being in place and the hammer down, to replace the sear spring, locate its lower end in the cut in the receiver with the end of the long leaf resting on the sear; then insert the mainspring housing until its lower end projects below the frame about ⅛ inch, replace the grip safety, cock the hammer, and replace the safety lock; then lower the cocked hammer, push the mainspring housing home, and insert the mainspring housing pin.

(d) In assembling the safety lock to the receiver use the tip of the magazine follower or the screwdriver to press the safety lock plunger home, thus allowing the seating of the safety lock. It should be remembered that when assembling the safety lock the hammer must be cocked.

(e) When replacing the slide and barrel on the receiver care must be taken that the barrel link is tilted forward as far as possible and that the barrel link pin is in place.

CARE AND CLEANING

The entire mechanism must be kept cleaned and oiled to avoid jams. Care must also be taken to prevent rust or the accumulation of sand or dirt in the interior. Pistols are easily disassembled for cleaning and oiling. Damp air and sweaty hands promote rust. The pistols should be cleaned and protected after every handling. Special precautions are necessary when the pistols have been used on rainy days and after prolonged exposure to the elements.

To clean the pistol, rub it with a rag which has been lightly oiled and then clean with a perfectly clean dry rag. Swab the bore with an oily flannel patch and then with a perfectly dry one. Dust out all crevices with a small, clean brush. Immediately after cleaning, to protect the pistol swab the bore thoroughly with a flannel patch saturated with sperm oil, wipe over all metal parts with an oily rag, applying a few drops of light oil (sperm oil is preferred) to all cams and working surfaces of the mechanism.

After cleaning and protecting the pistol, place it in the pistol rack without any covering whatever. The use of canvas or similar covers is prohibited in the armed services, as they collect moisture and rust the metal parts. While barracks are being swept, pistol racks will be covered with a piece of canvas to protect the pistols from dust.

Care and cleaning after firing presents a special problem. When a pistol has been fired the bore will be cleaned thoroughly not later than the evening of the day on which it is fired. Thereafter it will be cleaned and oiled each day for at least the next 3 succeeding days. To clean the bore after firing, first remove the slide and barrel, insert the muzzle of the barrel in a vessel containing hot water and issue soap, hot water alone, or cold water; the cleaning rod with a cloth patch assembled is inserted in the breech and moved forward and back for about 1 minute, pumping the water in and out of the bore. When the bore is wet, a brass- or bronze-wire brush, if available, should be run all the way through the bore, then all the way back three or four times. Water should again be pumped through the bore. Then wipe the cleaning rod dry, remove the barrel from the water, and using dry, clean flannel patches, thoroughly swab the bore until it is perfectly dry and clean. Examine the bore carefully for metal fouling.

It is especially important that after firing the bore must not be oiled before it is cleaned. Saturate a clean patch with sperm oil and swab the bore and chamber with the patch, making certain that the bore and all metal parts of the pistol are covered with a thin coat of oil.

On the pistol range, always clean at the end of the day's shooting. A pistol that has been fired should not be left overnight without cleaning. Never fire a pistol with any dust, dirt, mud, or snow in the bore. Before loading the pistol make sure that no patch, rag, or other object has been left in the barrel. During range firing in the armed services, a noncommissioned officer will be placed in charge of the cleaning of pistols in the cleaning racks.

During cold weather, oil is used sparingly on the working parts. It is not part of the usual instruction given in the armed services, but many Arctic explorers have reported that the use of powdered graphite as a lubricant permitted the pistol to function when all else failed.

After a gas attack, the pistols should be cleaned as soon as possible. Oil will prevent corrosion for about 12 hours. Clean all parts in boiling water containing a little soda, if available. All traces of gas must be removed from ammunition with a slightly oiled rag; then thoroughly dry the ammunition. Rust-preventive compound resists gas corrosion more than light oil. In many exposures, especially those of long duration, ammunition treated with sperm oil shows more severe corrosion than unprotected cartridges.

Some points to be observed in handling the pistol are: Never leave it uncleaned overnight after a day of firing. Keep it clean and well lubricated, but not gummy with oil. Do not place the pistol on the ground where sand or dirt may enter the bore or the mechanism.

Do not plug the muzzle of the pistol with a patch or plug. This might be forgotten and cause a bulge or a break in the barrel when the pistol is fired. A pistol kept in a leather holster may rust from moisture absorbed by the leather from the atmosphere, even though the holster may appear to be perfectly dry. If the holster is wet and the pistol must be carried therein, cover the pistol with a thick coat of oil.

The hammer should not be snapped when the pistol is partially disassembled. The trigger should be pulled with the forefinger. If the trigger is pulled with the second finger, the forefinger extending along the side of the receiver is apt to press against the projecting pin of the slide stop and cause a malfunction when the slide recoils. Pressure on the trigger must be released sufficiently after each shot to permit the trigger to reengage the sear. To remove cartridges not fired, disengage the magazine slightly and then extract the cartridge in the barrel by drawing back the slide.

The magazine must not be dented or otherwise damaged. When the magazine is inserted, be sure that it engages with the magazine catch. Never insert the magazine and strike it smartly with the hand to force it home, as this may spring the base or the inturning lips at the top. It should be inserted by a quick, continuous movement.

FUNCTIONING

Method of Operation.—A loaded magazine is placed in the receiver and the slide drawn fully back and released, thus bringing the first cartridge into the chamber. If the slide is open push down the slide stop to let the slide go forward. The hammer is thus cocked and the pistol is ready for firing.

If it is desired to make the pistol ready for instant use and for firing the maximum number of shots with the least possible delay, draw back the slide, insert a cartridge by hand into the chamber of the barrel, allow the slide to close, then lock the slide and the cocked hammer by pressing the safety lock upward and insert a loaded magazine. The slide and hammer being thus positively locked, the pistol may be carried safely at full cock and it is only necessary to press down the safety lock (which is located within easy reach of the thumb) when raising the pistol to the firing position.

The grip safety is provided with an extending horn which not only serves as a guard to prevent the hand of the shooter from slipping upward and being struck or injured by the hammer, but also aids in accurate shooting by keeping the hand in the same position for each shot and, furthermore, permits the lowering of the cocked hammer with one hand by automatically pressing in the grip safety when the hammer is drawn slightly beyond the cocked position. In order to release the hammer, the grip safety must be pressed in before the trigger is squeezed.

Safety Devices.—It is impossible for the firing pin to discharge or even touch the primer except on receiving the full blow of the hammer. The pistol is provided with two automatic safety devices: (1) The disconnector, which positively prevents the release of the hammer unless the slide and barrel are in the forward position and safely interlocked. This device also controls the firing and prevents more than one shot from following each squeeze of the trigger. (2) The grip safety which at all times locks the trigger unless the handle is firmly grasped and the grip safety pressed in. In addition, the pistol is provided with a safety lock by which the closed slide and the cocked hammer can be positively locked in position.

Detailed Functioning.—(a) The magazine may be charged with any number of cartridges from one to seven.

(b) The charged magazine is inserted in the receiver and the slide drawn once to the rear. This movement cocks the hammer, compresses the recoil spring, and when the slide reaches the rear position the magazine follower raises the upper cartridge into the path of the slide. The slide is then released and being forced forward by the recoil spring carries the first cartridge into the chamber of the barrel. As the slide approaches its forward position, it encounters the rear extension of the barrel and forces the barrel forward; the rear end of the barrel swings upward on the barrel link, turning on the muzzle end as on a fulcrum. When the slide and barrel reach their forward position they are positively locked together by the locking ribs on the barrel, and their joint forward movement is arrested by the barrel lug encountering the pin on the slide top. The pistol is then ready for firing.

(c) When the hammer is cocked the hammer strut moves downward, compressing the mainspring, and the sear under the action of the long leaf of the sear spring engages its nose in the notch on the hammer.

In order that the pistol may be fired the following conditions must exist:

1. The grip safety must be pressed in, leaving the trigger free to move.

2. The slide must be in its forward position, properly interlocked with the barrel so that the disconnector is held in the recess on the under side of the slide under the action of the sear spring, transmitting in this position any motion of the trigger to the sear.

3. The safety lock must be down in the unlocked position so that the sear will be unblocked and free to release the hammer and the slide will be free to move back.

(d) On squeezing the trigger, the sear is moved and the released hammer strikes the firing pin which transmits the blow to the primer of the cartridge. The pressure of the gases generated in the barrel by the explosion of the powder in the cartridge is exerted in a forward direction against the bullet, driving it through the bore, and in a rearward direction against the face of the slide, driving the latter and the barrel to the rear together. The downward swinging movement of the barrel unlocks it from the slide and the barrel is then stopped in its lowest position. The slide continues to move to the rear, opening the breech, cocking the hammer, extracting and ejecting the empty shell and compressing the recoil spring until the slide reaches its rearmost position when another cartridge is raised in front of it and forced into the chamber of the barrel by the return movement of the slide under pressure of the recoil spring.

(e) The weight and consequently the inertia of the slide augmented by those of the barrel are so many times greater than the weight and inertia of the bullet that the latter has been given its maximum velocity and has been driven from the muzzle of the barrel before the slide and barrel have recoiled to the point where the barrel commences its unlocking movement. This construction therefore delays the opening of the breech of the barrel until after the bullet has left the muzzle and therefore practically prevents the escape of any of the powder gases to the rear after the breech has been opened. This factor of safety is further increased by the tension of the recoil spring and mainspring, both of which oppose the rearward movement of the slide.

(f) While the comparatively great weight of the slide of the pistol insures safety against premature opening of the breech, it also insures operation of the pistol because at the point of the rearward opening movement where the barrel is unlocked and stopped the heavy slide has attained a momentum which is sufficient to carry it through its complete opening movement and makes the pistol ready for another shot.

(g) When the magazine has been emptied, the pawl-shaped slide stop is raised by the magazine follower under action of the magazine spring into the front recess on the lower left side of the slide, thereby locking the slide in the open position and serving as an indicator to remind the shooter that the empty magazine must be replaced by a loaded one before the firing can be continued. Pressure upon the magazine catch quickly releases the empty magazine from the receiver and permits the insertion of a loaded magazine.

(h) To release the slide from the open position, it is only necessary to press upon the thumbpiece of the slide stop, then the slide will go forward to its closed position, carrying a cartridge from the previously inserted magazine into the barrel and making the pistol ready for firing again.

SPARE PARTS AND ACCESSORIES

Spare Parts.—Spare parts are provided to replace those parts that become unserviceable through breakage or wear. They should be kept clean and lightly oiled. They are divided into two groups: spare parts and basic spare parts. Sets of extra parts provided with the pistol for replacement of the parts most likely to fail are simply called extra parts. Basic spare parts are sets of parts provided for the use of ordnance maintenance companies and include all parts necessary to repair the pistol.

Accessories.—Accessories consist of the holster, lanyard, and pistol-cleaning kit, and where they are needed, arm lockers and arm racks are also classed as accessories. The pistol-cleaning kit contains cleaning brushes and rods, pistol screwdrivers, an oiler, and a small brass can in which the set of spare parts is carried.

AMMUNITION

The Caliber .45 Ball Cartridge, M1911, is for use in caliber .45 automatic pistols and submachine guns, although submachine guns eventually will be entirely replaced by the M14 Rifle, as stated previously. This cartridge is 1.275 inches long. The bullet consists of a gilding-metal-clad steel or copper-plated steel jacket and a slug of lead-antimony. The length of the bullet is 0.68 inch.

The average of the mean radii of all targets (at the time of acceptance of the ammunition from the manufacturer) at a range of 50 yards is not greater than 2 inches when the pistol is fired with a muzzle rest.

Penetration, using either Model 1911 or Model 1911 A-1, in white pine, is as follows:

Range in Yards	Depth of Penetration in Inches
25	6.0
50	5.8
75	5.6
100	5.5
150	5.2
200	4.6
250	4.0

XXXIV. The Revolver

A TYPICAL Colt revolver is shown in Plate 85. The barrel is screwed to the frame. The front sight is brazed on the barrel. The rear sight is a longitudinal groove in the upper surface of the frame.

The frame contains the lock mechanism which consists of the hammer with its stirrup, stirrup pin, strut, strut pin, and strut spring; the trigger and its pin; the rebound lever with its spring; the hand with its spring; the cylinder bolt and its spring; the locking lever; and the mainspring.

The hammer, rebound lever, and trigger are each pivoted on pins fastened in the left side of the frame. The upper end of the mainspring engages the hammer stirrup and the lower end of the mainspring fits into a slot in the frame. The force of the hammer blow is regulated by the mainspring tension screw.

The rebound-lever spring pin secures the lower end of the rebound lever spring to the frame. The upper, free end of the rebound lever spring bears under the rear end of the rebound lever, permitting the latter, upon the release of the trigger after firing a round, to carry the hammer back to its safety position and force the trigger forward.

When the revolver is fired in double action, pressure upon the trigger causes its upper edge to engage the hammer strut and hence raises the hammer until almost in the full-cock position, when the strut escapes from the trigger, and the hammer, under action of the mainspring, falls and strikes the primer of the cartridge.

When the revolver is fired in single action, the hammer is pulled

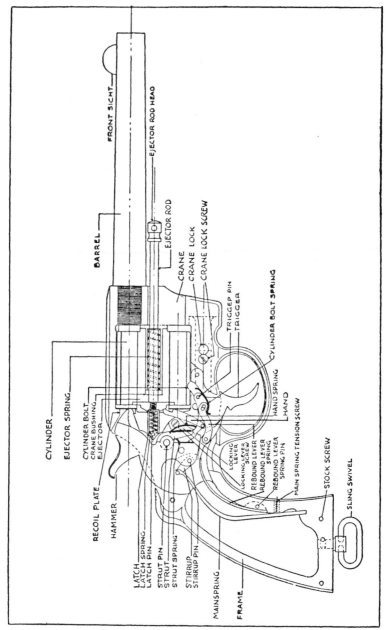

PLATE 85. THE REVOLVER.

back with the thumb until the upper edge of the trigger engages the full-cock notch in the forward end of the lower part of the hammer. Pressure on the trigger will release the hammer, which, under the action of the mainspring, falls and strikes the primer of the cartridge.

This being a 6-chamber revolver, a projection on the upper part of the trigger, working in a slot in the frame, prevents the cylinder from turning more than one-sixth of a revolution at a time by entering one of the grooves nearest the rear end of the cylinder surface. When the cylinder is swung out of the frame the slot in the rear of the crane pivot turns so that the projection on the forward part of the trigger is unable to enter it, thus locking the trigger and preventing cocking the hammer.

The cylinder bolt is pivoted on the trigger pin, and the cylinder bolt spring, bearing on the rebound lever arm, causes the nose of the bolt to go through a slot in the frame preparatory to entering one of the rectangular cuts in the cylinder surface. The nose of the bolt is withdrawn from the cylinder during the first phase of the movement of the trigger in cocking the revolver, thus permitting free rotation of the cylinder. The cylinder bolt prevents rotation of the cylinder while the revolver is being carried. The removal of the cylinder bolt will not prevent the functioning of the revolver.

The hand is attached to the trigger by the hand pivot. As the trigger swings on the trigger pin when the hammer is being cocked, the hand is raised, it revolves the cylinder, and locks the cylinder in its proper position for firing. The longitudinal axis of the bore is therefore an extension of the longitudinal axis of the chamber which contains the cartridge in position for firing. The hand spring makes certain the engagement of the hand with the ratchet. A projection on the side plate supports the rear of the hand spring.

The locking lever pivots on its screw in the left side of the frame. The head of the locking lever enters a recess in the latch, so that the lower end of the locking lever, when the latch is pushed back, moves forward until it is over the part of the hand pivot that protrudes on the left side of the trigger. In this manner, the trigger is locked, and the hammer cannot be cocked unless the cylinder is positively closed and locked by the latch.

The cylinder revolves around a central arbor of the crane; the latter fits into a recess in the frame under the barrel and turns on its pivot arm, which rotates in a hole in the frame under the crane lock screw. The ejector rod goes through the center of the crane arbor, comes out under the barrel, and its forward end is the ejector rod head.

The ejector, including the ratchet, is screwed on the back end of the ejector rod, using a left-hand thread. The ejector is then made fast by upsetting the metal. The ejector spring is coiled around the ejector rod in the crane cylinder arbor. The front end of this spring bears on a shoulder of the ejector rod. The rear end of this spring bears on the crane bushing, the latter being screwed with a left-hand thread into the cylinder arbor, thereby closing the latter.

The latch thumbpiece is on the left side of the frame where it slides longitudinally. The barrel of the latch fits in a hole in the frame. The latch spring is coiled inside the barrel latch and is held there by the latch pin, the latter also securing the latch and limiting its field of play. As the cylinder is swung back into the frame, the latch barrel, acted on by the latch spring, enters a recess in the ejector and thereby locks the cylinder in place for firing.

The recoil plate is driven into the recoil plate recess in the frame and made fast there by upsetting the rim of the plate to a slight extent.

The following precautions are observed:

1. Do not try to cock the hammer unless the cylinder is closed and locked in the frame.

2. Do not try to open the cylinder when the hammer is cocked.

3. Do not tighten the tension screw unless the primers are not exploded by the action of the mainspring, because too much tension increases the trigger pull and, even more important, it pierces the primers.

4. In removing the side plate, strike it with a wooden block on the left side of the frame where it is under the stock. Do not strike it with a metal hammer or pry it loose with any object.

5. When the side plate is replaced during the assembly, work it forward from the rear just enough for the side plate pin to be in the rear of the hand spring, for if the side plate pin is forward of the hand spring the latter will be ruined when the hammer is cocked.

The revolver is disassembled by removing parts in the following order: crane lock screw and crane lock; crane with cylinder; stock screw and stocks; side plate screws and side plate; hand and hand spring; mainspring; hammer; rebound lever; rebound lever spring; cylinder bolt and spring; trigger; locking-lever screw and locking lever; latch pin; latch; and latch spring. In the armed services, the crane and cylinder are not further dismounted except at ordnance depots. The gunsmith seldom needs to dismount these parts. The revolver is assembled by reversing the above order.

To eject the shells and load, push the latch to the rear and swing the cylinder to the left, out of the frame. Press against the forward end of the ejector rod head to empty the chambers. The cylinder is now ready for loading. Place cartridges in the chambers and swing the cylinder into the frame, being careful to revolve the cylinder so that its bolt will enter one of the rectangular cuts in the surface of the cylinder.

The revolver in the illustration is caliber .38. It weighs 2 pounds 1 ounce, it is 11.5 inches long, the barrel is 6 inches long, and the bore diameter is .357 inch, although earlier models had a bore diameter of .363 inch. There are 6 grooves, each of which is .156 inch wide and .003 inch deep. There is one turn of rifling in 16 inches. The lands are .03406 inch wide. The cylinder is 1.499 inches long, with a diameter of 1.52 inches. There are 6 chambers, each with a diameter of .3825 inch. The front sight is .6045 inch above the axis of the bore, although this height may be varied somewhat to meet individual requirements.

CARE AND CLEANING OF THE REVOLVER

The care and cleaning of the revolver follows, in general, the principles and rules explained in chapters on other firearms, but the following points are important:

1. To clean the bore and chambers after firing, release the latch and lift out the cylinder, and proceed as you would with any other firearm, bearing in mind that the chambers must be treated in the same manner as the bore.

2. The hammer, the inside of the frame at the top of the breech block, the inside of the frame where the barrel extends into the

frame under the ratchet at the breech end of the cylinder, and all other metal parts are given a thin film of oil, the same as the bore and chambers, after cleaning.

3. The hammer must not be snapped when the weapon is partially disassembled.

4. Oil is used in very small amounts on the working parts during cold weather. Lubricants such as graphite are used instead of oil in extremely cold regions.

SELECTION OF REVOLVERS

Make.—The author owns and fires both Colt and Smith & Wesson revolvers. The selection of a Colt revolver for discussion and illustration in this chapter does not mean that the author favors the Colt over the Smith & Wesson. In addition to these two famous manufacturers, there are several others who make reliable revolvers.

Caliber and Type.—Most law-enforcement officers prefer to carry the Caliber .38 Special cartridge and revolvers chambered for this cartridge while on duty. Those working in plain clothes may carry either the regular .38 Special Revolver or the so-called "Detective" model with a short barrel, of the same caliber. Some officers carry the Caliber .357 Magnum Revolver on special assignment, or have it available in automobiles for use when needed. Very few law-enforcement officers carry the so-called "automatic pistols," which are actually semiautomatic and not fully automatic. They regard revolvers as more reliable, handier, and generally more effective than "automatic pistols."

XXXV. Pistol and Revolver Problems

TRIGGER-PULL adjustment, barrel changing, and other topics common to all types of firearms have been discussed elsewhere. In this chapter we shall concentrate on the special problems relating to hand guns.

Misfires.—Revolver misfires are usually caused by a defective mainspring. It may have been filed thin in a mistaken attempt to reduce the trigger pull, in which case the remedy is to replace the old mainspring with a new one, either bought from a supply house or made in your own shop. Piano wire, or any other suitable steel, can be filed to shape, hardened, and tempered.

Leaving the gun cocked for several months weakens the mainspring. Replace the spring, or stretch the old mainspring to about 30 per cent more than its original length, harden, and temper.

Cutting down the hammer to hasten the lock time weakens the hammer so much that misfires may result. Replace the hammer, or use a heavier mainspring to give the hammer increased speed to make up for its light weight.

The firing pin spring in hammerless automatic pistols drives forward the firing pin. If misfires are traced to this spring, replace it with a new one or stretch, harden, and temper it.

Where the firing pin is separate from the hammer, examine the firing pin for size and shape, and observe the indentations made on the primers of fired cartridges. Compare the marks made on the primers when misfires occurred with the marks left when there were no misfires. A good firing pin leaves a full, hemispherical indentation without puncturing the primer or driving it into the cartridge. The indentation left by the firing pin or hammer nose on a fired shell is deeper than the indentation when the primer fails to function because the explosion and resultant recoil cause a certain amount of primer flow.

If the firing pin is too short, or has the wrong shape, replace it with a new one. Tool steel, filed to size and shape, hardened, and drawn to a blue color, results in a satisfactory part when a factory-made firing pin is not available. Shape the point carefully with a slip-stone under a magnifying glass. Work slowly and try the firing pin on primed empty cartridge cases, improving the shape gradually after each primer is fired and observed.

When the firing pin is too loose in its hole, the replacement should be slightly larger. When the firing pin is the correct size and shape, but the hole in the revolver frame is too big, misfires result from the firing pin hitting the edge of the primer. Skilled gunsmiths enlarge the firing pin hole in the frame with a drill, insert a steel bushing, and then check to see that the firing pin comes through the exact center of the bushed hole, but this is too difficult for an amateur.

Cylinders.—If the cylinder lock drags as it turns, examine the cylinder between the locking notches and you will find that the surface is scratched in a bright line. Some gunsmiths polish the upper surface of the cylinder lock with a small Arkansas slip-stone to remedy this condition, but we do not recommend this practice. For example, the Smith & Wesson cylinder stop returns immediately into contact with the cylinder after it has been retracted and presses against the cylinder, and it is this fact that permits the tremendously fast function without "cylinder throw-by"; any alteration of the face of the stop may result in "throw-by."

When the cylinder does not lock properly, and is easily moved out of position, stone the sides of the cylinder lock until it will enter the recesses in the cylinder deep enough to lock.

Too much side play in the cylinder when it is locked may mean that the recesses in the cylinder are worn on the edges, or that the cylinder lock is worn down. A new and thicker cylinder lock, dressed with a small stone to fit the cylinder accurately, is the remedy.

Cheap revolvers are neither carefully made nor accurately inspected. They sometimes have a high spot on the forward end of the cylinder which collects metal and powder fouling until it becomes difficult to turn the cylinder. The remedy is to file off the high spot.

Another trouble with cheap revolvers is that lead shavings from the bullets may accumulate between the top strap of the frame and the top of the barrel extension until they bear against the cylinder at its upper edge and slow its rotation. The remedy is simply to keep the revolver clear of the lead shavings. Either or both of the faults we have just mentioned may also be found in small caliber revolvers that are well made, but they are more common in the weapons sold on a price basis.

Poor cylinder rotation may also be due to the recoil plate in a center-fire revolver becoming so loose that dirt collects behind and pushes it against the bases of the cartridges in the cylinder. Remove the plate, clean out the hole through which the firing pin protrudes, straighten the plate, and replace it.

The cylinder ratchet, or the hand which turns the cylinder, may be worn. This is discovered if, when the revolver is fully cocked by pulling back the hammer, the cylinder can be turned by hand and the cylinder lock clicks into its recess. Slight wear is not alarming, but when the wear is pronounced, replace the hand with a new one or heat the old hand, pound it out longer with a hammer, and be sure that the barrel and cylinder line up accurately when the hand is back in place. A worn ratchet may be overcome by having a hand slightly longer than the original, filed and stoned to fit.

Owners of the U.S. Model 1917, Caliber .45 Revolver, either Colt or Smith & Wesson, sometimes want to replace the cylinder of this revolver, which takes the .45 caliber automatic cartridge, with a cylinder which will take the old .45 caliber Colt cartridge, as used in the Colt New Service Revolver. We do not advise performing this operation because it requires more skill and time than the job is worth. Instead, the owner of the Model 1917 revolver should either learn to be content with the automatic cartridges, or if he strongly objects to the steel clips in which those cartridges must be loaded for firing in the Model 1917 revolvers, he can obtain in normal times special rimmed cartridges.

Ejection Difficulties.—Large automatic pistols sometimes eject the fired cartridge cases upward and backward toward the shooter's face. Replace the old, worn extractor with a new one. If a new extractor is not available, remove the old one and stone the lower edge of the hook to a slight bevel at the end, thus causing the fired case to be released at the base first and eject to the right and rear, where it will not hit the shooter.

Stone the extractor very slowly. Replace it after a few strokes, fire a cartridge, observe the ejection, and keep this up until the problem is solved. If this fails, bevel the front face of the ejector to the right and rear, working extremely slowly and carefully with test shots between strokes of the oilstone. If all goes well, you will change the angle at which the ejector trips the fired case out of the extractor. If you are careless, you may not only fail to cure your trouble but you may also cause the gun to jam at every shot.

Another cause of ejection trouble is the accumulation of dirt, grease, and corrosion at the face of the breech, permitting the cartridge cases to become stuck so that the extractor slips over the rim instead of engaging the rim and pulling it to the rear where it is tripped out of the extractor and hurled out of the gun by the ejector. The remedy is ordinary cleaning.

Hammer Alterations.—To reduce the height of the hammer spur of the single-action Colt revolver, proceed as follows. Remove the hammer; force out the drift pin which retains the firing pin; drive out the firing pin from the rear; and hold the hammer between soft jaws in a vise, with nothing but the spur exposed above the upper edges of the soft jaws. Heat the spur to a red heat with a torch down to its junction with the main body of the hammer. Hold a copper rod against the spur and gently tap the rod with a hammer until the height of the spur has been reduced sufficiently. When the spur is cool, touch up the checking with a three-square needle file and also file down any roughness that has developed in the surface, or any bulged area. Finally, caseharden the hammer, including the spur. Be sure that the main part of the hammer is not bent or the firing pin will strike off-center.

If a wide, low spur of the Bisley type is desired, prepare the spur as explained above, heat until soft, and cut it off, or if you want to work it cold, it can be ground away. Weld a piece of steel to the hammer to form the new spur, grind and file to shape, check with a three-square needle file, and caseharden.

Grips.—If you decide to make your own grips of wood, select the wood according to the principles discussed in the chapter on wood for gunstocks. Scrap pieces from gunstock blanks are economical and usually sound, but avoid pieces of American walnut that have soft spots, wide grain, and poor figures.

Saw the blanks much larger than they are to be when finished. If possible cut both grips from the same block. Roughly shape both sides of the block and then saw it through the middle to produce the right and left grips. Make special forms for holding the grips in the vise out of soft wood. Use small carving chisels, small half-round files, and a small rasp for inletting the front and back straps and shaping the grips to the frame. Work slowly, rub lampblack on the bearing surfaces of the metal, press it against the wood, examine the high spots in the wood, and work them down.

Drill the holes for the stock screw and alignment pins; counter-bore holes for the escutcheons. If necessary, provide a new and longer stock screw. When the blank grips are fitted to the frame, start to shape the wood to fit the hand, using the chisels and files. It is usually better, however, to remove the rough grips from the gun, screw them to a wooden block, and place the block in the vise. When the desired shape is reached, sand the wood smooth, and finish as you would a rifle or shotgun stock.

An excellent pattern for grips can be made with plastic wood. Make rough grips of soft wood, attach them to the gun, spread plastic wood on the grips, oil or grease your hands, and aim the gun as though you were actually going to fire it. This will leave grooves that fit the fingers and thumb perfectly. Trim away any excess plastic wood, let it dry, file and sand to the desired final shape, and you have a model that can be used to make grips out of any material—wood, aluminum, ivory, bone, or plastics.

Checkering Metal Parts.—Triggers, back straps, spurs, safety grips, and other metal parts may be checkered to give a better grip with the hand and to improve the appearance. Use a three-square escape-ment file, or a 6-inch needle file with a knife edge (about No. 0 cut) or both. First, cut lines with the knife-edged file, and then go back over them with the three-square file to deepen them and point the corners of the squares or diamonds or triangles. If you cannot space the lines evenly or cut them straight, practice on a piece of scrap metal until you attain skill. If the resulting surface is too sharp, hold it against a circular wire wheel driven by a motor, but be careful that the wire wheel is not so hard that it cuts the metal down rapidly; a brass wheel is therefore better than one made of steel wire.

The most beautiful metal checkering is accomplished with engraving tools, as described in the chapter on etching and engraving, but no matter what tools are used, it is always well to practice on scrap material, and work very slowly and cautiously on the actual gun parts.

XXXVI. Shotgun Problems

Gauge.—Originally, a piece of ordnance that fired a round lead ball weighing 1 pound was described as having a 1-gauge bore. A weapon that fired a round lead ball weighing ¼ pound was a 4-gauge gun; if it fired a round lead ball weighing ⅛ pound, it was an 8-gauge weapon, and so on. In other words, the gauge was the number of round balls that could be made from 1 pound of lead, each ball to fit the bore of the weapon. Today, gauges are no longer determined in this manner, and it is sufficient to say that, in general, shotgun gauges designate bore diameters just as rifle and pistol calibers do for those arms.

The popular gauges are 12-, 16-, 20-, and the new 3-inch .410 gauge, but the most commonly used is the 12-gauge, which is represented by a greater variety of shotguns and ammunition than any other. The 20-gauge lags far to the rear in popularity but ranks next to the 12-gauge.

Barrel Length.—A short barrel is light in weight, handy in the brush, quick to get on the mark, and is better than the long barrel for some purposes. The gunsmith should not determine the barrel length unless he is working on his own shotgun. Gauge, barrel length, choke, stock dimensions, shotgun selection, the care and repair of shotguns, and other subjects of interest to both the shooter and the gunsmith, are explained in detail in the author's new, revised edition of *Field, Skeet, and Trapshooting,* published by A. S. Barnes and Co., Inc.

gauge increases, thus: A 28-inch or 30-inch or even a 32-inch barrel may be used with a 12-gauge; a 26-inch or a 28-inch barrel goes well with a 16-gauge; and a 26-inch barrel works well with a 20-gauge. Barrels less than 26 inches are not commercially marketed.

Choke.—The choke of a shotgun is the amount of taper or constriction from the rear of the tube to the muzzle; it may also be described as the relationship between the diameter of the bore at the muzzle and the diameter of the bore at or near the breech. If the diameter at the muzzle were the same as the diameter throughout the barrel tube, the gun would be described as having a true cylinder bore, or a cylinder bore, but no manufacturer turns out an absolutely true cylinder bore, except on special order; all so-called cylinder bores have a slight constriction at the muzzle to make the barrel throw the shot evenly and not in bunches.

As the amount of constriction is increased, the choke is described as improved cylinder bore, quarter choke, half or modified choke, three-quarters or improved modified choke, and full choke. The greater the choke up to a certain limit, the more the lead pellets will be concentrated within a small pattern. The standard is a circle having a 30-inch diameter at a range of 40 yards. The approximate percentage of the shot from a load that will strike within the standard circle at the standard range is as follows: Improved cylinder bore or cylinder bore, 50 per cent. Quarter choke, 55 per cent. Half or modified choke, 60 per cent. Three-quarters or Improved modified choke, 65 per cent. Full choke, 70 per cent. These figures are conservative; some authorities would add 5 per cent to each of the percentages given here.

Standard Stock Dimensions.—The so-called standard stock dimensions for shotguns are: 14 inches long; drop at comb 1⅝ inches (some prefer 1½ inches), drop at heel 2⅝ inches (some prefer 2½ inches). These dimensions result in a stock that does not fit anyone perfectly but fits everyone fairly well. A more complete discussion of this topic will be found in the chapter on Stock Design.

Number of Barrels.—Advocates of single-barrel shotguns plea that they cannot aim well over twin barrels, but those who prefer double barrels protest that they find it more difficult to line up the target with a single barrel. If the shotgun is not a repeater, the aiming argument by itself is of no moment. Those who argue for a single-barrel gun are usually thinking of an automatic, but since the restriction on automatic fire to a three-shot magazine, which was made by the government to conserve game, the double-barrel shotgun has led the field in popularity.

The real argument for the double-barrel shotgun is that the barrels can be bored with different degrees of choke, thus permitting both short and long shots. The forward trigger fires the right-hand barrel, which should have a smaller amount of choke; the rear trigger fires the left barrel, which should have a greater amount of choke. The first shot gives a fairly large pattern at close range while the game is near; the second shot gives a smaller pattern but sends it farther. If the left barrel were fired first, the concentrated pattern of pellets would tear up the game too much.

Shot Size.—Smaller pellets are used to kill small birds, larger pellets to kill large birds. There is an old rule-of-thumb that it takes three pellets to kill a bird. Since more small pellets than large pellets can be loaded in the same space, and a greater percentage of pellets is delivered to the target with an increased choke, it looks easy in theory to kill a small bird until it is remembered that it is difficult to hold the aim on a flying bird. Practically, the best combination for all purposes is an improved cylinder for the right barrel and a modified choke for the left barrel of a double-barrel shotgun. A single-barrel gun is fired once, when the game is close; it should have a wide spread of shot, and hence a modified (one-half) choke is indicated.

Shotgun Types.—Shotguns are classed as to type as follows: single-barrel single shot; single-barrel automatic repeater; single-barrel slide-action repeater; single-barrel single-shot bolt action; single-barrel repeating bolt action; double-barrel (side-by-side); double-barrel over-and-under; and combinations of rifled bores with smooth bores in the same shotgun. It is not necessary for the shotgun to fire pellets or "shot" to be classed as a shotgun; it is the design and construction that determines the name and not the projectile, as shown by the fact that a gun may be used to fire nothing but a single ball, bullet, or slug, such as the Brenneke shotgun slug.

REPAIRS AND ADJUSTMENTS

Having presented a brief review of the general facts about shotguns, we shall now discuss the problems more or less peculiar to shotguns. The reader is reminded that fundamental operations common to rifles, revolvers, pistols, and shotguns are presented in other chapters, and that repairs, alterations, and adjustments for other arms are in many instances performed in a like manner on shotguns.

Pins.—Pins can be ordered from a gun-supply house, removed from other weapons, or made from drill rod. Cut the rod to the required length, round the ends with a file, and polish. Harden at a cherry-red color in oil, and then temper to a medium straw color in water. If it is slightly too large, polish it to size with emery cloth; if it is still too large, make a new pin from the next smaller drill rod. In ordering from a supply house, if the old pin is available and fits, place it in a drill and wire gauge which will give both its gauge number and its diameter in thousandths of an inch. If the old pin has been lost, insert the shank of a drill in the hole; if it fits correctly, measure the drill shank in the drill and wire gauge, or if the drill is marked, get the gauge number directly.

Screws.—If a machine screw is lost and another cannot be obtained easily, drill and tap the old hole for a larger screw, but caseharden the screw before inserting. If a wood screw is lost, marred, or broken, cut the point off an ordinary wood screw, imitate any decoration on it by making a few file cuts, insert in the screw hole, drive it in straight and flush. If a wood screw does not fit tight, use a larger screw, or drill a slightly larger hole, plug with wood, and then insert the screw.

Firing Pins.—Firing pins made separate from the hammer may be lost or broken. Make a new one from drill rod of the same diameter as the maximum diameter of the firing pin, file down to size and shape if you have no lathe, or turn to size and shape if you have a lathe, harden in oil at a cherry-red heat, keeping the metal the same color throughout, and draw the temper to a blue color.

A firing pin made integral with the hammer may break. It is better to obtain a new part, but the face of the hammer where the firing pin emerged can be drilled, and a new pin fitted tightly.

Make the pin similar to the separate firing pin already described, but start with a much larger drill rod and work it down from the center toward both ends so that the pin has a shoulder bearing against the hammer nose to absorb some of the shock of the blow when the hammer falls.

In making either type of firing pin, make it a little too large at first and then gradually file it down (before heat-treating) until it fits the firing pin hole. You can tell where to file away metal by coating the surface of the firing pin with lampblack or Prussian blue and noting where the coloring rubs off when the gun is snapped. In this connection, never snap on an empty chamber, but use a fired shell with a piece of fiber in the primer pocket.

Broken Hammers and Tumblers.—Broken hammers and tumblers should be replaced with new ones, but they can be repaired or replaced with ones made in the shop. Broken ones should be welded, not brazed, and it is important to use the oxyacetylene process of welding, not electric welding. Use a file to scarf the edges of the break open on the sides, with the broken edges coming together only in the center. After welding, file and emery the surface of the weld smooth, harden, and temper, using oil for both hardening and tempering. Shade off the color during the tempering from dark blue on the bottom to blue at the nose of the hammer.

Tumblers in hammerless shotguns are often described as inside hammers. They can be repaired as explained above, but in tempering, draw the sear notch at a yellow straw color and draw the nose at a blue color, thus making the latter soft enough to avoid breaking while the sear is hard enough to resist wear.

Hammers and tumblers can be filed from tool steel by an energetic gunsmith, and then processed as described above. Also, parts that are the wrong size and shape may be softened by the proper heat treatment, filed to size and shape, and then reheat-treated to restore their necessary properties.

Loose Forearms.—The forearms of the lower-priced shotguns frequently become loose. The old one may be tightened, or a new one obtained complete from a supply house. The most common type of forearm is the one that snaps into place on the barrel and is held there by a curved, flat-type spring steel lever which is pivoted into the forearm at one end and bears against the end of the lug on the under side of the barrel at the other end of the lever.

This type of forearm is loose because the spring has become too short from wear on the end. If it is soft enough for cold-working, draw it out by striking it along the end with a ball-peen hammer, starting about an inch back from the end and working to the end.

If the spring is too hard for cold-working, heat it to a cherry red, straighten it, let it cool, draw out its length while cold with the blows of the ball-peen hammer, heat and bring back to the original curved shape, reharden, temper it, and then replace it in the forearm and see if it fits. File the point until the forearms will fit tight when snapped into place. Be sure the temper of the spring is correct; if there is any question about it, reharden and temper again in oil at cherry red, flashing off the oil twice.

Sometimes the forearm has a spring that is too soft, with too much curve, thus taking up some of the length with the increase of the curve, and not from wear as in the former situation. The remedy here is to place the spring in a vise, tighten the jaws slowly against the curve, remove the spring and try for fit. Repeat this process until enough curve has been removed to restore the proper length and a tight snap fit. One practice is to take out a little more curve than necessary; this makes the spring too long to fit. It must be rehardened, tempered, and filed on the end until it fits.

The inside sliding forearm catch may be worn and loose. Remove it, heat and forge it longer, file to length, reharden, and temper at a light straw color. When this fails, make a new catch from tool steel, hardened and tempered carefully.

A worn barrel lug is rarely the cause of looseness. Hammering lightly on the sides while the lug is resting on a steel block or an anvil should lengthen it enough for a tight fit.

Resoldering a Loose Rib.—To resolder a loose rib, lift the loose portion and hold it up with one or more small wooden wedges. Clean under the rib and along the top of the barrel, moving the wedge along as you work. A small soldering copper with its tip flattened out for an inch or two is used to tin the barrel surface and the lower side of the rib, with powdered resin as a flux. Remove the wedges and wrap the barrels at two places on each side of the loose rib; then wrap wire around the barrels over the loose section.

Place small wedges under each wire-wrapping around the barrels, both on the lower and the upper ribs. Place some powdered resin and fine solder shavings along the sides of the loose section of the rib, heat the loose section and the barrels in that area with a small, low flame from a bunsen burner, alcohol lamp, or similar source of heat, until the solder melts and flows. Use a small three-cornered scraper to take off excess solder after it has cooled. If necessary, reblue the barrel, but with a little care this may be avoided.

Raising and Lowering Shot Patterns.—To raise the shot pattern, lower the rib at the muzzle; this also lowers the front sight. On a double-barrel shotgun, loosen the rib for a few inches behind the muzzle and file a little off the sides of the rib, to make it narrow and thus permit it to set lower. Resolder. On a single-barrel shotgun, loosen the rib, file metal from the bottom of the rib, and resolder.

To lower the shot patter, raise the rib at the muzzle. Loosen the rib, solder a piece of steel under it to raise the rib to the required height, and solder the rib to the piece of steel. If the barrel is of the ventilated rib type, cut the steel addition the width of the rib supports and the job is done. On a single-barrel shotgun with a hollow rib, and on a double-barrel gun with a raised rib, fill in the sides with solder.

Another method for raising or lowering the pattern is to scrape metal from the top or bottom of the bore, at the muzzle. Use a reamer that is a little smaller than the bore, place a shim under or over the reamer to protect the surface that is not to be reamed, and work slowly. If a shim is not used, round and polish one-half of the reamer so that it will not cut the metal on both sides at once. Instead of the reamer, a round or half-round carborundum file can be used.

Cutting Off Barrels.—Mark barrels for sawing with a machinist's square. Whittle out a wooden plug larger than the bore at the big end and tapered to a diameter a little smaller than the bore; wrap carborundum cloth around this plug and hold it there with glue. Place the plug in a barrel and saw the barrel off square. The purpose of the plug is to prevent burring the sawed edge. Having sawed the barrels to the desired length, file them square across, using the square again.

The opening between the ribs of a double-barrel shotgun that has been shortened must be refilled with solder. Scrape the opening clean for about ¼ inch behind the muzzle, press a piece of tin that fits this opening into place, and fill the opening above the tin with resin core solder. When it has cooled, file it square across the muzzles, using the machinist's square again, and polish with fine emery or carborundum cloth.

Since the shortening of the barrel removes the front sight, it is well to replace it before the opening between the ribs is filled. Locate the center of the rib, drill a vertical hole, tap it, and turn in the original sight, a special shotgun sight obtained from a dealer, or one of your own construction; if the sight does not screw in, it must be driven in, friction tight, with a light blow from a mallet. Manufacturers usually make recommendations regarding the mounting of sights, and they sometimes furnish a reamer of the size appropriate to the hole.

When the barrel is shortened, most, if not all, of the choke is removed because it lies in the first few inches behind the muzzle. If the barrel is not too thin, it can be rechoked by enlarging the bore. Leave the first 1½ to 2 inches back from the muzzle as it is, and then enlarge the bore for a distance of about 2 inches behind that, increasing the diameter of the bore about .008 inch. If the barrel is too thin, increase the diameter of the bore .005 inch, or whatever amount less than .008 inch you think the thickness of the barrel will permit. At each end of the enlarged section, taper for about 1 inch down to the diameter of the rest of the bore; the length of this taper at each end should be 1 inch, more or less, the object being to avoid leaving a shoulder at each end of the enlarged section. Finally, the bore is polished.

Precise directions for choke-boring are not given because the only way to check progress is to test-fire the gun and observe the pattern. Too short a taper may make the pattern irregular. Increasing the diameter of the enlarged section too much may concentrate the pellets in a small area so much that they deform one another in flight. Therefore, the safe course is to work awhile, test-fire, using the load you will use in the field, observe the pattern, continue the work, and repeat this process of check-firing and observing until the desired pattern is obtained.

A shotgun gauge is a handy instrument for determining both the gauge and the amount of choke. It is a cone-shaped piece of hardened steel with nickel-plated surface, marked on one side in regular shotgun gauge sizes, and on the other side into $\frac{1}{10}$ mm. graduations. When dropped tip first into the muzzle of the shotgun, the desired information is easily read.

Another instrument available to the gunsmith is the choke bore reamer, which is adjustable and designed for cutting choke in shotgun barrels by means of loosening one screw on one end and tightening on the other, thus adjusting the cutter for the desired diameter of the enlarged section of the bore. Some instruments of this type are available only for 12-, 16-, or 20-gauge only, while others are available for any of these gauges or 28- or 32-gauge. The shank is usually designed so that it may be fitted into the chuck of any lathe, or where a lathe is not available, a hand or breast drill may be used.

Shotgun chamber reamers come in two types: first cut reamers and finishing reamers. They are ordinarily available for all gauges from 10 to 410, and they must not be confused with choke bore reamers.

When a choke bore reamer is not obtainable, a substitute can be improvised in the shop, using a Tomlinson shotgun cleaner of the appropriate size for the gauge of the gun. Remove the brass-wire sides, coat the wooden strips with rubber cement, and press strips of No. $\frac{1}{2}$ carborundum cloth on the wooden strips, unless there is considerable rust and several fairly large pits in the bore, in which case a slightly coarser cloth is needed. Thread a steel rod to fit the screw end of the Tomlinson cleaner, paint a red line around the rod about 2 inches back of the cleaner, and work down the other end to fit the chuck of a lathe, or a breast or hand drill. The tool is lowered into the bore until the red line is even with the muzzle, and then it is revolved rapidly by the available power or hand tool. As carborundum cloth is worn smooth, it is replaced.

Start the work from the muzzle. Test-fire and observe patterns, if possible, but if not, use inside calipers to measure the bore section being enlarged, and compare the measurements with the ones desired. When the bore has been enlarged in the rebored section about one-half of the planned increase in diameter, use a long shank with the Tomlinson cleaner and work from the breech. Gradually move the cleaner back and forth, slightly enlarging the bore behind the choke and straightening the sides at the same time. Check the straightness of the bore according to the methods explained in the chapter on Rifling, illustrated on Plate 27.

The next step is to rough polish (sometimes called draw polish) the bore. Cut a slot 3 or 4 inches long in the end of a steel rod; in this slot place a piece of carborundum cloth as wide as the slot is deep; and wrap the cloth around the rod in the direction opposite the one in which it will be turned. Mount the other end of the rod in a lathe chuck, or in a hand or breast drill. Work the rod back and forth, like a cleaning rod, until there are no rough, uneven patches in the bore behind the choke. Keep out of the choke and also avoid polishing the chamber of the gun at this time. Start with No. ½ carborundum cloth, replace it as it becomes worn with finer cloth. If no other rod is at hand, a steel cleaning rod makes an excellent shaft for this rough polishing tool.

The final polish is accomplished in a similar manner. Start with No. o carborundum cloth, then use No. oo carborundum, follow with No. ooo emery cloth, and finish with crocus cloth. Light oil can be used advantageously with carborundum and emery cloth, but the crocus cloth is applied dry. The barrel is held in a vise or a lathe and the rod is worked back and forth, just as it was in the rough polish operation, but this time the rod is carefully revolved to make sure that the surface is very smooth and even, almost like a mirror in its perfect polish.

Some gunsmiths follow the above treatment by working lead sheets back and forth through the bore. Felt dipped in oil, rouge, rottenstone, and many other substances may improve the finish. Experimentation is desirable, but it should be done on old guns. A slight scratch left by a harsh material may slip by unnoticed in the shop, but the pattern on the target reveals the defect.

Instead of altering the Tomlinson cleaner, many gunsmiths have successfully employed a rubber expanding mandrel. On a steel mandrel with a solid head, about 6 inches long, rubber about 1¾ inches long is mounted over the arbor and against the head, so arranged that carborundum cloth can be cemented over the rubber and still permit the complete mandrel to enter the muzzle of the shotgun barrel with a snug fit. A long nut screws onto a threaded portion of the shank of the arbor to allow the mandrel to be placed in the choked part of the barrel before the mandrel is expanded. Then, when the mandrel is in the enlarged section of the bore, it can be expanded by tightening the nut. The polishing action of this expanding mandrel is similar in principle to that of the altered Tomlinson cleaner, but the expanding mandrel gives better results. The mandrel can be used in a hand or breast drill, or the arbor upon which the mandrel is mounted can be held in a chuck of a lathe spindle and revolved while the barrel is held against it with the hands. Likewise, the mandrel can be revolved in a drill press, or in a drill chuck mounted on the spindle of a motor.

Enlarging The Factory Choke.—When the pattern is too close, the factory choke may be enlarged by making the bore bigger at the muzzle. One method is to cement carborundum cloth to the expanding rubber mandrel or to the Tomlinson cleaner, insert the tool in the enlarged section of the bore, expand the mandrel or cleaner, start it revolving, bring it slowly out to the muzzle, run it back again, and continue to keep the tool revolving until the bore is enlarged sufficiently, as shown by the shot pattern.

Another method is to plug the barrel with waste, at a point about 6 inches below the muzzle, to catch the metallic particles to be removed, and use a reamer as the enlarging tool. An automobile piston-pin hone will do. Most hones of this type are adjustable for size, and it is also possible to obtain them equipped with burnishing blades. Professional gunsmiths often use a fine-toothed spiral-fluted reamer, although some of them favor a six-bladed expansion reamer which is straight, without taper. The reamer is inserted into the bore, adjusted, and then slowly turned with any suitable handle held in the hands, such as a large tap wrench.

Pioneer gunsmiths lubricated their tools and barrels during the reaming process with hard white soap and lard oil in the ratio of 1 pound of the former to each ½ pint of the latter. The soap was dissolved in water over a low heat, brought to a boil, and then stirred while the lard oil was added. When the mixture cooled, it was bottled and used as needed for reaming. Sometimes baking soda was dissolved in water and added to the soap and oil while the mixture was boiling, but often the soap and lard oil were the only ingredients. Modern gunsmiths use some heavy oil as a reaming lubricant.

Removing Dents.—Dents are removed from shotgun barrels with either solid steel mandrels, sometimes advertised as "shotgun rectifying cylinders," or with expanding mandrels, sometimes advertised as "shotgun dent raisers." These can be purchased from gunsmith-supply houses, or they can be made in the shop by a good machinist. The solid shotgun rectifying cylinders are sold in sets of five cylinders; the diameter of the first cylinder is .006 inch less than true barrel size; the second is .004 inch less; the third is .002 inch less; the fourth is true caliber size; and the fifth is .002 inch oversize. These cylinders are available for 12-, 16-, 20-, 28-, and 32-gauge shotguns ordinarily, and sometimes for other gauges. They are made of tool steel, hardened, ground and polished, about 3 inches long with ends tapered off to 15 or 20 degrees of curvature, so that they will force up the dent without harming the bore. In use, the cylinder and the bore are oiled with a light oil, such as sperm oil, and the cylinder is then driven into the barrel, under the dent, with either a heavy hardwood plug or a steel rod, driven by light blows from a hammer.

A solid cylinder (mandrel) may be needed to prepare the way for an expanding mandrel, since the expansion and contraction of the expanding mandrel is somewhat limited in scope, hence it is advisable for a professional gunsmith to have both types of dent-raising devices on hand. Also, he should own a hammer with a composition or plastic head, or some type of hammer with a very soft face. This is pounded lightly against the outside surface of the barrel, around the dent, while the mandrel of either type is being used inside the barrel, to reduce the stresses created in removing the dent, and to produce a smooth, even surface at the completion of the process.

A simple expanding-type dent raiser is made as follows: Cut a tongue on one flat piece of tool steel, and a groove to match on another piece of the same material. Temporarily fasten the two pieces together with solder. Place the joined pieces in a lathe, with one end ⅛ inch off center above the surface and the other end ⅛ inch off-center below the surface. Turn the joined pieces of steel into a plug about 3 inches long, tapered at the ends as described before. Heat until the solder melts, remove all the solder, and polish the two pieces of steel thoroughly.

When the tongued piece is slid into a union with the grooved piece, the two pieces form a plug of the size and shape of the bore of the shotgun in the dented region, but when the two pieces are only partly joined by their tongue-and-groove, they form a plug that is smaller than the bore. Notice that the purpose of the off-centering of the ends of the joined blocks during the turning process on the lathe was to give each of the two parts a taper lengthwise. If the two parts were simply two halves of a cylinder, when joined by the tongue-and-groove they would be too big to insert in the barrel.

To use this device, two driving rods are needed. The device is inserted under the dent with the parts only partly joined; a driving rod is inserted from each end of the barrel; and each driving rod is hammered to move the part on which it is acting. In this manner, the two parts close to form what is practically a solid plug, and in doing so the dent is raised.

Removing Bulges.—To remove a bulge from a shotgun barrel, first make a steel mandrel a little longer than the bulged region, with a diameter such that it will snugly fit in the bore of the bulged region when the mandrel is oiled and driven in place with a heavy rod and a hammer. Second, provide two brass blocks with curved grooves in each, so designed that they fit the outside of the shotgun barrel without the blocks quite touching each other when placed around the barrel.

Place the mandrel in the bore, and place the shotgun barrel between the brass blocks, in a padded vise. Tighten the vise slowly; loosen the vise; slide the barrel around in the blocks so that the blocks now grip at different points, and repeat this process until the bulge is ironed out completely.

An easier and faster method is to insert the mandrel, and iron out the bulge by placing the barrel between the rollers of a roller-type pipe cutter which has had the pipe cutter removed and a roller substituted for the cutter.

Curing Cross-Firing.—When the right barrel of a double-barrel shotgun throws pellets to the left and the left barrel throws to the right, the condition is called cross-firing. If it takes place at less than

40 yards, return the gun to the factory to have the barrels refitted to the face of the breech. If it takes place at a range greater than 40 yards, the condition can be corrected in the home shop.

The cure is to place a small piece of steel between the barrels to force them apart. The distance that they should be separated must be found by experiment. Measure the distance between the barrels as they are already. Then, remove the barrels from the gun, lay them on the open end of a soapbox in which notches have been cut to receive the barrels, and sight in on vertical lines drawn upon some upright object located within the usual firing range. This should give an idea of the way they point.

Use a large hot soldering iron, or a small torch, to remove solder from the ends of the ribs at the muzzle and loosen the upper and lower ribs for about one foot back from the muzzle. Lay the barrels back on the box, push a wedge between them at the muzzle, and sight in on the target lines again. Move the wedge back and forth until the barrels are separated correctly. Measure the distance between the barrels now. Place a piece of flat steel between the barrels as a permanent separator. It must be thick enough to give the desired separation and so designed that the top rib remains at its original height to prevent changing the height of the shot pattern. Solder the ribs back in place, following instructions given elsewhere in this chapter for rib soldering, but notice that it may be necessary to fill in solder under the top rib.

Improper Ejection.—Autoloading and pump shotguns occasionally eject loaded cartridges from the magazine out through the bottom of the action instead of carrying them to the barrel, due to the failure of the magazine shell-stop to function properly, which failure may in turn be brought about by various conditions, or it may be caused by a defective shell-stop itself.

Inspect an autoloading shotgun to see if the shell-stop or the shell-stop spring is missing or broken. If not, see if the breech bolt and the carrier which lifts the cartridge from the magazine to the barrel are coordinated so that the carrier is raised when the breech bolt is opened. If not, examine the carrier tip and the carrier tip spring. If any of the above named parts is missing or broken it must be replaced.

Improper ejection from a pump shotgun may be caused by any of the above defects, but in most pump guns the shell-stop is missing or defective. If the shell-stop has lost its elasticity, bend to shape, harden, and give it a new temper. If the shell-stop is too sharp on its front edge, dull it slightly with an oilstone. If the shell-stop appears to have no defects, clean the stop, the stop spring, and the recess in the receiver wall where the front end of the stop fits when the breech block is closed.

Ejector and Extractor Troubles.—A broken or defective ejector should always be replaced with a new one, and if there is any serious ejector problem the gun should be returned to the factory, since very few gunsmiths, amateur or professional, have either the equipment or the experience needed to perform this work.

When trouble occurs with the extraction in an autoloading or pump shotgun, replace the old extractor with a new one, but if that is not possible file the hook of the extractor to a sharper angle. Also, look for a broken spring, too much dirt under the extractor, or poor ammunition having a case that is not of standard shape and size.

Mainsprings.—Shotgun mainsprings are usually stocked by supply houses in ten standard sizes and illustrated in their catalogs full size. If a replacement is needed and none of the standard sizes are exactly right, order a spring a little larger than the one it is to replace and file it down. File from the tips of the leaves inward toward the thick part, try the spring for fit, and continue to file slowly until it fits the action. Any reduction in thickness that is not gradual along the length of the spring will seriously weaken it.

An old flat spring may be rehabilitated by changing its shape and heat-treating. Heat to a light cherry red before changing the shape, harden, and temper. A small piece of steel driven into the crotch of the spring while the spring is hot will force the leaves farther apart and increase the tension of the tips of the leaves on their bearing surfaces.

Coil springs, when weak or broken, should be replaced with new ones, but they can be made by winding piano wire around a steel rod by hand, being sure that the rod is smaller than the spring is to be after it is removed from the rod, or coil springs can be wound on a lathe. Ordinarily tempering is not necessary for piano wire, but if there is difficulty in winding, anneal, wind, harden, and temper.

Dismounting Locks.—To disassemble the typical shotgun, open the gun, remove the barrel and the forearm; remove wood screws from the back end of the guard; and remove the guard from the frame. The removal of the guard from the frame varies in method: in some guns, turn counter-clockwise and unscrew; in others, push the guard back or forward and unhook; in still others, remove the guard from the frame by giving the bayonet lock on the end of the guard a quarter-turn to the left and up. If the removal is not accomplished by one of these methods, examine the construction and proceed slowly, without using force.

Side locks are removed by withdrawing the screw near the rear which extends through both plates. Bend the end of a small brass rod to form a hook, insert through the screw hole, lift up while tapping the stock gently to loosen the connection, move the plates backward, and release the front ends of the plates from the body of the action.

Take out the wood screws at the rear of the trigger bar, and the long screw which enters from the top under the upper lever, holding the lever to one side while the big screw is withdrawn. Remove the trigger bar. Remove the tang screw, take out the screw holding the plate to the bottom of the body of the action, lift the trigger plate out with the triggers still attached, and remove the stock from the action.

However, if the gun has a box lock, remove the sears after the trigger plate is removed and before you attempt to separate the action from the stock. Push out the sear pin with a drift punch, but hold the thumb over the sears to keep the springs from flying across the room. After the sears and springs are removed, the action can be separated from the stock easily. A box lock is removed and reassembled with the hammers not cocked, while a side lock is disassembled and replaced with the hammers or tumblers cocked. As the bottom plate of the action is removed, keep it upright while loose parts are withdrawn.

Before disassembling the Blitz lock, found on many medium priced shotguns, especially on 3 and 4 barrel guns, cock the gun. The hammer and hammer springs, as well as the trigger action, lie on the trigger plate. If the gun is not cocked first, the hammer engages the housing and cannot be removed.

In disassembling any firearm, lay out the parts in order as they are taken from the gun; place the parts of any subassembly in order with other parts of the same group; place the subassemblies in the order of their withdrawal. In reassembling, work backwards from the order of disassembly. These rules seem obvious, but they are frequently ignored by amateurs.

Rusty parts should be rubbed with fine emery cloth and then polished with crocus cloth, being careful that the emery does not reduce the size or alter the shape of any bearing surfaces. Rusty parts, or those covered with gummy oil and grease, can be soaked in gasoline, scrubbed with an ordinary fiber brush, dried, and lubricated with a light oil.

The sears are extremely important. Examine their points to see if they are broken, nicked, or worn. In case of doubt, replace with a new sear. If the replacement sear is not exactly the same size and shape as the original, use the old one as a pattern to file and stone the new one to the correct size and shape, remembering not to copy any defect such as a point worn below its useful working shape. Insert the new sear in the mechanism and try it before working it all the way down, because you can always remove metal, but once it is gone it cannot be replaced. A more complete discussion of sears is given in the chapter on Triggers.

Loose Actions.—The hinge joint between the action and the barrel or barrels of a high-grade shotgun seldom gives any trouble, but on the low-priced guns looseness may develop. If a new hinge pin is needed, the old one may be drilled out on a lathe, using a drill about $\frac{1}{16}$ inch smaller in diameter than the pin, and the remaining metal is removed with a reamer, being careful not to make the pin hole any larger than it was originally, and also not to ream out any threads in the pin hole where such threads are there to receive a screwed-in type of hinge pin.

It is not always necessary to drill out the old pin. If it is the screwed-in type, it may be removed with a screwdriver if there is a screwdriver slot. Also, look for small screws used to lock the hinge pin. These may be at the end or on the sides of the hinge pin, according to the ideas of the manufacturer. The hinge pin may also be a simple pin, pressed into place. It may or may not also have small locking screws. If the latter are present, remove them before attempting to force out the pin. Heating the frame to a temperature immediately below the color-changing point often helps when the pin fits tightly and the gunsmith does not wish to drill it out. Having removed the old pin, replace the new pin while the frame is still hot. It will make matters still easier if the new pin has previously been packed in ice to shrink it slightly.

Some gunsmiths ream the pin hole until it is from .005 inch to .01 inch larger than it was originally, and then use an oversize pin turned down until it is about .001 inch larger than the hole. Since the hinge pin holds the barrel or barrels to the action, it must be very strong, and hence should be made of chrome-vanadium steel and not drill rod or some other comparatively weak steel.

Having used a hinge pin larger than the original, the semicircular notch in the barrel lug is filed out to fit the pin snugly. Work slowly and try the fit several times during the progress of the work. The use of Prussian blue, lampblack, or some other coloring material will show where the metal is "high" and must be removed.

Where the steel is casehardened, it may be necessary to remove the hardness, according to the heat-treating methods described elsewhere in this text, followed by casehardening to restore the original condition. Unless this is done the steel may be too hard to drill, file, or ream.

The owner of a cheap shotgun may not care to meet the expense of replacing the hinge pin, in which event the gunsmith uses a ball-peen hammer to peen the lug or lump near its semicircular recess at the front end where it fits the hinge pin. The purpose of this treatment is to lengthen the lug, take out forward and backward motion, and give a tight fit. The edges of the recess must not be battered, and any roughness left on the sides should be smoothed with a file. This peening treatment has temporary value only.

After removing the to-and-fro looseness, if there is an up-and-down motion when the action is locked, peen around the locking notch in the rear of the barrel lug, striking the lug lightly below the notch and around its lower, inner corner. Avoid battering the edges of the notch, and follow the peening with careful filing to remove roughness.

If the peening operation fails to take out the up-and-down play, insert snug-fitting steel plugs in the chambers to keep the barrels in shape, and squeeze the notch together between the jaws of a vise, using some soft material between the vise jaws and the metal, such as lead, brass, etc. Also, protect the rib extension by placing some soft metal over the breech, immediately forward of the rib extension. If this protective treatment is not accomplished for a gun having a cross bolt, the latter will not fit through the rib.

Shotgun Shooting.—Field, Skeet, and Trap Shooting, by the author of this text, was published in 1949 by Coward-McCann, Inc., New York. In 1962, it was revised and published by A. S. Barnes & Co., Inc. The old edition was revised with the co-operation of the Amateur Trapshooting Association, Vandalia, Ohio; the National Skeet Shooting Association, Dallas 19, Texas; the National Rifle Association of America, Washington 6, D.C.; Alex Kerr, Beverly Hills, California, who is an outstanding authority on shotgun shooting; and other experts.

Any gunsmith, amateur or professional, who works on shotguns, must know the requirements of men who use shotguns for skeet and trap shooting, and also those who fire shotguns only while hunting game.

XXXVII. Field Kits

GUNSMITHS are frequently asked for advice about tools and materials for field kits. Such outfits may be divided into two classes: first, shooting kits, which are intended for marksmen at target ranges; second, field or emergency repair kits, which are intended to be carried on hunting trips by at least one member of the hunting party, or to be taken to the target range by the gunsmith invited to take care of repairs during the match.

The container for the shooting kit is made of wood, leather, or steel, and divided into compartments for storing items such as oil-cans, cartridges, cartridge blocks, cleaning rods, cleaning-rod detachable tips, cleaning patches, tubes of grease, shooting gloves, ear stoppers, rifle rests, shot-hole gauges, sight-blackening material, micrometers for setting sights, bottles of solvent, and extra parts. Spotting telescopes and telescopic sights are usually carried in separate cases, although they may be carried in a properly designed shooting kit.

The container for the field repair kit should be a waterproofed canvas roll if it is to be taken on hunting trips or to a target range located at a distance from the usual means of transportation. Boxes are satisfactory for use at most rifle and pistol ranges, but if the gunsmith is to work either at a range or in the field he should select the canvas roll.

Gun-supply houses stock a standard gunsmith's field kit which consists of eighteen high-grade special gunsmith's tools, sufficient for amateur repairing, placed between adjustable straps in a leather-bound waterproof canvas case. This kit is normally sold for less than fifty dollars, but one price fluctuates with the rise and fall of tool prices. Since it is intended to satisfy most amateurs fairly well, it does not exactly meet the specifications of any very particular individual, amateur or professional. Most expert gunsmiths make up their own kits for each hunting trip or target range assignment, choosing their tools and materials to meet their immediate needs.

The following tools and materials will cover most situations where a gunsmith is expected to make emergency repairs. They can be taken from the workshop, or they may be items kept in the kit solely for field use. In general, it is well to have an entirely different set of tools for field use so that upon returning from a hunting or marksmanship trip one can go to work in the shop without unpacking the field kit; otherwise, neither the workshop nor the kit will be complete.

1. Waterproof adhesive tape is needed for wrapping a split or shattered stock of a rifle or shotgun, or a cracked pistol butt.

2. A broken-shell extractor makes it possible to remove broken cases from the chamber of a rifle, but it is seldom needed and can be safely omitted. If the base of a high-power cartridge breaks off, an accident calling for both a major ordnance repair job and the services of a surgeon may take place.

3. An old toothbrush comes in handy for cleaning the chamber. Bristle and brass brushes for cleaning rods are indispensable and should be selected according to the caliber or gauge of the weapon.

4. Black lacquer in a can with a tight lid is useful for blackening temporary sights. Any of the commercial bluing materials that can be applied quickly and easily are of value, but black lacquer is better suited to field conditions.

5. An extra rifle bolt is sometimes carried, but unless it has been previously tested for head space, gauges for that purpose must be available, hence this item is not ordinarily taken along.

6. One small cold chisel and one small wood chisel are invaluable when a need for them arises, but most gunsmiths leave them home.

7. A cleaning rod with detachable tips takes up little room if it is of jointed construction, but many prefer either a straight steel rod or a cleaning rope. The threads of the jointed rod may strip just when you need it the most. A straight rod is too long. The only

alternative is to have a field cleaner of the government type, consisting of a bristle brush with a detachable cord and weight for dropping through the barrel, and a separate slotted wiper for pulling through a dry or oiled cloth patch.

8. We have already mentioned the carrying case, but it is easy to forget it until the last minute unless it is in the itemized list of equipment.

9. A drift punch can be used to knock out pins, etc. Select several, of appropriate sizes.

10. A drill chuck is handy for holding small parts while they are being removed or replaced.

11. A small funnel is needed if the bore is to be cleaned by the hot water method.

12. Files are very important. A set of 6-inch needle files in a special container, one 6-inch flat mill file, and one 3-square file will be sufficient.

13. Gun grease in a tube should not be omitted.

14. A stick of prepared glue will be needed for repairing wooden parts.

15. There should be two hammers, one ball-peen, and one with a soft head.

16. A narrow hook saw frame and an 8-inch blade are often needed, but the blade alone is better than no sawing tool.

17. Two knives are needed, one an ordinary pocketknife, and the other a short hunting knife. If the pocketknife is of the Boy Scout type with accessories, it is even better.

18. There should be two oilcans, one for light and one for medium oil.

19. A set of small oilstones is needed for adjusting actions, sights, etc.

20. A pair of 6-inch, side-cutting pliers is indispensable.

21. A rifle rest, which is simply a U-shaped pair of prongs on the end of an upright, can be carved from a forked stick in the field, but a metal one cast in the home workshop gives more security. This is commonly carried on a target range, but gunsmiths also find it helpful.

22. A piece of rubber hose, 5 or 6 feet long, fitted with a metal

tube, 1 or 2 feet long, can be used to create a powerful draft in a campfire when intense heat is needed.

23. Screwdrivers should have short handles and should be appropriate in number and size to the screws on the arms to be repaired.

24. A small putty knife will serve as a scraper for removing splinters from wooden replacements, and for other purposes.

25. Spare parts are extremely important. Pins, screws, sights, strikers, firing pins, and extractors are always being broken or lost. Be sure, though, that they fit the guns you will repair.

26. A small soldering copper with a supply of acid-core wire solder can be used in making and repairing sights, repairing broken wooden parts, etc.

27. Three vises will prove very handy. These are a clamp base vise, weight about 2 pounds; a pin vise; and a hand vise.

28. Trigger weights (or a trigger-testing device) are needed by the amateur for any trigger-adjusting job, but a professional knows about how many pounds' pull is being exerted by the feel, and hence he uses trigger weights only when required to do so at a rifle or pistol match.

29. An extra front sight cover always should be carried because it is easy to lose this device while firing.

30. Special sight spanners and wrenches, made to fit the sights on the guns to be repaired, are important, especially for work on telescopic sights.

31. A roll of No. 24 gauge copper wire is needed for making emergency front sights, wrapping a broken stock, etc.

32. Last, but not least, in importance is a small first aid kit. A gunsmith is in more danger of getting hurt than a shooter because he works with edged and pointed tools, saws, hammers, etc.

33. Although it is not absolutely essential, a small portable bench can be purchased from gun-supply dealers or made at home by any man who has enough mechanical aptitude to do any type of gunsmithing. Whether or not a portable bench is carried on a shooting trip, it is a good practice to work at home with the field kit only before it is taken into the field for the first time, because handling a reasonably complete set of tools in a home workshop is much easier than using the field kit on a hunting expedition or on trap or skeet grounds.

XXXVIII. Restoring Antique Firearms

ANTIQUE firearms are valuable from several viewpoints. First, they have sentimental and historical value for those who realize that the United States was made and preserved as a nation through the force of arms. Second, they have value as firearms which, when properly restored, can be used in marksmanship matches that promote the highest ideals of good sportsmanship. Third, they have monetary value. Fourth, they are important to those who like to collect arms of beautiful design and construction, as works of art. Fifth, they are fascinating to those who collect weapons which are examples of advances in mechanical design and operation. Sixth, they are treasured by hobbyists who collect antique arms for the same reason that some people collect stamps, coins, or old shaving mugs—which probably is a diversion from their occupations. Finally, all these values and motives are combined when the owner of antique arms assembles a wisely selected group of weapons into a collection that reflects his pride of possession.

All these phases of gun collecting are thoroughly discussed in several books by the author of this text. These are: *The Complete Book of Gun Collecting; The Gun Collector's Handbook of Values; Guns of the Old West; U.S. Martial and Semi-Martial Single-Shot Pistols;* and *Guns and Girls of San Francisco.* These books all contain not only background historical information associated with firearms but also detailed technical descriptions and illustrations of antique firearms. A gunsmith, amateur or professional, needs such information in order to repair or restore weapons for collectors.

Both amateur and professional gunsmiths also must understand the problems of shooters. The author of this text has provided such information in his other gun books, such as *The Boy's Book of Rifles; Field, Skeet and Trap Shooting,* a book on shotguns; and *The Art of Shooting,* which covers pistol, revolver, and rifle marksmanship for target shooting, hunting, self-protection, and law enforcement.

Supply and Demand.—The law of supply and demand affects the value of antique firearms. *Hand guns,* which is a term applied to pistols and revolvers, are more popular than *shoulder arms,* a group including rifles, carbines, muskets, musketoons, and shotguns. For some strange reason, shotguns have never been very popular and are not valued highly by collectors. Generally speaking, U.S. martial and semimartial single-shot flintlock pistols are more in demand than U.S. martial and semimartial single-shot percussion (cap-and-ball) pistols. Percussion revolvers are normally worth more than cartridge revolvers. Dueling pistols, both flintlock and percussion, are single-shot pistols in great demand, especially if they are available in matched pairs in their original cases, complete with all accessories. Of course, there are exceptions to all these statements.

Colt percussion revolvers, particularly those made at Paterson, New Jersey, are in great demand. The Paterson-made Colt revolvers usually are sold at higher prices than flintlock revolvers, which are much more rare, probably because few people know of the existence of flintlock revolvers but most gun collectors have read about Paterson Colts.

Condition.—*Fine* means at least 50% of the original factory finish is present; markings are distinct; all parts are original; the arm is in perfect working order; and the amount of original finish is definitely known. *Good* means there is little or none of the original factory finish; markings are absent or indistinct; the barrel may be rusted or pitted slightly; the stock may be scratched, bruised, or cracked, but sound and complete; the gun shows wear but no abuse; it is in good working order; and the amount of rusting or pitting is definitely known. There are other condition descriptions, but these two give an idea of the trend.

Translating the above facts into practice we find that a certain Paterson Colt revolver, worth $2,000 in *good* condition, is worth

$3,000 in *fine* condition, while the same revolver in *fair* condition is worth not more than $1,400. If it were in *factory new* condition it would be worth $5,000.

Ethics of Restoration.—In repairing and restoring old guns there are ethical traditions. Since condition is so important in determining value, the gunsmith must be careful not to destroy more value than he creates. He should not substitute a new part for an original one unless the new part is necessary for the proper functioning of the weapon. He should not reblue a barrel when there is any of the original blue present, and it is sometimes inadvisable to reblue at all. Rust may be removed. Bruises, scratches, and cracks may be treated to improve the appearance of the gun. Markings, such as the name of the maker, the model, the serial number, etc., should not be removed.

Stripping the Gun.—Before disassembling the firearm, inspect to see if it is loaded, because it is quite common to find powder and ball still in the bore, and even this ancient charge may explode. The barrel may be removed and the charge pushed out from the rear. If the barrel cannot be removed easily, weld or braze a corkscrew of an appropriate diameter to the end of a steel rod, tamp it into the bullet with a mallet from the muzzle, and pull it out like a cork. The old powder may then be scraped out with the end of the cork-screw.

Having made sure that the gun is not loaded, proceed to disassemble. Do not use force unless absolutely necessary. As you remove the parts, place them on a table in a row so that you can assemble the gun by starting with the first part removed and end up with the last one removed. If you do not keep the parts in order, when you try to assemble you may find yourself in the childhood position of having an alarm clock that is assembled and apparently running but with several parts left over.

The barrel is usually the first part removed. On early muzzle-loaders it was often fastened to the stock with a wedge pin in the forearm; and a tang protruding from the breech plug, held to the stock by a screw extending downward into the trigger plate. On later muzzle-loaders there was a hook at the end of the breech plug which engaged what may be described as a false breech; the forearm fastening is removed and the barrel is lifted and removed from its rear fastening.

The Colt Old Model Pocket Pistol, a percussion weapon, is disassembled by removing the parts in the following order: barrel and barrel lug, barrel bolt or key and screw, ramrod plunger and screw, ramrod lever and screw, trigger guard and screws, mainspring and screw, frame or lock frame, cylinder, backstrap and screws, cylinder-locking bolt and screw, trigger and screw, trigger and bolt spring and screw, hand and handspring, and the hammer and screw, grips.

It would require several volumes to explain the disassembly and assembly of all the arms that a gunsmith may receive. Old catalogs, obtainable from book dealers and antique arms dealers, sometimes give assembly and disassembly directions, and they often illustrate the component parts. Books on guns, whether intended for marksmen or collectors, are also sources of information on this subject.

The Barrel.—When the barrel has been removed, take off any attached parts, such as the sights, the breech pin, the nipple, and the nipple plug (in the case of a percussion muzzle-loader). Inspect the bore. It is probably clogged with rust and dirt. Place a bronze-bristle brush on the end of a steel cleaning rod, dip the brush in powder solvent, and work the rod back and forth several times. This loosens the rust.

Clean out the loose rust by pouring gasoline into the muzzle through a funnel and letting it run out the other end into a pan. The same gasoline can be used several times but it should be changed when it contains much rust and dirt. Having removed most of the rust, run several clean white patches through the bore and examine to see if the bore is pitted.

To remove badly caked rust and dirt, dip a cloth patch in emery powder and oil, wrap it around the bristle brush, and work the rod back and forth. Flush out the bore with gasoline, wipe it out with clean patches and inspect again. The bore should now be clean enough to satisfy a collector. If the weapon is to be fired, it may be necessary to lap the bore, deepen the old rifling, or cut new rifling, following methods explained for modern arms in other chapters of this book.

The Lock.—The first step in disassembling an antique gun lock is to compress the mainspring and keep it compressed while it is taken out. Use a small hand vise (pad the jaws if the gun is a valuable one with polished springs). Tighten the vise around the mainspring until the hammer is no longer under tension, press down the sear spring, release the hammer, and take out the mainspring without removing the vise. The remaining disassembly steps are usually apparent on inspection.

Nipples.—A nipple is a short tube upon which the percussion primer is placed in a cap-and-ball arm. It is screwed in or out of position with a nipple wrench, sometimes called a tube wrench, which can be purchased from a gun-supply house or made in the home shop. Since the nipples vary as to length, cross-sectional shape, coarseness of the threads, and the size and shape of the head, it is important to use only a wrench that will fit the nipple. If the nipple breaks, it can be removed with a very small drill like any screw.

Ramrod Thimbles or Pipes.—Ramrod thimbles or pipes are devices for holding the ramrod in place on the stock when it is not in use. They are made of brass, sheet iron, silver, or other soft metal. A replacement for a broken or missing thimble can be made by cutting a strip from a metal sheet, rolling it over a steel rod, and pounding it to shape with a mallet. The new thimble is then temporarily mounted by wiring it in place so that the ramrod will fit. Remove the ramrod and solder or braze the thimble to the desired spot.

Ramrods.—Ramrods for ancient arms were usually made of hickory which was split straight, formed either straight or tapered with a draw knife or a spoke-shave (whichever was handier), planed square, the square corners removed, filed and sandpapered to final shape. After being formed, the ends of the ramrod were turned down, and brass tips were mounted on the ends. One brass tip was made concave to fit the lead ball used as a bullet, and the other tip was shaped to hold a brush, a slotted section for holding a cloth patch, or a wormer, which was a corkscrew attached for removing bullets and powder charges from the bore of a muzzle-loader.

Furniture.—The term "furniture" when applied to an antique arm usually means all metal parts except the barrel and the lock, examples of such parts being the trigger, trigger guard, butt plate, patch box, etc. When broken, these can be duplicated in the gunsmith's own shop or they can be taken from other old guns. Grease can be removed by boiling the parts in a strong solution of lye or caustic soda. Rust is removed by dipping them in a solution of 2 part sulfuric acid to 10 parts water and then rinsing thoroughly to stop the action of the acid. Some gunsmiths boil such parts in the acid bath and rinse in boiling water. Having removed the grease and rust, the parts are polished with emery or crocus paper by hand, or on a buffing wheel with emery paste.

Replacement steel parts can be made by forging and filing. Brass parts are made by using the broken member as a pattern, arranging a sand mould in a frame, and pouring molten brass into the mould. The details of this process are beyond the scope of this text but they are clearly explained in any text on pattern-making, moulding, and casting. When it is not desired to make a part of brass, but a brass appearance is preferred, make the part of steel, clean and polish, dip it into molten brass, remove it quickly, and let it cool in the air.

Antique Finish for Wood.—To give any wooden part the appearance of great age, start with the following mixture: Pour about 30 grains of steel filings into 11 parts by volume nitric acid; when the acid and filings have cooled, add 3 parts by volume tincture ferric chlorid, and 1 part by volume distilled water. Strain the mixture into a wide-mouthed bottle. Steel wool works as well as steel filings.

Meanwhile, dip a swab into ammonia and run it over the wooden part enough to give the whole surface a light coat. Let the ammonia dry. Using another clean, dry swab, coat the surface with the above mixture and let it dry. If it is not dark enough, repeat the process. If it is dry enough, rinse the wood with water to stop the action of the mixture and dry thoroughly. Next, go over the wood with fine steel wool and sandpaper. Use No. 3/0 steel wool with No. 5/0 sandpaper, if possible, but similar grit numbers will be satisfactory. Follow this by polishing with rottenstone (also called tripoli powder).

The next step is to make a finishing oil composed of the following ingredients: 1 pint raw linseed oil, 1 ounce alkanet root, 25 c.c. turpentine, and 175 grains lampblack. These are boiled together, allowed to cool, and poured into a bottle. Swab the stock liberally, let it stand two or three days, and swab again with this mixture. Continue the process until the wood is saturated with it. Let the wood stand for five or ten days, polish with steel wool No. 3/0, and complete the whole treatment by polishing with rottenstone, as at the end of the first phase. It is assumed that this treatment is not given until any old finish has been removed from the wood, and it is also assumed that wood has previously been given its final shape.

Rottenstone is applied with a rubbing pad made by gluing a strip of felt around a wooden block and anchoring the ends of the felt with tacks. Soak the pad in a dish of water, dip it into the rotten-stone, and rub the rottenstone over the surface of the wood with a gradually increasing pressure, working with the grain. To avoid caking the rubbing pad, wash it out in clean water from time to time.

An alternate procedure for refinishing an old stock is as follows:

Wash the surface of the wood with a rich, white soap lather on a sponge or a rag, wipe dry quickly, and then rinse off the soap with a rag wrung out in warm water. Dry the stock quickly again, and place it near a low, steady heat for a few minutes, where it will dry thoroughly without actually heating the wood more than a few degrees.

Next, dip a small rag in linseed oil, then dip it in finely powdered pumice and rub the stock with very light pressure until the old film of dirty and gummy grease is removed. Wipe off the stock twice with linseed oil, using a fresh rag and fresh oil each time. Follow this with the application of a finishing oil composed of 1 part white shellac dissolved in alcohol, 1 part light gun oil, and 1¾ parts raw linseed oil. To each quart of this mixture add 2 teaspoons-ful acetone, 5 teaspoonsful turpentine, and 2 ounces alkanet root. Where alkanet root is not available, oil soluble red can be used as a substitute in either this finishing mixture or the previous one.

Shake the mixture vigorously and rub it over the stock briskly. Use clean, soft rags and change them as fast as they become dirty. When the surface of the stock no longer dirties the rag, rub the mixture into the wood with your bare hands, being sure that they are clean and very dry. Finally, polish the wood with a soft woolen cloth or a pad made of very fine felt.

Both of these finishing processes are legitimate methods for giving wood an antique appearance. In no sense of the word can they be regarded as "faking" tricks. They can be applied equally well to the stocks of modern arms, but neither is equal to the oil finish explained in the chapter on Stock Finishing.

Forearm Tips.—The tip or socket into which the ramrod was inserted on the forearm (or fore-end) of old muzzle-loading rifles was made of lead, tin, brass, silver, or German silver. A pattern was carved from soft pine. The mould was made of sand, clay, or plaster of Paris. Molten metal was poured into the mould and when it cooled the casting was filed to the desired size and shape, drilled, and polished. Trigger guards and butt plates were often cast in the same manner, but they were usually made of brass.

Some gunsmiths cast the tip directly around the forearm instead of casting separately and then fitting. When this is done the wood should be cut to a cone-shaped tenon at its end, the larger diameter of the cone being to the front. A short dummy ramrod is placed in the ramrod groove and wrapped with paper to protect it from the hot metal. The barrel is similarly protected. When all is ready, the rifle is placed upright and the molten metal is poured over the forward end of the forearm in a quantity large enough so that when cool it can be filed down to the desired size and shape. We do not recommend this method because it may damage the forearm and leaves too much to the artistic ability of the gunsmith when a graceful tip is desired. Casting is by far the better method.

Precautions for Handling Old Guns.—Flintlock arms were made of iron or soft steel; percussion weapons showed some improvement in the quality of the steel but many of them were likewise made of soft metal. For this reason, when they are being cleaned they should be gone over by hand with fine emery cloth or fine steel wool with oil, and the pressure should be light. The use of a steel brush with a high-speed motor is dangerous because it will cut into the metal before the operator is aware of what is happening.

Screws, pins, bolts, and other small retaining parts may be rusted into place and they are often brittle. Soaking them with kerosene may loosen them enough so that they can be driven out with hard wooden pins struck by a soft mallet. Springs should be treated just as carefully.

The patina acquired through the years by metal is an asset in the case of arms for a collector; it should not be removed, but sometimes its removal cannot be avoided when rust and dirt are being taken from the surface. There are methods for giving metal an artificial patina, but these are not always successful enough to fool an expert and they are always unethical.

The author has found worms and insects in the wooden parts of old guns. They can be killed by placing the wood in a fuming chest where a formaldehyde candle is burning, but the chest should be placed where the fumes will not reach animals or people and the candle flame will not start a fire. If the worm holes are extensive enough to weaken the stock, the gun should not be fired. For exhibition purposes, worm holes can be filled by carving little pins from a new piece of the same kind of wood, swabbing them with glue, and driving them home with a mallet. Their ends should be filed down flush with the surrounding wood and they should then be darkened when necessary and given an appropriate finish.

Ethical Repairs and Restorations.—Replacement parts for a collector's weapon should be of the same size, shape, and material as the originals, wherever possible. Examining the necessary parts on other weapons, or studying the illustrations in gun books will guide the gunsmith in his work. Preservation of the period style of the piece is the underlying principle. Screws, for example, should not be used where pins were the original retaining devices. A lock plate from a rifle should not be placed on a pistol.

Assembling what appears to be an authentic piece from various discarded parts is especially dishonest. A less grievous crime, but still an objectionable one, is the assembling of a weapon from two different models. Etching or engraving inscriptions to falsely indicate ownership is pure fraud.

Whenever an original part is replaced with a new one, or with one that belongs on a weapon of another make or model, the one who makes the substitution should record the fact and pass on the record to any subsequent owner. Such information may be lost in time, but at least an attempt is made to avoid deception. Failure to indicate the substitution of a part, or the alteration of the design or finish, arouses the suspicion of an expert appraiser who then suspects the authenticity of the whole piece.

XXXIX. General Safety Precautions

A PERSON who understands firearms seldom has an accident, but a careless beginner is a source of danger not only to himself but also to everyone in the vicinity. It is the duty of all of us who are familiar with firearms to diplomatically but forcefully pass on our knowledge of safety precautions to the youthful, the ignorant, the careless, the foolish, and those who are vicious show-offs.

Firearms are made to kill. True, thousands of people use guns only to hit targets, but that does not contradict the fact that the ultimate object of any gun is to kill an animal or a human being. These are blunt words but they are necessary. Death by the accidental discharge of firearms is sixth in the list of the greatest causes of accidental death in the United States in times of peace, and it ranks still higher during a war. In a single typical year before the beginning of the Second World War, nearly three thousand people were killed in firearms accidents in the United States. Of this number, more than five hundred of them were children under the age of fifteen years. None of the more than five hundred children dead from gunfire were members of properly supervised and well-trained rifle or pistol clubs. Members of such clubs receive instruction in safety precautions. They know how to kill if it becomes necessary, but they also know how to avoid killing themselves and others accidentally.

Soldiers, bluejackets, marines, coast guardsmen and other members of federally trained and supervised armed services are seldom killed or injured in firearms accidents because they are not permitted to fire a shot until they have been instructed and examined in safety precautions.

Gunsmiths, both amateur and professional, handle firearms frequently and it might be thought that they do not need to be told anything about safety, but such unfortunately is not true. Familiarity breeds contempt. Since most of the guns they handle are empty, they unconsciously grow to believe that unless the opposite is known to be true, it is safe to assume that a gun is empty.

A gentleman well known to the author killed his only child accidentally while he was working in his gunshop. He was a very intelligent, cultured, thoughtful, and cautious individual. He graduated from a great university with distinction, served as a regular officer in the armed services for many years, and looked back on an active experience with firearms of all types for more than twenty years.

One day, in testing the head space of a rifle, he loaded what he believed to be a dummy cartridge into his rifle, closed the bolt, and squeezed the trigger. At that very moment, his daughter happened to step into the line of aim. When the trigger was pulled, the cartridge, which was really a live round, was discharged and the bullet went through the girl's brain, killing her instantly.

For days, all that the grieving father could say was: "I thought it was empty!" He gave away all his firearms, retired from the society of his friends, declined attractive offers of employment, and devoted himself to the care of his wife who suffered seriously from the shock of losing her only daughter.

Long after the death of his daughter the unfortunate father could talk of nothing but the tragedy. He would stop everyone he knew and advise them to be careful in handling firearms. Then he would explain safety rules in detail, even if his listeners were not interested in guns. Many of his friends thought that the publicity in the newspapers about the case and the father's crusade for safety might save lives, but within a month after the accident more deaths from the careless handling of guns occurred.

Special precautions have been given in the chapters on various arms. They are supplemented by the general rules of firearm safety presented here:

1. Treat every weapon as though it were loaded until you, *yourself*, have inspected it to see that it is not loaded.

2. Do not take someone else's word for the emptiness of a gun. Inspect it yourself.

3. Each time you pick up a weapon, even if it is one you knew to be empty when you laid it down a second ago, inspect it.

4. Do not leave a loaded weapon around where someone else may unknowingly pick it up.

5. When you put a weapon away, inspect to see that it is empty.

6. Do not aim or point a weapon at anyone unless you intend to kill him. Do not fire over his head, under his feet, to one side, or in any other direction but at his body, and then only if you fully intend to kill him, lawfully, morally, and without personal anger. Do not use a firearm as a club or as a tool, but only as a death-dealing implement of human destruction, the exception being target practice, but even then remember that a cartridge as small as .22 caliber will kill a man.

7. Load only when you expect to fire immediately, unless you are in the armed services and have orders to load.

8. Learn how to use the safety devices on your weapon before loading.

9. When your weapon is loaded and you are not firing, keep the safety lock on, particularly when advancing, as you may catch your trigger in the brush or in your clothing and kill yourself or a comrade.

10. Do not pick up shells, bombs, hand grenades, and similar explosives until you have been instructed and authorized to handle such material.

11. Do not pick up any shell or other metal object which you may see on the battlefield, on the firing range, or in the active war zone. It may be a "dud" (an unexploded shell), which may go off when it is disturbed.

12. Be cautious about picking up anything on the battlefield, or in the active zone where the enemy or his agents may operate. A magazine, newspaper, can of food, watch, purse, or piece of jewelry may be the "bait" for a "fool's trap" or "booby mine" which will explode when touched or picked up.

13. Always point the rifle or pistol upward when snapping the trigger, but look first to be sure that there is no person on an upper

floor of a building, in a lookout tower, in a tree, or in an airplane, who may be endangered.

14. Do not fire a weapon with any grease, cleaning patch, dust, dirt, snow, ice, mud, sand, or other obstruction in the bore. To do so may burst the barrel.

15. Be sure that all ammunition is clean and dry. The introduction of foreign matter, grease, or excessive oil will subject the firearm to the danger of bursting.

16. Do not put grease or oil on ammunition or in the walls of a rifle while it is ready for firing.

17. Do not expose ammunition to the direct rays of the sun for any length of time. This builds up hazardous chamber pressures.

18. Never turn around while firing on a range or while hunting if you have a loaded weapon in your hand, because by so doing you may point it at a person near you.

19. Do not lower the hammer on a loaded cartridge in a pistol, or let the firing pin of a rifle down by hand on a cartridge in the chamber.

20. Keep the finger out of the trigger guard unless you intend to fire or snap for practice.

21. In campaign, or while hunting, when the early use of a firearm is not foreseen, it should be carried with the magazine fully loaded, but with the chamber empty. When early use is probable, the weapon should be carried loaded and locked.

22. Safety devices should be tested frequently, because a safety device is a dangerous device if it does not work when expected.

23. When armed with a revolver, and its early use is not foreseen, have an empty chamber under the hammer, unless the revolver is a hammerless gun or one having a positive safety block operated by the trigger, such as the Smith & Wesson Patent Safety Hammer Block, the Colt Positive Lock, or the Iver Johnson Hammer-the-Hammer Safety.

24. Be sure that the head space of your rifle is correct. This is explained fully in another chapter.

25. Do not use high-pressure cartridges in a weapon designed for low-pressure ammunition.

Special Precautions for Gunsmiths.—Since the gunsmith works not at one trade but at many trades in the wood and metal working branches of science, any discussion of safety precautions for him would be encyclopedic in scope if we were to even attempt to list the hazards which confront the machinist, the pattern-maker, the cabinetmaker, the finisher, and the heat-treater, to say nothing of the other capacities in which a gun specialist operates. All that we can do is to point out a few of the more common sources of accidents.

Weakening the firearm is a serious undertaking. In order to save weight, modern firearms are made with as little metal as possible. Removing metal from any part of an action may reduce its resistance to stresses and strains which accompany the explosion of a cartridge. Drawing the temper of receivers and breech actions without restoring the temper is risky. Welding and brazing attachments to an action or receiver may draw the temper and weaken the gun. Remodeling a gun to take a different cartridge from the one for which it was designed, or to increase the powder load, is not to be approached without careful thought and research.

Flintlock and percussion arms were not intended to take modern loads. Black powder was used in the early guns. Smokeless and semi-smokeless powders will ruin guns designed to use black powder. Also, shotguns with "Damascus" barrels were designed for black powder. Unless you have expert knowledge of the correct type and charge of powder for an antique, do not fire it. There are many clubs which shoot muzzle-loaders but the members know what they are doing.

Do not become a member of the hay-wire school of gunsmithing. One of the requirements for admission is to replace a broken firing pin with a nail. The gun is safe until it is fired, but then the nail pierces the primer, the gas rushes out at the back, and the nail is driven into the shooter's face.

Another way to join the hay-wire club is to work down the trigger pull until you can fire the gun by breathing on the trigger. If hair triggers were safe, all triggers would be made as hair triggers. You may lose a customer temporarily, by refusing to work a trigger pull down past the safety point, but you may lose him permanently to the mortician if you lighten the trigger too much.

Do not assume that ammunition has lost its force merely because it is ancient. Some cartridges made and carried during the Civil War will still explode. A person can be just as dead from the effects of the accidental discharge of an antique as he can when shot with a modern automatic.

An old single-shot breechloader may have a charge part way down the barrel. If you are curious about immortality, load a fresh round in the chamber, fire the piece, and hope that your widow can collect the insurance without having to fight the insurance company about the fine-print clause that makes the policy void for such an accident.

When a working part is known to be defective, do not load and fire a fresh round as a means of remedying the stoppage unless you are working with a Browning Machine Gun of the heavy, tripod type. That operation happens to be the remedy for a first position stoppage of that weapon, but it is not prescribed for hand and shoulder arms.

Do not experiment with high-pressure loads unless you have adequate facilities and equipment, an ample reference library, and enough skill and knowledge to know what you are doing. Advanced research in the loading of ammunition is an expensive pastime that should be left to trained engineers working in laboratories. Ordinary reloading, and the loading of cartridges within the usual pressure range, are comparatively safe operations when surrounded with common-sense restrictions.

Do not attempt to repair or remodel firearms which are basically unsound in design and construction or which are assembled from obsolete, damaged, or poorly made parts. Mail-order shops advertise and sell obsolete martial arms, and also weapons made in Belgium, Germany, Spain, Japan, and other countries which the governments of those countries would not permit their citizens to shoot.

Some of the "bargain" weapons were made under the cottage system where one family made triggers, another made hammers, etc., with little regard for safety factors or tolerances. Other imported arms were assembled from parts picked up on battlefields. Still others were imitations of well-known, reliable arms, such as the Colt and the Smith & Wesson arms, produced in Spain to resemble the originals, even to the trade marks, but carelessly made from poor materials, without supervision or inspection beyond the requirement that they fit together well enough to fool a sucker.

The labor spent in repairing one of these pieces of junk may come to several dollars, and the cost of the material and parts may be as much. When the job is done, the weapon is still a piece of Belgian, French, Spanish, German, or Japanese junk. When it blows up in the owner's face, jams just when he needs it, or hangs fire and then goes off in a friend's chest, the gunsmith rightfully gets the blame. As you value your reputation, avoid working on junk, foreign or domestic.

The cause of gun trouble may not be in the gun itself, but in some accessory or attachment. For instance, many owners of automatic pistols complain that their pistols "jam" easily, but a close inspection of the magazine will show that the lips have been spread apart and that a fine crack exists on one or both sides of the magazine, near the back edge of the lips. This causes the lips to spread apart and leads to 90 per cent of all automatic pistol "jams."

WAR RELICS

Members of the armed forces of the United States brought home from World War I, World War II, and the Korean War, thousands of firearms. Most of them are fit only for wall decoration. Some can be fired after careful inspection, with the proper ammunition, and if the head space is correct; but the safe rule is this: *In case of doubt, throw it out!*

XL. How to Get a Gunsmithing Job

A BANK clerk of our acquaintance had reached the peak of advancement in his vocation. He had gone to work in a branch bank upon graduating from high school, he had completed several courses in banking and finance at night schools and by correspondence, and his efficiency rating was high, but the small salary raises he received each year did not make up for the increased cost of living or the additional expense due to a growing family.

Joe (that was not his true name, of course) liked to tinker with guns in his basement shop as an outlet for his frustrated feelings. We had helped him design gun stocks and follow through the various woodworking and finishing processes leading to completed stocks, but where he really stood out was in metalworking. He could make a pistol barrel from a scrap piece of high speed steel, blue it, mount it in the frame, and attach sights of his own construction. When he sought our advice, we urged him to look for a job as a gunsmith.

Joe made the rounds of hardware and sporting goods stores, gun and key shops, and similar establishments; nobody seemed to want a full-time gunsmith, although everywhere he went there were offers of part-time employment at piece rates. One chain-system store dealing in automobile parts, with guns as a sideline, wanted him to mount telescopic sights for customers; a hardware store had a small but steady demand for repair work on rifles; and a shooting gallery needed a man who would properly clean and lubricate their much-abused weapons.

It seemed like fun to be paid for doing things that had previously been regarded as an avocation. Joe had a little trouble at first in fixing his charges, but gradually he learned to estimate the time and material that it would take for each job and he made out a regular schedule of fees—so much per hour for cleaning and lubricating the rifles at the shooting gallery, another rate for mounting sights, etc. As his customers grew to depend upon him, the word got around town that Joe could be relied upon to do a good job at a fair price. Business increased. Soon he had more than he could do at night and on week ends. He was tempted to quit the bank job, but his natural caution came to the front and he wisely kept his position while he surveyed the situation.

Joe's big "break" came when one of the pillars of the community died and willed his collection of antique firearms to the local library with the provision that it be suitably displayed and kept in good condition. Casting about for a part-time curator, the library board could find no one available except Joe, whom they engaged to catalog, clean, and display the collection, with a promise that he would be paid a small but respectable sum each month for going over the guns with an oily rag and delivering an occasional talk on the historic background of the old pieces.

The local newspaper published a feature article about the donor of the collection, exaggerating, of course, the cash value and the sentimental legends of the weapons. Joe received scant attention at first, but when the excitement over the passing of the leading citizen subsided another feature story played up Joe as a man with a colorful hobby. His fame spread. Collectors, hunters, and marksmen who had never before heard of his existence came to his home and even visited the bank with their prized possessions. Most of the callers merely wanted to talk guns with a fellow enthusiast, but a few came back for repair jobs.

By now the tail was wagging the dog. Joe resigned from his bank job, rented a small shop around the corner from the bank, inserted an advertisement in the newspaper and brought his tools down from his home. The first month he barely cleared enough to pay his rent. His wife begged him to go back to the bank, but he stuck to his new trade, ran advertisements in the sporting magazines of national circulation, and soon had enough mail-order business to bring in a net income that was greater than that received by his former boss, the branch bank manager.

Three years went by. Joe acquired a national reputation for his gun-bluing jobs, gained confidence in himself, and studied heat-treating from every book he could buy or borrow. When the Second World War started, there was a rush of business from home guardsmen, officers called to the colors, and similarly patriotic-minded citizens. Even the police department hired him for two nights a week to take care of its arms and train rooky patrolmen in the proper use of their weapons. Gradually, as men left for the armed services, business with hunters, marksmen, and collectors fell off, but home defense activities more than made up for the loss.

In 1943, Joe was offered an attractive job with the heat-treating department of an aircraft factory. Another offer came from the employment office of the United States government in a nearby city. This job was in an arsenal, and it meant a U.S. Civil Service status; but Joe decided that he was needed just as much in the armed forces. He tried to enlist but was rejected because of a heart condition. He took the examination for the arsenal job but was rejected because of his physical condition. For a few weeks, Joe was depressed, but eventually he decided that God intended that he should be a gunsmith in his own shop.

Joe's avocation became his vocation. His story is typical of gunsmithing. Every town is not large enough to keep a gunsmith busy with gun work alone, but even in the country villages a skillful and enterprising craftsman who advertises nationally can find enough to do to devote his full time to firearms. Those who are content to remain unknown outside of their own neighborhoods can always supplement their gun work with such traditional sidelines as bicycle repair, locksmithing, key-making, and saw-filing.

Sideline jobs of this type are practically trades in themselves, but gunsmithing develops skills which make it easy for their owner to branch out into hitherto unknown trails. A man may much prefer to work on guns, and he may be a specialist in one or two gunsmithing processes, but the ability to conduct a general repair business when the gun work is slack may mean the difference between making a bare living and enjoying prosperity.

Police Department Jobs.—Gunsmithing is a part-time activity for the police departments of small towns and villages. The local government may pay a gunsmith a monthly salary to keep the weapons in order, he may be paid by the hour or job, or he may be hired to train one of the patrolmen to make minor repairs and adjustments, but training a policeman to perform the simpler operations is usually the first step toward eliminating the police department as a source of business.

In order to obtain a full-time job as a police gunsmith, it is necessary to become a regular member of the department. In this situation, three possibilities exist:

First, the gunsmith may be required to perform the duties of a patrolman and work on guns after coming in from his tour on the beat. However, in the larger towns and smaller cities there is so much gun work that the gunsmith will usually be taken off the patrolmen's roster as soon as he learns something about practical police procedure.

Second, the gunsmith who joins the department of a medium-size city may be assigned to the identification division of the detective bureau where he learns to identify firearms used in the commission of crime, and functions as a laboratory detective. Gradually, as he becomes more proficient, the firearms expert is permitted to assign the cleaning and repair of the police guns to an assistant who, in turn, may work his way up to the higher status.

The identification of firearms is a specialized science in itself. Those who go into court and give evidence that may cost the defendant his liberty, and even his life, should have a background of mechanical engineering, forensic chemistry, criminal law, medico-legal jurisprudence, and other subjects which it takes years to learn in theory and still more years of practice to master. Being an excellent gunsmith is not enough to qualify a person morally and intellectually as an expert witness in the identification of firearms used in crime, even though some thoughtless judges have held to the contrary. However, a gunsmith is certainly better qualified than the average layman for this purpose, and there is no doubt about the value of gunsmithing as a firm foundation for further advancement.

Third, in the largest cities of the United States, a gunsmith in a police department may be classified as an armorer and devote his entire time to the cleaning, repairing, and adjusting of the department's firearms, including not only the ordinary pistols and revolvers, but also the riot-type shotguns made with a 20-inch plain barrel, bored cylinder; and various automatic weapons.

There is also a tendency today to train the police department armorer in chemical warfare, both defensive and offensive. He learns to care for and fire gas guns, gas grenades, smoke grenades, and similar weapons. He also becomes proficient in the use of the various types of gas masks, and he may be required to train other members of the department in the handling of chemical-warfare equipment.

From the duties of an armorer and a chemical-warfare technician to the responsibilities of an expert on arson, sabotage, and plant protection is a short jump in many instances, but with a broader field of usefulness come pay increases and promotions in rank.

County Gunsmithing Jobs.—Jobs under county governments which a gunsmith can hold are usually in the sheriff's office. Like the police jobs, they may be strictly gunsmithing positions, or they may involve firearm identification, and assignment to arson, demolition, or riot squads. The man who is willing to serve as a special deputy sheriff on holidays and other special occasions usually has a better opportunity to gradually work into a full-time job with the sheriff's office than he would have with a police department, because the latter is normally not in the habit of hiring men by the day for regular police duties.

State Jobs.—The various state governments have many men armed with firearms which need the attention of a gunsmith. State police, state guards, the National Guard of a state in time of peace, liquor-license officials, tax collectors, and many types of investigators may be required, or at least permitted, to carry arms in the execution of their missions. The state employees may be instructed in the care of their weapons, and yet parts are constantly being broken or lost, and complaints about arms that do not function properly are common.

Jobs for gunsmiths exist in each of the branches of the state government where arms are carried, either at the state capital or at one of the headquarters of subdivisions of the governmental branch. Firearm identification experts are on the staff of the state identification bureau at the capital, or assigned to the attorney general's office, or to the office of one of his deputies.

Federal Jobs.—The greatest opportunity for a gunsmith who wants a civil service job is offered by the United States government. In general, gunsmithing jobs may be divided into several classifications: manufacturing, inspecting, cleaning and repairing, and identifying. Manufacturing and assembling take place at arsenals such as those at Springfield, Massachusetts; Rock Island, Illinois; and Benicia, California, although the latter two have sometimes been reduced to the status of repair and supply depots in days of peace. Inspecting is done at the government arsenals, at factories producing ordnance for the government, and elsewhere. Cleaning and repairing are processes which must be carried on wherever firearms are received or issued for use. Identifying firearms is a function of the Federal Bureau of Investigation, Department of Justice, and it requires more than a knowledge of gunsmithing, as already explained.

Applications for Civil Service Jobs.—Postmasters have up-to-date lists and descriptions of U.S. Civil Service jobs for which vacancies exist. Information may be posted on the bulletin board, but it is advisable to inquire personally about such openings and not depend entirely on the posted announcements.

An applicant should also write to the U.S. Civil Service Commission, Washington, D.C., requesting notification of any examinations to be held in the near future. If he leaves his name on file with the Commission, together with an address where he can always be reached, and a statement of his qualifications, he may receive special announcements before they are published in newspapers, announced over the radio, or posted on the bulletin boards of post offices.

Gunsmiths should realize that the gunsmithing trade is really a combination of several skilled trades which fall broadly into two groups: woodworking and metalworking. It is not sufficient merely to ask about openings for gunsmiths; it is better also to inquire about vacancies for cabinetmakers, pattern-makers, wood-finishers, heat-treaters, machinists, welders, blacksmiths, etc., in all cases where the applicant is actually skilled or semiskilled in any of these occupations.

In addition to writing to the U.S. Civil Service Commission and visiting the post office, the applicant should also write to or visit the United States Government employment offices and fill out their questionnaires. Such employment offices publish notices of vacancies in newspapers circulating in the surrounding territory and release information through radio stations.

States also have employment offices and civil service commissions, but they are usually not conducted with as much efficiency and publicity as the employment agencies of the national government. Inquiries should be sent to the Civil Service Commission, State of ———, at the capital of the state, and also to any branch offices, the location of the latter being determined by inquiring at any large library or newspaper office.

Most of the above suggestions also apply to the civil service commissions and employment offices conducted by county and municipal governments, which are normally located in the county courthouse and the city hall, respectively, although they may be housed in separate buildings.

Gunsmiths in the Armed Services.—A conscientious and skilled gunsmith is welcome in all of the armed services, and he can be sure of splendid opportunities for advancement in pay and rank. In the Navy, he may be rated as a Gunner's Mate, a Chief Gunner's Mate, as a Gunner (warrant officer), or as a Chief Gunner (commissioned warrant officer). In the Army, he may start as a private, but eventually he may become a Master Sergeant or a Warrant Officer. In the Marine Corps, similar opportunities exist.

The gunsmith, amateur or professional, who joins one of the armed services should seek expert advice before expressing a preference for assignment. The professional gunsmith may have a better opportunity for promotion in a unit where he is the only technician of his kind, but the amateur gunsmith will lay a firm foundation for advancement by seeking duty where he will work with and under more experienced craftsmen.

At one time, a gunsmith in the Infantry dealt principally with rifles, pistols, and automatic shoulder weapons, but today he may work on machine guns, mortars, howitzers, and even weapons that were once regarded as the exclusive property of the artillery. A similar situation exists in the Cavalry and other arms of the service.

Officers trained and experienced in personnel-assignment problems are on duty at induction centers, recruit depots, and other places where personnel are classified and recommended for future assignment. Instead of relying solely upon the advice of his comrades, the gunsmith is advised to obtain an interview with such an officer and then abide by his suggestions and orders.

Civilian Jobs.—The account of the career of "Joe," given in the opening of this chapter, is typical of the experiences of many civilian gunsmiths who started as amateurs and advanced to a professional standing. Another avenue of advancement, especially for the young man who is ineligible for military-naval duty, is a job as an apprentice to a master gunsmith, but he should try to work under an all-round gunsmith rather than one who is a specialist in one or two narrow divisions of the trade, unless, of course, he actually wants to become the same kind of gunsmith.

Specialization is an advantage for a gunsmith who wants to work in a large shop where the labor is divided among several men, or for a man who has an aptitude for a particular line of work and intends to solicit business in that line as an independent gunsmith, but the beginner should endeavor to learn as many branches of the trade as possible before choosing a specialty.

For this reason, it is well to serve as an assistant to an independent, all-around gunsmith in a small shop, even though the wages are low and the hours are long. Under such conditions, the apprentice may work on sights the first hour, adjust a trigger the second hour, remove an obstruction from a barrel in the third hour, and spend the rest of the day inletting an action.

It may take a few weeks or a few months for the apprentice in a small shop to discover where his talents are best directed, but then he can go to a larger shop and obtain a job as an assistant to a specialist, or he can open his own shop, in either a store catering to sportsmen or in a building of his own.

The old complaint of the job-hunter is, "I cannot get a job without experience and I cannot acquire experience without a job." The answer is that the amateur can gain experience by first doing simple jobs for his friends at little or no cost; then performing more difficult operations for regular pay for both friends and strangers; and finally working as a semi-professional in his home workshop at night and on week ends. His satisfied customers will gladly write letters of recommendation and they may even lend him their arms, on which he has worked, for him to display to prospective employers, although it is probably asking a little too much to borrow such property.

In conclusion, the job-hunter is advised to enlist the law of averages on his side. He should telephone, write, and visit every possible employer and everyone who might know of a job. He should tell all of his friends and relatives that he is looking for a job, the kind of work he prefers, and his qualifications. When an interview is granted and he is told that there is no present opening, he should ask permission to call again later, and be sure to return after a reasonable period of waiting. The speed with which a job is obtained is in direct ratio to the number of contacts and applications made by the applicant.

BIBLIOGRAPHY

ANGIER, R. H. *Firearm Blueing and Browning.* Harrisburg, Penna.: The Stackpole Co., 1936.

ARNOLD, RICHARD. *Automatic and Repeating Shotguns.* New York: A. S. Barnes & Co., 1960.

BAKER, CLYDE. *Modern Gunsmithing.* Harrisburg, Penna.: The Stackpole Co., 1933.

BRAVERMAN, SHELLEY. *The Firearms Encyclopedia.* Athens, N. Y.: Shelley Braverman, 1959.

BROWN, PETE. *Guns and Hunting.* New York: A. S. Barnes & Co., 1960.

BROWNELL, F. R. *Encyclopedia of Modern Firearms.* Montezuma, Iowa.: F. R. Brownell, 1960.

CHAPEL, CHARLES EDWARD. *The Art of Shooting.* New York: A. S. Barnes & Co., 1960.

———. *The Boy's Book of Rifles.* New York: Coward-McCann, Inc., 1948.

———. *The Complete Book of Gun Collecting.* New York: Coward-Mc-Cann, Inc., 1961.

———. *Forensic Ballistics.* Chicago: Institute of Applied Science, 1933.

———. *The Gun Collector's Handbook of Values.* New York: Coward-McCann, Inc., 1963.

———. *Guns of the Old West.* New York: Coward-McCann, Inc., 1961.

———. *U.S. Martial and Semi-Martial Single-Shot Pistols.* New York: Coward-McCann, Inc., 1962.

DUNLAP, ROY F. *Gunsmithing.* Harrisburg, Penna.: The Stackpole Co., 1952.

FFOULKES, C. *The Gun-Founders of England.* New York: Cambridge University Press, 1937.

FRAZER, PERRY D. *Elementary Gunsmithing.* Harrisburg, Penna.: The Stackpole Co., 1938.

GLUCKMAN, ARCADI, and L. D. SATTERLEE. *American Gun Makers.* Harrisburg, Penna.: The Stackpole Co., 1953.

HATCHER, JULIAN S. *The Book of the Garand*. Washington, D.C.: Infantry Journal Press, 1948.

———. *Firearms Investigation, Identification and Evidence*. Harrisburg, Penna.: The Stackpole Co., 1962.

———. *Hatcher's Notebook*. Harrisburg, Penna.: The Stackpole Co., 1962.

HAYES, TOM. *Hunting the Whitetail Deer*. New York: A. S. Barnes & Co., 1960.

HOWE, JAMES V. *Amateur Guncraftsman*. New York: Funk & Wagnalls Co., 1938.

———. *Modern Gunsmith*. New York: Funk & Wagnalls Co., 1941.

———. *Professional Gunsmithing*. Harrisburg, Penna.: The Stackpole Co., 1946.

KAUFFMAN, HENRY J. *Early American Gunsmith, (1650–1850)*. Harrisburg, Penna.: The Stackpole Co., 1952.

LENZ, ELLIS C. *Muzzle Flashes*. Harrisburg, Penna.: The Stackpole Co., 1944.

MACFARLAND, HAROLD E. *Gunsmithing Simplified*. New York: A. S. Barnes & Co., 1950.

MACKAY, JOHN W. *Good Shooting!* New York: A. S. Barnes & Co., 1960.

NEWELL, A. DONALD. *Gunstock Finishing & Care*. Harrisburg, Penna.: The Stackpole Co., 1949.

ROBERTS, NED H. *Muzzle-Loading Cap Lock Rifle*. Harrisburg, Penna.: The Stackpole Co., 1952.

VICKERY, W. F. *Advanced Gunsmithing*. Harrisburg, Penna.: The Stackpole Co., 1940.

WHELEN, TOWNSEND. *Why Not Load Your Own?* Washington, D.C.: Combat Forces Press, 1957.

WHITE, HENRY P. and BURTON D. MUNHALL. *Center Fire Metric Pistol and Revolver Cartridges*. Washington, D.C.: Infantry Press, 1948.

WILLIAMSON, HAROLD F. *Winchester—The Gun That Won the West*. New York: A. S. Barnes & Co., 1952.

INDEX

case, ruptured, removal of, 394;
Cartridge, chambering, 382-383;
Cartridge, feeding, 382; Cartridge, packing, 336, Chambering cartridge, 382-383; Cleaning, 379-381; Cocking, 387; Cold climate operation, 376-377; Controls, operation and maintenance, 368-376; Cycle of operation, 381-388; Damp climate operation, 378; Disassembly and assembly, 343-354; Dry climate operation, 378; Echelons of maintenance, 340-341; Extracting, 385; Feeding cartridge, 382; Field maintenance, 341; Field stripping, 343-354; Firing, 372-376, 383-384; Firing mechanism, 354-360; Functioning of, 381-388; Head space, 266-272; Hot climate operation, 377; Landing operations, in, 378-379; Loading, 364-367; Locking, 383; Magazine, assembly and dissassembly, 359-360; Magazine chargers, 336; Magazine loading when out of rifle, 367-368; Main Groups, 343-344; Maintenance echelons, 340-341; Muddy operating conditions, 378; Muzzle velocity, average, 332; Nomenclature, 341-343; Operation, normal, 364-368; Operation under unusual conditions, 376-379; Organizational maintenance, 340-341; Preventive maintenance, 388-390;

Range, maximum, 332, Rifle controls, 368-390; Ruptured cartridge case, removal of, 394; Salty atmosphere, operation in, 378; Sandy operating conditions, 378; Semi-automatic fire, 372-373; Semi-automatic fire, cycle of operation, 382; Semi-automatic and automatic fire, conversion for, 360-362; Sight, rear, controls for, 369-370; Sight, rear, disassembly and assembly, 351-354; Tactical use of, 337-339; Tool, combination, 349, 366; Troubleshooting, 390-391; Unloading, 376; Unlocking, 383; Velocity, average muzzle, 332; Zeroing or targeting, 371

U.S. Rifles: Models 1892, 1896, 1898, 1899, 323, 327-329; *See also* Krag Rifle

U.S. Submachine Gun, Cal. .45 (Thompson), 339

V-tool, 93, 100
Values, antique firearm, 343-344
Vandyke printing, 50
Varnish, 107; remover, 107
Vee-blocks, 18; 205
Velocity, average muzzle, M14 Rifle, 332
Vickers test for hardness, 211
Vises, 39
Visible outline in drawing, 53

Walnut, 72, 73
War relics, 457